From the Presocratics to the Present
A Personal Odyssey

DANIEL KOLAK

The William Paterson University of New Jersey

MAYFIELD PUBLISHING COMPANY

Mountain View, California

London • Toronto

For Joe, Mike, and Hope—three beautiful ships
built for our faring-forth

Library of Congress Cataloging-in-Publication Data

Kolak, Daniel.
    From the Presocratics to the present : a personal odyssey / Daniel
Kolak.
        p.   cm.
    ISBN 1-55934-975-1
    1. Philosophy—Introductions.   2. Philosophy—History.   3. Kolak,
Daniel.   I. Title.
    BD21.K63   1997
    190—dc21   97-36991
                                                              CIP

Manufactured in the United States of America
10 9 8 7 6 5 4 3 2 1

Mayfield Publishing Company
1280 Villa Street
Mountain View, California 94041

Sponsoring editor, Ken King; production editor, Carla L. White; manuscript editor,
Margaret Moore; text designer, Donna Davis; cover art, Tom Murray; art and design
manager, Susan Breitbard; manufacturing manager, Randy Hurst. The text was set in 10/12
Berkeley Book by TBH Typecast, Inc. and printed on 45# Baycoat Velvet by Banta Book
Group, Harrisonburg.

Contents

Preface

This is the book I wish I had as a student and that as a philosopher I need. Written as a historical introduction to the subject, it offers the most important insights of the most important philosophers—not watered down but *distilled*. It is the story of philosophy told through the philosophers: their lives, their loves, their fears, their hatreds, their dreams, their theories, their explanations, their answers, and, most of all, their questions. The goal is to wake the student up and reawaken the teacher to a common point of embarkation.

This book can be read on its own or be used in conjunction with any of the leading introduction to philosophy texts. I have tried to make it neither too long nor too short, with enough overview and detail to take the discussion a little deeper than what usually is contained in introductory texts. It is written in a clear style and is free of unnecessary jargon. I do not emphasize the differences among philosophers—that story is well enough familiar as wars, intellectual and otherwise, make good press. I try instead to reveal the common ground.

Agree with it or disagree, so long as you read this book you will have a good idea of what philosophy is: sure-footed, mystical, frustrating, edifying, and sometimes plain odd. Philosophy is sometimes tough to understand but, then, what isn't? Often it is quite shocking or downright unbelievable and impossible to defend yourself against (for that you need the philosophers). It can be a metaphysical tidal wave of words, thoughts, ideas, a maelstrom that swallows you up. Then, again, philosophy can lay you right back down gently onto the shore of your belief as if nothing had happened. But there is wisdom, even in its whispers.

Most of philosophy's practitioners, it is true, have been men. At least the Oracle at Delphi was a woman. Of course, it was her pronouncement that brought Socrates to the hemlock. Still, let us openly admit: it is not Mars but philosophy that needs women.

I like philosophy and I hope you like this book. It may not be "the greatest story ever told" but I think it is a worthy substitute. Because of its brevity, there are lots of mistakes in it—every time I read it I find another and as best I can I fix them. Be assured: none have been put there on purpose (well, perhaps one or two).

I am grateful to all the friends, colleagues, and students who over the years have offered me insights that in one way or another may have wound up in this book, especially: Neil Florek of Purdue University Calumet, Raymond Martin, Marshall Missner, Mike Russo, Joe Salerno, Hope May, Garrett Thomson, Freeman Dyson, Burton Drebin, Willard Quine, Bill Boos, Victor Velarde, Tom Nenon, John Archibald Wheeler, and Jaakko Hintikka. I thank Cunard for having invited me as Professor of the Cunard World University to travel around the world and chat philosophy on wonderful ships such as the Queen Elizabeth II, the Vistafjord, and the Royal Viking Sun. I also thank the many people who have read previous versions of this book or my other books against which this book sometimes borrows. You may not exist (thanks, Hume) but at least at this moment you know who you are.

CHAPTER ONE

Ancient Philosophy

Thales: Navigating the Cosmic Ocean

As I write this I sit on deck aboard an ocean liner making its way along the Dardanelles, the narrow straits of Asia Minor. It is night. Somewhere off to my right is the coast where Thales once walked; to my left is the birthplace of Heraclitus. Except for the glowing computer screen and the soft glow of the ship's electric lights, it is pitch black. Across the water I see only moon shadows and waves. Behind me, the ship's three radar antennas calmly and confidently spin in the ark beneath the moon and stars. Peering out over the deck I wonder: what an impossible feat such travel must have seemed to the sailors of ancient Greece! How many a ship had crashed upon unknown rocks?

Ancient Greece was not just a land, the Greece of Europe, but also a sea, the Grecian sea, with all its coasts from Asia Minor to Sicily and from Cyrene to Thrace. This sea, peopled since the earliest recorded time, linked the three great continents from the Black Sea to the Pillars of Hercules. Up to the time of Thales, commercial trade and exploration by sea was limited to ships hugging the coast by day and anchoring at night. Traveling after sunset or venturing beyond sight of landmarks was virtually impossible. Ancient navigators tried to solve the problem by improving the maps of coastlines, making better anchors (all ships had to anchor at night), and organizing sailing chains: while one ship kept land in sight on the horizon, a parallel ship could venture out to the first ship's opposite horizon. Once sight of a ship was lost, however, the chain would be broken and many ships in this way were lost at sea.

Reflecting on the beginning of philosophy, I am awed yet again to realize that the person most often credited as being the first philosopher, Thales (624–546 B.C.E.[1]), also just happened to solve the problem of how to sail the seas at night! What amazes me about this as I sit here in the dark beneath the stars with the waves pounding against the ship's bow is that philosophy demands so much abstract thinking and esoteric knowledge, while navigating a ship requires practical know-how and concrete experience. But of course the two are not unrelated, and in Thales we have a paradigm example, from the very dawn of philosophy, to reveal why philosophy is as difficult to understand as it is wonderful to master.

Instead of thinking up new and improved ways of seeing by the light of day, Thales explored the darkness. To navigate by the seen coastlines in the light of day, one must constantly realign oneself with the changing sights; one cannot go far. But when the sun sets the stars come out. The dim stars, obscured in the light

1

of day by the sun, are in relation to each other permanent and fixed. They are of course there during the day, only we cannot see them. Studying the stars, Thales noticed what many who looked up into the heavens saw: patterns, regularities, that repeated with the seasons. Looking in the upward direction, into the starry night, Thales conceived of a way to correlate one's position with the mapped sky above. The end result was his nautical star guide, which showed Grecian seafarers how to navigate the seas using the stars.

Align yourself not with the light, the bright appearances made vivid by the light of day, but with what can be seen only in the dark. Then you can be guided not by the verisimilitudes of earthly maps but by the permanence of the heavens, under cover of darkness, making your way as if by magic, guided by the gods. What better metaphor to give us a glimpse into the mysterious beginnings of philosophy?

Entire epochs in human history have been named after the raw materials that had subsequently come to be viewed as definitive of the age—stone, iron, atomic. It is therefore appropriate that philosophy was born in what subsequent ages have called the Age of the Seven Wise Men. There have been some variations as to who they were,[2] but Thales makes every list. He lived in the early part of the sixth century B.C.E., several generations before Socrates and Plato, more than 2,600 years ago, in Miletus, a sprawling seacoast city of white stone and olive groves, with labyrinthine streets of villas overlooking harbors full of ships. In its heyday, Miletus was the leading seaport on the west coast of Ionia in Asia Minor (present-day Turkey). Its cobbled highways stretched north and south and east as far as the eye could see; one could walk, or ride, all the way to the Orient, where the four great Eastern sages of antiquity—Gautama Buddha, Confucius, Lao-tzu, and Chaung-tzu—were all alive at the same time. Why philosophy should have blossomed with such synchronicity in these vastly different civilizations remains an unsolved mystery.

In riddle, in anecdote, in epigram, with "winged words" the Wise Men traveled throughout the ancient world, espousing wisdom to anyone who would listen. What they said varied, but there are at least two sayings that we know they had in common: "Know thyself" and "Nothing in excess" or "Everything in good measure." One wonders whether the first imperative, "Know thyself," prompted the warning comprising the second. Could there be such a thing as too much self-knowledge?

One wouldn't think so. But perhaps too much philosophy was too much even for these early wise men. Certainly, philosophy was not all they did. Thales was no exception. He was both a metaphysician concerned with the question of what reality consisted of and a natural scientist who revolutionized nautical science. His understanding of geometry and the laws of nature was astounding. He showed how to calculate the height of a pyramid by measuring its shadow at the time of day when a man's shadow is equal to his height and even predicted the solar eclipse of May 28, 585 B.C.E. During the Persian Wars he showed the army how to cross a wide river by building a dam and diverting its flow into two narrower rivers across which bridges could then be built. Indeed, in most of Thales' work one finds the underlying theme of water and navigating beyond the limits of the seen into the dark, steering through the unknown.

Due in part to the achievements of Thales and others like him, Miletus became the most powerful center of commercial activity of the ancient Greek world. Riches and knowledge poured in from Europe and Egypt and the Orient. Private and public wealth acquired from trade gave the citizens of Miletus an unprecedented amount of leisure. Perhaps for the first time in the history of the world, ordinary people were freed from the pressures of daily needs long enough to turn their hearts and minds to art and science, to speculate about themselves and the world, to discuss, argue, and wonder about everything. Religious, political, social, and scientific beliefs were openly discussed without the primitive bloodshed going on at the time on the European continent because business was the rule of the day. Milesian courts drew poets from all over the world, the city's leaders founded libraries and supported every movement in art and science. Lyric poetry replaced old universal religious and political sentiments, giving way to new ideas of personal and individual expression. Satirical poetry arose alongside the lyric, expressing keen and cleverly developed individualism, often critical of the lyrical passions and excitement, even of one's own traditions and culture; it was no less than the birth of self-criticism. There also emerged at this time the so-called gnomic poetry, wise sayings and reflections on moral, practical, and metaphysical principles advocating moderation between the passions and the intellect through the establishment of enlightened rules about life not derived from the gods as espoused by religious authorities, but achieved through independent, personal, individual reflection.

According to legend, at one point Thales gained control over the entire economy of Miletus. Plato writes in his *Theaetetus* that this happened after a young woman laughed at Thales when he "was looking up to study the stars and tumbled down a well. She scoffed at him for being so eager to know what was happening in the sky that he could not see what lay at his feet." Aristotle, too, tells the story in his *Politics*:

> There is . . . the story which is told of Thales of Miletus. It is a story about a scheme for making money, which is fathered on Thales owing to his reputation for wisdom. . . . He was reproached for his poverty, which was supposed to show the uselessness of philosophy. According to the story, observing from his knowledge of meteorology while it was yet winter that there would be a great harvest of olives in the coming year, he gave deposits for all the olive-presses in Miletus and Chios, which he hired at a low price because no one bid against him. When the harvest time came, and there was a sudden and simultaneous demand for the olive presses, he let out the stock he had collected at any rate he chose to fix; and making a considerable fortune, he succeeded in proving that it is easy for philosophers to become rich if they like, but that their ambition lies elsewhere.[3]

Aristotle goes on to identify Thales as the originator of the idea that some underlying material substance forms the basis of the existence of all things: water.

The seas of time, however, have unfortunately not been kind to Thales. None of his original works have survived. Moreover, philosophers and historians of philosophy and science have used Thales' cryptic statement, "Everything is made of water," as an example of primitive thinking about the nature of the world. Rarely, if ever, is it asked how such a statement could have had the profound effect on subsequent thinkers that history records, and why someone with Thales' obvious brilliance and acumen would have made it. Even Aristotle treated Thales' statement like an intellectual antique and, giving a collegial pat on the back to the poor ancient fellow, seemed to say, "Nice try." Why?

Part of the problem, I think, is that such histories are written from their own present. Another is that philosophers themselves are rarely at ease with the strangely dualistic nature of philosophy that I have already mentioned, which is nowhere more evident than in Thales, who both explained the known and ventured into the unknown, clarified and mystified the minds of his students, all in perfect proportion. To understand Thales as an individual is to understand the wholeness of philosophy. Like the work of the many great philosophers after him, his work both solved practical problems and stirred intellectual puzzlement, in equal measure. It is one thing to teach your fellow Greeks how to navigate at night by the stars; it is quite another to tell them that "everything is made of water." So keep in mind, as we navigate through the entire course of Western philosophy, that our journey begins not with a way of thought, not with a concept or theory, but with an individual, *Thales.* He was not a divine being, just a brilliant and hard-working human one, a real person who once lived somewhere off the starboard side of our ship, an explorer who made travel by sea possible at night, a deep thinker who started a metaphysical conversation lasting three millennia. Our interest is not in intellectual antiques but in the journey of ideas that the history of philosophy is, an odyssey of wondering about ourselves and the world.

So: *everything is made of water.* Now, what could Thales have meant by this cryptic statement? And what effect did it have on Thales' contemporaries? To understand, try to imagine what it must have been like to be alive in the early part of the sixth century B.C.E. You're an ordinary citizen of Miletus. What is your view of the world? What sorts of things do you believe? How do you live your life?

Like most Milesians then and most people today, you accept without question the answers you've been given by your authorities. You trust them completely the way young children trust their parents. It's not that you merely believe what the priests and oracles say; rather, it never even occurs to you to question their authority. As far as you are concerned, the priests' knowledge comes directly from the oracles who themselves speak in the voices of the gods. The oracles were without exception women. We know nothing about these female oracles. How were they initiated? How did they pass down their secrets?

One day, a fellow famous throughout Asia Minor for his wisdom and great deeds announces that he will reveal the ultimate truth about all things to anyone who dares listen. Naturally, you go. The square is teeming with the devout and the curious. A robed figure appears. It is Thales. A silence falls upon the crowd.

"I have come to enlighten you," he says, "about the world, about yourselves, about all things. Gather round. Listen."

You feel a strange excitement. This man is known to you, he is known to everyone as one of the wisest among you. So what does this wise man, Thales, have to say about the world? What is his great truth that will enlighten all of mankind?

"Everything is made of water," he pronounces.

Really try to put yourself in the shoes of our ancient Milesian who has just heard these words for the first time. What is your reaction? What do you think about this statement, what do you feel? *Everything is made of water.* How do you respond? If in projecting yourself via your imagination into the soul of our ancient Milesian standing in the square listening to Thales you say to yourself something like, "Well, yes, I can see how that might have made sense to someone back then—they lived by the sea, there was water everywhere, everyone must drink water to survive—people back then didn't know any better," then think again. First, notice that when you do say something like that to yourself, in the back of your mind—subtly, just beneath the surface of conscious perception— you're quietly, innocently, reassuring yourself that our present state of knowledge is an advance over the past, that today's understanding of ourselves and the world so outstrips our ancestors' understanding of themselves and their world that compared to contemporary wisdom their ancient views are laughably naive, even absurd.

Second, notice that Thales didn't say, "Many things are made of water," "Water is very important for our survival," or anything remotely like that. Presumably, figuring out how best to put it would have been a small feat for someone who could calculate the height of a pyramid by measuring its shadow, figure out how to navigate at night at sea using the stars, and accurately predict solar eclipses (can you, thousands of years in the future, with all your sophisticated education and access to hundreds of thousands of books on all subjects that then did not even exist, do any of the sorts of things that Thales did or anything even remotely like them?).

Let us assume that you, the Milesian standing in the square listening to Thales, knows perfectly well what the word *everything* means. It doesn't mean "many things" or even "most things." It means all things that exist. And you also know perfectly well what water is. You see water. You swim. You drink. You've just been told that *everything* is made of the one substance you probably are more familiar with than any other: water. Rocks are made of water. Air is made of water. Light is made of water. Fire is made of water . . . certainly it does not seem to be the case that all of these things are made of water. So why would Thales say this? We have seen a good deal of evidence to suggest that Thales was neither an idiot nor crazy, but was one of the smartest people of the time. So what could he mean?

Notice that unlike most cryptic statements, you can do something about his statement right away. You can try to *test* it. And you can do it yourself, you don't have to defer to some other authority. No faith required. No special training. You can try to find out for yourself whether the statement "Everything is made of water" is true or false, simply by testing it using your own experience and reason! I thus conjecture that the first and immediate effect Thales' statement had on his listeners was nothing like what common sense might suppose. Rather, it went something like this. A great wise man, the voice of the gods, has just uttered an obviously false statement. Our ordinary Milesian citizen went home after having heard one simple declarative sentence from Thales and nothing would ever be the same again. All of your life you've accepted the wisdom of the priests. You believe in the gods. You also believe that the gods do not lie. Everything made of water? You think: suppose you locked Thales up in a room and when he got thirsty and asked for water you gave him a cup of pebbles. Would he thank you and drink it? Or would he ask for some water? Does Thales wash himself using fire? Hardly. No, something profound has just been made perfectly clear to you. Thales didn't just say something profound and enlightening. He showed you something. What, though? Well, in a sense, he sacrificed himself as your authority so that you might begin thinking for yourself. His words cannot simply be accepted at face value— except by a fool at his own peril. An obvious way to respond would be to say that Thales spoke only "metaphorically," that he was just trying to communicate in a way that ordinary people would understand. But I think such a response misses the point. The first philosopher is indeed trying to communicate some profound truth to others, but he is also trying to make them profoundly aware that no one has a perfect monopoly on the truth.

In other words, once you—our ancient Milesian—have really thought about what you've just heard one of the most respected priests say, you realize that even if the gods do exist, you cannot know for certain whether any priest or oracle has direct access to the gods. Thales said he would enlighten you. What a revolutionary way of enlightening you—not by telling but by showing.

I believe that's the first thing to be learned by Thales' statement: a person in authority is showing you that to be wise you cannot simply be a follower of truth; you must yourself become a seeker of truth. At the heels of this first initial response to his statement there is another thing to learn. Not only has Thales evoked in you the desire to prove him wrong, you—an ordinary person—can do so. This second point is extremely important, as revolutionary as the first. Instead of being given a monologue that you are expected to obediently accept, you not only can enter into a dialogue, but you are forced into reacting, thinking, responding, debating, disagreeing. Can you see what a profound shift this is? Usually, even today, when you are in the presence of someone who is deemed very knowledgeable, a great expert in something, or wise, and you want to get the benefit of the knowledge or wisdom, you listen and try to remember what the person has said. Suppose a physicist tells you, "$F = ma$." That's a very important statement, a formula linking force with mass and acceleration. You learn the formula and you apply it—that's the purpose of the physicist telling it to you in the first place. Or the doctor tells you that your blood pressure is too high; you better remember to do something about it. As a child, you learned what to eat and what not to eat. In most cases, the purpose of making statements about things is to tell you something you need to record and remember. Statements made in science, mathematics, geography, and so on, are designed for that purpose. But look now at the difference between that and the purpose of philosophical statements. The purpose of philosophical statements is not merely to give you an answer you are supposed to record and remember (though sometimes that can be the intent), but in addition to awaken your awareness, to make you wonder, to make you look for yourself: in a word, to understand through questioning.

Scientific and mathematical statements will often lead to the same result. Great scientists and mathematicians often engage in philosophy when they begin to question the statements they have been taught to accept as true. Often, such activity leads to new breakthroughs in science and mathematics, to overturning longstanding theories and replacing them with revolutionary ones, and creating whole new areas of inquiry. In other words, physics and mathematics is not invented by physicists and mathematicians per se, any more than the English language is invented by the British or the German language is invented by the Germans. Rather, as history bears out, physics and mathematics are invented by philosophers. Sometimes, as in the case of Pythagoras, Descartes, Leibniz, and Russell (whom you will meet in later pages), they are philosophers first who come to the other disciplines with specific questions that bring new insights and developments. Other times, they are scientists or mathematicians first who become true philosophers when they begin to question their systems of knowledge and frameworks of understanding (what "systems" and "frameworks" are and how they "work" is one major aspect of philosophy that we shall explore throughout this book).

There is also a third and a related fourth thing that can be learned from Thales' statement, so profoundly important that in many ways these overshadow the first two. Look again at the statement "Everything is made of water." The first two responses are mainly negative and predicated on the observation that the statement is obviously false; we now turn to the statement's positive aspect. That is, let us now assume for the moment that Thales, who we have every reason to believe was extremely wise, knows what he is doing and so besides evoking in us the desire to find out for ourselves and to question, there may be some truth in what he says about the world. It then occurs to us that, in whatever sense the statement is true, it does not seem to be the case that everything is made of water. In other words, appearances are deceiving. But more than that: In what way are they deceiving?

Looking around, you see many different sorts of things: tables, chairs, rocks, stars, people, air, fire, and so on. The ancient philosophers whom you will meet in the upcoming pages will often talk about this aspect of the world by referring to "the many." In speaking of "the many," they are simply referring to the things you see around you. They also will speak of "the appearances." In speaking of "the appearances," they are referring to the way everything appears. And the way things appear is not always the way they actually are. For instance, standing on railroad tracks, it looks as if the two tracks converge, which you know is false: in actuality the tracks are parallel. Likewise, things that are closer seem bigger than things further away, which is not always true (but sometimes is). But that's not even the whole of it. Not only are appearances deceiving, the least obvious and most deceptive way in which the appearances are deceiving is that they do not appear to be appearances! They appear to be things. But think about it. Do things shrink and grow as you move closer to or further from them? No. Only the appearances do. Of course, as always in philosophy, language is especially tricky here in that the word *appearance* is ambiguous; for there is the sense in which my hand (i.e., the image of my hand) appears to get smaller as I move it further from my eyes and there is the sense in which my hand does not "appear" to change in size at all: that is, only by paying special attention do I notice relative size differences. Under ordinary circumstances there is what is called "object constancy," the mind's ability to interpret varying image relations in such a way as to make the visual appearances appear more constant than what is given by their actual visual geometries. So there is an important sense in which the objects that appear before the mind can't be the things themselves as they exist "out there" in the world independently of the mind but, rather, are only objects as they appear to the mind. Most things don't appear to be water. Thales is saying that the way things appear is not the way they are. He is saying that the appearances are not the things themselves. Reality is something beyond mere appearance.

In other words, an aspect of the appearances that Thales draws attention to is that they appear as a many. In saying that everything is made of water, he is saying that what appears to be a many is, in reality, a one. The appearances are but different aspects of one and the same thing. But why water? If you think about it and do some experiments, you will see that water has no shape, no "form" of its own. Pour it in a round container, the water takes on a round shape. Pour it in a square container, it takes on a square shape. And so on.

But, still, one may wonder: why water? Here's the metaphysical[4] surprise: the fact that some substance has a constantly changing shape (as liquid does) makes it the prime candidate for underlying unity (and water's ability to quickly change from a liquid to gaseous state may be deeply relevant).[5] So the idea Thales is trying to communicate is that behind the appearances, which present themselves to us as a many, there is an underlying unity. Reality is to be understood as some sort of underlying unity. Ultimately, everything is made of one single substance.

Thales calls this universal substance "water." If you think this idea is scientifically naive, then consider this: for the next twenty-five centuries, the whole history and development of philosophy and science has altered Thales' statement by one word! That history goes something like this:

Everything is made of water.

Everything is made of air.

Everything is made of the indeterminate boundless.

Everything is made of fire.

Everything is made of numbers.

Everything is made of atoms.

Everything is made of quarks.

Consider tables, chairs, books, rocks, people, cars . . . what are these things? From the perspective of our looking at them (how they appear to us), these seem to be very different things. But what are all these things made of? Tables are made of atoms. Chairs are made of atoms. Books are made of atoms. People and cars are made of atoms. Everything is made of atoms! And what about the atoms themselves? They're made of the ultimate subatomic particles: quarks! Indeed, in the twentieth century, post-Einsteinian physics has come to understand all matter in terms of one universal substance, mass-energy. Some quantum physicists have even come up with theories equating mass-energy with space, one universal medium, a single reality underlying all things.[6]

Lest you think that all of these ideas form an unambiguous map for our journey through the evolution of Western thought, keep in mind that there is but one other statement made by Thales that has been attributed to him: "Everything is full of gods."

Anaximander: The Infinite Boundless

If somebody told you that everything is made of water, the first and most obvious thing you could do is try and prove that the statement is false. This, in fact, is exactly what one of Thales' young students, Anaximander of Miletus (d. 546 B.C.E.), did. Our historical information about Anaximander comes from one of Aristotle's students, Theophrastus (370–287 B.C.E.), who wrote many volumes of ancient history of which only a few fragments remain. In the first, he quotes directly from Anaximander's otherwise lost book (which also is our only source, by testimony, for what Thales said).

Anaximander agreed with Thales that all individual things derive their existence from one eternal, indestructible universal something into which they ultimately return when they cease to exist as individual things, but he disagreed about what that ultimate source of existence is. How and why the Milesians came to think that everything in the world reduced to some single, underlying substance is as mysterious as the question of where any ideas—right or wrong, true or false, important or unimportant—come from. And that question is one we shall explore in more detail later (John Locke in the seventeenth century, for instance, will write an essay, "Where Our Ideas Come From"; see Chapter 3). But we can to a certain degree trace the reasoning by which Anaximander moved away from Thales' conception of water as the ultimate substance to the infinite boundless, for Anaximander's argument is preserved by Aristotle. In a way that would become a pivotal bone of contention among philosophers up to the present day, Anaximander disagreed with Thales regarding the degree to which truth can be expressed using the terms of ordinary language. If you think about it, you will realize that language was not invented by people but is something that evolved over time. That is, it developed naturally through the activities of people, not through the sort of conscious design involved in *invention*. That is the clear sense in which the Germans did not invent German, the English did not invent English; so how did language arise?

One leading theory is that language arose as a way of making noises consistently to refer to various things among our perceptions. Consider, for instance, the sounds (not the words) "water," "fire," "air," and so on; these noises are made consistently to stand for something we wish to refer to in our experience. Experience consists of appearances. If, as Thales and his students all readily assert, the appearances are deceiving (because there is, according to them, an underlying reality beyond appearances that is radically different from things as they appear to us through our senses), then isn't language, too, deceiving? That is, since language evolved to describe the appearances, how can we use it to get at what is beyond the appearances? This is the question Anaximander asked and then answered in the negative.

According to Anaximander, philosophy can solve this problem by creating new terms to stand for new concepts. These new, "technical" terms will not simply be an attempt to refer to immediate appearances. He thus takes what he thinks to be the essential aspects of water and abstracts from them their underlying concept to create a new, "nonvisualizable," abstract concept. In thus trying to capture the abstract "idea" of water, he comes up with the abstract concept: the "infinite boundless." This is the key ideal aspect of the type of thing water is, which makes water such a good metaphor for the underlying substance, the "stuff of reality." But water is just a metaphor, and the infinite boundless is, paradoxically, the more literal truth. In other words, the concrete empirical concept is, for Anaximander, not the literal truth but the truth expressed metaphorically. Individual things have a specific, finite shape; water has no shape. Individual things have an intrinsic, built-in boundary; water has no such boundary. The basic idea is that the world exists as an undifferentiated, infinite substance, a cosmic, frothing ocean in which individual things arise through its various, internal motions, among which are the appearances as reflected in the mind's eye, the human soul.

Anaximenes: A Question of Language

Philosophy progresses, it evolves, it rarely stands still. Though philosophers build upon the work of their predecessors, they continually revise and often overthrow the views of their predecessors—sometimes, even those of their own teachers. One of the most famous examples will come in the sequence from Socrates to Plato to Aristotle; here, at the very beginning of philosophy, still centuries before the golden age of Greece, we can see this evolutionary process of thought begin to unfold in the progression from Thales to Anaximenes. For just as Anaximander made his mark by disagreeing with and rethinking his teacher's philosophy, so his own young student, Anaximenes (585–528 B.C.E.), found the notion of an infinite boundless unintelligible.

Anaximenes argued that Thales had originally been on the right track. To discover the ultimate truths about ourselves and the world, we ought, according to Anaximenes, rely solely on known terms (water, air, etc.) as they arise in common language. We ought to avoid inventing new terms and the abstractions of thought that such a purely theoretical language would evoke. In other words, he claimed —as some philosophers in the twentieth century have claimed (the "ordinary language" philosophers)—that moving away from ordinary language into abstract terms should be avoided because such terms are *meaningless*. Only words as they arise in reference to specific objects found in our experience are legitimate. Anaximenes thus used simple, ordinary terms in an unpretentious, lean writing style very different from the lyrical, poetical prose of Anaximander. He wrote a book that has since been lost but was celebrated for many centuries for the lucidity of its prose. Theophrastus devoted a long passage to the work, which at least gives us a glimpse into Anaximenes' ideas, if not his style.

According to Anaximenes, the primary, infinite substance underlying all things is "air." He thought this notion was a great improvement over both of his predecessors, retaining the best aspects of their ideas. Air, like water, has properties that also evoke even better the abstract idea of a substance that is an "infinite boundless" because air is invisible. You cannot see air, you can see only its effects. Yet "air" is a perfectly ordinary term, familiar to all. Whereas Anaximander used the problematic concept of motion (see the upcoming section on Zeno's paradoxes of motion) to explain differentiation within the single primary substance underlying all things, Anaximenes used ideas like "rarefaction" and "condensation" to explain how "air that is condensed forms winds . . . [and] if this process goes further, it gives water, still further earth, and the greatest condensation of all is found in stones."

So what we see here, at the earliest beginnings of recorded history, is that from the very start philosophy involved discussions and debates not just about truth, but about our methods of inquiry into truth. That is, what distinguishes philosophy from straightforward scientific inquiry is that in philosophy the issue isn't merely about what the truth is, but about how we can *know* what the truth is. This central aspect of philosophy has remained a central issue to the present day. The physicist knows things, the biologist knows things, the poet knows things; the philosopher asks, *How* does the physicist know? *How* does the biologist know? *How* does the poet know? We thus see from the very beginning of philosophy the emergence of inquiry into *methods of inquiry* that have remained central themes to the present day not just in philosophy but also in science and mathematics.

It is for this reason that philosophy is often described as a second-order activity: thinking about thinking, knowing about knowing, and so on. But this clarification of what philosophy is should not obscure the equally important underlying idea being put forth by Anaximenes, already well established in Presocratic views, that everything in the world reduces to one underlying substance. The related question of what sort of language to use to describe truth—whether we should create new, technical terms and concepts or whether we should stick to the familiar terms of ordinary language—is still a living issue today, along with the perplexing question of what constitutes meaningful versus meaningless expressions and theories.

Pythagoras: Everything Is Numbers

In the light green-blue Aegean Sea between Miletus and Athens lies a tiny island called Samos that during the time of the ancient Greek philosophers was the main commercial rival of Miletus. It was also the birthplace of its leading philosophical rival, Pythagoras (572–497 B.C.E.), whom Bertrand Russell (Chapter 5) called "intellectually one of the most important men that ever lived . . . one of the most interesting and puzzling men in history."

Small wonder that a powerful politician named Polycrates, the tyrant of Samos, banished him from the island. Pythagoras migrated to Crotona, a Dorian colony in southern Italy where he and his students formed a religious brotherhood based on ancient Orphic rites, similar to the Hindu religious tradition, designed to purify the soul so as to free it from the "wheel of birth." Pythagoras's philosophy owed much to the religious traditions of the time, many of which relied almost exclusively on mystical rituals, as well as to the views of the Milesian thinkers from whom his philosophy would develop in sharp contrast. He created a syncretic unique blend of what today would be considered opposites: mysticism and mathematics. His mathematics became the avatar of the demonstrative deductive argument that Pythagoras invented and which is still the foundation of mathematical thinking today; while his mysticism[7] became the basis of a new religion in which mathematics and a new type of music, also developed by him, became the methods by which he and his followers tried to attain philosophical enlightenment.

Thales was still alive, teaching sailors how to sail the seas at night, when Pythagoras invented the Western musical scale. Music as we know it was born on Pythagoras's discovery that, by measuring the appropriate lengths of string on a monochord, musical intervals correspond to simple numerical ratios between the first four integers: the lengths in the ratio 2:3:4 emit a tonic, its fifth, and its octave, respectively, and the major triad has relative frequencies expressible in the ratio 4:5:6. Pythagoras not only invented new string instruments (like the one that became the basis for the guitar) but also showed empirically that these ratios hold for vibrating strings as well as for resonating air columns, thereby laying the foundation for the subsequent construction of pipe organs. His students, sworn to secrecy about his musical, mathematical, and philosophical discoveries, swore oaths on the tetractys, a series of dots summarizing the musical harmonies:

octave (2:1)   •

                           •   •   fifth (3:2)

fourth (4:3)   •   •   •

            •   •   •   •

The Pythagoreans were so impressed by the tetractys that they saw in it the secret insight that all of nature can be understood through mathematics—an idea that would influence later thinkers for centuries to come and still today is accepted by most scientists. It was also Pythagoras who showed for the first time how the concept of number can be used to explain musical harmonies. For instance, the first four integers, 1, 2, 3, and 4, are essential in that they can be represented in an equilateral triangle of ten dots as arranged above. He and his students had a secret oath to the mathematical God of the cosmos, which began, "By him that gave to our generation the tetractys which contains the fountain and root of eternal nature. . . ."

Pythagoras thought that by using the concept of number and the methods of mathematics he could decipher the inner workings of the mind. Further, he believed that by using mathematical philosophy he could perfect the mind's intellectual and perceptual abilities by "purifying" it of its many deceptions and errors. Thus, according to Pythagoras, it is not religion but philosophy, mathematics, and science that teach the real instruments of enlightenment.

His famous theorem, which still today bears the name, the *Pythagorean theorem,* revealed to the world for the first time the intimate and important relationship between arithmetic and geometry—between number and magnitude. It lay the conceptual foundation for subsequent philosophers and scientists to create systems of thought based on the view that the structure and order of the universe can be completely understood by the human mind—provided that its logical and reasoning abilities are perfected along with its powers of mystical insight. Unlike today, when these two tendencies of the human mind are viewed in sharp contrast, the Pythagoreans tried to create a complete understanding of themselves and the world through combining mathematics, philosophy, and mysticism into an integrated system of thought. The most important and fundamental aspect of their thought, with intriguing implications for us today, is that the point of contact between the rational and the mystical was mathematics. This is because the universe and everything in it, according to the Pythagoreans, revealed itself as consisting of numbers.

Just as Thales said that "everything is made of water," Pythagoras argued that "everything is made of numbers." There is both a striking difference between the two statements and a striking similarity. Obviously, Pythagoras's proposition is a variation of the same formula, according to which all separately existing things in the universe—"the many"—ultimately consist of the same sort of thing, though of course it must be kept in mind that numbers are not "things." Similarly, it certainly doesn't *seem* as if everything is made of numbers. Thus, once again, the fundamental idea is that appearances are deceiving. But, notice that according to Pythagoras the underlying oneness is not some sort of *stuff* or *matter,* as Thales, Anaximander, and Anaximenes (the Milesian philosophers) thought; indeed, reality is not a *thing* at all. This is one of the most important philosophical insights of all time: the recognition that there is a distinction between tangible *things* and intangible *ideas.* Think about it: if numbers are not things and everything is made of numbers, then everything must ultimately be made not of *things* but *ideas.* The profound importance of this move can best be understood in contrast to the Milesian view that the world is some sort of undifferentiated, unified, single substance —"water," "the indeterminate boundless," "air," and so on. For while Thales, Anaximander, and Anaximenes could only allude to what accounted for the differentiation observed among all things using complex and obscure notions,

Pythagoras could explain the observed differences among things with the all-important concept of *ideal form,* based on his concepts of *limit* and *proportion,* both of which can be understood in purely numerical terms. The concept of ideal forms will turn out to be the key notion in the philosophy of Plato. Further, it is the numbers themselves that represent the application of a specific *limit,* or *form,* to the *unlimited* stuff of the world (matter or substance). This line of Pythagoras's thought paved the way for the philosophy of Plato.

Philosophy students often wonder what makes the Pythagorean theorem so special. Here is the theorem: Let a triangle in the plane have sides of length a, b, and c. Then this triangle is a right triangle whose hypotenuse has length c if and only if $a^2 + b^2 = c^2$. This formula says that the sum of the squares of the lengths of the legs equals the square of the length of the hypotenuse:

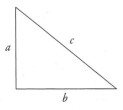

Now, why is this theorem so important? It is of course nice as a tool to calculate distances. But Thales was already able to do this, and Pythagoras is merely formalizing his predecessor's methods. What is so *philosophically* astounding about that? And yet this proof has had a great impact on philosophers over the last twenty-five centuries. Consider, for example, the case of the great early modern philosopher Thomas Hobbes (1588–1679; Chapter 3). Hobbes's friend John Aubrey writes that Hobbes "was 40 years old before he looked on geometry, which happened accidentally. Being in a gentleman's library Euclid's *Elements* lay open, and it was the Theorem of Pythagoras. Hobbes read the proposition. 'By God,' says he, 'this is impossible!' So he reads the demonstration of it, which referred him back to such a proposition, which proposition he read. That referred him back to another, which he also read. *Et sic deincepts,* that at last he was demonstratively convinced of the truth."

What did Hobbes see? Well, you may have noticed that the proposition "The sum of the squares of adjoining perpendicular lines having lengths a and b respectively is the square of the line connecting their endpoints, length c," which is what $a^2 + b^2 = c^2$ of the Pythagorean theorem says, is not obviously true. In other words, you can't tell just by looking at the two sides of a right triangle that the ratio of the length of the hypotenuse to the sum of the two sides is as Pythagoras proves it must be. Indeed, one can *see* no reason why the ratio must be so. And yet it must be so. Hobbes's initial disbelief isn't just that the ratio is as Pythagoras says it is, but that it can be proven by *showing what cannot be seen.* If you recall the previous discussion about the appearances, you will see the significance at once: we are discovering, through mathematics, truths that cannot be seen. We are seeing beyond the appearances. A theorem, like Pythagoras's, is a type of proposition. *Propositions* are statements that are either true or false. Some propositions, like "Two points determine a line," can be seen to be true without proof. These are sometimes called "self-evident." Self-evidence is a deeply influential notion; for instance, when the authors of the U.S. Constitution wrote, "We take these truths to be self-evident," they were evoking this ancient notion and applying it to the domain of prescriptive, moral claims. In mathematics, such fundamental propositions are called *axioms*. Once the axioms are stated, then further propositions can be proven to be true by using the *axiomatic method;* the propositions proved in this manner, as in the case of Pythagoras's proposition, are called *theorems.*

The axiomatic method begins with axioms and moves step by step, using other axioms, to derive some new proposition, called the *conclusion.* This is in part what Pythagoras gave to mathematics and philosophy. The whole procedure is called an *argument.* The type of argument Pythagoras gave to the world, which has been the foundation of mathematical thought and much of philosophy for the last twenty-five centuries, is the *demonstrative deductive argument.* You may have noticed, for instance, that Hobbes's reaction to Pythagoras's proof shows that he is amazed how each proposition leading up to the conclusion is intuitively obvious, whereas the conclusion is not at all intuitively obvious. This is the cornerstone of the deductive method of reasoning. Yet it is also what gave impetus to Pythagoras's mysticism. The idea is that you can take one intuitively obvious step after another until you end up with an intuitively unobvious conclusion which is itself known to be true with perfect certainty. This method will have a profound influence on all subsequent Western thought, especially on the work of Plato.

As Pythagoras neared the end of his life, his students and devoted followers began to argue among themselves. They eventually split into two rival factions. The *akousmatics* followed the mystical and ritual side of his teaching. They considered Pythagoras to be an enlightened guru who could teach them how to join their minds with the cosmos, to make them one with the universe. The other group called themselves the *mathematicians.* They believed literally in Pythagoras's statement that everything is made of numbers, ruled not by mystical forces or gods but that the cosmos itself is logical, and they laid the foundations of mathematics as it is practiced today.

Pythagoras deeply lamented the division of his philosophy into factions. To him, music, mathematics, and mysticism were all part of a unified cosmos to which the individual philosopher must aspire holistically. Today, most people are of the opinion that the world is far too complex to be comprehended by any single individual. They believe that the knowledge-seeking enterprise, as practiced in today's colleges and universities, must be strictly compartmentalized to function properly. How remarkable to realize that the unifying vision lies not at the end of our journey but at the beginning, in the open hearts and minds of sages like Pythagoras who conceived, designed, and built everything from virtually nothing, lovers of wisdom who before they died launched the ships for our faring-forth.

Heraclitus: The Flux

Anaximenes, the youngest of the first three great Milesian philosophers, was already an old man by the time Heraclitus (540–480 B.C.E.) was born in Ionia, which today is called Turkey. Heraclitus grew up and lived on the west coast, where jagged rocks jut into the sea like meteors from outer space, in Ephesus, a city halfway between Miletus and Colophon. Unlike his predecessors, who were commoners elevated to their respective positions of authority by their learning and achievements, Heraclitus was of noble descent from the earlier kings of Ephesus. He was a rich nobleman who renounced any pretense to the throne and gave up all family privileges to his younger brother, and he did it out of love for philosophy. And very much unlike Thales, Anaximander, and Anaximenes, who were respectful of their society and their positions as figures of authority, Heraclitus was profoundly the first of a long tradition of philosophers who openly criticized their societies and fellow citizens, including other philosophers. For instance, when his fellow Ephesians put one of Heraclitus's teachers, Hermodorus, on trial for corrupting the youth and raising questions about the accepted gods—a foreshadowing of the similar fate awaiting the future philosophical rebel, Socrates—Heraclitus declared: "The Ephesians would do well to hang themselves, every adult man, and bequeath their city-state to adolescents." In other words, the leaders, being full of ignorance and pretense, should give way to the youth because the youth have not yet been corrupted. We shall see this same theme again in the trial and death of Socrates.

What remains of Heraclitus's major philosophical work, published around 500 B.C.E.—about 100 fragments as quoted by subsequent writers—reveals the vivid, cryptic, and prophetic style that earned him the nickname "the Obscure." Because we have no continuous narrative, to glimpse his thoughts we must rely solely on brief statements taken from his surviving aphorisms. Here, for instance, is his definition of wisdom, based in part on the Milesian premise of cosmic unity: "Wisdom is one thing: to understand the thought which steers all things through all things." Again, as with his Milesian predecessors, we find the idea that beneath the multitudinous, scattered, and fragmented world of appearance lies an underlying oneness, except for a tangential but crucial difference. Heraclitus intuits the unity hidden behind the veil of appearance not as the Milesians did, in terms of some persisting physical substance, but as the Pythagoreans did, as an ideal, formal, ultimately mathematical reality.

There is some reason to believe that Heraclitus knew, perhaps even studied with, Pythagoras. But whereas the Pythagorean approach reduces everything to mathematics, the Heraclitan approach reduces everything to logic. Indeed, as we shall see in Chapter 5, Bertrand Russell's attempt in the early part of the twentieth century to reduce mathematics to logic can be viewed as a modern-day attempt to bridge the Pythagorean and Heraclitan world view.

Heraclitus observed the things you can observe by paying close attention to your own immediate experience, not by thinking about them but by looking at the act of looking: the appearances are in constant flux and undergoing constant change. All things, mental phenomena when you carefully look at them and physical phenomena when you carefully think about them, correspondingly come into being and pass away. The idea that one or the other sort of phenomena —either physical (as for the atomists) or mental (as for the idealists)—were enduring objects over time, perhaps even a primary aspect of being itself, would become the cornerstone for the complementary view of Heraclitus's great contemporary, Parmenides. The difference between these two antithetical but complementary thinkers, often exaggerated merely as polar opposites, comes down to a question of emphasis. According to Parmenides, it is the apparent changes observed in experience—the ephemeral, the transient—that must be explained away as illusory, in terms of some unchanging, permanent substance. According to Heraclitus, on the other hand, it is the apparent permanencies observed in experience that need to be explained away as illusory, in terms of eternal, fixed laws of change and motion. In many ways, as we shall see, modern thought until the end of the nineteenth century, especially in science, was fundamentally Parmenidean, whereas the twentieth century, which saw the advent of quantum mechanics (Chapter 4), was a return to a fundamentally Heraclitan perspective.

One of Heraclitus's most famous aphorisms is "You can't step into the same river twice." He couches this in terms of unity found through the discovery of the world order via a uniting of opposites, much in the way that centuries later the proponents of a variety of dialectic philosophers would claim. He writes:

> All things come into being through opposition, and all are in flux like a river. Upon those who step into the same rivers flow other and yet other waters.

The recurrent theme of water is reminiscent of Thales:

> Cool things become warm; what is warm cools; what is wet dries out; what is dry becomes moist.
>
> Sea water is very pure and very impure; drinkable and healthful for fishes, but undrinkable and destructive to humans.

Essential to Heraclitus's thinking is the process of the coming together of opposites which, when properly understood, reveals the hidden cosmic unity not in things, which are themselves ephemeral, but in the idea (form, or shape) of things expressed through universal laws of change that cannot be understood except in terms of their own opposites:

> The path traced by the pen is straight and crooked.
>
> In a circle, beginning and end are common.
>
> The way up and the way down are the same.
>
> This world-order, the same for all, no god made or any man, but it always was and is and will be an ever-living, all-consuming fire, kindling by measure and going out by measure.

Once we understand such opposites as manifestations of common principles as revealed through reason, the mind learns that the world was neither created nor can it be destroyed, for it is ceaselessly coming into being and passing away according to the laws of chaos and chance. When Heraclitus describes the world as represented in the appearances allegorically as an "ever-living, all-consuming fire," he means that the only order among the chaos, the only permanence among the impermanence, the only thing that does not change, is change itself, as manifested by the underlying laws governed by reason, the *logos,* an eternal pattern of cosmic flux. In doing so, he foreshadows in an important way the modern concept of uniform law as the basis for the nature of the cosmos.

When the ancient Greek philosophers referred to the world as a whole, they called it *cosmos,* meaning "ordered whole." In Heraclitus's philosophy, the human mind must ignore the world of deceptive appearances so as to be guided by the invisible logic of its own operations, in order to apprehend through the dark light of reason the hidden, underlying logic of existence. In this way the mind becomes a mirror of the cosmos through the universal, cosmic law: the logos (whose etymological origin is discussed below). This is possible because the mind as logos can perceive regularities from out of the flux of ever-changing and ephemeral sensations so as to think and speak about them. And this, in turn, is possible because the mind as logos and the world as cosmos are inextricably linked by the same principle: the logos and the cosmos are one being (for which there is no word). The human mind as logos and the world as cosmos are ultimately guided by the same laws and principles, according to which all the many separately existing things in the world are united. The appearances show the individual things of the world to be many and in constant flux, but reason reveals a hidden cosmic unity beneath the apparent diversity.[8] This mystical insight cannot be seen directly, however; it must be intuited. It transcends the subjective opinions of those barely conscious souls who sleepwalk through life. Heraclitus writes:

> To those who are awake the world-order is one, common to all; but the sleeping turn aside each into a world of his own. We ought not to act and speak like men asleep. We ought to follow what is common to all; but though the logos is common to all, the many live as though their thought were private to themselves.

The word *logos* is derived from a verb meaning "to speak," but had several different meanings in ancient Greek. Most important, it referred both to the words used by a speaker and to the thought, or meaning, thereby expressed, which exists independently of the words. It thus signified reason or order both in words (which makes language and thought possible) and in things (which makes existence and the world possible). The logos thus is both what guides the world and what makes the world intelligible to the human mind. It is at once the source of all natural processes and of human reason. The Stoics will use this notion in their view of the world as a living, breathing unity, supremely perfect in its conjoinment between individuals and the whole. The logos according to the Stoics gives rise to the concept of divine Providence as well as to the idea of Nature conceived as an ordered course of events. Subsequent thinkers went on to conceive the logos as an immaterial instrument, the personal agency through which God guides the course of events in the world. In Christian philosophy, the logos became the second person of the Trinity, Jesus Christ. The fourth Gospel of the New Testament begins with the cryptic statement, "In the beginning was the word," where "word" is a translation of "logos." And "the word became flesh."

Heraclitus's idea that the inner workings of the human mind and the inner workings of the world are structured by the same underlying reality will find its fullest expression in the work of Immanuel Kant. Unfortunately, according to Heraclitus, the majority of people ignore the logos, even after it has been explained to them. This is because the human mind, not fully awake or enlightened to its own presence in the world, tends to constantly divide its understanding into oversimplified, black-and-white thinking, disagreeing with itself. Its own naive concepts suggest that things must be one way or another, never both. The problem, in other words, is that we think in simplistic, rigid terms using words that are limited and incapable of expressing the whole truth except through reasoning. Our concepts are divisive of the whole and therefore cannot render the world as it really is. Thus according to Heraclitus we must learn to make room for what to the unenlightened mind will seem like utterly perplexing contradictions.

Is the cosmos one or many? Heraclitus says: both. How is that possible? It is a question of perspective. From the point of view of our perceptions—the appearances, the images the mind makes in response to its senses—what we see is a many. This is because our perceptions consist of opposites: small and large, infinite and finite, hot and cold, dead and living, wet and dry, and so on—all of which constantly undergo change, going from one state to the other. But why then does everything not vanish? The fact that it doesn't, says Heraclitus, suggests that there must be something behind everything, keeping it all going, always present but nowhere to be seen: the logos. It is reason that corrects our ever-flickering view of the world due to our constantly changing perceptions, revealing that despite all the changes something must nevertheless remain the same.

We shall see Heraclitus's ideas about the nature of the world and the mind's attempt to comprehend it resurface again and again in the thoughts of Plato, the Stoics, Kant, Hegel, Nietzsche, and Wittgenstein.

Parmenides: All Is One

Parmenides (515–445 B.C.E.) was born in Elea (called Velia today), a town of labyrinthine streets in southern Italy, on the other side of the known world from where Heraclitus and the other Ionians lived. The journey of ideas from Thales to Anaximander to Anaximenes culminates in Parmenides. As a young man he went to study with the followers of Anaximander in Athens, which was situated just about at the center of the then-known world. Afterward, he joined Pythagoras's religious and philosophical brotherhood in Crotona, where he began to formulate his version of cosmic unity, a view in which all borders and boundaries between things dissolve, leaving a single, unified totality: being, of which it can only be said, "All is one."

All that remains of Parmenides' writings are 160 lines of a poem he wrote in honor of his most illustrious student, Zeno. His style is Pythagorean mysticism combined with myths and allegories. He may have written the work to confound and mislead the uninitiated while passing on to his initiates the secret teachings of the wise and enlightened masters. It describes a journey from darkness into light and beyond, in which Philosophy, the goddess of wisdom, appears to him as she one day would to Boethius. She then proceeds to enlighten him about the true nature of reality. She tells him he must not only learn about the absolute truth, about which there can be no disagreement, but also acquaint himself with all the misleading opinions among which there can be no truth so that he will know the difference and not be deceived.

Philosophy tells him that there are three ways to try to discover the truth about reality. The first is to inquire into what does not exist: "It is not, and there must be not-being." But this is impossible. What does not exist cannot really be thought of: thinking is itself something. The second way is to inquire into "what is" and to say both that "it is and is not" or "it is the same and it is not the same." This is the Heraclitan way. The third and only correct path to truth according to Philosophy is to start from the fundamental proposition, "It is, and not-being is impossible."

The idea is that while it seems we can think about either what is or what is not, in reality we cannot think about what is not. We can think only about what is since whatever we think about is, itself, an object of thought. This is what Parmenides means in identifying thought and being as one and the same. Thoughts themselves—even the thought "Goblins exist"—exist and have being regardless of whether the things described by the thoughts exist. When we think that goblins exist, for instance, we are merely thinking something false about what exists, namely, that the world contains goblins. We are not thereby thinking about not-being, but about something that exists (albeit only in our thoughts). Not-being is not a possible object of thought for it is not an object, it is nothing. And since nothing is not, we must reject the first of the three ways of inquiry into truth.

By similar reasoning we should reject the second way of inquiry, as advocated by Heraclitus. To say of "what is" that it is both "the same and not the same," as Heraclitus does, is according to Parmenides a grave mistake. Such a false way of thinking comes about because the mind is seduced by the power of its own appearances. We must therefore rise above the senses and rely solely on reason in determining what the truth is. If we do this, Parmenides claims, we will find that the world as a whole exists in and of itself, eternal and uncreated. Ultimate reality is permanent and unchangeable; it is whole, indivisible, and everywhere continuous.

Like Heraclitus, however, Parmenides identifies being with the thought that recognizes it. In this way, all the things our ordinary, commonsense conception predicates of reality—generation and destruction, being and not-being, change of position, change in qualities—are mere illusions. The way out of the illusion is to move beyond the realm of the senses and rely solely on reason to deny the reality of what our senses tell us is true of the world. In this way, the true nature of the cosmos, the world as a whole, will reveal itself, and the philosopher will see reality as it exists in and of itself, always identical with the thought that recognizes it.

Zeno of Elea: The Way of Paradox

It is one thing to come down off the mountaintop or out of the desert and make mystical proclamations about the nature of reality that fly in the face of common sense. Your audience either likes what it hears or not; as with poetry and religion, people can choose whether to believe or even listen. It is another thing to offer proof, not in terms of miracles, holy scriptures, reliance on authority, or hearsay, but with an explicit, logical, rational, mathematical demonstration. Poetry, myths, and allegories may seduce the heart and mind with beautiful metaphors, but mathematics goes straight for the brain. In none of the Presocratic philosophers was this more apparent than in Zeno of Elea (490–430 B.C.E.) who, like his teacher Parmenides, was initiated into both the Pythagorean mysteries and mathematical methods. Zeno entered the philosophical fray armed not with allegory or myth but with precise demonstration; like Pythagoras, he enlightened not with poetry but with mathematics.

According to Parmenides, reality is nothing like the appearances. Appearances are a many; Parmenidean reality is a one. You and I and everything in the world are in the eyes of Parmenides an undifferentiated, numerical unity. To most people such a view seems obviously false. The reason is itself obvious: it seems one can tell, just by looking, that a lot of different things exist, separated by space from other things; just open your eyes and Parmenides' view looks, literally, to be sheer nonsense. But it's even worse than that. Parmenides can argue all he wants that "all is one," but will this statement make you doubt the reality of what you see? Perhaps, in some intellectual sense, it might, but not in any practical sense. His theory does not alter the nature of appearance; there seems to be an inescapable primacy in the appearances themselves, fixed in our experience, that no amount of theorizing or argumentation can ever dispel. Arguing, believing—even knowing—that the appearances are an illusion in no way dispels the illusion. One could therefore ask, What good are Parmenides' theories and arguments if what he says makes nonsense of our actual sense experience and, further, can make no difference to our sense experience? Parmenidean arguments might fly in the face of common sense, but common sense flies in the face of Parmenidean philosophy. At best, Parmenides can support the view of an unseen reality beyond the appearances that *contradicts* the appearances but does not *alter* the appearances. That thinking and reasoning about the supposedly illusory nature of the appearances does not in any way alter the character of the appearances might therefore be taken as evidence that the flaw lies with Parmenides' argument, not with the commonsense view of reality. This, in fact, is exactly what most of his Greek contemporaries thought.

Zeno's response to such criticism based on common sense is as powerful as it is subtle: he shows that the commonsense view of reality based on the appearances is *itself* nonsensical! Further, the commonsense view is even *more* nonsensical than is the view of Parmenides! Zeno put forth such a carefully reasoned proof that it gave rise to a new form of argument, known as *dialectic,* the invention of which both Plato and Aristotle attribute to Zeno. In Plato, we find the following description of Zeno's book:

> In reality, this writing is a sort of reinforcement for the argument of Parmenides against those who try to turn it into ridicule on the ground that, if reality is one, the argument becomes involved in many absurdities and contradictions. This writing argues against those who uphold a Many, and gives them back as good as and better than they gave; its aim is to show that their assumption of multiplicity will be involved in still more absurdities than the assumption of unity, if it is sufficiently worked out.

Only fragments remain of Zeno's book, but even they contain paradoxes so deeply puzzling that they have confounded and confused not just laypersons but philosophers and mathematicians, up to the present day. As the twentieth-century philosopher Alfred North Whitehead notes, "No one has ever touched Zeno without refuting him, and every century thinks it worthwhile to refute him."

Zeno tries to prove Parmenides right by proving that the reasons you may have for thinking that Parmenides is wrong are bad reasons, that the absurdity which you might think is involved in Parmenides' view applies even more to your own commonsense view. In other words, instead of directly supporting Parmenides' view of reality, Zeno offers proofs that go against your own beliefs about what you take to be the commonsense reality. He does this by presenting paradoxes, which means "beyond" or "above" (*para*) "belief" (*doxa*). He invented about forty paradoxes designed to show that the ordinary, commonsense view of reality is nonsensical, that it is more absurd to believe what the appearances tell us is real than what Parmenides tells us is real.

To see why, let us consider one of Zeno's most famous paradoxes, that of motion. Nothing seems more obvious than the fact that things move from one place to another. That is one of the most fundamental tenets of the ordinary, commonsense view of things: the universe is a space (perhaps infinite) of many (perhaps infinite) things all moving about in a variety of motions. For instance, you get up and walk across the room. First you were there, now you are here. Parmenides says that in reality nothing changes, Being always remains the same. But isn't that a change? *Something* changed: the position of an object within the universe. Doesn't that make it obvious that the universe is not one undivided thing, but a plethora of different things, each one separated from the other, undergoing constant change and motion?

Zeno then asks: how did you get from there to here? Obvious answer: you moved. Zeno asks: before you got to the wall, did you first go halfway? Of course you did. After all, you did not simply pop out of existence over there and materialize over here. There is a space between you and the wall. And you can't cross that space unless you first go halfway. Zeno then asks: when you were at the point halfway to the wall—call it point 1—did you then reach the wall without first going half the *remaining* distance? Of course not. You first had to cross half of the remaining half distance—¼ distance—before you reached the wall. Call that point 2. Now, Zeno asks: when you were at point 2, did you cross the remaining ¼ distance to the wall without first going halfway between point 2 and the wall? Again, of course not; you would have had to first go ⅛ distance past point 2, to point 3. At that point you were halfway between point 2 and the wall, with only ¹⁄₁₆ meter remaining between you and the wall. Did you *then* suddenly appear all the way at the wall without first going half the remaining distance, to point 4, ¹⁄₃₂ of the original distance to the wall? No. And so on.

But look: to say it once, as Zeno was fond of putting it, is to say it forever. How many such points are there between you and the wall? Well, how high can you count? At point 1 you have halfway to go. At point 2 you have ¼ way to go. At point 3 you have ⅛ way to go. At point 4 you have ¹⁄₁₆ way to go. At point 5 you have ¹⁄₃₂ way to go. At point 6 you have ¹⁄₆₄ way to go. Do you see how this keeps on going? Do you ever run out of numbers? No. Is there ever a point at which you can't further divide the fraction? No. In fact, you can see the pattern in the explicit formula

$$d = \frac{1}{2^n}$$

where d is the remaining distance from point n. Thus, at point 6 you have

$$\frac{1}{2^6} = \frac{1}{64}$$

distance remaining, and so on forever. No matter how close you get to the wall, there is always another midpoint, halfway between wherever you are and the wall, still remaining!

Now, an obvious response to the paradox is this: *but I do get to the wall.* Well, but if you didn't get to the wall—if you actually never arrived—there would be no paradox, would there? Zeno's point is that our *appearances* do not accord with our commonsense thinking about what is going on, even in something as simple as crossing the room. It's easy to miss the depth of the problem because while experience keeps telling us that objects move and reach their destinations, at some point we can no longer see what is going on in the minute distances where the remaining fractions are very, very small:

But imagine that you have an infinitely powerful zoom microscope, which works as follows. In the viewfinder you see the tip of a needle approaching a grain of sand. The closer it gets, the more the microscope zooms in at exactly the same rate at which the needle is approaching the grain of sand: for every reduction of the distance between the needle and the sand by a factor of 2, the magnification increases by a factor of 2. What would you see? In the viewfinder the tip of the needle and the grain of sand get bigger and bigger, but the space between them remains the same. Or, to make things even more complicated, suppose that you have shrunk down to a microscopic size between the needle and the sand, and as the needle approaches you keep shrinking. What would you see? At some point, let us imagine that the atom at the front of the tip of the needle and the atom of sand closest to you are each, relative to you, the size of a planet. They keep getting closer and closer, but you keep shrinking. Would you ever see them touch?

Ever since Zeno posed his original paradoxes, subsequent philosophical reflection on such puzzling thought experiments has over the centuries challenged both mathematicians and scientists to try to answer what to this day remains unanswerable.[9] For instance, the idea of a derivative in calculus involves exactly this type of image. Infinitesimal calculus and quantum physics both try to offer theories that move us beyond the realm of object spaces as ordinarily conceived. In standard calculus, the real numbers are used. In infinitesimal calculus, new types of quantities are used. Quantum mechanics postulates that the ordinary concept of space and time completely breaks down at some point.

To recognize that Zeno's paradoxes are still not solved does not mean that our concepts of space, time, motion, and identity are completely worthless or that we should therefore give up rationality and the pursuit of knowledge. Sometimes, Zeno and Parmenides are interpreted in exactly that erroneous way, as extreme skeptics. The point, rather, is that even when our answers become good enough for practical purposes, we must not let them blind us to the ever-present mystery hovering just beyond the edge of perception, we must not hide behind our answers what is unanswerable. The philosophical method developed by Zeno extends our attention beyond our commonsense answers to the unanswerable, forcing us to be aware of the discrepancy both between reality and our concepts and between reality and our perception of reality. That is the point made by all the ancient Greek philosophers, from the Ionians, Zeno, and Parmenides to Protagoras and the Sophists and, as we shall see, even Plato.

And yet, at the same time, we must not forget that Zeno intended to use his paradoxes to defend Parmenides. In other words, he apparently believed in the positive thesis that "all is one," that the world in its entirety consists not in a collection of many things but in a single, indivisible unity. What, then, in light of Zeno's paradoxes not being solved, ought we to make of Parmenides' claim that "all is one"? Well, Zeno's paradox has just shown us why the commonsense notion of the universe as an ever-changing collection of many different things, separated from other things, all constantly moving about in space, is deeply paradoxical. And if we were to accept Parmenides' view, then there is still a paradox: namely, why does the world not appear as it is? That is, why do we experience the world as a many (or at least think we do) instead of as a one?

The deeper philosophical problem is this. There is what we might call "our experience of reality." This is just our experience as it unfolds and which we take (rightly or wrongly) to be real. When we think about what reality *really* is like, even when we do so on the basis of our experience, we often come to the conclusion that reality is vastly different than how it appears to us in experience. Let us call this our "view of reality." Thus, even if we accept Zeno's paradox as a true refutation of our "experience of reality," and we accept Zeno's and Parmenides' "view of reality," there appears to be no way to reconcile these two opposites. We shall now consider the first of many subsequent attempts to do exactly that.

Protagoras and the Sophists

Protagoras (480–410 B.C.E.) was born in Abdera, a coastal town in the northernmost hub of the Aegean Sea. Along with Anaxagoras and Zeno of Elea, he enjoyed the patronage of Pericles (495–429), the enlightened political leader and military general most responsible for the development of the Athenian democracy and the rise of the Greek Empire. Protagoras spent most of his adult life traveling throughout the empire, teaching anyone for a fee. His exposure to many different societies, with a lot of different customs, laws, and religions, no doubt impressed on him the vast latitude of ideas that the human mind could accept as true. As a teacher of Pericles, who defended democracy in Athens against the plutocracies of neighboring Corinth and the military warrior nobilities of Sparta, Protagoras showed the great leader the extent to which religious and moral codes were based not on nature or some God-given truth but on socially constructed conventions. Rhetoric, the art of persuasive speech, could and should therefore be used, according to him, to influence people's opinions and change them in ways that great leaders like Pericles could see would be best, at least relative to the interests of the society. In that way, Protagoras anticipated Plato's concept of the philosopher king.

As the oldest and generally regarded the wisest of the sophists who came to Athens, Protagoras wielded a huge influence. The word *sophist* appears in the word *philosophy*, which consists of the Greek *philein*—"to love"—and *sophia*—"wisdom." The word *philosophy* means "love of wisdom," and *philosopher* means "lover of wisdom." Thus the early "sophists" were, literally, "wise men." They appeared in the Greek city-states during the fifth century B.C.E. as "traveling teachers for hire," who taught the youth of the aristocracy who aspired to power. With the advent of democracy in that century, a new and profound power shift had occurred among the ruling class, one that had a definite and positive affect on the birth of philosophy. Whereas before to attain power you had merely to have inherited a political position, wealth, or land, now to attain positions of political authority you had to demonstrate your intellectual skills and earn the right to power. This required skills of argumentation and rhetoric; you had to win your case in open debate. The sophists came from all over the known world, often from nondemocratic localities where their brand of disputation had often gotten them in trouble with the authorities, to take advantage of these new freedoms by seeking employment for their knowledge and abilities.

Thus the word *sophist* did not originally have the pejorative connotation it has today, that of someone who uses a superficial grasp of knowledge and truth to confuse, confound, and manipulate, which is due mainly to the influence of the sophists' great adversary, Plato. The sophists came to Athens at a time when there was no education as we know it today. It was not until Plato's Academy—built in part as an alternative to the way of the sophists—that the first university was born, one which is still the model of most institutions of higher learning today. Up to the time of Plato, education in ancient Greece was for the privileged and the few; the sophists, however, had already begun to tip the balance by teaching anyone, noble or commoner, who could afford their rates. Since success in Athenian society depended on oratory skills and appealing to the masses, the sophists —much like the lawyers of today—became highly sought by everyone who sought a position of power.

Plato's own teacher, Socrates, was educated by the sophists and originally made his living as one, distinguishing himself at a young age as the most skilled of all the sophists. The one sophist for whom Plato seemed to have great respect, however, probably because of his theory of perception, which in many ways was very similar to Plato's, was Protagoras, to whom Plato devoted an entire dialogue. Like his most famous student, Socrates, Protagoras raised doubts in the minds of the youth about the gods they had come by tradition to accept, saying, "About the gods, I am not able to know whether they exist or do not exist, nor what they are like in form; for the factors preventing knowledge are many: the obscurity of the subject, and the shortness of human life." What influenced Protagoras more than anything else he learned from the Ionians who preceded him was the ancients' discovery that we do not directly perceive the external world. From Thales to Zeno, one point that had been driven home, time again, was that the mind does not have direct access to the world but only to its own images of the world. Keenly aware of this, and not yet able to try, as Plato and subsequent epistemologists would, to find a way of transcending such limitations, Protagoras summed up his philosophy in his famous proposition: "Man is the measure of all things." This idea was expressed and developed in his book *On Truth,* of which only the first sentence remains: "Of all things the measure is man; of existing things, that they exist; of nonexistent things, that they do not exist."

In Plato's dialogue *Cratylus,* Socrates ponders Protagoras's cryptic meaning. The dialogue is named after another of Socrates' enigmatic sophist teachers, Cratylus, who not only refused to write anything down, just as Socrates did, but went further: Cratylus refused even to speak. He wagged his finger occasionally to acknowledge that it seemed to him that sensations were occurring.

> Socrates: So what is true of existing things, according to Protagoras, is this: what each thing itself is depends on the individual perceiving it. This is what Protagoras means when he says "Man is the measure of all things." The way things appear to me is the way they are for me; the way things appear to you is the way they are for you.

Protagoras's philosophy had important pragmatic repercussions for his theory of education, which is remarkably similar to the theories of nineteenth-century American pragmatists William James and John Dewey (Chapter 5) and their German avatar F. C. S. Schiller. This pragmatist slant comes out in Plato's dialogue *Protagoras,* in which Protagoras responds to Socrates' criticism that if truth and knowledge are relative in the way Protagoras is claiming, then no one is wiser than anyone else. But Protagoras denies this, saying that in fact there is a special responsibility that the wise man has, due to the freedom that the understanding that truth is man-made confers upon the enlightened. The suggestion is that insofar as I can bring myself to realize that the world I live in is to a large extent one of my own making, I can alter it in positive ways and have a better life.

Protagoras's Bucket Experiment

The sophists, while propounding their negative views about truth and knowledge, laid the foundation for much of subsequent philosophy because they all relied on perfecting their methods of demonstration and argument. Protagoras even devised an experiment to demonstrate his point. He assembled an audience in front of a stage and then took three volunteers to a secluded area behind the stage. The first put his hand in a bucket of cold water, the second put his hand in a bucket of hot water, and the third put his hand in a bucket of lukewarm water. After a few minutes, Protagoras brought them back on stage where they all put their hands in the same bucket of water at air temperature. Much to the audience's surprise, each claimed the same bucket of water was a different temperature—cold, hot, or lukewarm!

It would be easy to try to dismiss Protagoras's demonstration by saying that the only reason the same water felt differently was because the three people had gotten used to three different temperatures. But Protagoras's argument goes much deeper. After all, he himself openly revealed what accounted for the differences, because his point isn't that he is "manipulating" what each person feels. Rather, the words *hot, cold,* and *lukewarm* refer to actual sensations experienced by each mind involved in the experiment. These sensations are something the mind conjures up among its perceptions in response to some stimulus. Protagoras's subtle point is that the stimulus itself is neither hot nor cold nor lukewarm! This is an incredibly advanced insight about the nature of the appearances—perception—in relation to the world beyond the appearances.

Indeed, today science tells us that temperature is a measure of the relative motion of atomic particles. Now, think about it: the motion of particles, by itself —is this the feeling of warmth or coldness? One can try to reduce, via a scientific theory, the sensation of warmth to the motion of particles, but warmth as an experience certainly does not seem to be the same thing as motion. And that the same motions, or vibrations, can give rise to different sensations is precisely the sort of relativistic truth that Protagoras is after. Insofar as the appearances themselves consist not of physical things as they exist independently of the mind but of mental phenomena, they are not a direct apprehension of objective reality but constructions by the mind relative to the observer. It is to Protagoras's credit that he could make such a sophisticated type of argument using something as simple as three buckets of water.

Gorgias

What is most remarkable about all the sophists is that while they agreed on the principle of relativism, they drew radically different conclusions from it. Gorgias (480–375 B.C.E.), who came to Athens from Sicily as an ambassador of the city of Leontini, started out as a philosopher in the tradition of Thales and Parmenides. He was, however, so taken by the other sophists that he gave up his former views to become the most radical of all the sophists. Whereas Protagoras argued that everything is true in the sense that truth is relative to the perceptive world of each individual mind, Gorgias argued from the same premise of relativism that there is no truth. Relying on the reasoning methods developed by the Eleatic philosophers, especially Zeno, Gorgias claimed that

1. nothing exists,
2. if anything exists it is incomprehensible and unknowable, and
3. even if it is comprehensible or knowable, it cannot be communicated to others.

Just as numerals are not numbers—the numerals being the symbols used to denote, or refer to, the (intangible) things (numbers) themselves—and perceptions (the appearances) are not the things perceived (the "things" out there in "the world"), so Gorgias argues that words, which are but symbols or signs for the thing represented, can never properly be used to denote the things they stand for. True communication is therefore impossible. This view is not merely a type of skepticism, which we shall encounter many times along the way in our historical journey, and which holds only that we cannot know anything. Gorgias is making the even stronger claim: there is nothing there to be known, no truth at all.

Thrasymachus

The third of the three great sophists, Thrasymachus, appears in Plato's great dialogue, the *Republic,* as the defender of yet a third type of response to the same principle of epistemological relativism. Instead of arguing that there is no truth, as Gorgias did, or taking the Protagorean position that truth is man-made and so everything that anyone believes is true, Thrasymachus argued for a view describable, in a nutshell, as "might is right." Just as laws are made by rulers for their own interest and then define in that society what is right, so the most powerful are the ones who can determine by their authority what is "true." This extends to the moral realm: there is no morality beyond the subjugating of truth and right for one's own personal gain and interest; whether one succeeds is determined in a competitive struggle against all other contenders for the truth and the law. Thrasymachus's philosophy would achieve its most eloquent and sophisticated (no pun intended) exposition in the nineteenth century in the brilliant and influential writings of Friedrich Nietzsche (see Chapter 4).

Disgusted with the sophists' abandonment of the pure and disinterested search for truth, Socrates left the sophists in search of higher wisdom. His greatest contribution, no doubt, came in the form of his most famous student, Plato, who almost single-handedly ended the influence of the sophists and for the next several centuries put philosophy on the path to certain and absolute knowledge. But before turning to Plato we must look at another great master of the time whose belief in ultimate truth and the search for method to attain it not only paralleled Plato's but became the paradigm for all subsequent physical science: Democritus and the view that everything is made of atoms.

Democritus: The Birth of Materialism

Democritus (460–360 B.C.E.), like Protagoras, was born in Abdera, Thrace. Twenty years younger than Protagoras, ten years younger than Socrates, he overlapped with the young Plato, who makes no mention of him nor of his atomic theory of physical reality. And this in spite of the fact that Plato's star pupil and philosophical successor, Aristotle, wrote knowingly about Democritus. Democritus himself complained that, unlike Protagoras, who received a great welcome in Athens, "I went to Athens, and no one knew me." The ancient biographer Diogenes Laertius, from whom we get much of our biographical information on the Presocratics, claims that Plato so despised Democritus that he wanted his books burned. It would have been quite a task, for Democritus was as prolific a writer as Plato, with more than fifty books to his credit. All his writings were indeed destroyed, not by Plato but by the Christians in the fourth century C.E. (Common Era).

Democritus studied with Leucippus at his highly influential School of Abdera at about the same time as Protagoras. Leucippus had based his theory of reality on Parmenides but with an original twist: he took the primary aspects of being which Parmenides had ascribed to the whole of reality and applied them not to the whole but to the ultimate parts. Parmenides argued that if there is a separation between two beings (between two existent anythings), it cannot be nothing (for that is no separation) for that is not-being; so not-being cannot be ascribed to it. Being has the following properties:

1. unity
2. indivisibility
3. indestructibility
4. eternity

Thus you will recall that according to Parmenides and Zeno the cosmos is one complete totality without any parts and everywhere completely full. Not-being, in the sense of some sort of void between things, is according to them impossible, for the following logical reason. To say that there is a "void" is to say that the "void" has existence; if it has existence, then it is a type of being. Of course, void means something like "emptiness" or "lack of being," but these Greeks realized the importance of not using a term that means, in effect, "not X" to refer to "X" (substitute "being" for "X")—a lesson that has often been cleverly forgotten by mathematicians and scientists as a way of ignoring deep philosophical problems. Parmenides and Zeno thought it absurd to say that a nothing (the void) exists. It is this sort of logical precision and correctness of language that leads to the startling paradoxes of Zeno that we discussed earlier.

But the sophists, demoralized on the one hand by the inability of logic, reason, and language to make sense of the world, and on the other hand inspired by the extreme differences between the various philosophies that had thus far developed, gave up the search for truth and turned instead to the practice of rhetoric and the attainment of power through persuasion. The idea that there is some ultimate truth about the way the world is and the nature of human existence became subjugated to ancient myths, legends, and religious imagery that drew sharply divisive lines between the worldly affairs of the human intellect and the cosmic truths accessible only to the divine.

Democritus tried single-handedly to remedy the situation by teaching his students about both the Ionian philosophers (Thales, Anaxagoras, Anaximenes, Pythagoras, Heraclitus) and the Eleatic philosophers (Parmenides, Zeno), hoping thereby to create a new synthesis of apparently irreconcilable philosophical positions. This is the ideal to which Democritus devoted his entire, long life (he lived to be one hundred). He took the atomic physical theory of Leucippus and combined it with Protagoras's representational theory of the mind. In Leucippus's view, the Parmenidean properties of being apply not to the whole of existence but only to its ultimate, indivisible, eternal units, or atoms (literally, a[non]tom[divisible]). To the question of what separated atoms, Democritus gave a brilliant answer: not *nothingness* but *emptiness*. Thus the concept of nothing, or not-being, gave rise to the concept of space. But whereas Parmenides had claimed that reality is a single, undifferentiated, and indivisible unity—the *one*—which is completely full, Democritus claimed that there is an infinite number of separate, individual things—atoms—each one of which is completely full and contains no void (no empty space). Because the atoms are so small, they are invisible. Being themselves eternal, the atoms are neither created nor destroyed. In other words, reality consists not of one type of being but of two very different types of beings: existent things and existent non-things. Atoms are existent things, but space, which is a non-thing, also exists. Space is a vacuum having only the property of extension. In this way the atoms can freely move about such that their motions give rise to the various physical objects, which we perceive as representations.

In this way, Democritus was the first to try to use atomic theory to circumvent Zeno's paradoxes. Motion, according to Democritus, is possible because everything consists of atoms that combine and recombine themselves in empty space into the various shapes and forms we see. In the same way that Pythagoras relied on ideal objects—numbers, represented as dots—to explain the formation of various shapes, Democritus used the minimal physical dots of existence: atoms. He thus combines Leucippus's atomic theory not just with mathematics but also with Protagoras's theory of perception.

According to Democritus, the various arrangements that atoms can make account for the qualitative differences among perceived objects. These perceived qualities do not belong to the atoms themselves but only appear at the level of perception; they are the result of the subjective manner in which the mind of the perceiving subject (the observer) constructs the representation. But the behavior of these atoms is purely mechanical, the result of laws of motion that are always and everywhere the same. Democritus's philosophy is thus the first multiperspectival philosophy, in that there is according to him both an absolute reality (beyond the perceptions) and a relative reality which we perceive; the two are related by cause: the physical causes the mental.

Democritus was convinced that an atomic physical theory and the void could answer Zeno's objections to the possibility of motion. At the same time, this theory raises and then tries to solve the Parmenidean problem of how to reconcile appearances with ultimate reality so that we could have true knowledge of the world. Democritus's brilliant solution takes both the Heraclitan (Ionian) and Parmenidean (Eleatic) philosophies—as his colleague Protagoras would similarly claim—to be true. But both philosophies are true not simply in the subjective way that Protagoras and other sophists had claimed. Rather, the Parmenidean and Heraclitan views are both *objectively* true of the world! So, according to Democritus, the objective world contains both material reality ("the physical world") and ideal reality ("the ideal world").

Such a dualistic view of reality persists to this day. Most people today believe that there exists an objective, external, physical reality consisting of atoms in motion through empty space, as well as a subjective, internal, mental world of perceptions, ideas, and thoughts. Which is the more fundamental reality? According to Democritus, the mental world is itself to be explained in terms of the mind-independent reality of the physical world. In that regard, he was the first thoroughgoing materialist: the mind and all of its phenomena are ultimately of derivative reality, to be explained the same way that the physical phenomena of nature are explained: by the movement of atoms. The materialist world view, overshadowed for centuries by the emerging philosophies of Plato and Aristotle, came into its own again in Epicurus, Epictetus, and the Stoics. During the Middle Ages it disappeared but then resurfaced in the seventeenth century, when it became the foundation for the newly developing physical sciences, especially in Newton's work.

These two supposedly opposing metaphysical systems, idealism and materialism, have one deeply fundamental common principle: rationalism.[10] Each system in its own way tries to encompass the entire scope of the scientific and philosophical knowledge of the time. Although Democritus agreed with Plato concerning the Protagorean theory of perception, he held steadfastly to the more ancient idea of rationalism as espoused by Parmenides and Zeno. This type of rationalism must be contrasted with yet another type of rationalism, namely, that of the natural science theory of sense perception.

The Greek notion of "rational" is exemplified in the concept of rational numbers. A number is rational insofar as it can be expressed as a ratio, or measured proportion, of other numbers. Similarly, a thought or an idea is rational insofar as it can be expressed as a ratio, or measured proportion, of other ideas (Aristotle will rely on a similar idea when he defines virtue and excellence in terms of a rational mean between various extremes). In other words, what Democritus had in mind in forging the concept of rationality was something along the following lines, as is well evidenced by his attempt at creating a balanced synthesis of all opposing philosophical viewpoints. Unlike Protagoras and the sophists, who viewed philosophical differences as incommensurable and each subjectively valid, Democritus tried to find a ratio among the opposing viewpoints by, in effect, holding them all up at the same time for view. It is almost as if the multi-perspectival view that he sought (see below) came about as a sort of intellectual and conceptual interference pattern from a multiplicity of apparently opposing viewpoints.

Like perception, thinking in Democritus's view consists ultimately of nothing more than the motion of atoms. This too was a pivotal idea in that it suggested there may be mechanisms of a logical sort underlying our thought processes, themselves ultimately the result of atoms in motion. Remarkably, Democritus's elaborate theory about perception and the nature of thought is in many ways similar to modern theories of the electrochemical functioning of the brain. In his view, the influence of external things upon us can come about only through contact among various types of atoms via mechanical principles. He distinguished the ordinary atoms constituting non-minded physical objects from the even finer, "fiery" atoms responsible for thoughts and perceptions. Inspired no doubt by Heraclitan ideas about the fundamental role of fire in the cosmic scheme of things, Democritus viewed sensations as the effect of "fire atoms" upon the sense organs. Sensation, he claimed, cannot give us true knowledge of the external world because our perceptions as such consist only of subjective qualities like color, taste, and temperature, not of the objective quantities of true reality: we see colors and shapes, not atoms; likewise, when we pay attention to our minds we experience images and sensations, not the firing of atoms.

Sense experience thus cannot present objective truth as it really is, only indirectly, through an obscure, subjective view of the actual world consisting of visual, tactile and auditory images that are not the things themselves "out there" in the world but, at best, imperfect representations. True, objective knowledge, which would mean knowledge of the atoms, which are themselves as imperceptible to our senses as empty space is, can be arrived at only by thought. And only thought that is fundamentally rational, in the sense of being properly balanced with full knowledge of all views, is the key. This is very different from taking an empirical approach to epistemology—the theory of knowledge—and that is why I stress that Democritus's brand of materialism has much in common with Plato's rational epistemology, as we shall soon see.

Socrates: Knowing the Unknown

It has often been pointed out that what the character of Jesus is to Christendom, the character of Socrates is to Western philosophy. Both became tidal forces for opposing sides of a revolutionary seachange. Some scholars have gone so far as to claim that the Jesus story is just a rewriting of the Socrates story. Christianity has been called, by Bertrand Russell and others, "Platonism for the masses." Certainly the similarity of themes is striking: both supposedly sacrificed themselves for their respective causes, having been sentenced to death for crimes against their respective states. Neither Socrates nor Jesus wrote an autobiography, leaving it to oral historians and subsequent writers to interpret their lives.

Socrates came first. He lived in Athens, a city-state in ancient Greece, from 470 to 399 B.C.E. According to Plato, the unexpected events that turned Socrates into a philosopher began at the temple at Delphi. Plato tells the story like this. While still a young man, Socrates—like many a young person at the time—traveled about seeking wisdom by asking questions of everyone who would talk to him, questions about anything and everything. Socrates thereby—to his own surprise—got a reputation for being extremely wise. One day a friend of his went to the official oracle (the high priestess through whom supposedly the gods spoke) and asked whether anyone in Athens was wiser than Socrates and "the Delphic prophetess answered that there was no one wiser."

How did Socrates react to this? According to his testimony as told to us by his student Plato, Socrates did not believe the oracle. So he set out to prove the gods wrong. His method was simple: go to those you think are wiser than you and question them until you demonstrate to yourself their superiority. In Plato's *Apology,* Socrates gives a moving and eloquent statement about how he thereby stumbled upon the true meaning of wisdom: all the supposedly "wise" people Socrates questioned invariably pretended to know more than they actually knew.

Socrates went to the leading scientists, religious leaders, educators, artists, and politicians. He found what is still true today: that authorities rarely like to be questioned. Socrates found that they could answer him better than laypersons but only up to a point and then they began to evade. Often they ended up pointing Socrates in the direction of another authority, such as some other expert or a book. But, because Socrates had something to prove—namely, that the gods were wrong about him—he persisted. When the people he questioned used terms he didn't understand, he would ask them to clarify their language. This they could also do only up to a point beyond which it seemed to Socrates even they did not fully understand their own words or, if they did, they could not make their meanings clear. Soon Socrates began to get a strange, nagging suspicion that somehow they were trying to pull the wool over his eyes, that there were some fundamental unknowns they were covering up. But why would all of these knowledgeable experts be covering up their unknowns?

He went from expert to expert, authority to authority. When they failed to convince, or to demonstrate, or to justify, or to explain, he demanded that they do so. They couldn't. He kept questioning. They made statements they could not justify. Inevitably, they would begin to go beyond what they knew yet they spoke with the same authority. Or, what Socrates noticed happened often, they sounded even more certain! The more he persisted, the angrier they became. Finally, they refused to talk with him anymore.

In the end, Socrates drew an inexorable conclusion. Certainly many experts knew more than he did. They could describe in great detail a variety of views and theories. He did not have anything like that under his command. But then, at some point, invariably the experts seemed to go beyond what they knew. They made statements that were not known by them to be true, and they did so with the same air of authority as when they talked about what they did know. Past a certain point they seemed to become defensive. That's when Socrates began to suspect that they were pretending to know more than they actually knew.

How strange, he thought, how ironic. It's not that they don't know anything. Far from it. It's as if their very knowing has somehow corrupted them. You've heard it said that power corrupts and absolute power corrupts absolutely. Maybe something like that is true with knowledge? Knowledge corrupts and absolute knowledge corrupts absolutely? Could something like that really be true? Surely Socrates must have wondered about this.

Perhaps the gods were not wrong after all! Socrates had begun simply assuming that wisdom and knowledge are the same thing. But maybe wisdom and knowledge are only somehow related and not the same thing at all. Unlike all the great knowers with whom Socrates spoke, he knew perfectly well what he did not know and—unlike them (at least that's how it seemed to him)—he did not pretend to know more than he actually did know. Might that be wisdom? Knowing how little you know? Knowing the limitations of knowledge?

Further, it seemed to Socrates that the pretense of the authorities he questioned was not even conscious. That is, in pretending to know more than they knew, the politicians, poets, philosophers, and artists—the "experts," the "authorities"—weren't merely lying to Socrates. They were lying to themselves. And they were lying to themselves successfully. In other words, they did not just lie that they knew what they did not know, they actually believed it. They were self-deceived. Socrates, on the other hand, realized that he knew perfectly well how little he knew. He did not pretend to know more. He was not self-deceived about what he knew and what he didn't know. Socrates calls this "wisdom."

Wisdom, so the old saying goes, cannot be taught. But then, the more hopeful students sometimes ask, What about the fact that Socrates was the teacher of

Plato who was the teacher of Aristotle who was the teacher of Alexander the Great who by the age of thirty-three had conquered the known world?

Thus spake Zarathustra: "Even old sayings are sometimes right."

The Unexamined Life

One of the most famous and most often quoted sayings in the whole of philosophy is Socrates' "The unexamined life is not worth living." This statement is so uncompromisingly extreme that many have tried to water it down over the ages so as to make Socrates a little more palatable. What, after all, is a typical person to make of such moral extremism? Suppose you are a nicely respectable middle-class person, happily married with children, with a good job, friends, security, are admired by your neigbors, and so on. One day, the doorbell rings; you answer it.

"Have you examined your life?" the stranger asks.

"No."

"Then here!"

It's not a door-to-door salesperson but Socrates, who hands you a rope with which to hang yourself because according to his dictum your life is absolutely *worthless.* Now, surely, there must be something wrong with this picture—but what? The statement is, after all, the ultimate philosophical ultimatum: examine your life or die! Surely that is not what Socrates meant!

Let us take Socrates, as we did Thales, to be smart enough to say what he means. And he did not say, "The unexamined life is not worth much," or, "It is better to examine your life than not," or any of a thousand other much more palatable ways he might have put it. He is saying in no uncertain terms that unless you examine it your life is *worth zero,* utterly *valueless.* But how could that be? It seems any human life, after all, is worth *something,* that no life is without *some value*—which brings us to the crux of the issue: *values and the meaning of life.* And the upshot of Socrates' famous dictum, if we take it seriously, reveals something deep about the nature of such values.

Suppose you are a student in college. If you are like most students, probably the reason you want a degree is that you want a job that requires a college degree. In that case, the value of the college education for you is *derivative, instrumental,* and *extrinsic* to the degree itself. That is, the piece of paper certifying your degree is not worth anything; it is what this piece of paper can get you that is worth something. The diploma *derives* its value outside itself, in what it can get you, external to the having of the diploma. (Suppose, for instance, that you were the last person on Earth, doomed to live out your life alone. Would you try then to satisfy degree requirements for a diploma? Probably not: you would regard it as a worthless and futile exercise.) The diploma is an *instrument* for attaining something valuable: a higher-paying job. That's why we call such values *instrumental, derivative,* or *extrinsic.*

What is the value of the job afforded by a college degree? Obviously, more money. What is the value of money? Money is a prime example of derivative, instrumental, extrinsic value; unless you are a coin collector, money has no value in and of itself. It is an instrument for attaining valuable things; the value of money comes from what you can buy with it. Money *derives* its value, it has no value in and of itself. Suppose I have a million dollars in a Swiss bank account that I know I will never cash—*not ever.* How much is that money worth? The obvious answer is "a million dollars." But suppose that I will never spend a penny of it, will never leave it to anyone, will never borrow against it, and so on, so that it will sit in there for as long as the bank lasts. Then, in a very important sense, that money in the bank has no worth to me.

Now, what about the things that money can buy? What is *their* value? Eventually we get to something like "Having lots of nice things makes me happy." Suppose someone asks, "Why do you want to be happy?" If you now answer, "to make more money, because I work better when I am happy," you are caught in a strange loop. At this point one does not have to be a Socrates to ask about the meaning of life and wonder whether your life really has value. It would be like making money and *never spending it.* To make money and *never* spend it defeats the purpose of money, which has no value in and of itself. *Happiness,* on the other hand, is a prime candidate for something having *intrinsic* value: the buck, *literally,* stops there.

All of this brings us to what I think is Socrates' point. Things having derivative value have no value unless they are cashed out in terms of something having intrinsic value. Now, what in life is of intrinsic value? Here I think Socrates is most profound. He doesn't really say. What he does say, instead, is that unless you examine your life it will be worthless because there will then be no value in it. He directly implies, in other words, that *the meaning of life is something you must discover and choose for yourself, through critical self-examination.* Anything less is a derivative life and not your own.

And that is why the unexamined life is not worth living: because it is worthless. It may look pretty, like a paint-by-numbers picture, but it will not have the intrinsic beauty of a painting. Critical self-examination puts you in the responsible and perhaps anxious role of the creative artist who throws away the hand-me-down coloring books and faces the blank canvas with brush in hand to ask: Who am I? Who—what—do I want to be? What meaning do I want to give my life? How should I live? How should I relate to the world, to others, and to myself? What really matters? What is truth and how can I know it? *What statement do I want to make with this work of art?*

The work may be great and inspiring and valuable to others, or not. But it will be your own. This is the Western philosophical legacy.

Plato: Out of the Cave and into the Footnotes

Unlike his mentor Socrates, who wrote nothing, Plato (428–348 B.C.E.) was prolific. He produced more than two dozen dialogues on nearly every philosophical topic; so great has been his impact on Western thought that one prominent twentieth-century philosopher, Alfred North Whitehead, has claimed that the entire history of philosophy has been "a series of footnotes to Plato."

Plato was born in Athens to a prominent aristocratic family, the son of Aristo and Perictione. His father was of the Codrus family, and his mother traced her lineage back to Solon, a great seventh-century warrior and statesman who not only wrote many of the Athenian laws and created constitutional reforms but also was the earliest Athenian poet. Solon's poems, which celebrate both the individual and loyalty to the democratic state, were a popular vehicle for social and economic reforms. With both the benefits and drawbacks of such a noble lineage, Plato grew up during the 27-year Peloponnesian War between Athens and Sparta. From early on he received the finest education possible. He was trained by the best tutors available in mathematics, science, and philosophy, with the idea that he would when ready embark on a great political career. He excelled in poetry and music and became a young champion in wrestling.

When Athens surrendered to Sparta in 404 B.C.E., Plato—disillusioned by the overthrow of the world's first democracy—rejected the political life for which his family had prepared him, in favor of philosophy. But it wasn't only losing the war that moved him away from the public into the private life of contemplation. He had recently come under the influence of the Heraclitan sophist Cratylus, he studied the Eleatics, Protagoras, and Heraclitus, and he finally became a disciple of someone who himself began as a sophist and was as famous as he was unpopular: Socrates.

Plato was only twenty-eight when Socrates was put to death by the Athenian government for "corrupting" the youth and raising doubts in their minds about accepted "gods." No doubt, the trial and death of his beloved mentor had a profound effect on young Plato and may well have changed his mind about the role of writing. We do know that Plato left Athens shortly thereafter. For nearly ten years he traveled in southern Italy and Sicily, where he began writing his famous dialogues, in which Socrates appears as a philosophical gadfly seeking human excellence. He enlightens not by offering solutions to philosophical problems but by goading his adversaries into offering a definition of some term, such as justice, courage, intelligence, piety, and so on, and then drawing inferences from his opponents' responses so as to elicit explicit contradictions. In this way, Plato's Socrates shows the profound ignorance in which most people live. By unmasking their pretense, he frustrates his adversaries not into some better view of reality but into his own befuddled state of puzzlement and unknowing. This was probably the method used by the real Socrates, but we have no way of knowing how much of it was Plato's, since most of what we know about Socrates comes directly from the works of Plato.

Not only does Plato's Socrates avoid trying to get people to agree with him, to conform to some fixed system of thought (as in orthodox religious traditions), he shuns the extraordinary types of mystical experience usually codified by religious rituals. Remarkably, the measure of correctness in the Socratic tradition as passed down to us by Plato consists in the consistency and accuracy of one's own statements tempered by one's own reason through free and open discourse. One of the best examples of this Socratic method is Plato's *Euthyphro*. This dialogue takes place shortly before Socrates' infamous trial and subsequent execution in 399 B.C.E.

Euthyphro is a religious prophet so highly pious that he has come to court to prosecute his own father, a rich landowner, for having caused the death of a slave who in a brawl had murdered another slave. Apparently, Euthyphro's father bound the murderer and left him in a ditch while he went to fetch the authorities, but the slave died. Euthyphro then accuses his father of murder and comes to court seeking justice. If we take Socrates' words in the dialogue at face value, he is so impressed by the lengths to which Euthyphro has gone in the name of moral justice that he says he wants to become Euthyphro's "disciple" and learn from him the true meaning of piety[11] so that he can better defend himself against the charge of impiety. This scenario is often presented as clever tongue-in-cheek, but this is not at all clear. Perhaps Socrates means it! He says that if anyone knows what piety is, then surely an acknowledged prophet like Euthyphro knows, having gone to such extreme lengths in the name of piety.

However, under Socrates' persistent questioning, each of Euthyphro's answers fails. The problem is not that Euthyphro's beliefs are inconsistent with Socrates'. Rather, Euthyphro, using his own reasoning, sees that he himself ultimately disagrees with himself! (This self-disagreement, by the way, is in my opinion the source of the leading resistance many people have to doing philosophy: they don't mind so much being in "error" against some external authority; indeed, they may pride themselves on it. What they don't like is being in error against the authority of themselves.) First, Euthyphro claims that piety means doing what he is doing: prosecuting an unjust person (in this case, his own father) for some wrongdoing. Socrates asks whether any such example of piety, even if a good one, would—in Euthyphro's own view—be a sufficient definition of piety. Obviously not; no example can provide a general meaning of piety. An example is not a definition. What one needs instead is a general statement that can then be used to tell whether some particular action is pious or impious.

The problem, in other words, is this. To know a general concept such as piety, one would have to do more than merely cite examples of pious actions, since the meaning of a general concept is necessary before the example can be understood. In response, Euthyphro gives a more general statement. Pious actions, he says, are those that please the gods, whereas impious actions are those that displease the gods. Does this work? Well, we now have a definition instead of an example, which is the right type of answer. But is the answer right? Socrates does not say whether it is or isn't. Instead, he asks another question: Do the gods sometimes disagree? Euthyphro says that they do. Socrates then points out that an action that pleases some gods will anger others, so a particular action can on Euthyphro's definition be both pious and impious, which is contradictory. Again, Euthyphro is undermined not by Socrates' better view or understanding, but by the incoherence of his own view.

What is wrong with being self-contradictory and incoherent? Well, such inconsistency is itself a *demonstration*, in the sense we discussed in the section on

Pythagoras. If you claim to believe some statement X and then as I examine your beliefs it is revealed that you also believe some other statement Y, which itself implies that X is false, *you are in disagreement with yourself*. That means I don't need to demonstrate the falsity of X (if I am arguing against you) by providing evidence to the contrary, and so on: I have instead demonstrated that there is a very important sense in which *you do not really hold X to be true*. You only think you do. It is a bit like thinking you are worth $1,000 because you happen to have a bank statement that says you have that much in the bank, and then finding you have a credit card bill for $1,000 that's due. You're actually broke. (In some ways, the Socratic method is like taking account not of your monetary assets but of your beliefs and opinions to see what is actually there. You cannot just go part way, for in both financial and philosophical contexts that could be seriously misleading. One must, as Socrates is always painstakingly prepared to do, go all the way.)

Euthyphro suggests, in his own defense, that on some things all gods agree. Interestingly enough, at this point Socrates could have raised a number of difficult questions about whether the gods really do agree on anything universally, how we could know this, and so on. But this line of questioning would have relied on factors external to Euthyphro's own point of view. Had the author of this dialogue been a lesser philosopher, the argument might have taken such a turn, and the result would have been a debate between, say, a religion-based ethical system and a secular one. Probably, at that time, such a debate could not have been resolved by reason. In any case, what Plato gives us instead is one of the most devastating assaults ever mounted against a religion-based ethics, in the form of a simple, piercing question: Is an action pious because it pleases the gods, or does it please the gods because it is pious? In other words, is some action, X, right because God says so, or does God say so because X is right?

This question cuts so deeply to the heart of the issue at hand that contemporary philosopher Anthony Flew has remarked that "one good test of a person's aptitude for philosophy is to discover whether he can grasp its force and point." Socrates' famous question forces Euthyphro into a dilemma (literally, "two-forked path"), each fork of which leads to a contradiction from within Euthyphro's own point of view. For instance, if being honest is right because it pleases the gods, then it is not the merits of honesty that make it right or wrong; rather, it is the collective moods of the gods that make honesty a good thing. But this makes the difference between right and wrong arbitrary, which in Euthyphro's own understanding seems wrong! What if it pleased the gods to see innocent people tortured? On Euthyphro's definition, it would then be right for us to torture innocent people.

Euthyphro sees the problem and so instead takes the second horn of the dilemma. He states that, obviously, it must be the nature of the pious act itself that makes the gods love it, and not their love for that act that makes it pious. That is, the gods' love is the effect, not the cause, of the action being pious. But now the problem is even worse! For, on Euthyphro's own view, this makes the approval of the gods absolutely irrelevant to what piety itself is. It is then the nature of the pious action itself, not someone's view of it (not even a god's view), that makes the action pious. Once again, through Socrates' persistent questioning, Euthyphro comes to see that he does not understand what he thought he understood, that he knows far less than he believed. The dialogue ends, famously, with Euthyphro at the key point at which he could have begun to have some insights into himself, his actions, and his world, excusing himself and running away.

Plato's *Apology* and *Crito* describe Socrates' trial and subsequent imprisonment. Already in his seventies, Socrates was by then famous throughout the Hellenic world. Plays had been written about him, the most famous of which, the *Clouds* by Aristophanes, satirized Socrates and his students, making them the objects of public ridicule. The *Apology* (the Greek word *apologia* means "defense," not "request for forgiveness") begins, as was traditional at the time, with a defense by the accused. After repeating the charges against him, Socrates discredits his accusers, especially Meletus, whom he catches in contradiction, and then goes on to insult his audience and ridicule his accusers. In the end, he suggests what his punishment should be: a lifelong pension! He is then found guilty by a vote of 281 to 220—more voting against him now than before his apology!

In the *Crito*, sentenced to die in prison by drinking the infamous hemlock, Socrates awaits execution. Here we find that the citizens of Athens apparently expected Socrates would not take the poison but would flee to another country. But Socrates, always the gadfly, does not flee. He stays, and the *Crito* ends with Socrates choosing death instead of exile. Socrates' final conversations with his students can be found in the *Phaedo*.

These early dialogues of Plato complete the initial formulations of his philosophy. They mark not only the end of one philosophical journey and the beginning of another, but are in many ways an omen of things to come. In many ways, the trial and death of Socrates was symptomatic of the flaws inherent in the Athenian system of government and the level of intellectual and spiritual corruption to which the city-state had fallen. In losing the war with Sparta, the Athenian democracy was overthrown by a totalitarian city-state. Subsequently, the democracy was restored, but it was so wrought by corruption that it lasted only briefly. The golden age of Greece ended in utter disarray, followed by the Roman Empire. After that came centuries of the so-called Dark Ages, rampant with religious repression. One can only wonder at what might have happened had the Athenians voted more wisely.

Why Plato wrote his dialogues is a mystery, especially since Socrates apparently not only shunned the written word but claimed that to try to write down philosophy would be unphilosophical. Even his own greatest works, such as the *Republic,* contain explicit arguments against the very types of books Plato wrote. No doubt the early dialogues were inspired by a desire to record for posterity the trial and death of Socrates. But in subsequent dialogues we find a marked turn in Plato's thinking away from the Socratic method to a much more Pythagorean approach. In the *Meno,* for instance, Plato argues not only that knowledge is possible, but that it is completely innate. All human knowledge is nothing more than recollection. He illustrates this by showing how a slave, completely ignorant of mathematics, has already within him a storehouse of knowledge that he has forgotten. Once awakened, this inner knowledge allows him to learn what otherwise would be impossible. This idea—that knowledge ultimately comes from within, that it is already in you, waiting to be discovered—will become one of the most recurrent themes in subsequent philosophy.

From this point on, all of Plato's dialogues carry on this positive theme. Although they focus on many of the same questions as the earlier dialogues, the method, style, and conclusions are different. Instead of the dialectical cross-examination by Socrates leaving his interlocutors without any viable solutions, the character of Socrates is now much less adversarial and offers positive answers to even the most difficult philosophical questions. Relying on the Parmenidean distinction between reality and appearance and using the method of Pythagorean mathematics, Plato thus moves beyond the Socratic state of unknowing to the direct knowledge of the ideas as revealed "through a glass darkly," the "mind's eye."

A Brief History of Ideas

Before we go on to discuss Plato's theory of *ideas* (translated sometimes as *forms*), let me make clear the various ways the term *idea* has been used throughout the history of philosophy. The Presocratics used the Greek word *idea* to mean the form, fashion or mode, or class or species of an existent. (An *existent* is simply any object or thing that exists, whether independently of or dependently on the mind.) For Plato and Socrates, an idea is a timeless essence or universal, the dynamic and creative archetype of an existent. In Plato's system, ideas comprise a metaphysical hierarchy and organic unity in what he simply calls "the Good"; they are themselves ideals or patterns of existence manifested in the objects of perception and the objects of human desire.

The Stoics, on the other hand, regard ideas as class concepts that exist only in the mind, whereas the Neoplatonists will regard them as archetypes that exist in the cosmic mind or world-soul, which according to them was the *nous* or *logos*. The early Christian and Scholastic philosophers will take this same approach, except that the ideas as conceived by the Christians exist as eternal archetypes in the mind of God.

The modern philosophers, beginning with Descartes, treat ideas as if they were subjective, logical concepts of the mind. Locke, for instance, not only treats them as subjective or mental, but regards all the objects of consciousness as ideas. The "simple ideas," which are the source of all complex ideas, arise out of either sense perception or reflection. Likewise, Berkeley treats all sensed objects as objects of perception, ideas that exist only in the mind. Hume considers ideas to be "faint images," or memory copies, of sense impressions, themselves mental constructs.

Plato's Theory of Ideas

According to Plato, the objects of our knowledge do not exist among the appearances. Indeed, the objects that appear to us only obscure the true nature of the real objects that are themselves nowhere to be seen. Real objects exist beyond appearances, in the world of pure, formal ideas. Plato explains this relationship between appearance and reality allegorically. He argues that the objects we perceive are at best but shadows of real things and that most real things are not *things* but *ideas*. Using his allegory of the cave, the simile of the sun, and the divided line, he presents his theory of ideas in what many regard to be his greatest dialogue, the *Republic*. Set during a pause in the Peloponnesian War, ten or so years before Socrates' trial, while Athens was still a democracy, it is the one work he kept revising for the rest of his life.

"The many," says Socrates in the *Republic*, "are seen but not known; and the ideas are known but not seen." By *the many*, Plato simply refers to all the various things that appear before you as a multitude. In referring to them as "many" rather than "things" or "objects," he is trying to refer to the world of appearances as neutrally and philosophically as possible. Look around: what you see appears to be not a one but a many. In your field of vision you see no noticeable gaps, but a lot of visual borders mark what you automatically perceive as boundaries between objects: color gradations, changes in shape, and so on, are automatically interpreted by your mind as many different things—books, people, furniture, rocks, and so on. Now, in saying that the many are seen but not known, Plato is drawing your attention to the fact that all of these appearances before you do indeed appear in a certain way: you see them as a variegated multitude of somethings. They are not known, however. But in what sense are they not known? You see tables, chairs, people, and so on. So you do know these objects in the sense of being able to name and distinguish them. But what are all of these objects that seem so familiar that even to question whether you know what they are seems, on the face of it, absurd? If you reflect a moment, you will realize that you "know" these objects only in the superficial way of being acquainted with their presence. Certainly you make the same sounds that others make in referring to them, and so on. But what are these objects really? Why do they exist? How did they come to be? What are they made of?

The moment you begin to engage with such questions you have moved away from the appearances themselves (as they appear) and have entered the realm of what Plato is calling ideas. This book that you hold in your hand, for instance, why does it exist? You answer with the idea of an author, a printing press, a publishing company, and so on. But notice that at this very moment, as you read this, such thinking relates you not to *things* as they exist out there in the world independently of your mind, but, rather, to your own ideas. For instance, you may in your mind have an idea of me, the author of this book, but you do not presently see me. And even if I was in the room with you, would you see an *author* or a *man*? *Author* is an idea. But would you even see a *man*? Isn't "man," too, an idea? You may see a body or, more precisely, an image of the surface of a body, but certainly that is not what a man is. Likewise, you may have an idea of the printing press. Or, to shift directions slightly, you may have an idea of what this book is made of, such as atoms, but presently you do not see them. And yet all of these ideas are known to you. But what, exactly, is it that is known? Your idea of me is an idea of an author. That you know; you know that this book has an author. That too is an idea. It is an abstract entity, a concept that as such is nowhere to be seen.

Again, suppose you meet me. Have you now met an idea? Have you even really met an author? No, Plato would say: even if I am in your presence, it is an idea of an author that somehow is involved in my being, in my existence, but authorship is not, itself, an appearance like colors, temperatures, shapes, and so on.

From the start, Plato thus has us reflecting beyond what merely appears, what is given to our sense experience. Why should knowledge be of things that are not seen and not of things seen? This is the very foundation of Plato's rationalist epistemology, in which he bases knowledge in a realm utterly removed from experience, in pure reason. For this step leads him to ask one of the most profound and devastating philosophical questions. The question has two, related, parts. First, what do you see the appearances with and, second, with what organ, or faculty, do you apprehend knowledge? Plato's simile of the sun suggests that there is something other than the seen objects themselves that makes vision possible: the sun, which is the cause of light. Likewise, something other than the known objects themselves is the cause of knowledge: Plato calls it the mental faculty of *understanding*. It is the understanding that is responsible both for the objects of perceptions and for what you know about them. This is because the immediate cause of what you are looking at is itself nowhere apparent among the appearances. It is like when you are dreaming; what do you see the objects in your dreams with? What illuminates the objects in your dreams? What makes you see and understand that, say, a dog (in the dream) is chasing you rather than, say, a dragon? The objects in your dreams appear to be particular items; they look as they do rather than some other way.

All of this is made possible by the existence of something within you analogous to the sun. Indeed, it is this eternal sun within the mind that gives light to everything within what you call your world. But you cannot see what this is any more than you see things as they really exist in and of themselves. For, as Plato describes in one of the most famous images in the whole of philosophy, the allegory of the cave: you live in a cave of darkness, the objects you see are but shadows of reality (ideas), inaccurate and illusory representations:

> And now let me show in a figure how far our nature is enlightened or unen-
> lightened: Behold! Human beings living in an underground cave, which has a
> mouth open towards the light and reaching all along the cave; here they have
> been from their childhood, and have their legs and necks chained so that they
> cannot move, and can only see before them, being prevented by the chains from
> turning round their heads. Above and behind them a fire is blazing at a dis-
> tance, and between the fire and the prisoners there is a raised way; and you will
> see, if you look, a low wall built along the way, like the screen which marionette
> players have in front of them, over which they show the puppets. . . . Men pass
> along the wall carrying all sorts of vessels, and statues and figure of animals
> made of wood and stone and various materials, which appear over the wall . . .
> and suppose further that the prison has an echo which comes from the other
> side, would they not be sure to fancy when one of the passers-by spoke that the
> voice which they heard came from the passing shadow? . . . To them the truth
> would be literally nothing but the shadows of the images.[12]

What happens when someone leaves the cave? He becomes, literally, enlightened. But he has lived so long in the darkness, among the shadows, that his eyes have grown accustomed to the dark and so at first he cannot see the truth, the real sun; reality blinds rather than illuminates him. But then if he does not give in to fear but remains in the blinding light that obliterates everything, if he can stand being surrounded by an apparent nothingness until he, literally, comes to his senses, a new and brilliant world of absolute truth and ultimate being reveals itself. If the philosopher is a true lover of wisdom and unselfish, he does not remain outside the cave. He goes back into the cave to try to enlighten the others, and so he stumbles back into the dark. When he tries to enlighten the others, they think he is a fool; they want him to prove that he has attained true wisdom and enlightenment by, for instance, predicting the patterns of the shadows on the cave wall. He cannot even see them! He clumsily knocks into things, he is blind in the darkness they call light.

Plato develops his theory of ideas far beyond such mythological rendering, however, and creates one of the most elaborate and influential systems of metaphysics and epistemology. The concepts of knowledge in Plato's view are very different in both origin and content from the objects of perception. In perception, what comes into consciousness is a world of change and appearance. In conception, however, we intuit the permanent and unchanging essence of real things: the objective content of conceptual knowledge is the idea.[13] True knowledge is given not in our perception of reality but in our conception of reality, and this is knowledge of what really is. Because the relative truths of sense perception consist in our translating the changing relations observed in the perpetual process of becoming (further discussed below), the absolute truth of conceptual knowledge consists in the fact that we conceive in ideas true being, independently of any change. Thus, for Plato, there exist two different worlds corresponding to our two ways of knowing: the world of ideas, which is the true reality, and the world of relative actuality, the ephemeral objects of sense perception.

Plato's two worlds exist in a unique superposition of the Heraclitan and Parmenidean views of reality. Parmenidean being belongs to the idea as the object of true knowledge: it is permanent, fixed, and unchangeable. The Heraclitan flux of continuous change and destruction manifests itself in the individual objects of perception. And the fundamental principle in Plato's metaphysical epistemology is that these two worlds must be distinguished; one world *is* and never *becomes*, the other world *becomes* but never *is*. One is the object of reason, the other is the object of sense perception. And since the objects are as separated as the methods of knowing are distinct, ideas stand as incorporeal forms in contrast to the material things as perceived by the senses. Ideas cannot be found in the world of space and matter. Ideas exist purely for themselves and cannot be grasped by the senses but only by thought; they are purely *formal* and exist in the intelligible world.

Ideas exist for a purpose. They set forth the logical character of the class concepts, thereby revealing the common qualities of the particulars comprehended by the class concepts. (Plato is clear that without ideas there would be no particulars.) In this way, Plato regards the process of thinking not as an analysis of reality or an abstraction from reality, but as a sort of *synoptic intuition of reality presented in single examples.* In marked contrast to the view that will be developed by his most illustrious student, Aristotle, an idea according to Plato cannot be contained in its perceived phenomenon. (Aristotle will argue that it can and is.) An idea cannot be found in appearance; material things do not include ideas; they include only the copies or shadows of ideas. In other words, the objects found in perception do not include ideas as separable, integral parts but are only the occasions for the apprehension of ideas, similar to the object of perception but in no way identical with it. Further, since an idea cannot be created by reflection, it is an original possession of the soul that the soul remembers into actual presence when it sees its copy in the world of appearance. But how does this happen? How can the mind recognize among the world of appearance what is nowhere apparent, what cannot be seen, what has never been perceived?

In the *Phaedrus,* one of his most mystical dialogues, Plato uses the examples of love and beauty to present his theory of the immortality of the soul and of ideas, which are the cause of the particulars, the many. As the ultimate constituents of reality and the proper objects of mystical contemplation, ideas make enlightment possible. Plato claims that your soul has indeed once gazed directly upon ideas with its supersensible faculty of understanding. This happened before you were born. You now remember ideas only upon the perception of similarly corresponding phenomena. Now he subtly includes the following secret marker among your psychological states that is, in accord with the Socratic imperative for amazement and wonder, the prime Platonic imperative to philosophical inquiry: the sensation of awe and wonder. For it is out of the uncomfortable, even painful, sense of befuddlement and astonishment at the impossible gulf between an idea and its phenomenon that the philosophical impulse is created within the soul, the longing love for the supersensible idea, oneness with true reality. It is this love that can guide you out of the cave, through the labyrinthine transitoriness of sense experience, into the immortality of the ideal world.

Plato's *Philebus* lays the metaphysical foundations for the myths about the natural world as put forth in his *Timaeus.* There Plato suggests that the sensible world of appearance consists of an infinite space, itself imbibed with the particular mathematical forms required to represent ideas. Because no conceptual knowledge can be given of how ideas inform space and matter, in the *Timaeus* Plato personifies this purposeful, teleological world and object-forming force as the "demi-urge," or God. This demi-urge is the good and because of its good will creates the world of becoming, the world of appearance, in which individual souls exist as reflections of the ideal world. In the act of creation, God sees all the pure unitary forms of ideas and uses them to create the most perfect, best, and most beautiful copy possible, using divine reason and goodness. But the world made by God is not perfect. The reason is that although ideas correspond as closely as possible to their copies, the copies are themselves limited in that they must exist in space, which cannot be known either through thought or by the senses. That is, space is neither a concept nor a percept, neither an idea nor a sensed object. Although space has no being as such, without it the appearances could not appear and ideas could not be copied into the sensible objects. Out of this "nothingness" God creates the sensible world, the cosmos.

The demi-urge then creates within the cosmos a world-soul, imbibed with reason and intelligence. This world-soul is the life-principle of everything, the mean between the indivisible eternal being (ideas) and the divisible, ephemeral realm of becoming (space), possessing the opposite qualities of sameness and change. The world-soul contains all numbers, all dimension, and is itself the mathematical form of the cosmos. The demi-urge distributes the world-soul into its various harmonious and disharmonious relations, thereby setting the entire cosmos into motion. Through this motion, permeating the whole cosmos and then returning to itself, the world-soul in turn creates in itself an individual consciousness, perception, and thought.

Thus by no means did Plato regard the world of appearances, the shadows in the cave, as mere illusions. Indeed, despite his lofty pronouncements he did not completely forsake the world of appearances with mystical pronouncements on how to attain freedom from illusion or transcend the apparent for the real, ideal world. Although the shadows are far less real than ideas, they are related and the nature of this relation became the model for Plato's social, ethical, and political theory. Indeed, in his wordly actions Plato was very much a practical realist, with a keen eye to where the human soul finds itself in relation to other souls as they interact in the world of appearances. Thus his ethical and political philosophy as expressed in the *Republic* is far less concerned with, say, the happiness of some particular individual citizens than with the attainment of a perfect social state that would empower all citizens to enlightenment and happiness.

Much of Plato's ethical and political teachings concerned directly the problem of how to build such a state. Indeed, he is adamant that, regardless of the natural or historical origins of the state, its ultimate purpose must always and everywhere be the same: to ensure a way of life in which all citizens may attain happiness through virtue. This requires that the relations of society be structured according to the principles of human moral nature. Thus the ideal (and perfect) state should be divided into three distinct parts, just as the individual human soul is:

1. workers
2. warriors
3. administrators

The majority of citizens would be workers who must provide the material foundation for the life of the state by caring for all of its day-to-day needs. They are driven by their own needs and desires to perform their tasks and duties. The warriors and administrators carry out the unselfish fulfilment of duty; they guard the state from external enemies by repelling invaders and guard it internally by executing the laws of the state. Unlike the workers, who are driven directly by self-interest through their needs and desires, the warriors and administrators act unselfishly in their duties, purely through each individual warrior's and administrator's noble sense of responsibility to the whole. The administrators, however, as the rulers of the other two groups, must determine according to their own insights what the proper and best principles are of legislation and administration. And how is the perfection of the entire state attained? Only when all individual citizens have the means at their disposal for getting what are their rights, through justice. Justice, in turn, consists in the three classes having a proper measure of power fairly distributed among the individuals of the class in proportion to their function. Therefore the rulers of the state must have the highest levels of education, wisdom, and culture and the warriors must have been trained in complete devotion to duty, while the people are trained to be obedient so as to curb their natural desires.

This three-part division leads Plato to advocate the ideal state as one ruled by an aristocracy in the strictest sense of the word. It is ruled by the wisest, the most virtuous, and the best. All legislation, along with the direction of the entire society, lies in the hands of the leaders. Therefore the famous Platonic saying, "There will be no end to the sorrow of humanity until the philosophers rule or the rulers are philosophers."

It should therefore not be surprising that the Platonic state would accordingly serve as an institution for the education of society. The highest aim would be to prepare individuals *using the materials of the sensible world* for the ideal life in the *supersensible world beyond the appearances*. Throughout his life Plato devoted a good deal of his energies to building a bridge from the world of appearance to the real world, between the world of becoming that never is and the ideal world of being that never becomes. It is in this spirit that he founded the Academy, a center for the advancement of wisdom and a training ground for future philosophers. Under Plato's direction, the Academy spawned a slew of scientific and mathematical innovations, linking fifth century B.C.E. Pythagorean mathematics with Egyptian geometry and arithmetic done in Alexandria.

The Academy lasted over a thousand years. It was destroyed at the start of the Dark Ages but since then has been resurrected. You are no stranger to it. Like democracy, whose first incarnation began and ended in Athens, the Academy too is alive and well, having become the avatar of many of today's colleges and universities.

Prior to Plato most Greek education floated on the paradigm that everything beautiful is good. By reversing this paradigm, "Only the good is really beautiful," Plato would reverse forever the course of the Western river of thought. The ideal state must accept the myths of religion as educational material for the third class of society, and partly for the second class (especially in early childhood), while expunging from them all immoral enticements and enchantments, except in the symbolic representation through art for the purpose of teaching. Most important, the religion of the philosopher must be completely free of all myths and enchantments so that the philosophers' mind can within itself attain the likeness of the idea of the good—the Godhead.

It may be significant for us to note that while the Western conception of God and the human soul owes much to the fruits of Plato's early philosophical labors, it was Plato as an old man who in pessimism and despair gave birth to the idea of *evil of the soul,* the Devil. The young man saw philosophical enlightenment as merely the guiding of souls from ignorance to wisdom; the old man became convinced of the badness of the world and came in the end to believe in an evil world-soul that works against the divine soul. As a result, for centuries and millennia to come the human enterprise would be inspired to join the cosmic battle of good versus evil.[14]

Aristotle: From Two Worlds to One

During his forty years of teaching, Plato had gathered many of the greatest minds in the known world into his Academy. But the one he singled out as the greatest was Aristotle (384–322 B.C.E.), who came there to study at the age of seventeen. So impressed was Plato by his young student from Macedonia that after only a few years he gave him the nickname "The Brain."

Born at Stagira, in Macedon, a Greek colonial town settled by the Ionians, Aristotle had been sent to the Academy by the king of Macedon as a favor to Aristotle's father, the king's personal physician. Much to everyone's surprise, the royal doctor's son not only quickly became Plato's most prodigious pupil but soon began developing his own metaphysical system sympathetic with but in marked contrast to Plato's. Together their complementary systems stand to this day as the two main opposing pillars holding up the edifice of the Western philosophical tradition.

So great were Aristotle's achievements that for the next thousand years other writers would refer to him simply as "The Philosopher." In his lifetime, Aristotle went on to systematize the whole of knowledge. Like Plato, he was prolific. Although only fragments remain of his published writings, his unpublished writings have survived in the form of lecture notes or texts used by his students. He produced ground-breaking texts not just on metaphysics and logic but on virtually every subject: physics, astronomy, meteorology, taxonomy, psychology, biology, ethics, politics, and aesthetics.

At the time when Aristotle entered the Academy, Plato was in his final period of philosophical creativity, trying to subdivide the ideas further and further in an attempt to reach the *infima species,* the final and indivisible unit of division. Plato's goal was to explain how ideas, which were universals, or class concepts, were related to the particular individuals that exist as immediate objects of perception. Take, for instance, the class concept "horse." The pony my daughter rode yesterday is a particular individual example of a horse; how are the two related? The problem is that for Plato class concepts are like numbers, abstract entities that do not exist in space and time (but they do nevertheless exist). But it's even more mysterious than with numbers; if I wonder how the number 2 is related to the numeral "2," which I just used to express the number, the answer is more simple: my mind takes the symbol "2" to stand for the concept 2, which of course can be expressed by other particular symbols, such as the Roman numeral II, the word *two,* or the word *deux.* The interface between the class concept and the particular object falling under the class concept is, in the case of numbers, the mind. But not so with the horse example—at least not obviously. And what plagued Plato is that he was forced by his elaborate metaphysics to place the class concept "horse" completely beyond the world of appearances, outside of space and time, in the eternal realm of being. (Lest you think that it is obvious that no such realm exists, ask yourself what 3 + 2 would equal if there were no universe, no space, no time, just nothing; would it equal 0? 7? No: 3 + 2 would still equal 5. No one would be there to know or be aware of it but, still, that is what it would equal. But where are such truths "written"? What holds them in place? What makes them true? Do you see the problem?) So then how could the idea of a horse, which like the number 2 exists nowhere in the phenomenal world of appearance, interact or cause or bring about or affect in any way the existence of this particular pony on which my daughter sat bobbing?

In the ethical domain, Plato got around the problem in a clever and profound way, by making the individual human soul directly involved in choosing to be virtuous and thereby partaking in, and bringing into the world, the idea of the good. Thus the moral devices he puts forth in the *Republic,* for the purpose of creating the right sort of individual and state, are part of his elaborate metaphysical plan. Plato thus circumvented the epistemological dualism inherent in his theory of ideas by putting forth plausible, if ultimately rather dogmatic, imperatives concerning social and political norms. This way he could keep his premise that the idea of the good is the cause of everything in the sensible world of appearances, even though it turns out that the good itself cannot be scrutinized via any adequate explanation or analysis. And the mediating role between appearance and reality played by the individual soul within the world is buttressed beyond the world with a rather traditional religious concept of the Godhead who oversees both worlds and acts as a bridge between them. But Plato could find no such similar move in his attempt to understand the events within the world of becoming and destruction in relation to the good, for the same reason as before, that the realm of being cannot be the object of dialectic or true knowledge. Thus Plato's theory of ideas presupposes in a fundamental way a completely teleological view of nature (of the empirical world that appears to exist as a sequence of events in time) and yet can offer no knowledge of nature itself.

Working both together and in creative opposition, Plato and Aristotle will now produce a fork in philosophy's path, a conceptual and methodological juncture that in some ways is an ancient version of the analytic-synthetic distinction (Chapters 4 and 5) and foreshadows the split between humanities and science on the one hand and between religious and secular philosophies on the other. Plato was analytic, a humanist, and religious, with an eye toward mathematics; Aristotle was synthetic, a scientist, and thoroughly secular in his epistemology, with an eye toward logic (the foundations of which he himself invented).

The philosophical differences between the final views of Plato and Aristotle are deep and fundamental. The major difference is that what Plato tried to do for the rest of his life, Aristotle claimed was impossible: Plato's theory of ideas could never explain the existence of empirical facts. There was no way to relate the ideas to the particular individual objects found in experience, except through tenuous myths and allegories. And the fact as Aristotle saw it was that despite the mythological and religious imagery found in Plato's later works (such as the *Timaeus* and *Philebus,* discussed earlier), Plato simply could not harmonize the existence of particular perceptions, the world of sense, with the ideas. The problem, in Aristotle's view, can be solved where it begins, with Plato ascribing a separate reality to the world of ideas. This, according to Aristotle, was Plato's great insight but also his great mistake. He claimed that in making the ideas transcendental, Plato was unnecessarily duplicating the empirical world. We therefore ought to reject the ideal world as unreal. To solve the problem, Aristotle conceives ideas as existing not in a different realm from the objects of experience, but as the particular essences of the individual objects of existence. Ideas exist as the essence of individual objects, determining from within the content of each and every appearance.

It is deeply ironic but philosophically illuminating to understand that indeed the greatness of Plato's philosophy consisted in his recognition of the necessity for the existence of two worlds, a dual realm of being, whereas the greatness of Aristotle's philosophy lies in the recognition that two worlds are *not* necessary, that the transcendental world of ideas and the sensible world of appearance can be regarded as the same world. In Aristotle's philosophy, Plato's two worlds are identical, there is but one world. And what makes this concept so illuminating is that by collapsing Plato's world into one view, Aristotle inadvertently gave to the Western world something no other world had: multiple *philosophies.* Indeed, the subsequent history of Western thought can and should be called the history of Western *philosophies.* But let us return to our story.

Because in Plato's view the world of appearances is ultimately a variety of illusion (albeit an important one), true knowledge (of ideas) could be sought only through the mind's eye, by the inner light of pure reason. (Recall the "through a glass darkly" image.) Such ideal knowledge, as we saw, could in Plato's view be communicated by philosophers but only abstractly, without technical rigor, using myths and metaphors. Aristotle agrees with Plato that knowledge acquired through the senses is not sufficient, but he claims it is the only real path to wisdom. Whereas Plato, under the influence of Pythagoras, relies on the notion of geometrical forms and the abstract rules of numbers to explain his theory of Ideas, thereby aligning his philosophical method closely with mathematics, Aristotle aligns himself with the methods of natural science. His classifications of genera and species lead him to physics, organic biology, physiology, and so on; he then uses the rigorous methods of formal logic to further analyze individual objects, well beyond the scope of appearances, into their constituent categories. Aristotle thus develops for the first time a dynamic theory of change, according to which individual objects exist as composites of idea and substance. Knowledge then becomes possible not through contemplation and pure reason but through observation.

Aristotle's *Metaphysics* opens with the famous passage "All men by nature desire to know." He thus claims that we desire knowledge not through education but through our own natures. That is, our desire for knowledge is innate, we are born with it. He suggests, as did Plato, that we are seduced away from our natural desire to know. Nor is it merely practical knowledge that we want. The human mind craves knowledge for its own sake. He gives the example of our senses, which are of course very useful, but there is also the "delight we take in our senses; for even apart from their usefulness they are loved for themselves." Thus the highest levels of knowledge are like beauty, having not instrumental but intrinsic value; that is, ultimate knowledge has value in and of itself. Although there are different levels of knowledge, the highest form of knowledge is wisdom. Although Aristotle, unlike Plato, allows that knowledge can be attained through the senses, he agrees with Plato that knowledge gained through the senses is the lowest form of knowledge and is not wisdom. Knowledge gained through the senses tell us only the "that" of a thing, not the "why," it cannot teach us the causes of things. For instance, to know that breathing is essential to consciousness and to life is practical knowledge with little wisdom to it. But to know exactly why breathing matters and in what way is a higher form of knowledge. To explain why breathing matters requires much more than merely noticing that without breathing we pass out or die: it requires understanding the underlying causes of life and consciousness.

Wisdom, in Aristotle's view, as in Plato's, requires us to see beyond sense experience, to learn about the underlying first principles and causes of things. This wisdom gives us knowledge not merely of the appearances but of that which is behind (or within) the appearances and causes them to be as they are. This knowledge then becomes the central goal of Aristotelian metaphysics: to construct beyond the Socratic-Platonic conceptual philosophy a theory explaining the phenomenal (mental) world of the appearances. Plato's philosophy had tried to explain, for instance, the relationship between the conceptual reality of ideas and the perceptual reality of perceived objects using allegories like the cave: the perceived objects are but shadows of ideas, reflections of reality, mere representations. This theory, however, in no way explains *why* experience is as it is rather than some other way; it lacks an explanation in terms of Aristotle's first principles: it does not explain the causes of the phenomena. The ultimate task of Aristotle's metaphysics is to discover those first principles from which all the other sciences are derived. This is the goal of what Aristotle calls *first philosophy,* or *metaphysics,* which he claims is the most abstract and, at the same time, the most exact of all the sciences. "Secondary" sciences like physics ask what things are and why they are as they are. Metaphysics—the primary science, the first philosophy—asks far more general types of questions, such as, What does it mean to be anything whatsoever? What is it to be? Metaphysics is thus "the science of any existent, as existent."

What is the cause of being itself, whether in the particular or in the universal? Why is there existence—any type of existence—at all? Aristotle argues that Plato's ideas cannot explain the existence of empirical facts (such as that presently you see a book in front of you). Nor can ideas explain their own existence: Why are there any formal ideas to begin with? To claim that ideas are eternal is hardly sufficient: Why are they eternal? What causes ideas to be eternal rather than ephemeral? To suppose that ideas exist as a higher level of being, even to think of them in theological terms, such as being God-made entities, does not satisfy Aristotle. Regardless of whether God exists, the metaphysical problem is exactly the same. The problem is with being itself, any being. Aristotle's solution is to claim that the world of Plato's ideas is but a conceptual and unnecessary duplication of the empirical, phenomenal world of the appearances. Plato's big mistake, according to Aristotle, is to distinguish these worlds as two different realities, one that is more fundamental and more real than the other. There is one reality, one world: the world of ideas and the world of sense experience are the same world. Ultimately, in Aristotle's view, Plato's theory of ideas fails to explain anything and, further, it is impossible to prove the existence of ideas.

What has primary reality for Aristotle is *substance* that exists as individual entities, such as you and I, tables and chairs, rocks and planets, and so on. Because the essence of individual entities is known by means of class concepts like "man," "horse," "table," and so on, the fundamental problem of Aristotle's philosophy and his solution to the problems posed by Plato is found in the relationship of the universal to the particular. Thus, in his *Categories,* Aristotle criticizes Plato's theory of ideas by arguing that universals, like "man" or "blueness," do not exist independently of particular individuals. Each individual thing is a "primary substance" whose species and genera are "secondary substances" that make the thing what it is rather than some other thing.

It should be kept in mind that the actual word used by Aristotle, *ouisa*—usually translated as "substance"—can also be translated as "reality." Thus, to argue that particular individuals are a type of primary *substance* is to claim that they are themselves primary *realities.* This of course contradicts Plato's theory that the objects of sense experience are, at best, only partly real reflections of ideas. Thus, instead of the a priori analysis of ideas that Plato envisioned as the true function of the philosopher, Aristotle focuses on an empirical study of the structure of the objects that appear in the sensible world of ordinary experience. He then analyzes both the concept of ideas and the concept of substance from the perspective of the language used to describe them. He gives the first logical definition of substance, one that influenced philosophers throughout the Middle Ages. Plato aimed at knowledge of the essential nature (*ouisa*) of things through knowledge of universals such that the essence of individual things considered as intelligible is the universal idea of the many—and this was for Plato the substance of things, what they primarily *are.* Aristotle, on the other hand, in addition to the universal intelligible being of things, aimed primarily at the investigation of the being of things from the point of view of their generation and existence; since according to Aristotle only individual things are generated into existence, substance is conceived in primarily individualistic terms. The Aristotelian notion of substance is a *this* (something ostensibly referred to in experience) that, in marked contrast with the universal or secondary substance, is not predicable of the many. Moreover, the understanding of substance can be exposed from four different points of view:

1. *Grammar:* The nature of substance as the ultimate subject of predication can be expressed in common language by using the noun (i.e., noun substan-

tive) as the subject of a sentence to signify some individual entity that "is neither present in nor predicable of a subject."

2. *Physics:* The independent nature of being can be seen as a fundamental characteristic of substance in the analysis of change.

3. *Logic:* The analysis of change creates a division of being into the Aristotelian categories, with a clear distinction between the category of substance and the accidental categories (quantity, quality, place, relation, etc.). The category of substance itself is prior to the other categories and completely independent of them.

4. *Metaphysics:* Substance is the presence in an individual that is the cause of its being and unity.

Thus the substance of a thing is according to Aristotle always intelligible, so that while there are sensible substances (substances that can be sensed directly) the substance of the things thereby sensed is not sensible *except* insofar as the *activity* of the intellect is involved. (See Chapter 2, on medieval philosophers, especially the section on Averroes, for a discussion of the role of the active intellect in his interpretation of Aristotle.)

Aristotle thus lays the foundation for his view that—contrary to Plato—the soul, or mind, does not exist as a separate substance from the body. Rather, the soul is an integral part of the living process. Plato had argued in the *Phaedo* that the soul is eternal and immortal and that like the eternal ideas, the soul can exist without the body. Indeed, the mind, or soul, is according to Plato more real than the body. Aristotle, in his *On the Soul,* argues to the contrary. First, the soul is not a separately existing entity from the body. The soul cannot ever exist apart from the body. The soul is but the ideal principle of life, "the primary actualization of a natural organic body." The human soul builds a body for itself out of matter and is an integral part of it, rather than some metaphysical substance that enters the finished material body. The immaterial soul, for Aristotle, informs the physical body and is everywhere apparent in it. *One might say eyes are not windows to the soul but merely its outermost organs.* Further, the soul is the principle of independent motion inherent in each individual, bound to the matter that is the possibility of its activity. And it is in the soul's relation to its matter that the soul has desires and wills itself to action.

Souls are individuated by the variety and complexity of their functions, which in turn correspond to individuating differences in the organic structures that embody them. Fundamental functions, common to all living things including plants and animals, are nutrition, growth, and reproduction. At the next level are sensations, desires, and locomotion. Finally, at the highest level, unique to human beings, is the most important function of the soul: rationality.

Rationality, in turn, has several faculties. The most important is perception, which is the faculty of receiving the sensible idea of outward objects without their matter. These perceptions are the phenomena. Aristotle coined the term *common sense,* meaning a sense common not among people but within an individual person. It is the unifying sense common to the five senses of perception. This "common sense" makes it possible for the unification of data by the five separate senses into a single apperception. The common sense also accounts for the soul's awareness of its own activity of perception and all of its other states. Hence it is the common sense that is directly responsible for consciousness. Reason, as a separate faculty from perception, allows the soul to apprehend the universals and first principles necessary for all knowledge, but it is useless without sense perception. Reason is not limited to what can be experienced but can, through the faculty of the understanding, grasp the universal and ideal. We thereby can achieve true and absolute knowledge.

Aristotle classifies knowledge into three categories: (1) theoretical, whose aim is impartial and disinterested knowledge, (2) practical, whose aim is to influence and guide human conduct, and (3) productive, whose aim is to offer guidance to the various arts. The primary science, fundamental to all three types of knowledge, which he called the *analytic,* is logic. The purpose of the Aristotelian analytic, or logic, is to set down the necessary and sufficient conditions for any discipline whose aim is truth. The purpose and function of science, for instance, is to determine the underlying causes of particular existences, the individual perceptions, the actual (but transitory) objects found in our experience. Aristotle distinguished four types of causes: (1) material cause, "that from which, as its constitutive material, something comes, for example the bronze of the statue"; (2) the ideal (formal) cause, what the particular statue is, its essence or nature, such as its being a bust of Plato; (3) the efficient cause, that by which it initially comes into existence, "the source of the first beginning of change," as in "the father is the cause of the child"; and (4) the final cause, its "end" or purpose, "that for the sake of which" something is done, such as "health is [the final cause] of walking around." His method for attaining knowledge of these causes is deductive logic, the syllogistic deduction from premises known to be certain.

Aristotle's logical method is a marked contrast to the other two prevailing methods of discourse at the time, the *dialectic* method, which starts from probable premises, and the *eristic* method, whose purpose is not truth but rhetorical victory (this was the method used by the sophists to train young lawyers and politicians). Aristotle invented the *syllogism* as the most basic and simplest tool in his method of reasoning. A syllogism, consisting of three statements, says: if something is so and something else is so, then something else must be so. The first two statements, or *propositions,* are sentences that assert something to be so; they are called *premises.* The third statement, which in a valid syllogism must necessarily be true if the first two statements are, is called the *conclusion.* Syllogistic inference works on the principle that the term common to both premises, the middle term, must be related as either subject or predicate to each of the other two terms. Thus the conclusion is necessarily forced regarding the relation of the two terms to one another. For instance, consider the following syllogism:

> All philosophers are wise.
>
> Socrates is a philosopher.

Therefore,   Socrates is wise.

"Philosopher," the middle term, is related (as subject) to "wise" and (as object) to "Socrates" in such a way that "Socrates" and "wise" must necessarily be conjoined as in the conclusion. Notice, of course, that this valid argument (one in which *if* the premises are true the conclusion cannot be false) is not necessarily a good argument. A good argument must be both valid and sound. A sound argument is a valid argument whose premises are in fact true. And the first premise, while it may be true, is not obviously true. This is just one example in which we see that reasoning by pure logical validity is not sufficient for knowledge; Aristotle would certainly have agreed. However, Aristotle gave such a thorough analysis of the subject-predicate relation and all syllogistic forms that his method, now called *deductive logic,* has virtually remained unchanged to this day. But he didn't stop there; he also developed the method of logical induction, in which knowledge is attained even when the conclusion cannot be known to be true with absolute certainty but only with probability. This method involves passing from the particular individuals found in sense experience to the universal, necessary principles involved in sense experience.

Unlike Plato, who had to rely on the dubious concept of the demi-urge, Aristotle used his theory of the relation between the physical world of matter (the realm of appearance) and the world of ideas to explain change. The Presocratics conceived change in terms of passage from not-being to being. This idea seemed absurd to Parmenides. If ever there was nothing there would be nothing still, since nothing can come from nothing. Aristotle tries to get around this problem by saying that what first has only potential being is transformed, through its corresponding idea, into actual being, which he calls *entelechy.* Physical reality is thus conceived as a synthesis of the active and the passive, mind and matter; he thus conceives the world as a dynamic evolutionary system within which change is not illusory but real, spontaneous, continuous, and teleological. Change is the product of discoverable causes.

Since in Aristotle's view the essence of everything is known by means of class concepts, the key problem—one that generated research for subsequent centuries and continues to this day—is to fully understand the mysterious relationship between universals and particulars. Indeed, Aristotle makes this question the fundamental principle of scientific thinking: the derivation of the particular from the universal becomes the ultimate goal of science. The problem of universals and particulars was of course already recognized not just by Plato but even by Socrates. But it took Aristotle to fine-tune the puzzle with his science of logic as the foundation for a universal theory of scientific method, still very much in use in the present. Moreover, by turning the human thinking process into a separate object of philosophical contemplation and investigation, he made *methods* of inquiry an essential part of the human inquiry into the nature of things.

In this way, for Aristotle, as for many subsequent thinkers (such as Hegel), the historical and psychological development of human knowledge corresponds to the metaphysical and logical connection among things, except inversely: bound to its own sense perception and developing from it, the mind receives the phenomena from which it then advances by induction to form a conception of the true essence of things, the cause of the appearances. Since, according to Aristotle, this is how the objects of our perception first arose, all aspects of their existence can from that point on be explained through the logical process of deduction. Accordingly, the human mind can attain absolute knowledge of the true (essential and permanent) reality through an exact and careful examination of the empirical facts to which it has access in its own direct experience by asking, What is their cause? As we shall see, more than two thousand years later, Immanuel Kant (Chapter 4) will try to achieve exactly this result with a similar question: What are the necessary conditions for having experience?

Unlike the Platonic theory of ideas, the Aristotelian system of ideal concepts has no overarching unification like Plato's idea of the good. Rather, Aristotle's concepts fall under one of ten categories of being that may be asserted as a predicate of a proposition: (1) substance, (2) quantity, (3) quality, (4) relation, (5) place, (6) time, (7) position, (8) state, (9) action, and (10) passion. So, while "man" and "horse" are examples of substances, terms like "is six feet tall" or "weighs 165 pounds" are examples of the category of quantity. Examples of relation are terms like "greater," "smaller," and "double." "In the room" or "on the moon" are examples of place, while "yesterday," "now," and "tomorrow" are in the category of time. "Lying" and "sitting" are examples of position; "happy," "hungry," and "armed" are in the category of state. "To kill" and "to run" are examples of action. "To be wounded" is in the category of passion.

Thus, instead of the a priori analysis of ideas as envisioned by Plato, Aristotle organizes an empirical study of the structure of the objects of the sensible world. In this way, the role of both the good and the demi-urge in Plato's metaphysics is replaced by the most basic and fundamental presupposition of Aristotelian metaphysics, based on the Heraclitan notion that the mind as *logos* and the world as *cosmos* were inextricably linked. The identity of thought with being is an idea that would continue to influence many philosophers throughout the centuries, to this day. The mind is not merely an instrument for the study of nature but is one of the essential aspects of nature so that through direct reflection the mind apprehends and perceives being. But Aristotle does not merely express such ideas in the abstract, he develops intellectual and logical tools for the analysis of thought through language so that these essential structures and realtions of being can be understood and explored by the philosopher. For in listing the possible predicates of an object, Aristotle had discovered a natural and surprising progression from the quantitative and qualitative to spatial and temporal relations to causal relations and dependence that corresponds to the grammatical distinctions of substantive, adjective, adverb, and verb. Aristotle in this way lays a detailed conceptual map for subsequent theories based on a correspondent relation between the structure of language and the structure of reality. We shall see this theory emerge again in nineteenth- and early-twentieth-century debates regarding the nature of the relationship between syntax and semantics, sense and reference, in the works of Wittgenstein and in our present-day philosophy of language.

Again, it must be stressed that for both Plato and Aristotle the only object of true knowledge can be an ideal form, a conceptual universal, because absolute reality consists of conceptual universals. The difference is that Aristotle argues that such universals cannot have the sort of higher, or transcendental, being in relation to sensed objects as Plato envisions. According to Aristotle, there can be no such transcendental reality detached from the appearances. To talk as if there were such a higher reality Aristotle regards as mere reification or hypostatization of class concepts (i.e., making "things" out of noun substantives). This, says Aristotle, is the great flaw of Plato's two-tiered hierarchy. Thus, for Aristotle, the true metaphysical reality is located right here in the one and only world that exists, an amalgam of mind and matter; existence is made up of the conceptually determined individual things and knowledge must be sought in the relationship between passive material existence and active mental existence, in the existential shift from *possibility* to *actuality*. That is how objects come into existence, by passing from possibility into actuality through the conceptual workings of the mind. Matter, which contains all possibilities in itself, yields through the mind's class concept to the ideal form that already exists, from the start, not in some transcendental realm but within it. *Space itself is the containing source of being.* Aristotle takes this to be the greatest achievement of his system in relation to the Heraclitan and Eleatic theories. He argues that all the previous systems that had been based on permanence and being had been unable to explain becoming. He solves the problem with the idea that what possesses being is the substance that realizes itself and is conceived in the process from possibility to actuality in the very act of becoming a perceived object in time—an idea we shall encounter again in the strange amalgam of nineteenth-century German idealism and twentieth-century physics (especially the so-called Copenhagen interpretation of quantum mechanics).

God, too, in Aristotle's elaborate metaphysics is brought down from the transcendental realm as conceived by Plato as an idea, to a more worldly manifestation. The essence of God, as in Plato, is still immateriality, perfect incorporeality, pure spirituality, just as for the Heraclitans: God is conceived as the *nous*. Except God according to Aristotle is the absolute spirit who desires nothing and does nothing; God is the unmoved mover who moves the universe, the pure idea of contemplation that manifests itself in each being as *self-consciousness.* This deeply mystical aspect of Aristotle's philosophy we shall see emerge again, most notably in the philosophy of Averroes.

Aristotle's ground-breaking work on ethics, the *Nicomachean Ethics,* named after Aristotle's son Nicomachus (himself named after Aristotle's father), is generally regarded as one of the greatest works ever written on moral philosophy. In it, Aristotle extends his teleological view of the world (according to which each and every thing exists for some purpose toward which it tends by its own special and unique nature) to the meaning of life. The final end, or good, of human life is, according to Aristotle, the fulfillment of human nature. This he defines using his concept of essence as the unique characteristic of something which, for humanity, is the rational faculty of the soul. Rationality is the essence of human life because rationality is unique to humans. The highest good for human life therefore, in Aristotle's view, consists in the improvement and actualization of rationality and rational behavior.

Like Plato, Aristotle defines a good human character in terms of moderation, justice, virtue, and courage, and he claims that knowledge of what is good can be attained through rational means. He too says that the good and virtuous person will be an essentially happy person. The key difference between their approach to ethics stems from Aristotle's rejection of Plato's ideas as separately existing entities: unlike Plato, Aristotle claims that absolute knowledge in the moral realm can never be attained. He describes human virtue in terms of various traits that help us to achieve happiness and live well. This cannot be achieved unless there is a rational harmony in the social sphere, within the larger human community. He thus claims that social institutions are a necessary ingredient to human happiness. Indeed, in his view moral individuals as such cannot exist independently of their political and social setting. It is the society at large that enables individuals to develop virtues for the good and happy life. But he is careful to distinguish between moral virtues and intellectual virtues. Whereas intellectual virtues can be taught, moral virtues must be learned through living. The goal of every human action, however, is a good realized by some activity; this goal, however, is only a means to the highest goal of human existence, which Aristotle defines as happiness. And the highest ideal of human activity is reason. It is through the proper use of reason that human individuals become great and virtuous in relation to each other, their surrounding world of appearance, and the Godhead.

In his *Politics,* Aristotle argues, following Plato, that only those sufficiently intelligent or well educated—the "natural masters"—should govern the rest—the "natural slaves." The good life, however, is not defined by the political life nor in any other type of practical activity, such as the arts. Rather, the good life consists in theoretical inquiry and contemplation of impartial, disinterested truth for its own sake. Only this activity can bring complete happiness because it is the highest and noblest part of the soul, that which is least dependent on the external world: namely, intuitive reason, or *nous.* In such rational and theoretic contemplation of first principles, the human mind participates directly in the activity of pure thought constituting the eternal perfection of the soul.

In his *Poetics,* Aristotle presents bold new theories on poetry, drama, and literary criticism. Unlike Plato, who took a dim view of art, Aristotle claims that poetry "is something more philosophic and of greater import than history, since its statements have the nature of universals, whereas those of history are singulars." For Plato, art was but the cheap imitation of illusory appearances, at best three times removed from reality: a painting of Socrates, for instance, is a copy of Socrates who is himself but a copy of an idea. Since according to Aristotle the ideas themselves exist in particular things, by studying and imitating nature the artist is communing directly with the ideas, which he can then communicate to others by rendering them more vividly in his work, thereby expressing and illuminating the universal truths hidden in the particulars.

The king of Macedonia, much awed by what the royal doctor's son had become, asked for a return favor: would Aristotle come and be the personal philosopher to his own son, the thirteen-year-old crown prince, a curious and precocious little boy named Alexander? Aristotle agreed. Six years later, little Alexander became Alexander the Great, conqueror of the ancient world from Greece to India.

Upon his return to Athens, Aristotle set up his own school, the Lyceum, called the Peripatos (hence Aristotelians are often called "Peripatetics"). Like Plato's Academy, it lasted nearly a thousand years. While Plato's Academy led in the development of mathematics and geometry, Aristotle's Lyceum centered on applied scientific research in the natural sciences and logic. Not being an Athenian citizen, however, Aristotle had to rent the land on which the Lyceum operated. Although he was widely regarded as one of the greatest minds of the time, many Athenians resented him for having trained the Macedonian who had become their conqueror. So when in 323 B.C.E. Alexander suddenly died and the Macedonians were ousted from power, the Athenians turned against Aristotle.

Ironically, Plato's greatest pupil, like Plato's teacher Socrates, ended up being arrested by the Athenian government and charged—like Socrates before him—with atheism and impiety. Sentenced to death, Aristotle—unlike Socrates—chose to escape. A year later, he died on the island of Euboea.

Epicurus

In 323 B.C.E., the same year that Aristotle escaped, an aspiring young would-be philosopher named Epicurus arrived in Athens from Samos, the birthplace of Heraclitus, hoping to attain guidance from the great master. Little did the wide-eyed eighteen-year-old know that already the philosophy of Aristotle and Plato was quickly becoming the legacy of a dying Greece to future generations. The philosophical, scientific, and spiritual decay of Greece, already begun at the loss of the Peloponnesian War, was well underway. The next half dozen centuries, despite some noble efforts by Stoics, Epicureans, and Skeptics, would be a pale version of the golden age. Indeed, from here on the Greek mind produced little more than philosophical criticism and readjustment in comparison to its past glory.

Philosophy in the Hellenic and Roman periods after Plato and Aristotle branched into three distinct movements: Epicureanism, Stoicism, and Skepticism. The first of these is named after its founder, Epicurus (341–270 B.C.E.). An early proponent of the view still held widely today that the universe consists ultimately of physical particles called "atoms" (literally, "indivisibles") moving about in a void, Epicurus used his version of atomism as the basis for his moral theory. Following in the footsteps of his father, who was a teacher, he tried but failed to secure a teaching post in Mytilene and Lampsacus. He was considered by his superiors to be not well educated enough and too colloquial in his presentation. So in 306, at the age of thirty-five, he began teaching in Athens from the porch of his garden. So popular were these lectures that soon his garden became a renowned school that, unlike Plato's Academy and Aristotle's Lyceum, included women. There, teaching in the privacy of his garden, Epicurus and his students created a unique theory of life that integrated their atomic view of the physical world with ethical principles designed to liberate humanity from the superstitious terrors of religion. So in harmony was his teaching with the spirit of the time and so successful in producing learned students that soon he won the respect of even the most serious schools of science.

According to Epicurus, the soul, which like the rest of nature is made of physical atoms, is born, grows, and dies with the body. Like Democritus, Epicurus did not believe that God created the universe, nor that—contra Aristotle— human life (or anything else, for that matter) existed for some purpose. Further, though in Epicurus's view gods do exist, they cannot exert any causal influence on human affairs. We therefore need not fear death or the gods. Epicurus argued that seeing the sober truth about ourselves and accepting it, rather than hiding behind the veil of spiritualism or religious faith, liberates us from the fears imposed by religion and allows us to live, without fear or postponement, in a way that maximizes pleasure and minimizes pain in this world, in this life.

Unlike Democritus, however, whose atoms behaved as Newton would someday imagine, with perfect determinism, Epicurus's atoms moved partly by pure chance; a random swerve ("clinamen") in their path brought indeterminism and chance into the universe by making the atoms swerve from their course. Strict causality from one part of the universe to another could therefore not hold; the future did not come about through fate but was a random occurrence. Putting stock in metaphysical and religious theories to guide one's actions was therefore pointless, since everything could and would change haphazardly, guided by pure chance.

Except for a few letters and some fragments, most of Epicurus's voluminous writings have been lost. In his famous letter *To Herodotus,* Epicurus explains how everything comes about through the random collisions of atoms falling through empty space. This knowledge not only has the power to free us from the misery imposed on us by religious conditioning but also can spare us from fear of death. According to Epicurus, the gods are merely collections of physical atoms in empty space and have no effect on our lives unless we are led by fear of the gods to act in ways we think will please them. According to the common wisdom of the time, the gods not only ruled over all human affairs but also directly caused human happiness and misery. Epicurus denied this, claiming—as would the atomist Hobbes in the sixteenth century—that we ourselves are responsible for our misery as well as our happiness. Unlike Democritus, who believed in strict determinism, Epicurus held that while some events happen necessarily by chance, some are within our causal control. Belief in destiny, he argued, was more repressive than belief in the myths about the gods; the latter at least gives us hope, whereas determinism leads only to despair. But once you understand that neither gods nor destiny affect our lives, you "shall live like a god among men."

In his equally famous letter *To Menoeceus,* Epicurus expounds his major ethical theme: everyone should always seek pleasure. According to him, this is not just some cavalier formula but requires great skill and wisdom. One must be virtuous and prudent, knowing the values of various sorts of pleasures—how to weight them, how to attain them, how to forgo some pleasures to achieve greater pleasures, and so on. However, contrary to subsequent popular belief, he did not tolerate the gluttony that has come to be symbolized by his name; he in fact argued just the opposite: prudence in life frees us from the ills brought about by desire. This, in turn, requires learning philosophy so that one can be free of moral anxiety and superstitious fears brought about by religious worship of the gods. Having supposedly attained the ideal life in which the soul is released from its anxieties into real happiness, Epicurus was worshiped by his followers as "a god among men." Many regarded him as the founder of a new religion; his school, which lasted into the fourth century C.E.[15], had a number of influential and devout followers, among them Metrodorus, Hermarchus, Colotes of Lampsacus, Apollodorus, Demetrius Lacon, Zeno of Sidon (Cicero's teacher), and the great Latin poet Lucretius (99–55 B.C.E.), who also worshiped Epicurus and whose *De rerum natura* (On the nature of things) is widely regarded as one of the greatest didactic poems ever written. In rendering Epicurus's atomic theory from the abstract Greek prose into Latin hexameters, Lucretius made especially poignant Epicurus's ideas about the role of pleasure in the realm of ethics that would later influence the utilitarians, especially Bentham and Mill.

Like most of the philosophers during the Hellenic-Roman period, Epicurus expressly limits philosophy to the practical search for the means of attaining individual happiness. Science and virtue, in fact the whole of knowledge, are worthless in and of themselves and must also be subservient to the practical human need for pleasure, but not just positive pleasure in the sense of satisfying some need. Rather, the more valuable pleasure is the state of *painlessness,* which can be attained only in a state of nearly perfect rest. Pleasure attained from the satisfaction of desire is less perfect than happiness found in a state in which every desire is absent. Epicurus distinguished three types of desires: (1) natural and indispensable (food, survival, etc.), (2) natural and perhaps dispensable (sex, love, admiration, etc.), and (3) imaginary, which are neither natural nor indispensable (fame, wealth, etc.). We cannot live without the first; without the second, we cannot be happy; and the third we can discard. The attainment of Epicurean enlightenment has thus much in common with Stoic enlightenment (see below), in that it makes the individual human being as free as the gods.

In many ways, the selfish utilitarianism of Epicurus was a revival of the early sophists, except that Epicurus developed it into a fully political and social system that became the commonsense philosophy of the Roman world. It subsequently became the leading principle of political compact in the Enlightenment of the seventeenth and eighteenth centuries, in which the "social contract" was conceived as the product of the selfish reason of individuals who live without a state. As with such social contract theorists (again, especially Bentham and Mill), there is no such thing as right and wrong action except insofar as there exists some sort of agreement about universal utility between individuals.

Epictetus and the Stoics

Stoic philosophy originated with Zeno of Citium[16] (334–262 B.C.E.), a native of Cyprus who came to Athens as a young man to study philosophy. He developed a pantheistic system according to which reality is a rational order within the world-soul, subject to laws of reason fully accessible to the human intellect and thus making revelations from the gods superfluous. Around 300 B.C.E., Zeno and his students began teaching their views from a stoa, or porch, in the marketplace and that is how their philosophical movement, which lasted six centuries and continues to exert influence, got its name.

Early Stoics developed all Platonic and Aristotelian fields of philosophy, including logic, physics, and ethics. The only good, according to Stoic doctrine, is virtue, which is attainable not by faith but through knowledge, as Socrates had taught; the result is happiness. The truly wise use knowledge to achieve independence from both the external world of social and political forces and the internal world of their own passions and emotions. Stoic views appealed to all classes and found wide support even among rulers, exerting great influence on the Roman Empire; one of the greatest adherents of Stoicism was the Roman emperor Marcus Aurelius.

Though the Stoics developed their philosophy in opposition to Epicurean hedonism, they agreed with Epicurus that the way to the good and happy life is through the pursuit and practice of philosophy. Their claim that nothing could disturb the happiness of a true philosopher grew out of the views of Socrates, Plato, and Aristotle. According to Socrates, a good man cannot be harmed. Happiness for Plato consisted in a "harmony of the soul." In Aristotle's view, "the good is something proper to the person and cannot be taken away." Epictetus likewise argued that "men are disturbed not by things, but by the views they take of things."

Epictetus (55–135 C.E.) was born a Roman slave in Hierapolis, in Asia Minor (the peninsula comprising most of modern Turkey). While still a slave, he began studying with the Stoic philosopher Musonius Rufus. He quickly surpassed his teacher and so impressed his master that he was freed. Soon afterward he founded his own school in Nicopolis, Epirus. Like Socrates, Epictetus wrote nothing. His teaching, based on Stoic doctrines, has been preserved by one of his students, Arrian, who also wrote the history of Alexander the Great. The *Enchiridion,* or *Manual,* and the *Discourses* are both transcriptions of Epictetus's lectures.

Epictetus argues that both happiness and unhappiness are completely under our control. He relies on the Stoic distinction between what is within our power —"the use of the phenomena of existence"—and what is not within our power, namely, the phenomena of existence themselves. In other words, although we have no control over the objects of existence, we can to a certain extent control their use because we have the power to view objects as we choose, to form opinions about them, to fear or desire them. This control can be achieved only if we learn "how it is possible to employ desire and aversion without hindrance." Like Epicurus, Epictetus claims that the main purpose of philosophy is to help us achieve inner peace through a proper understanding of the world. Like the Stoics, he has a Heraclitan philosophy of nature, according to which change, the fundamental force of the universe, is governed by the *logos* as it manifests itself in human reason. Inner peace comes from conforming to the way the world is rather than to our own prejudice and then following reason in three stages: master your desires, perform your duties, and think correctly about yourself and the world.

Epictetus warns against boasting about philosophy or knowledge so as not to draw attention to oneself; in fact, he suggests that the wise ought not to simply teach their wisdom to whoever would have it. He even warns against revealing theorems, that is, propositions that are known to be true because they have been rigorously proven! He suggests that philosophy ought to reveal only its most conjectural claims and hide its certainties from those who have not been initiated into its secrets.

Following Plato, Epictetus points out that you cannot make yourself believe something simply by wishing it. For instance, if you try to make yourself believe on a bright day that it is the middle of the night, you will fail. Or try to make yourself believe that right now as you are reading this book there are exactly 1,720 other people reading it (there might be—you don't know). Still, you can't convince yourself. In other words, our beliefs and ideas about ourselves and the world are not of our own conscious choosing. We cannot simply believe what we wish, nor can we wish whatever ideas we want into our own minds. We therefore according to Epictetus are not responsible for the way the world is or for our own ideas. All that we are responsible for is reduced by Epictetus to the use we make of the ideas that present themselves to our minds: "Two maxims we must ever bear in mind—that apart from the will there is nothing good or bad, and that we must not try to anticipate or to direct events, but merely to accept them with intelligence."

Lame and physically weak from the time he had been a slave, Epictetus worked arduously in making his views known. He developed a large following, even among early Christians, and in 90 C.E. the emperor Domitian expelled him from Rome along with many other philosophers whose teachings he saw as dangerous to his tyranny. In his *Discourses,* Epictetus offers a powerful and ironic polemic against the illusion of freedom, no doubt inspired by his own experience of having been "freed" from slavery and then attaining fame and even power. Thinking that because you are not a slave you are free can be especially deceptive, he says, because unlike the slave who knows he is not the master of his own life, a "free" man is in the graver danger of being a slave without even knowing it. You are then powerless to act against your oppressor for you do not realize you are oppressed. How can you be a slave and not even know it? By being a slave to greed, vanity, and desire and thinking that these qualities are in your own self-interest. According to Epictetus, true freedom, the greatest good, can be attained only in ways similar to what five centuries later the Indian sage Gautama Buddha would espouse: free yourself from your desires and the greedy corruption of the self or ego so that you can attain that rare freedom from the self that eludes the mass of humanity. The Stoic philosopher seeks freedom through surrender to *what is,* taking as a guide neither the illusory reins of the internal authority of self nor the illusory whip of the external authority of society but instead following the correct principles that make the philosopher one with the actual world, fearless, and incorruptible.

Marcus Aurelius

Marcus Aurelius (121–180) was born to a prominent Spanish family in Rome. After the death of his parents, while still a boy, he devoted himself to his studies. By age twelve he was mastering geometry, music, mathematics, painting, and literature. Under the mentorship of private tutors, he learned fluent Greek and Latin and the whole of philosophy from the ancients through the Stoics whom he most admired. At fourteen he received the *toga virilis,* the white robe signifying adulthood and full citizenship in Rome. He showed so much promise and talent that when the emperor Hadrian picked Marcus's uncle Antoninus as his successor, he specified that Antoninus should designate Marcus to be the next emperor. Thus, by the age of seventeen Marcus Aurelius already had become the heir apparent to the imperial throne of Rome.

According to Plato, "philosophers must become kings or kings must become philosophers before the world will have peace." As the fourteenth Roman emperor (from 161 to 180), Marcus Aurelius was probably the closest thing to a philosopher king the world has ever known. By the time he became emperor at age thirty-nine, he had earned a reputation as a great statesman and philosophical visionary. During his nineteen-year reign, he brought about more political, social, educational, and economic reforms than any other emperor. He championed the poor, and because of his own experience as an orphan initiated many programs to aid young children. He brought about many reforms that improved the condition of slaves. He resisted what he saw as the corrupting trappings of power, remaining a sincere and simple human being capable of great kindness but a powerful and resolute leader as well.

As the commander-in-chief of the Roman legions, Marcus Aurelius successfully defended Rome against more invasions than any other emperor: he fought invasions from Syria, Spain, Egypt, Britain, Italy, and the Germanic tribes along the Rhine-Danube frontier. In Athens he financed all four great philosophical schools: the Academy, the Lyceum, the Garden, and the Stoa. Today there still stands, in Piazza Colonna in Rome, a column erected to his memory. Its spiral frieze contains dramatic, brutally realistic depictions of the Danube wars.

Marcus Aurelius regarded Christians as the most subversive and dangerous elements within the Roman Empire and violently persecuted them, warning that if Christianity were allowed to corrupt the intellect and souls of the citizens the entire Roman Empire would fall, destroyed in the end not by physical assault from external enemies but from within, ruined by the mental deterioration of its own people.

Meditations, written during military campaigns, is a twelve-volume compendium of his ruminations on life. Written not in Roman but in Greek, it reveals the mind of a Stoic philosopher of great eloquence, laying out his own path of self-discovery and enlightenment; he rejects, for instance, the Stoic doctrine of absolute truth, holding instead that we can at best have probable knowledge and that therefore to be virtuous we must always keep an open mind. His overarching theme throughout the *Meditations* is that only one thing can keep the "daemon within a man free" through the tumultuous trials and tribulations of life: philosophy. The work itself is a unique window into the mind of an enlightened Roman emperor who tried to integrate wisdom into the sphere of human politics. Most historians believe the work was written for his own eyes only, to inspire him and to keep alive within himself the Stoic philosophy that was his lifelong allegiance.

Sextus Empiricus and the Skeptics

The so-called Pyrrhonian skeptics are named after Pyrrhon of Elis (367–275 B.C.E.), according to whom it is absolutely impossible to attain knowledge about anything. He argued that we should, at best, suspend judgment about whether any statement is true or false. This includes the statement "It is absolutely impossible to attain knowledge about anything." Such a suspension of belief, according to Pyrrhon, leads not to insecurity and anxiety but rather to a tranquil, liberating state of indifference about the world. It should be noted that skepticism is not the same as nihilism. Compare, for instance, the philosophy of Socrates' teacher, Cratylus (450–385 B.C.E.), who claimed not only that knowledge is impossible but also that no one can ever say anything true about anything, and so refused to speak.

Indeed, the word *skepticism* does not mean "nonbeliever" or anything remotely like that. It comes from the Greek words *skeptesthai,* meaning "to consider" or "to examine carefully" and *skepsis,* which means "to seek." Thus, much like the early sophists and their successor Socrates, who in the *Apology* declares, "All that I know is that I know nothing," the Pyrrhonian skeptics claimed that before you should accept anything as true, you must subject it to careful, rigorous scrutiny, seeking proof based on clear and indubitable evidence. Such strict adherence to absolute certainty as a necessary condition for knowledge led them to extremely negative views about the possibility of absolute knowledge.

As a philosophical method, the Pyrrhonian movement grew out of the skepticism that had developed in Plato's Academy under its leaders Arcesilas (315–241 B.C.E.) and Carneades (213–129 B.C.E.), who presented a series of devastating arguments designed to show why nothing at all can be known except one thing: that nothing can be known. One should therefore live only by probabilities —a principle the Pyrrhonists regarded as too dogmatic, arguing that even the previous skeptical position, that "nothing can be known," cannot be known. The Pyrrhonians were thus led to suspend judgment about everything that is not immediately evident, never affirming or denying anything. Things appear a certain way, which the Pyrrhonian skeptic accepts at face value without knowing whether the appearances are as they seem and lives by following the laws and customs of society, with the peace of mind that comes from not having to judge anything.

None of the writings of the Pyrrhonian skeptics have survived, except the work of Sextus Empiricus (175–225). Trained not as a philosopher but as a medical doctor and teacher, he became the last leader of the Pyrrhonian movement. His written works are viewed by most historians as copies of lectures consisting of arguments worked out by previous skeptics. *Against the Mathematicians* and *Against the Dogmatists* contain detailed arguments against each area of knowledge: the liberal arts (grammar, rhetoric, geometry, arithmetic, astronomy, and music) and what then were the three branches of philosophy—logic, physics, and ethics. Ironically, these works are two of our most important sources of knowledge about the early history of astronomy, geometry, grammar, and the prevailing Stoic theology of the time.

His famous *Outlines of Pyrrhonism* is a general summary of the various Pyrrhonian arguments organized into a specific and precise philosophical method. Just as doctors use varying remedies of different strengths to cure the sick, depending on the severity of their illness, so the skeptical philosopher must use arguments of appropriate strength and measure to cure the dogmatic ills of dogmatic belief. The more entrenched you are in your beliefs, the stronger the skeptical argument should be applied to you until you see that you don't really know what you think you know. Sextus Empiricus thus distinguishes the Pyrrhonian position from the dogmatic position of Aristotle and Epicurus, who think they have discovered the truth, and that of those who think truth cannot be found. The purpose of his skeptical arguments is to cure people of both types of dogmatism—the dogmatism of those who believe they have attained knowledge and the dogmatism of those who believe that knowledge cannot be attained. The philosophically healthy position is never to draw conclusions; the healthy philosopher must always keep seeking. To this end Empiricus developed a "skeptical grammar," in which every sentence must end in "so it seems to me at the moment."

Plotinus: The Twilight of Philosophy

In the third century the philosophical tradition we have thus far considered, from Thales to Sextus Empiricus, ground to a screeching halt. To the enlightened citizens at the height of the Roman Empire, with the Hellenic philosophical genius behind them and the emerging political, social, and cultural advances before them, it must have seemed as if some great, cosmic awakening was about to happen, as if the next level of enlightenment within human consciousness was just around the corner. What they got instead was the Dark Ages: the burning of books, the closing of the philosophy schools, the collapse of the Roman Empire.

It is against this backdrop that the last of the great ancient philosophers, Plotinus (205–270), appeared on the scene. Born and raised in Egypt, Plotinus studied philosophy in Alexandria. He joined the Roman expedition in 244 against the Persians with the idea of learning about Eastern philosophies. After settling in Rome, he single-handedly tried to revive the classical Hellenistic philosophy as an antidote to the ruin and misery of the crumbling world around him. Because it was based on the views of Plato, the philosophical movement Plotinus founded came to be called Neoplatonism (though it was a full blend of both Platonic and Aristotelian views). Under the auspices of Emperor Gallienus, Plotinus became extremely influential throughout the Roman Empire, and for a time it seemed as if his mission would succeed. At one point the emperor agreed to let him build a second city near Rome, based on Plato's *Republic,* to be called Platonopolis. It would have been the center for the new philosophical revival. But then, suddenly, for reasons unknown, the emperor withdrew the offer.

Plotinus's works stand at the crossroads between the Greek tradition spanning the seven centuries from Thales to Sextus Empiricus and the beginning of Christendom. Although he did not begin writing until he was forty-nine, his works, edited posthumously by his student Porphyry into fifty-four books called the *Enneads,* covered every major branch of philosophy except politics. In them, under the influence of all the ancient thinkers, especially Parmenides and Pythagoras, Plotinus tried to resurrect Plato's philosophy. He used Plato's ideas to attack what he saw as the materialism of the Stoics and atomists, as well as to argue against the whole of Epicurean philosophy. He thought that, for all of their practical wisdom, the Epicureans were incapable of dealing with the base instincts driving the superstitious beliefs that suddenly seemed to be making philosophy irrelevant.

Catholic theology after the end of the Roman Empire and throughout the subsequent Christian era of the Middle Ages was importantly influenced by the works of Plotinus, especially by his distinction between three levels of reality. This distinction became the avatar for Christian views of the Holy Trinity. The Parmenidean One, in Plotinus's view, is equated not only with "God" but with Plato's good as well. Although the One precedes the good, the One is essentially undefinable and therefore no predicates can be attributed to it. All we can say about this highest level of reality is that "it is."

At the second level, below the One, is its image, nous, variously translated as mind, spirit, or intellectual principle. Nous exists because the One, in its quest to understand itself, attains the power of seeing, or vision; in a sense, nous is the "light" by which the One sees itself. Finally, the third and lowest level of reality is the soul, which in Plotinus's view is the creator of all living things, including the sun, moon, and stars and the visible world itself. The soul has two parts: the inner soul, which faces the nous, and the outer soul, which faces the external. The three metaphysical levels—the One, the nous, and the soul—correspond to three distinct levels of consciousness: discursive thought, intuitive thought, and mystical awareness—the soul, the nous, and the One, respectively. Relying on

Aristotle's notion that contemplation receives the idea of the object contemplated, Plotinus argues that the soul—which forgets that it is but an emanation of the One—can through contemplation transcend itself and glimpse that which it is the reflection of—the nous—and that which the nous is the reflection of—the One. Since, unlike the nous and the One, the soul can contemplate its objects only in succession, it gives rise to time, space, and matter; this quasi-reality of nature in turn contemplates but in a dreamlike state, ultimately deteriorating into the nonconscious level of matter.

Going in the other, "inward" direction, when the soul is "divinely possessed and inspired," it sees the next higher level, where there is the fragmented image of the One—"thought thinking itself." This is the nous, a "unity-in-diversity," where all ideas are present in every idea, and the soul then is able to have direct, mystical contact with the One. Plotinus then asks for the first time in a formal manner the question of why the mind is not aware of itself. He asks, "Why is the soul oblivious to itself?" In saying that without the soul there is no sun, he is of course relying on the idealist world view that began with Plato and will find its culmination among the modern British philosophers in Berkeley, among the Germans in Hegel, Fichte, and Schelling, and among the nineteenth-century American idealists in Royce.

Alexandria, Egypt, Plotinus's birthplace, was of course named after that student who was the last of a remarkable chain started by Socrates, Plato, and Aristotle. It was one of the most important ancient seaports and was home to the greatest and largest library in the known world, perhaps the largest of all time: the Library of Alexandria. Plotinus was one of its last readers, for it would soon be destroyed, consumed by fire during a civil war. One can imagine him making his way slowly through labyrinthine stacks containing untold numbers of manuscripts, of which we have but scraps, copies, and translations—authors with names like Thales, Anaximander, Anaximenes, Pythagoras, Heraclitus, Parmenides, Zeno, Protagoras, Democritus, Plato, Aristotle. One imagines him reading, thinking, wondering, writing, hoping to rekindle the inner mounting flame amid the growing darkness.

Except it was not to be. The dawn of philosophy had long since come and gone. Its first day, which had lasted six hundred years, was rapidly drawing to a close. Plato's sun had begun to set. Philosophy's first twilight descended rapidly across the known world. It was the beginning of the 600-year night.

---

1. Before the Common Era, which coincides with, and replaces, "B.C."
2. The lists vary somewhat, but four names appear on all of them, including Plato's (Protagoras, 343a): Bias of Priene, who saved the Ionians during the Persian invasion by helping them to migrate to Sardinia; Pittacus, the tyrant of Mitylene; Solon, a gnomic poet who became the "lawgiver" of Athens; and Thales.
3. From A. E. Taylor, *Aristotle on His Predecessors,* 1907.
4. The word *metaphysics* is an arbitrary coinage of Andronicus of Rhodes (c. 70 B.C.E.), who used it to refer to a collection of books Aristotle had written after (*meta*) his books on physics. It was only later applied to what Thales and others were doing; that Thales was *doing* metaphysics before there was a word for it is as revealing as the fact that people

learned to speak before they had a word for language. In other words, although it was centuries after Thales that we gave meaning (Bedeutung—see the sections on Frege and Wittgenstein in Chapter 5) to metaphysics, it was, in my opinion, Thales who gave it its sense (Sinn) and paved the way for our subsequent understanding of it as "the science of being as such," by which we mean to distinguish a certain type of cognitive inquiry from the "study of being" under some particular category or aspect. Hence the study of metaphysics, in the oracular words of the medievals, was the study of *ens* (being in the most general sense) *unqualified* by any term, in comparison to *ens mobile* (being in motion), *ens quantum* (quantitative elementary being), and so on, which are examples of the science of mechanics.

I think the word *science* is best understood in its classical sense, meaning "knowledge by causes," where *cause* has the sense (Sinn—see, again, the sections dealing with Frege and Wittgenstein) of the Greek *aitia* and *knowledge* is contrasted not with *ignorance* but with *opinion*.

In this way, we can arrive at the sense (Sinn) of metaphysics (and to see why it is illogical to call it nonsense—as the logical positivists will try to do—see Chapter 5). For the *objects* of metaphysical contemplation can properly be understood as what they are: the first *causes* in the natural order, the "first principles of being" conceived in the broadest and most general form possible; a more general form cannot be conceived by the unaided human intellect. (One should always leave room for one's descendants as, in this case, for a Turing machine running a Gödel code conceived in the Von Neumann architecture, sometimes referred to as a "computer.")

5. I owe this insightful point to Neil Florek.
6. See my "Quantum Cosmology, the Anthropic Principle, and Why Is There Something Rather than Nothing?" in Kolak and Martin, *The Experience of Philosophy*, 3rd ed. (Belmont, Calif.: Wadsworth, 1995), pp. 427–459.
7. The word *mysticism* has come to signify a variety of psychic and occult phenomena and in many "scientific" circles today connotes spurious knowledge. In other words, it has come to be as disassociated from its philosophical roots as the word *metaphysics* when used, say, in the context of Shirley MacLaine's books that, I take it, are not on the same subject for which Kant's *Prolegomena to any Future Metaphysics* was written.

   The word *mysticism* owes something to the "mystery religious," whose followers, who were initiated with the divine secret of the universe, were called "mystes." The idea was that God is an absolutely transcended being, beyond reason, thought, and experience, but could—according to the mystery religions as well as the Pythagoreans—be reached by extraordinary experience, thinking, or reasoning (it is not generally known that the later two were emphasized over the former in the "Pythagorean mysteries"). The early Christians substituted the word *contemplation* in this same context, for mystical states of mind (including, again, not just experience but also thinking and reasoning). The word *mystical* came into general usage in Western philosophy with Dionysius the Areopagite, during the end of the fifth century C.E., who used it to signify a type of theology in which thinking, experience, and reason were in fact suppressed so that the Godhead could be reached *via negativa*. (For a discussion of this concept, see Chapter 2.) It had much to do with the concept of *agnostia*, literally, "unknowing knowing," as it was used by the Neoplatonists as the conscious state in which the human mind attained unity with the divine mind of the Godhead.

   What these philosophical and theological etymologies have in common, which relates to the way the word *mysticism* came to be used by philosophers who would rightly consider themselves as espousing some type of mysticism, is this:

   1. Ultimate reality cannot be known, understood, experienced, or even talked about using conventional language, experience, knowledge, and so on.
   2. Ultimate reality is one unified totality, an indivisible, absolute whole, *or*
   2.a. Ultimate reality is absolute nothingness, a nothing.

   It is of course ironic that one has to put the second principle as a pair of opposites, but even the most casual survey of the literature conveys the distinct impression that although there are many mystically inclined thinkers who would agree as to the method, they tend to draw (speaking very loosely and roughly, of course) two very different sorts of conclusions. Perhaps one of the distinguishing characteristics of certain Eastern types of mysticism is shown in those religious systems that claim the ultimate "level" of "spiritual enlightenment" is to realize that there is no difference between 2 and 2a, such as one finds in some of the more interesting varieties of Buddhism (Theravada, Zazen, etc.).

8. How is reason related to mysticism? As I have already noted, contrary to common opinion, the Greek mystics considered special types of reason and thinking along with experience as conducive to attaining unity with ultimate reality. I say "special" merely to mean something analogous to ritualized, "unnatural" human activities. For instance, if you think about it, you may see that the sorts of physiological convolutions and special procedures usually involved in ancient rituals to achieve "enthusiasm"—meaning literally, "taking the gods within oneself"—have a counterpart in the intellectual realm in, say, mathematics, logic, and philosophical thinking as formally practiced by professional philosophers. In other words, it's not just reasoning in the way we may do it in our ordinary states of mind, when we are trying to figure out, say, what kind of car to buy, but the kind of reasoning as is involved in solving differential equations, proving a theorem in logic, or presenting a philosophical argument to other philosophers. These latter sorts of activities have nothing *natural* about them and require a ritualized form of training to achieve a minimal level of proficiency. And what the Pythagorean-inspired mystics had in mind can be viewed as a sort of intellectualized version of physical religious rituals.

9. For a more detailed discussion, see my "Incredible Shrinking Zeno," reprinted in *The Experience of Philosophy,* written with mathematician David Goloff, in which we explain why even the most sophisticated mathematical solutions do not work.

10. The word *rationalism* refers to a theory of philosophy that began with the Eleatics, Pythagoreans, and Plato, according to which reason is a self-sufficient intellectual system in which the criterion of truth is not experiential (empirical) but deductive. It's chief modern proponents have been Descartes, Spinoza, and Leibniz. Typically, the attempt to instill mathematical methods into philosophy has come to be associated with rationalism, a leitmotif that runs through the works of Plato, Descartes, Spinoza, Leibniz, Hegel, and the early Russell and is strongly adhered to by today's mathematically inclined philosophers.

11. To the Athenians of the time, the Greek term for piety had a meaning that went beyond the narrow religious sense of today's English; it meant responsibility, trustworthiness, and loyalty in terms of obligations binding an individual to others, such as his family and friends, the political and religious traditions of his state, and so on.

12. From Plato, *The Republic,* trans. Benjamin Jowett (London: Clarendon Press, 1892).

13. The Greek word *eidos* has sometimes, and in my view erroneously, been translated not as *idea* but as *form.* The reason, supposedly, is that the English word *idea* has too close an association to the subjective meaning of *idea* and that what Plato intended by *eidos* was not merely a subjective state of mind. I do believe that Plato did not mean to espouse such radical subjectivism as, for instance, some of the nineteenth-century idealists would do (see Chapter 4). However, the meaning of *form* goes so far in the other direction and fits so well in cahoots with the various varieties of naive realism as practiced by some unphilosophically minded philosophers, that in my opinion—especially when viewed in context with how the moderns, including Kant, have been (mis)treated as of late—the whole enterprise begins to look like a very clever philosophical conspiracy.

14. Bertrand Russell has famously remarked, in his *Why I Am Not a Christian* (New York: Simon and Schuster, 1957), that he considers Jesus to have been an immoral person for having preached Hell. But perhaps Jesus can be viewed as not having been entirely to blame.

15. Common Era, which corresponds to and replaces the locution "A.D."

16. Not to be confused with Zeno of Elea (490–430 B.C.E.), inventor of the paradoxes of motion.

CHAPTER TWO

Medieval Philosophy

By the third century C.E., the cities that once were the cultural centers of the Roman Empire, home to philosophers, artists, and political leaders, began to unravel because of economic pressure from the constant military campaigns. Large numbers of the wealthier citizens fled to escape the steadily rising taxes, health conditions began to deteriorate, and within a short period about a third of the population died from either wars or the plague. The militaristic elements of the Roman Empire gained supreme power, even over the emperors, in part the result of growing attacks by Germans from the north and Persians from the East, who sought to capitalize for what they perceived was a growing weakness within the empire. Meanwhile, from inside there came a growing sentiment among the citizens, who began to turn away from culture and education, seeking instead personal prestige and amassing wealth from within an ever-widening class system.

The distinctly antireligious sentiments of the Epicurean and Stoic philosophers, which had developed along with the rise of the Roman Empire, gave way to a slew of cults and emerging religions vying for people's beliefs. Among them, various Christian cults began gaining large numbers of followers. The Roman leaders, concerned more about the threat of external enemies than about fragmentation within their society, ignored the danger signs Marcus Aurelius had warned about. Superstition became rampant, along with a growing syncretism in which philosophies and religions were assembled haphazardly like a collage of prevailing opinions without a philosophical center. Further, instead of trying to lay a substantial foundation for its philosophical principles and methods, the Roman aristocracy began to worship its emperors as gods. Meanwhile, people divided themselves among the cults: Isis, which combined Greek and Egyptian gods into a sort of unitarian religion; the Mithraic cult, which worshiped the sun; and the Phrygian cult, which worshiped the Mother of the Gods. The Christians, no longer persecuted as they had been under Marcus Aurelius, were beginning to win more converts than all the other cults combined.

Catholic philosophy developed in part from philosophical views derived from Plato, the Stoics, and the Neoplatonists. It dominated Western thought for a thousand years, from the time of Augustine to the Renaissance. Of its four main Latin church founders—St. Ambrose, St. Jerome, St. Augustine, and Pope Gregory the Great—Augustine (Aurelius Augustinus of Hippo) had the deepest and most lasting influence.

Augustine: The Beginning of Christendom

Augustine (354–430) was born at Thagaste, near Carthage in North Africa. He studied and then taught rhetoric in Carthage, Rome, and Milan. As a teenager he joined the Manichaean religion, a synthesis of Christianity and Zoroastrianism that had spread throughout the Roman Empire and rivaled the growing Christian religion. Its founder, Mani (Greek Manes, Latinized Manichaeus), converted to Christianity from Zoroastrianism, an Indo-Iranian movement (also known as Mazdaism, Bah Din, and Parsiism) based on the teachings of Zarathustra, an ancient figure from the sixth century B.C.E. According to Zarathustra, the human struggle between good and evil is a manifestation of a cosmic duel between the divine forces of light and the demonic forces of darkness. Individual human spirits must, according to Zarathustra, fight personal battles between light and darkness, truth and falsehood, moral right and wrong, in order to gain either the salvation of eternal bliss or eternal agony. Mani synthesized Zoroastrian ideas with Christianity, claiming that Christ was an incarnation of the same spirit as Buddha and Zarathustra, the original soul of the first man created by the "mother of light" to help the rest of humanity become a major force in combatting the overpowering darkness.

Augustine finally rejected Manichaeanism when he came under the influence of the Skeptics, and for a brief time he turned to Skepticism. When he discovered Plotinus, however, he became a devout Neoplatonist, arguing on behalf of Plotinus's semireligious interpretation of Plato, which he embellished with Zoroastrian and Manichaean ideas about the human struggle between good and evil, sin and salvation. These ideas remained a central aspect of his thought even after his conversion to Christianity so that through his writings they became a central aspect of later Christian dogma. In 387, at age thirty-two, he formally converted to Christianity and returned to Africa, where he established many monasteries. He become a priest in 391 and in 396 was appointed bishop of Hippo, a city near Carthage.

Just as the history of philosophy contains variations on the themes of Plato and Aristotle, so the history of Christian thought consists in the variations on the themes of Augustine and Aquinas. Aquinas was primarily an Aristotelian and Augustine was primarily a Platonist, and thus the influence of Plato and Aristotle has remained central. In some ways, Augustine's philosophy is a return to the Socratic tradition in which metaphysics and epistemology are studied not for their own sake but as a way of enlightening the individual soul. The purpose of philosophy is salvation from suffering and the attainment of happiness, not just in this world but in the next world as well. From the Epicureans, Stoics, and Skeptics, Augustine thus took as fundamental the maxim that the ultimate aim of the various purposes of philosophy is the attainment of happiness. In addition, in the Neoplatonists he found "all things but one—the *logos* made flesh." Out of these combined views Augustine laid down a philosophy that became the foundation for subsequent Christianity. He gave a Christian reinterpretation to the Neoplatonic view that ultimate knowledge can be obtained only by a select few individuals via mystical intuition of ultimate reality (that is, "the supreme idea of the good, being, God," etc., itself a reinterpretation of Platonism) through mystical union with God. These special divine representatives have, according to Augustine, been preordained by God to act as the divine representatives of Being and there is nothing—no amount of sinning or doing "God's work" that can alter God's choice: it was fixed before the beginning of time.

Augustine's own and very dramatic conversion experience fits squarely into this latter caveat, for Augustine sees both the key role the desire for happiness plays in the mind's desire to know and its solution. Influenced by the Manichaean doctrine that final salvation comes through ascetic living itself derived from the views of the Stoics and Skeptics, Augustine argues that the path to salvation lies in turning away from the worldly pleasures—but not through the abstract detachment of the Stoics or the belief-free disinterestedness of the Skeptics. Augustine's answer is predicated on the understanding, provided in the philosophies of his Platonic predecessors, that what we call "the world" is not the real world but only our idea of it. Likewise, what you call your "self" is merely an idea within your own mind, not your real soul. It is the ability to see beyond both the external and internal world of appearances that one attains knowledge of ultimate reality, which Augustine calls God.

Under the philosophical influence of Plato and distinctly unlike much of the Christianity of today, Augustine's view is grounded, he claims, in reason. That is not to say that rationality is somehow par for the course in philosophy or even essential to it. We shall see many examples of philosophers who have argued, asserted, or even merely expressed that nothing can be argued for rationally, that everything—not just one's views of God—rests on faith. Yet there are many different meanings of the word *faith,* too, as used in different systems of thought in which it often plays a subordinate but important role. This concept is important because Augustine is asking for the kind of critical engagement with his arguments that, typically, the religious rhetoric with which you are familiar today has little in common.

Augustine criticizes the ancient Greek philosophers on grounds that to know the truth does not guarantee doing the truth. The problem is that the essence of humanity is not, as Aristotle had supposed, rationality but will. According to Augustine, no one can believe in the true God (whatever that is—we don't know yet what he means by this word) without first willing it. This is because no amount of rational argument can affect the will. Self-centeredness corrupts us away from truth and the "true reality" (the "true God") so that we fashion reality in our own image. Only when we are touched by "Divine Grace" can we will the true God—true reality—to be God—real for us. In other words, the true reality can be understood as real only when we understand what we take to be true reality—the world of appearances, for instance—to be false. Augustine's view, then, is that the sort of inner, transcendental revelation of truth, which he calls "faith," cannot be approached by reason. Rather, one must start with inner insights and reason from them to the truth (this will be exactly the procedure Descartes will later use). One cannot reason *to* faith, one must reason *from* faith. The cornerstone of his position is the famous dictum "I believe in order to understand." This view of religion replaced the previous theology (which put belief at the conclusion, not the beginning, of the journey) and dominated subsequent Christian thought for over nine centuries, until the advent of Aquinas's scholastic philosophy.

Reasoning from inner insight ("faith"), Augustine concludes that the mind cannot grasp reality on its own: without special conditioning into states of illumination, no one can know God. God must first illuminate the mind through inner revelation so that the truth can then be grasped. Knowledge of God is thus predestined by God, and there is nothing we can do to attain such knowledge. No amount of studying or learning will help, not even prayer makes any difference whatsoever. This is the actual view of one of the founders of Christian dogma, one of the religion's own "saints." Few, if any, professing Christians believe this today; Christianity today is in large part a religion that preaches that what you do can affect whether or not you attain knowledge of God. According to Augustine, however, such "illumination" either will or will not happen to you as preordained, in advance of anything you do, by God's own "grace." The idea, in other words, is that such illumination can be bequeathed only by God for no rational reason and it cannot be earned. Nor can the human intellect dispel the mystery of God's wisdom in choosing some human beings over others. We are, however, obliged, according to Augustine, to seek God even though we cannot know whether we will ever receive true knowledge or salvation. We must seek the truth, enlightenment, ultimate reality, and God, even though we cannot ever know whether this will lead us on a correct path because for us there is no "correct path."

Augustine's famous *Confessions,* written when he was forty-three, begins with a description of the tumultuous events of his life that led to his conversion. He was, before his conversion, anything but saintly. His mother, St. Monica, spent much of her life praying for the "sins" of her son; here is the advice Augustine says she gave him when he left for Carthage (Africa at the time had been described by one church commentator as "the cesspool of the world" and Carthage as "the cesspool of Africa"):

> She commanded me, and with much earnestness forewarned me, that I should not commit fornication, and especially that I should never defile any man's wife. These seemed to me no better than women's counsels, which it would be a shame for me to follow. . . . I ran headlong with such blindness that I was ashamed among my equals to be guilty of less impudency than they were, whom I heard brag mightily of their naughtiness; yea, and so much the more boasting by how much more they had been beastly; and I took pleasure to do it, not for the pleasure of the act only, but for the praise of it also.

When his mother tried to end his activities by getting him to agree to marry, she found for her 32-year-old wayward son a girl who so impressed him that he sent his current mistress back to Africa and promised to marry the girl in two years, when she would turn twelve. A few weeks of chastity was all he could muster, however, and soon took on a new lover, praying, "Give me chastity, but not yet!"

The *Confessions,* however, is much more than a colorful and very honest human diary. One of the most famous autobiographies of all time, it is directly addressed to God as an act of contrition. It contains a variety of deep philosophical questions of a variety that had never been asked before. For instance: "When I think of God, what is the object of my thought?" Suppose I am thinking about my death. You ask me, "What is the object of your thought?" This would be an analogous puzzle to what Augustine is here raising. We shall see Josiah Royce raise this question in exactly the same way, using similar examples (see Chapter 5). My death, like God, is not an object present before my mind the way a table or a chair is. It's not even so much a question of what I am thinking about as it is a question of what is present in my mind at the moment my thinking is going on. God is not present (at least not the way the chair is) any more than death (my own death) is present. What, then, is present? A concept? An idea? Whatever it is, it is present before the mind. Thus, the mind is engaging with a concept or an idea, each of which is present to consciousness (they are at that moment the "objects" of consciousness), of something beyond that which is immediately grasped by the mind (since neither God nor death is present to the mind at that moment). At the same time, however, there is operating within the mind a second sense of object, as an intention. You can ask, "What is the object of this thought (of God or of death)?" to mean "What is being intended by your mind when it is having such thoughts?" What might be intended is something completely different than anything of which I am consciously aware. Augustine, like many subsequent philosophers, goes to great lengths to point out this double function of the objects present to the mind. This second sense, "What is the object of your thought?" is like asking, "What is the function of this idea within the overall system of beliefs within which you operate?" In other words, Augustine here engages in what philosophers often call a second-order activity: thinking about thinking, wondering about wondering, knowing about knowing, and so on.

Similarly, Augustine asks what the actual object of his thinking, desiring, worshiping, or whatever, is when he contemplates God. This can most vividly be seen when he returns to a distinctly pre-Socratic perspective to ask "what everything is" and explicitly mentions Anaximenes: in addressing the objects he perceives to be the items of the world—the mountains, the sky, the air—he asks, "Are you God?" Imagine standing before a tree and asking, "Are you God?" The tree does not answer. Augustine understands the tree to be but a mental imagine within his own mind. So, really, what is he asking? He is using his own mind to inquire into what this, the object of his attention, is and asking his own mind to reveal to him, through thinking, whether what he is looking at is ultimate reality. It is a most profound philosophical activity in which he is engaged. And from within himself he gets his answer: "The whole air with its inhabitants answered, 'Anaximenes was deceived, I am not God.'" Augustine had the same access to the writings of Anaximenes that we do, which are but fragmentary, and Aristotle's commentaries. Anaximenes nowhere uses the term "God." Thus, in putting it this way, Augustine makes his intentions quite clear. Like most philosophers from Thales to Plato, he seeks to understand what ultimate, or absolute, reality is.

Augustine's God is the age-old quest for the ultimate ground, or source, of Being —the primary cause, or essence, of existence. And, like most philosophers, he is assuming that essence precedes existence. We shall see several more recent philosophers deny this, most notably in the nineteenth- and twentieth-century existentialist philosophers, such as Jean-Paul Sartre who claimed that "existence precedes essence."

Just as Plato argued that the objects of our perceptions are not real things in themselves but have only derivative existence (i.e., the "shadows"), Augustine argues that the things we see "are not God," meaning that they are not in and of themselves real. Without that which gives to the appearances their derivative reality—without God—the appearances (the objects we see, the world we mistakenly call real and which in reality is but illusion) could not exist at all, not even in someone's imagination. Augustine's argument consists mainly in a vivid demonstration that something other than the objects of our perception is responsible for structuring the appearances as they present themselves to us. It is an argument that we shall see again and again, most notably in the work of Bishop George Berkeley. This part of the argument, by itself (divorced from its explicitly religious implications), most philosophers before Augustine and after him would accept. Images don't control or cause images. Images are but the effects of something higher ("higher" here meaning merely that the latter causes the former but not vice versa). This, in Augustine's view, leads one to infer the existence of God: only God could be responsible for this being so. But the same form of argument can be used, and will be used, to claim that what is beyond (or behind, or the cause of) the appearances is a "transcendental" self, or nonconscious and superconscious mental structures or even just the physical brain.

Although he is not a relativist, Augustine goes on to reiterate the Protagorean point that each of us has access only to our own points of view on the world, not to the world as it exists in and of itself. What, then, accounts for the possibility of connecting our many different, often conflicting perspectives? Here, Augustine evokes the idea of God (i.e., the existence of some supreme, higher being of which this reality is only an image or imperfect representation). His main philosophical concern is, With what faculty of the mind can we know God? This question is not just about a religious concept per se, but about how it could be possible that the mind can reach out via either its percepts or its concepts, to gain access to what is beyond itself, beyond the mind. In this way Augustine enters upon what is probably the first introspective psychological analysis of the nature and function of awareness, consciousness, language, and memory, from both an analytic and phenomenological perspective, to see what it is about the mind's own structures that allow it by inner extension to "reach out" and thereby apprehend structures as they exist in themselves, outside the mind's reach. That this is even possible will be denied by many idealist philosophers, and so here we see that Augustine is squarely a realist, a position from which all subsequent Christian thought, even post-Thomistic (Aquinas), has never veered. Augustine's careful examination of the powers of the mind reveals to him how, when you ask yourself questions, answers come forth as if from out of nowhere. You direct your attention to ideas, events past and present, and your mind goes where its attention is directed by the words you use when you think. But where do the words themselves come from? The twentieth-century philosopher Ludwig Wittgenstein (Chapter 5) will remark, "Thinking is not something I do but something that happens to me." Augustine would agree. When we pay close attention to our own minds, we see ourselves not as the causal agents of our own mental activities but as their effects. In other words, as he concludes, "What is nearer to me than myself? And lo, the force of mine own memory is not understood by me: though I cannot so much as name myself without it." This careful consideration of the functioning of the conscious mind leads Augustine to give up the selfish life and to contemplate, instead, the acceptance of the supreme reality of what is beyond the ego, which he calls God.

Augustine's *Against the Manichaeans* contains his criticism of the Manichaean version of Zoroastrianism to which he had once belonged. He argues that we have no choice but to accept the existence of forces and powers beyond the grasp of the conscious mind and the intellect: God. But why, then, is the world so imperfect? Why is there evil, pain, and suffering? One way to respond would be to claim that God is evil, that the purpose of existence is negative. Some medieval theologians believed this to be the case and traveled through the land inflicting pain on others and each other, thinking that this is what God wants. Ingmar Bergman's film *The Seventh Seal* is a classic that poignantly explores this theme. Or one could claim that what we take to be evil, pain, and suffering are an elaborate type of illusion. Augustine does not take either of these ways out. He claims, instead, that evil and suffering are necessary tools by which God carries out God's plan.

In his *Enchiridion*, Augustine claims that while God is perfectly good not all the things God creates—such as human beings—are perfectly good. God created us knowing we would sometimes choose evil so that, through our evil acts, God's perfectly good will could be fulfilled in ways that we, in our finite wisdom, cannot understand. The subtle but deeply influential implication is that God needs human beings because we can do what God cannot; we are a necessary ingredient in the fabric of reality. We make it possible for God to carry out what otherwise God could not achieve. This aspect of Augustine's theology was largely an attempt to respond to critics who had claimed that the weakening of the Roman Empire was—as Marcus Aurelius had warned—directly brought about by Christianity. Many religious thinkers of Augustine's time claimed that belief in Christ had brought the vengeance of the "pagan" gods, whereas secular philosophers claimed that Christian belief in otherworldliness had ruined the minds of the citizens and weakened their hold on practical reality. Indeed, more than fifteen hundred years later, the same charge is echoed by Bertrand Russell in his *History of Western Philosophy*: speaking of Jerome, Ambrose, and Augustine, he writes, "It is no wonder that the Empire fell into ruin when all the best and most vigorous minds of the age were so completely remote from secular concerns." Russell does, however, acknowledge the powerful emotional appeal of Augustine: "On the other hand, if ruin was inevitable, the Christian outlook was admirably fitted to give men fortitude, and to enable them to preserve their religious hopes when earthly hopes seemed vain. The expression of this point of view . . . was the supreme merit of Saint Augustine."

In *The City of God,* Augustine depicts the entire spiritual history of humanity from the "fall of Adam and Eve" to the "Last Judgment" as a struggle between the " City of God" and the "City of Man." The latter is founded upon the principle of self-love, and its citizens are greedy materialists in pursuit of carnal pleasure; the former is founded upon the love of God and the contempt of self, and its citizens live as a "mystical and unanimous society of saints in Heaven and believers on Earth."

In *On the Trinity* (*De trinitate*), Augustine answers the question raised by Plotinus in Chapter 1 about why the soul is not fully aware of itself. The reason the mind is not readily known to itself, according to Augustine, is because in order to function properly in the world the mind must have images of things and take them to be not images but things; hence, through deceiving itself into taking its own representations as being not of its own self but of things in the world, the mind must operate under a false view of its own operations. To become illuminated to its own existence, the mind must detach itself, in the manner of the Buddhist, Stoic, and Skeptic, from both its own perceptions and the things to which it is attracted by desire, which means making itself aware of the seductive power of its own images. This process of enlightenment requires that the mind becomes aware of three separately functioning faculties within itself, each of which according to Augustine is a direct image of the Holy Trinity. These three divine faculties reflected in the human spirit are memory, understanding, and the will; they are, he claims, the direct image within us of the Holy Trinity.

In all of his works, Augustine displays his philosophical gifts in a context where they can and should be viewed outside the religious framework of most of the rest of his writings; *On the Trinity* is a vivid and extraordinary example. For instance, turning to the difficult question of how self-knowledge is possible and why it is so difficult to attain, he claims that most of the mind's own beliefs about itself are false. Arguing against the skeptics, according to whom we cannot know ourselves with certainty, he points out that even if one is a skeptic and doubts everything, the act of doubting itself requires thought and a thinker and therefore affirms the existence of the self. Augustine thus anticipates Descartes's famous argument of more than a thousand years later that the proposition "I think, therefore I am," can be known with absolute certainty. Indeed, these arguments were so influential to Descartes that studying them gives us a unique opportunity to understand firsthand the source of much subsequent thinking about the relationship between our minds and world and the nature of knowledge.

In seeking certainty through doubt, he moves deeply into the inward path cut by previous skeptical theories to arrive at the already established point that even the complete skeptic who denies the external reality of the content of perception (or leaves it as undecidable) *cannot bring into the category of doubt the internal existence of the sensation as such.* But then instead of taking the familiar relativistic or postivistic turn, Augustine presses forward into the jungle of self. In the inner darkness, he finds through introspection that along with the sensation there is not only the content, which has been established as doubtful, but also the *reality of the perceiving subject.* He finds that consciousness has a certainty in itself that follows first and foremost *from the very act of doubt.* He says, "In that I doubt, or since I doubt, I know that I, the doubter am: and thus, this doubt contains within itself the valuable truth of the *reality of the conscious being.* Even if I should be mistaken about all else, I cannot be mistaken in this; for in order to be mistaken I must exist."

Augustine does not stop there. He extends this fundamental, intrinsic certainty to *all states of consciousness (cogitare)* and then tries to show that all the various conscious states are already included in the act of doubt itself. I who doubt know not only that I live, but also that I remember, that I know, that I will. The foundation for my doubt rests upon ideas into which I may have been conditioned, but the *momentum*—the force, the will of my doubt—is driven by thought, knowledge, and judgment *not in the abstract but as developed by their particular content,* motivated solely by my desire for truth. Here Augustine offers one of the deepest and most original insights into the inner life of the human mind, by seeing that the various kinds of mental activity do not appear as separate spheres of consciousness (whether or not they are) but as aspects of one and the same conscious *act,* inseparably united. In this way, Augustine fills in the inner life of the soul well beyond the external contours sketched by Aristotle and the Neoplatonists: the soul mirrored in Augustine's self-vision is the whole of *personality,* a centered life that is a unity and which, through its self-consciousness, attains the certainty of its own existence.

Anselm: The New Scholasticism

Anselm (1033–1109), the archbishop of Canterbury in England, was not British but Italian; he was born to a noble family in Piedmont (Aosta), a town in the Italian Alps. His father had prepared him for a political career, but instead he joined a Benedictine monastery at Bec, Normandy, to study philosophy and theology. After graduating, he became the abbott. In 1093 he became the archbishop. Besides his three main theological works, *Monologion, Proslogion,* and *Cur Deus homo?* (Why God and Man?), Anselm wrote studies on semantics (*De grammatico*), truth (*De veritate*), and freedom (*Le libertate arbitrii*). In his final, unfinished work, called *On Power and Powerlessness, Possibility and Impossibility, Necessity and Liberty,* he tried to unravel the mystery of how a soul could come into existence. Upon learning that he would soon die, he wrote, "If it is His will I shall gladly obey, but if He should prefer me to stay with you just long enough to solve the question of the origin of the soul which I have been turning over in my mind, I would gratefully accept the chance, for I doubt whether anybody else will solve it when I am gone."[1]

Anselm's philosophy and theology, highly influenced by Greek rationality, laid the foundations for *scholasticism,* a method and system of thought based primarily on the works of Plato and Aristotle and embracing all the intellectual, artistic, philosophical, and theological activities carried on in various medieval schools as taught by its proponents. But unlike ancient Greek philosophy, which was essentially the work of individuals, scholasticism was an attempt to build philosophy as part of a "Christian society" whose purpose in turn was to transcend both individuals and nations. As the corporate product of social thought, scholastic reasoning depended on obedience to authority as espoused by the traditional forms of thought codified within the supposedly "revealed" Christian religion under the auspices of the church. As a result, philosophy was subjugated to theology and rigidly controlled by the authoritarian hierarchy of the church.

Anselm was one of the first to use a form of linguistic analysis to "solve" philosophical problems. In his *De veritate* (On truth), for instance, he shows that there are different senses of the concept of "truth," which are abused by various thinkers to achieve false ends. In *De libertate arbitrii* (On free will), he tries to identify the necessary and sufficient conditions for the concept of free will, a technique that would reappear in twentieth-century analytic philosophy. In *De casu diaboli* (On the devil's fall), he uses the idea of the fall from grace by a God-created Satan to argue that the existence of evil is compatible with the existence of an all-good God.

In his most famous work, *Proslogion,* Anselm relies on Aristotelian logic as developed by Boethius, along with a variety of Neoplatonist ideas, to create his famous ontological argument for the existence of God. Later thinkers divided over it vehemently. Philosophers such as Descartes, Spinoza, Leibniz, and Hegel, inclined toward a Platonic or Neoplatonic realism about universals in which the role of essences is emphasized over particulars, each accepted some form of the ontological argument as valid and profound. Others, most notably Aquinas, Hume, and Kant, under the influence of Aristotelian nominalism,[2] rejected the argument as mere verbal trickery.

In an attempt to equate the denial of God with a self-contradiction, Anselm quotes from Psalms 14:1, "The fool has said in his heart: There is no God." He tries to derive God's existence from the meaning of the word "God": the greatest conceivable being a greater than which cannot be conceived. Anselm then claims that since existence is greater than nonexistence, to say that "God does not exist" is tantamount to saying something like, "A being that cannot be conceived as anything other than existing does not exist," or "A being that exists necessarily does not exist," which is self-contradictory. Crucial to understanding Anselm's thinking is the distinction between an idea that exists in reality—in re—and an idea that exists only in conception—in intellectu. Anselm's argument is that if an idea is the greatest, then it must exist in re, not just in intellectu, since it is greater to exist in reality than merely in the conception. That is why any supreme or perfect idea, such as Being, exists in re, why reality itself has existence in actuality not just in concept (for instance, merely in intellectu in the mind of God). This line of argument, based on Plato's realistic metaphysics and buttressed by Augustine's Neoplatonic reinterpretation of Christian dogma, was inspired by a question that had puzzled many medieval Christian thinkers, namely, why God would have to create a world at all. If God is perfect, there would be no need for God to add to the realm of His own being.

Anselm's ontological argument was rebuffed by objections from another Benedictine monk, Gaunilon, from the Abbey of Marmoutier near Tours. Gaunilon claims, on behalf of "the fool," that Anselm's proof is bogus for two main reasons: first, we cannot properly form the concept of a necessarily existent being since there is nothing in experience on which to base such a concept; second, we can imagine a lot of perfect things defined as "perfect" but that in fact do not exist. For instance, why not argue for the existence of the perfect island or the perfect unicorn?

Averroes (Ibn Rushd): The Islamic Influence

After the fall of the Roman Empire, with Christianity in full swing, the philosophical schools of Athens were closed by Justinian in 529 C.E. The books were burned and Greek learning, denounced by papal authorities as pagan heresies punishable by death, virtually disappeared from Europe. Many philosophers escaped to Persia where Greek works, translated first into Syriac and then Arabic, had already begun to exert wide influence among Islamic and Jewish thinkers. Thus the Platonic and Aristotelian systems not only survived the five hundred years of the Dark Ages of Christendom in Europe, but continued to evolve on the other side of the Mediterranean.

Schools in Alexandria, Syria, and Persia became centers for the translation and study of Greek texts. After the Arab conquest of Spain, philosophy migrated back from across North Africa into Europe through Spain, where in Toledo and Cordova a group of brilliant Islamic philosophers rekindled the flame of the golden age of Greece within Christendom. Among them were Avicenna (Ibn Sina, 980–1037) and Averroes (1126–1198). Both are considered followers solely of Aristotle, due in part to a confusion of Platonic and Aristotelian ideas as espoused in an influential work of the time, the *Theology of Aristotle,* a Neoplatonic work that was really a compilation of Plotinus's *Enneads.*

Averroes (Mohammed Ibn Rushd) saw Avicenna's interpretations of Aristotle as colored on the one hand by religion and, on the other, by Stoic and Neoplatonic influences. He tried to purge these influences from his own interpretations of Aristotle, whom he regarded not only as the greatest of all philosophers but the "model of human perfection." He was born in Europe, in Cordova, Spain, the son of a *qadi* (judge). He studied theology, law, medicine, mathematics, and philosophy, which under Islamic protection centered on the masterworks of Plato and Aristotle as preserved by an evolving series of lengthy and often innovative commentators, ideas that by then had been banned for centuries and virtually forgotten in the adjoining Holy Roman Empire.

Averroes began his career as a judge, first in Seville and then Cordova. But his main interest was philosophy. According to legend, one night he and Prince Abu Ya'qub Yusuf were arguing over the origin of the world and the nature of mind. Supposedly, Averroes's ruminations on Aristotle's account of existence and the nature of the soul so impressed the prince that he commissioned Averroes to write an entire set of commentaries. Then, a few years later, the same prince appointed Averroes as his personal physician so that he would no longer have to be a judge. Averroes thus spent the rest of his life writing commentaries on virtually all of Aristotle's works.

Averroes wrote detailed and original reconstructive commentaries on Aristotle's *Metaphysics, Physics, Posterior Analytics, De caelo,* and *De anima,* as well as Plato's *Republic.* His main concern was not with subtle reinterpretations of ancient Greek wisdom according to then-current religious tenets (to which most previous Islamic commentators and most subsequent Christian commentators were prone), but rather to "reawaken philosophy's slumbering soul." Indeed, he argues that previous commentators such as Avicenna had completely misunderstood and corrupted Aristotle's ideas with theological concerns.

After the prince died, Averroes's enemies accused him of promoting the "pagan" philosophy of the ancients instead of following the accepted Muslim faith. Averroes spent the last years of his life in exile, first outside Cordova and then in Morocco. Ironically, just as five centuries earlier Justinian and the Christians had burned the philosophy books, so now the Caliph al-Mansur burned all available books on logic and metaphysics. He published an edict that anyone who believed that truth can be known by unaided reason, independently of divine revelation, would be sentenced by God to Hell.

After the Christian-Muslim wars pushed the Muslims out of Spain, the censorship of Averroes by the Islamic rulers marked the end of Muslim philosophy. Banished from the Mohammedan world, it was replaced by a rigid orthodoxy. And just as the Islam authorities once welcomed works banned by their Christian enemies, the conquering Christians were quick to seize works banned by the Muslims. Thus, in one of the greatest historical ironies, philosophy managed to pass hands from one opposing religion to another and then back again.

Averroes defended Aristotelian philosophy and "purified" it of its Stoic and Neoplatonic elements so well that scholastic writers called him "The Commentator." Thomas Aquinas, for instance, will use Averroes as a source while writing his own commentaries on Aristotle and the *Summa contra Gentiles.* During his lifetime, Averroes defended philosophy from various assaults by the Mohammedan orthodoxy. For instance, when al-Ghazali, a famous theologian of the time, published *Destruction of the Philosophers,* claiming that because all necessary truth is revealed in the Koran, philosophical speculation is completely unnecessary, Averroes responded by publishing *Destruction of the Destruction,* showing that religious dogmas are at best philosophical truths presented in allegorical form and amenable to an Aristotelian interpretation. Likewise, Averroes's *Ta-hafut al-Tahafut* (The incoherence of the incoherence) was a response to al-Ghazali's *The Incoherence of the Philosophers.* Al-Ghazali had criticized philosophers, especially Avicenna, for advocating views incompatible with religious faith. In his defense of the philosophers, Averroes attacks al-Ghazali's book without himself having to deny any of the doctrines of Islam.

Averroes does this by evoking a distinction that many later medieval philosophers would rely on to avoid direct conflict with the Christian counterparts of the orthodox Muslim authorities, the distinction between "revealed" theology and "natural" theology. The idea is that philosophy and theology each have a legitimate but distinct function based on a three-tiered class division of human beings, much like the Golden Lie espoused by Plato in the *Republic* about the three different classes of souls ("gold," "silver," and "bronze"). Like Plato's cave-dwellers, the lowest class of people—the vast majority—live by imagination, not reason. Unable to comprehend philosophy, they need the security of religious answers forced by obedience to an orthodox dogma into which they must be indoctrinated by eloquent or charismatic priests. The next, slightly higher, class—much smaller than the first—lives by the same sorts of beliefs as the lowest class but with more intelligence. They do not merely accept dogma because it is taught but try to establish intellectual justification for their beliefs. Theologians come from this class. However, since they too are ultimately prejudiced (they seek justification only for commonly accepted beliefs), they can never attain the truth, which requires complete impartiality from all orthodoxy. The third, highest level of intelligence, found in but a few extraordinary individuals who can discover directly for themselves the awesome truths that the rational theologians and the irrational believers can only go on seeking, allows one to see that religion does not and cannot ever provide a connection to truth. This highest level of intelligence is found only among the philosophers.

According to Averroes, philosophers know that to know the truth you must know it not by faith or by rationalization from premises accepted as true by faith, but directly on the basis of premises first tested by experience and justified by careful and logical reasoning. The most difficult of all truths, known by only a select few philosophers, is one that in a way contradicts all that has just been said about the three different levels of intelligence: namely, that the active part of the mind of each human being is not a distinct and separately existing individual but is the same, numerically identical unity. The greatest of all truths, hidden in the tradition passed down to us from Plato and Aristotle as revealed through Averroes's commentaries, is that each individual mind is numerically identical with all other individual minds, identical to the Agent Intellect, the mind of God.

God's existence and complete knowledge of God's attributes can, according to Averroes, be known directly by philosophers and demonstrated through reason. He argues against the individual immortality of the soul, at least of that aspect that Aristotle had called the passive intellect. Like Avicenna before him, Averroes claims that the individual human intellect, activated from without by the Agent Intellect (God), is itself the emanation of the Agent Intellect (God). But it has both an active and a passive part. The passive intellect, brought into existence through interaction with the Agent Intellect via the active intellect, does not survive the body. Only the active intellect, which is immortal, survives. It is this active intellect that is numerically identical (one and the same entity) within all sentient beings. Thus, in his *Commentary on "On the Soul,"* Averroes argues that the active intellect is not a personal faculty but is numerically identical to the Agent Intellect, the One that individuates itself into the Many by illuminating the passive intellects within each individual human being.

The distinction between the active and the passive intellect may be difficult to grasp, but it is rooted in the simple observation that the mind does not consciously need to do anything to represent objects to itself. You come to a tree and the mind represents a tree to itself, in the form of a visual perception. (Berkeley, in Chapter 3, will take this fact as evidence for the existence of God.) At the same time, the mind actively reflects on passive perceptions. These two faculties of the mind are referred to by Aristotelian metaphysicians as the "passive" and "active" intellects. The main function of the active intellect is to abstract the forms from things. The passive, or potential, intellect is a mental repository whose main function is to receive the forms as concepts or ideas represented in conscious perception. These active and passive intellects come together in individual human beings: the active intellect produces through its contact with the passive intellect a combined intellect that Averroes called the *material* intellect. The material intellect, however, is not a substance but an activity; it is the activity of the active intellect within each individual human. It is both one and many. That is why the same things aren't known by all minds even though they are the same mind in action. The passive intellect differentiates us and is not immortal, whereas the active intellect—nous—is not only immortal but everywhere identical: nous is numerically one and the same being manifested in all of us.

Averroes's monopsychism cut deeply against both Christian dogma and the Mohammedan theology within which Averroes presented it. His response to his own rulers was to claim that while reason compelled him to assert the unity of the intellect among all human beings, the belief in separate individual human intelligences could be accepted by faith. But he persisted in arguing that the ultimate culmination of reason led to what he took to be Aristotle's secret teaching as passed down through his cryptic remarks in *On the Soul*: the intellectual unity of all mankind.

Islamic theologians tried to reinterpret their understanding of Greek philosophy away from Averroes's monopsychism. Lacking any good argument, they simply banned it as a Muslim heresy. This brought it to the attention of Christians. Secular thinkers in northern Europe took interest, until a philosophical movement arose in the thirteenth century known as the "Averroists" or "integral Aristotelians." Their main proponents consisted of members of the faculty in Paris. These philosophers argued, following Averroes, that the ultimate conclusion of reason and the correct understanding of Plato and Aristotle lead to the same inexorable truth: the numerical unity of the active intelligences of all conscious beings. Christian theologians of the time, notably St. Albert and St. Thomas, saw in this idea the end not just of Islam but of Christianity as well and so, like their Islam counterparts, united as a front against Averroism until monopsychism was proclaimed a Christian heresy as well and condemned by the church in Paris in 1270—the same year as the publication of Thomas's *On the Unity of the Intellect Against the Averroists*—and formally added to the list of "forbidden propositions." Thus, Averroes's monopsychism had the added distinction of being declared heresy in two opposing religions. Although the Averroists continued to teach in secret what they took to be the only correct understanding of the ancient Greek wisdom—the unity of the active intellect within all minds—the idea became successfully repressed from Western philosophy until the present day. Indeed, as one twentieth-century philosopher put it, "We are all the same person."[3]

Maimonides (Moses ben Maimon): The Jewish Influence

Like Averroes, Moses Maimonides (1135–1204) was born in Cordova, Spain, while Averroes was still a boy. Unfortunately, the two never met. Maimonides came from a prominent Jewish family. In 1148 the Almohads conquered Cordova and life became very difficult for the Jews. His family escaped first to Morocco, then Palestine, and finally settled in Fostat (old Cairo), Egypt.

Maimonides became both a physician and a rabbi. He was such a good doctor that he was appointed royal physician to the king of Egypt. And as rabbi he became *nagid,* or head of the Egyptian Jewish community in Fostat. While still a young man, he began to publish widely read books, such as *Sharh al-Mishnah* (Commentary on the mishnah), also known as *Siraj* (Luminary), in 1168; *Mishnah Torah* (Code of Jewish law), in 1178; and *Treatise on Resurrection,* in 1191. Maimonides' most famous work, however, is now generally regarded as one of the greatest philosophical works of the Middle Ages: *Dalalat al-Ha'rin* (Guide for the perplexed, 1190). In it he tries to bring Judaism in line with Neoplatonic Aristotelianism as taught by al-Farabi (Abu Nasr, 870–950) and Avicenna. Written in Arabic for philosophers and theologians, not the general public, it is often deliberately obscure.

Maimonides argues that metaphysics is the supreme level of human activity, attainable only by those with a sufficiently high intellect. Unlike Averroes, however, who implied that the different classes of intellectual ability among people were predetermined, Maimonides offers a pedagogy by which individuals can evolve through the different stages of intellectual ability up to the highest level. This requires careful guidance through education. The work had tremendous influence over both Jewish and Christian scholasticism, especially Albertus Magnus and Thomas Aquinas, as well as, over subsequent centuries, Spinoza, Mendelssohn, and Leibniz. Maimonides' development of John Scotus Erigena's (810–877) *via negativa* method ("the negative way") was also deeply influential. The idea is to provide a method of finding out what something is even if it cannot directly be experienced. You can't do it by stating the thing's attributes, since the thing cannot be experienced. So instead of getting at the essence in positive terms, you try to find out what is left over after all positive statements about the essence of the unexperiencable thing are exhausted. The *via negativa* method can be used, according to Maimonides, to transcend the limitations of the human mind and attain knowledge of things beyond the direct reach of the senses or the intellect, such as God. The idea is that by stating all the things that God is not, we are in a position to intuit what God actually is.

The first part of his *Guide for the Perplexed* deals with problems of biblical anthropomorphisms and application of the *via negativa* method to discovering the divine attributes of God, along with criticisms of the Muslim Scholastic theology according to the method of *kalam,* in which philosophical proof is used to justify religious propositions already accepted to be true. The second part offers proofs of God's existence, an Aristotelian analysis of the relationship between matter and form, and an explanation of the role of prophecy. The third part contains studies of the problems of free will and determinism, evil, the nature of rationality, and an original defense of how to reconcile reason with divine revelation. If on some point the Old Testament is perfectly clear and no obvious philosophical arguments can be adduced to the contrary, we ought to accept the word of the Bible. If, on the other hand, the point seems dubious and a contrary philosophical argument easily presents itself, the biblical statement ought to be reinterpreted according to the dictates of rationality so as to be understood only in allegorical terms. This was an extremely revolutionary idea, and it paved the way for subsequent Jewish philosophers who wanted to emphasize reason over revealed scripture. It has had a lasting influence on the rational process central to rabbinical theology.

But the *Guide for the Perplexed* warns that students should not begin with the study of metaphysics. There are certain things the undisciplined mind cannot accurately represent to itself, neither as a perception nor as a concept. Trying to do so without the proper training is like trying to lift too heavy a weight or running too far before one is in the proper physical condition. The highest form of knowledge consists in the truths of metaphysics, but these cannot be comprehended by unaided perception or unaided reason without causing psychological and intellectual harm.

Although according to Maimonides the methods of religion and of science are insufficient for representing metaphysical truths, he reconciles their function in human society as preparation for metaphysics as practiced by philosophy, the only way by which human beings can attain a true understanding of God and the world. In this way, Maimonides offers to reconcile not just religion and philosophy but also science and metaphysics. These are but different ways of inquiry suited to the different aspects of the human mind and must function together in the proper order until the mind is ready to attain full intellectual illumination through true wisdom, which Maimonides defines as "consciousness of self." This event must take place through a gradual evolution, from the particular to the abstract; one must rely on faith where reason fails but always be prepared to give the upper hand to reason. In this way we can transcend the natural limitations of our own minds and attain complete knowledge of ourselves, the world, and God. As Maimonides puts it, "When you understand Physics, you have entered the hall; and when, after completing the study of Natural Philosophy, you master Metaphysics, you have entered the innermost court, and are with the king in the same palace."

Maimonides dismisses most commonly accepted notions of faith. True faith according to him is neither the acceptance of orthodox beliefs nor psychological affirmation of some theological dogma. Rather, true faith involves the leap of faith that truths represented in experience and supported by reason correspond to things as they actually are in the world. Whether or not this is so is something that cannot ever be known. He thus criticizes both Christian notions of faith and the Christian concept of God. God according to Maimonides is absolute unity, a pure One without any form, indivisible and everywhere identical. He dismisses the doctrines of the trinity and the corporeal embodiment of God in Christ as utter absurdities that lead the intellect into depravity and corruption. (Compare this notion with Kierkegaard's leap of faith, in Chapter 4.)

According to Maimonides, there can be no relationship between any aspect of the world, including the human intellect, and the absolute unity of God. People who think they have a relationship with God are deluded. There can be no such relationship between the relative world of potentiality and the absolute actuality. Even to say that "God exists" or that "God is One" must, according to Maimonides, be tempered with the knowledge that God exists without having the attribute of existence and that God is One without having the attribute of unity.

The idea is that God has no positive attributes. Yet God is not nothing. And in some mysterious way the universe does not exist independently of God but ultimately is a reflection of God. The universe, like God, is one individual being, everywhere identical to itself even though its parts are differentiated. Maimonides likens the unity of the universe to the unity of the body, in which through a joint activity the parts constitute one integrated whole whose characteristics cannot be found in any of its individual elements. *Guide for the Perplexed* concludes with an explanation of what he calls the "mysteries of the Law," suggesting that the true secrets of the universe must be kept secret, never revealed in writing, and passed on, if at all, "viva voce"—by word of mouth—only to those worthy disciples who have demonstrated that they have attained an appropriate level of intellectual maturity. The rest of humanity must be kept away from the mysteries, not guided to them. Philosophy is not for everybody.

Aquinas: The New Christian

Thomas Aquinas (1225–1274) was born in Italy near Aquino, between Rome and Naples. He was first educated at the Benedictine abbey at Monte Cassino and then went to the University of Naples. When in 1244 he joined the Dominican order of mendicant (begging) friars, his father, the Count of Aquino, was outraged. The Dominicans espoused complete poverty and traveled the country spreading the gospel as living examples of Jesus' teaching. His father had expected him to join the more respectable Benedictines, a powerful order founded by great corporate wealth. As a result, he locked young Aquinas in the family castle. Legend has it that his father offered him all sorts of bribes, including a beautiful prostitute, to join the Benedictines. To his father's great dismay, Aquinas supposedly refused even the prostitute and escaped to Paris. He went on to study both philosophy and theology in Cologne under Albertus Magnus

(1200–1280), a Dominican philosopher and theologian known as "Doctor Universalis" and "Albert the Great" because of his immense knowledge. From Magnus, Aquinas learned Greek and Islamic philosophy, and the natural sciences.

At the time, the Paris Dominicans were under suspicion by the church and the conservative university authorities because of their "heretical sympathy" with Averroist doctrine about the unity of the active intellect in all human beings. Recall that according to Averroes, it is not the human personality as exemplified by the individual soul that is immortal but only the active intellect, which is numerically identical in all sentient beings. It was Aquinas who helped defend the Dominicans with his Averroist arguments that there are two different sorts of truths—one based on reason and the other based on revelation—and that only through revelation could one know the "real" truth. Since Christian dogma is foundationally embedded in views antithetical to Averroes's monopsychism, its truths must therefore supercede the cosmic unity of all mankind as espoused by the internal Aristotelian philosophers of the Averroist school.

Conservative Christian theologians feared that Plato and Aristotle, whose works had conveniently disappeared from Catholic Europe, would now return to the philosophical scene, especially since the Islamic philosophers might have put their own spins and interpretations on the Greek works through the commentaries. The church therefore viewed the Greek works as a pagan and infidel threat to Christian dogma. Aquinas boldly took the opposite approach. He saw Aristotle not just as the greatest of all philosophers—he also called him "The Philosopher"—but as an opportunity to put Christian doctrine on a solid intellectual foundation.

Aquinas argued that Aristotle's metaphysics, cosmology, and epistemology could provide the solid theoretical framework for Christianity, provided that an account could be given of how the soul can preserve the individual human ego, personality intact, after death. In all of his early work, Aquinas tried to put the conservative theologians' fears to rest by showing various ways that Aristotelian philosophy could be made consistent with Christian belief. Often he ended up simply rejecting whatever parts of Aristotle's philosophy did not fit Christian dogma. Whenever he saw insoluble contradictions between the two views, he tried to prove that reason could force neither conclusion. The implication was that one needed faith to decide—a position that would be used again and again by conflicting systems, including that of Copernicus (see Chapter 2). For instance, on the question of whether God created the universe, as it was written in the Bible, or whether the universe is eternal and uncreated, as Aristotle had argued, Aquinas said that there was no way to tell: neither the creation of the universe nor the eternity of the universe could be confirmed or denied by reason. His conclusion is that we need *revelation* to know the truth. In the same way, instead of simply declaring Averroist monopsychism to be a false heresy or banning the heretical proposition, he argued that whether the individual human soul is mortal or immortal cannot be settled by reason. Such truths can be known only through revelation, and studying the "forbidden" philosophies is a way of strengthening the dogmatic theology.

Likewise, Aquinas enabled the study of Aristotle's argument against the immortality of the soul; such study can, according to Aquinas, only help make the point that without divine revelation there can be no knowledge. This brilliant and perhaps philosophically covert line of thought so pleased church leaders that they made the arguments of the philosophers against the very things that they held sacred part of the church's "proof" of the need for nonphilosophical ways of knowing truth! It is philosophy itself that establishes the necessity of revelation. Thus, whether advertently or inadvertently, Aquinas managed to appease the conservative critics of philosophy and revive Greek philosophy within the Christian domain.

Ironically, most of Aquinas's work, like that of his antithesis Averroes, consisted of commentaries on Aristotle. The most famous works are the *Analytics, De anima, De caelo, Ethics, De interpretatione, Metaphysics, Physics,* and *Politics.* When one compares Aquinas's and Averroes's interpretations of the same works, it becomes clear to what extent these early "spin doctors" could control the meanings of the great masterworks of philosophy. It isn't just that they wanted to suit their own metaphysical agenda; the fact is that even the most carefully written text (as would be discovered in the twentieth century), like the world itself, is always amenable to a multiplicity of interpretations.

Among Aquinas's best original writings are *De ente et essentia,* which explores the nature of being and essence and shows some independence of thought; *De principiis naturae* (On the principles of nature); and *De unitate intellectus* (On the unity of the intellect), where he argues against the Averroist interpretation of Aristotle according to which all human beings share the same, numerically identical, intellect. Aquinas's two most important theological works are the encyclopedic *Summa contra Gentiles* and *Summa Theologica.* The former, written between 1259 and 1264, attempts to speak to readers who are not already believing Christians and uses arguments without assuming, in advance, that Christianity is true. In it, he offers his five proofs for the existence of God, which many theologians and philosophers found convincing until Hume's devastating destruction of them (for a discussion, see Chapter 3). It was written between 1265 and 1274.

After being appointed a regent master (full professor) at the University of Paris, in subsequent years Aquinas served under the popes at Orvieto, Rome, and Vitergo in Italy. He continued teaching in Paris and Naples until his death.

Duns Scotus: The Logical Analyst

John Duns Scotus (1266–1308) was born in the village of Duns, Berwickshire. At the age of fourteen he entered a Franciscan seminary in Scotland at Haddington, Dumfries. After being ordained in 1291, he continued his studies in theology and philosophy at Oxford and Paris. Through his mentor at Paris, Peter of Spain, he was influenced by Islamic philosophy, especially the works of Avicenna and Averroes. He received his doctorate from Paris in 1305 and became professor at Cologne where he remained until his premature death.

Nicknamed the "Subtle Doctor," Scotus originated many subtle but important distinctions that have continued to influence philosophers as diverse as Leibniz, Heidegger, and Peirce. Yet he also concocted an idea that has since become one of the central tenets of Roman Catholic dogma and is believed by hundreds of millions of people: the Immaculate Conception. After much subsequent debate among Christian theologians, the councils of Basel (1439) and Trent (1546) finally sided with what came to be called the "Scotist opinion," and some years later Pius IX issued the bull *Ineffabilis Deus* declaring Scotus's notion of the Immaculate Conception to be a divine revelation that must under threat of Hell be believed without question.

Although Scotus's contributions to philosophy are somewhat less dramatic than those to religion, he is generally regarded as the most important of the British medieval thinkers. His voluminous writings, organized from lectures, drafts, and marginal notes passed down by his highly devoted students and numerous followers, make for extremely difficult reading because of Scotus's reliance on obscure Latin terms and technical words of his own invention. Reading even a brief selection from his *Ordinatio* (also called the *Oxford Commentary on the Sentences of Peter Lombard*) requires that you understand several terms in his vastly influential philosophy. Of primary importance is his complicated-sounding notion of the univocality of the world (as opposed to its equivocality—its multiplicity of interpretation and meaning): the world according to Scotus is not merely One (as Parmenides and so many others have already claimed); it has a single unmistakable, unambiguous single meaning discoverable by the human intellect through our own experience and reason.

Scotus sides with Aquinas against both Averroes and Maimonides that the world can be fully understood by the human mind—no special mystical or divine illumination is needed. What is needed is not mysticism but a new and more precise language. In Scotus's view, the philosopher is free, like the mathematician, to invent new distinctions and terms to capture subtle differences and thereby increase the resolution power of the mind until it can correctly apprehend being. According to Scotus, knowledge is not based on innate ideas (through which the forms might be directly intuited) but must begin from individual experience. He thus turns away from Platonic dualism (as captured for instance by the allegory of the cave, where the real world exists independently of the mind's representational images and ideas that are, at best, copies of reality).

According to Scotus, the primary object of the intellect—that is, what the mind directly apprehends when it is conscious of something of which it has knowledge (i.e., the "shadows on the walls of the cave")—is not a mere representation of some universal form, as Plato and Aristotle had each in his own way thought, nor is it the divine essence, as Augustine had claimed (and Berkeley will in his own way reclaim), nor material objects, as Aquinas had suggested. Scotus instead takes a brilliant and innovative stance on the doctrine of *hylomorphism*, the view that existent things are a combination of Aristotelian forms and primordial matter. He explains the existence of various individual things known by us—the objects in our immediate presence—in terms of a formal principle, which he calls *haecceity* (literally, "thisness"), of the same logical type as a universal. (See the discussion on universals versus particulars in Chapter 1.) In many ways this idea anticipates the sort of metaphysical move that would eventually find its culmination in Kant's synthesis of empirical and rational thought wherein empirical objects exist through a combination of the activity of mind (i.e., as representations in the phenomenal world) and the activity of things in themselves (Kant's *ding-an-sich*, the noumenal world). Thus, while rejecting universal hylomorphism, Scotus argues that material things exist as a conjunction of matter and form but that these are different principles. Each individual object—including the primary objects to which the intellect has access (perceptions, thoughts, ideas, etc.)—is *esse*, being as such. Everything that exists has esse—it can be predicated "univocally" of all things—and without it nothing is comprehensible. In other words, whereas for Aquinas "to be" means "to have being," for Scotus being as such is in reality always and everywhere.

Aquinas had argued that individual things cannot be known directly by the mind because the primary object of human knowledge is a form abstracted from matter and revealed through the universal concept. The universal or common term (for instance, "man")—because it is essentially conjoined to a "this"—makes the singular term intrinsically intelligible. So for Aquinas the mind apprehends individual things only indirectly, via representations such as visual perception so as to preclude intellectual intuition (i.e., perception) of the thing in itself. According to Scotus, however, the mind has a primary intellectual intuition of the individual thing in itself. His argument is that it would be impossible to abstract the universal idea from the individual thing unless we possessed a previous intellectual intuition of the individual thing; the abstraction is from the individual, not the universal. Thus being, which can be predicated univocally of everything, provides universal meaning to all things even though it is really separate. This is accomplished in Scotus's system with a subtle distinction among distinctions: a real distinction, between things, versus a merely logical distinction—that is, between aspects of the same thing made by the intellect.

To illustrate, consider that Socrates is human and that Plato is human. As distinct individuals they are different humans and yet there must be some amorphous aspect of their being—"humanness"—that allows distinct individuations: "Socraticity" and "Platoness," the "thisness" (haecceity) of each of them as a numerically distinct individual. Scotus painstakingly argues that it is possible to distinguish the individual concepts such as "Socraticity" and "Platoness" from general concepts such as "humanness." On what, then, is the distinction based? In no way is "Socraticity"—Socrates' individual essence, or nature—separable in actuality from his existence as a human being—his "humanness." Remove the human being from existence and you remove the individual Socrates. Destroy the individual Socrates and you destroy the human being. According to Scotus, not even God could separate the two. Yet the distinction is not merely verbal or a mental conundrum. It is what Scotus called a "formal objective distinction."

Crucial for understanding Scotus's subtle metaphysics is his notion of being, which involves not a genus but the concept of opposition to non-being, or nothingness. There are various types of oppositions to nothingness, from God to human to inanimate objects. This appreciation is partly manifested in the will, both divine and human; neither God nor individual human beings are bound by necessity to act according to the dictates of either deterministic providence or logically guided reason, as the Arabic Neoplatonic and Aristotelian intellectualist philosophers held, but they exist as autonomous individual agents in the universe. The world is apprehended through the primacy of being itself, for being is known directly, as such, by all conscious beings who are aware of anything. Being itself is something apprehended immediately and directly along with whatever else is known by whatever means it is known. Its method and domain is metaphysics.

Ockham: The Razor's Edge

Born in the village of Ockham in Surrey, near London, England, William of Ockham (1280–1349) studied first the arts and then theology at Oxford University. While working on his doctorate, he lectured on the Bible and the *Books of Sentences* by Peter Lombard (1100–1160), the official textbook of theology at nearly all universities well into the sixteenth century. Hundreds of philosophers and theologians wrote commentaries on the *Sentences* and so did Ockham. But although his commentaries contained fairly standard sorts of disputations (formal questions with replies and rebuttals) according to the style of the time, the chancellor of Oxford—an ardent follower of Aquinas—brought Ockham before the Holy See at Avignon on charges of heresy. Instead of retracting his opinion, Ockham took the opportunity to present explicit criticisms of current orthodoxy (such as whether Jesus and his followers possessed property, one of the major issues of the day) and to raise questions about the nature of the relation of the papacy to secular authority. Reprimanded for his publicist views but not officially condemned, Ockham went on to write half a dozen politically charged works, such as *Dialogus de potestate papae et imperatoris* (Dialogue on the power of the emperor and the pope, 1339–42) in which he argued against the temporal supremacy of the pope in favor of the idea of a secular state, laying the foundations for modern theories of government. Ockham continued his criticism of Pope John XXII in favor of the Franciscan General Michael of Cesena, with whom in 1328 he joined a branch of the Franciscans called the Spirituals and fled from Avignon to Pisa. But the Franciscans also found Ockham too independent of mind, expelling him from their order, and he took refuge in Munich with Ludwig of Bavaria.

As a philosopher Ockham is best known as the originator of *Ockham's razor,* a principle of ontological economy: "multiplicity ought not to be posited without necessity." That is, according to Ockham, as few entities as possible should be regarded as real and the rest should be dismissed as mere *ficta* (fictions), terms that have only intensional meaning without reference (i.e., without extension). This principle led Ockham to abandon the view of universals as mind-independently real entities. Taking as his starting point the views of Duns Scotus, whom he regarded as a realist about universals, Ockham offered an alternative view that has come to be known as *nominalism* (see Note 2), which his fellow nominalists (sometimes called "terminists") came to call the *via moderna* ("the modern way") versus the *via antiqua* ("the ancient way"). Ockham paved the way for terminist logic by taking an analytical, critical, and empiricist approach to the analysis of the functions of individual terms within propositions. Central to this effort was his pivotal distinction, which has remained influential to this day, between a term's meaning and that which it stands for, which he called *supposition* ("standing for"). (This concept will come up again, famously, in Frege—see Chapter 5.)

In the first book of the *Prior Analytics,* Aristotle defines terms by stating, "I call a term that into which a proposition is resolved (viz. the predicate, or that of which something is predicated) when it is affirmed or denied that something is or is not something." But what is the nature of the existence of such terms, especially when they seem to involve universal rather than particular entities? Ockham says that a term can stand for something in three different ways. In "This man Socrates is a philosopher," the term "this man" stands for a specific individual; in "Socrates is a mortal man," the term "man" stands for a class; and in "man is a noun," the term stands for the word. If I write the word down, it exists on paper; if I say it, it exists as an audible sound; but the third and most important aspect of the word is the concept. Concepts are to the written and spoken words that express them as numbers are to numerals; they are not the symbols themselves. Rather, according to Ockham, the symbol expresses a concept that is itself the mental content or impression possessing signification. In no case— such as "man is mortal"—does the term—"man"—stand for some mind-independent universal entity that all the individual instances have in common, as Plato and the Neoplatonists claimed. Only the meanings of terms themselves— names as such—have the property of being universal, not that to which they refer (not to any actual things themselves). All things exist only as individuals. Names that seem to stand for universals in reality are but signs for classes of individuals. Thus in his *Logic* he identifies conceptual terms and propositions as "mental words" that do not belong to any language. They exist only in the mind and cannot be uttered; they are but signs subordinated to mental concepts or contents.

Ockham does not mean by this distinction that spoken words are signs of mental concepts but merely that they signify the same things signified by mental concepts. A concept signifies something "primarily and naturally," whereas the word signifies it "secondarily," a distinction that would later be used by Locke in his explanation of the relationship between mind and world. Ockham claims that this is what Aristotle really meant when he said, "Words are signs of the impressions in the soul." Thus for Ockham and all subsequent nominalists influenced by him, to say that words signify, or are signs of, impressions in the mind simply means that they are signs that signify secondarily what the impressions of the mind import primarily. Whereas the designation of a spoken or written term can be changed at will, the designation of the conceptual term cannot be changed at will. In thus continuing the medieval tradition of advancing Aristotelian logic into a science of language capable of revealing what the mind is thinking about and how it is representing the world to itself, ever since Ockham one of the central tasks of philosophy has involved precise formulation of what words signify along with the mode of their signification.

Ockham thus lays the foundation for his empiricism, arguing that all knowledge must ultimately come from the senses and cannot be had without them. Whereas for Plato things outside the mind must correspond exactly to things inside the mind in order for there to be knowledge, and for Aristotle universals in the mind are based on the thing existing in reality independently of the mind but do not correspond exactly, for Ockham only individual, particular things exist such that each has its own nature. This means that there can be no identity among things, only similarity.

This view is in marked contrast to Duns Scotus's position that a common nature exists in things that is distinct from the individual things yet somehow contained in them. Thus, according to Scotus, the problem of individuation has no meaning, since each thing is singular in itself; ultimately, for Ockham, the distinction between essence and existence is itself fictitious: "Existence and Essence signify one and the same thing."

Ockham uses his concept of intellectual intuition to make explicitly clear that the perceptions you are now having are not of things in themselves but exist only in the mind; he calls it the "intuitive vision" much in the way that Kant will later talk of "intuitions." Following Augustine, Ockham further paves the way for the Cartesian method of finding certainty by finding certain propositions that cannot be doubted, such as one's own existence, based on having mental events regardless of whether they are actual or not; the mere fact that one is thinking is evidence for one's existence as something. He also provides the first clear statement of a theory of the mind in terms of intention, distinguishing two sorts: the first intention—"the sign of something not itself a sign," a "mental name meant to stand for its signified object"—and the second intention, "something in the soul which is applicable to things and is predicable of the names of things when they do not stand in personal supposition but in a simple one." Universals are thus to be understood as second intentions. They have only "logical being." That is, they exist in the logical realm, which for Ockham subsists in the soul but not as psychological entities such as sensations, images, or figments of the imagination. They exist in the logical realm just as external objects exist in the ontological realm and are thus real without existing independently of the mind.

Nicholas of Cusa and the Renaissance

We are approaching a time in European history that has since come to fall under the term "Renaissance." Although there was a fairly sudden intellectual and artistic growth that took place in Italy and Europe during the fifteenth and sixteenth centuries, the term "Renaissance" was first coined in 1860 (by J. C. Burckhardt[4]). Philosophically, these two centuries signified a period of transition from the medieval, theologically centered world view to the modern, scientific view. The emphasis on literature, art, science, and philosophy shifted from the relationship between God and the world to the nature of the relationship between the human mind and the rest of nature. Buttressed by the remarkable developments in logic and reason of the Middle Ages, each of the three philosophers of the period whom we shall study rejects in his own way medieval standards and methods of inquiry in favor of a return to ancient, pre-Christian thought enlivened by the advent of a new style and literary form.

One of the best early examples was Nicholas Krebs (1401–1464), better known as Nicholas of Cusa, a name he took in honor of his birthplace, the small German village of Cusa on the Moselle River. Nicholas showed such high promise as a boy that at the age of twelve he received a scholarship to study with the Brothers of the Common Life at Deventer in the Lowlands, a mystical group devoted to experiencing unity with God as inspired by a widely influential book of the time, the *Imitation of Christ,* authored by one of their fellows. Over the next twelve years he went on to study the arts, philosophy, law, mathematics, the sciences, and theology at the Universities of Heidelberg, Rome, Cologne, and Padua, from which he received a doctorate in law. In 1433, at age twenty-nine, he became an ordained priest and pursued a series of ecclesiastical appointments culminating in his becoming cardinal in 1448 and bishop of Brixen in 1450.

One of the leading church conciliators of the fifteenth century, Cusa used his knowledge of theology, law, and philosophy to negotiate among widely differing religious and political factions whose main bone of contention was whether the Church, Council, or Pope held the highest authority. Called a "mystic on horseback" because of the extensive travels he undertook in the cause of political and religious unity, he rode into Byzantium to help end the centuries-old rift between Latin and Greek churches. His earliest written work, *De concordantia Catholica* (On Catholic concordance, 1433), dedicated to his colleagues at the Council of Basel, argues for a global harmony of the church conceived as the supreme form of human society.

Amid all of his political and theological activities, Cusa worked continuously on behalf of the advancement of philosophy, where his achievements are so impressive that he is generally regarded as a key transitional figure between the Middle Ages and the Renaissance. As in his political and religious work, he created a philosophical synthesis of widely differing views. In his major philosophical work, *De docta ignorantia* (Of learned ignorance, 1440), the key element in his thinking is the concept of the identity of opposites (*coincidentia oppositorum*), according to which the distinctions and oppositions among finite beings resolve into unity at the absolute level. For instance, draw a series of bigger and bigger circles, all touching a line at the same point:

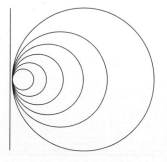

Notice that as the circles get bigger and bigger, the more the curve "flattens out" and approaches the straightness of the line. If you drew an infinitely large circle and placed it against the line, there would no longer be any difference between the "curved" line of the circle and the straight line. In this precise way, Cusa argues that in the infinite all the opposites become one: "an infinite line . . . would be at once a straight line, a triangle, a circle, a sphere; similarly, if there were an infinite sphere, it would at once be a circle, a triangle and a line; and it would be likewise with the infinite triangle and infinite circle." And thus his thesis that "everything is everything."

In other words, whereas essence and existence are distinct among finite objects, in God they are identical. This idea owes much to the previous doctrines of Thomas Aquinas and would later influence the nineteenth-century German philosopher Schelling's "philosophy of identity," in which Schelling views individual differences as vanishing points of the Absolute. Indeed, in many ways one can see in Cusa the early stages of the philosophy that would find its full force in nineteenth-century German Idealism.

A blend of Neoplatonic philosophy and thirteenth-century mysticism, this aspect of Cusa's thought grew out of an opposition to Scholastic Aristotelianism. In creating a synthesis of, on the one hand, mathematical and experimental knowledge and, on the other, mysticism and knowledge, he continuously makes use of analogies from mathematics, claiming much in the way that Kant would later do that the categories of reason, with their opposites and contradictions, can only give us a limited and inadequate representation of reality, which is beyond our direct access and understanding. He thus relies on a version of the medieval "negative way," in combination with what he calls "learned ignorance," a concept so important to his overall vision that he names his book after it. This should not be confused with the idea of "learned incompetence" or some such anti-authoritarian stance toward intellectual orthodoxy. Rather, what Cusa means by learned ignorance is very similar to, and is basically an elaboration of, what Socrates meant when he defined wisdom as knowing how little you know. In other words, Cusa means, in effect, something like "wise ignorance." That is, only through struggling in our efforts to understand the world do we realize precisely how and why the absolute truth about God, the world, and even our own natures transcends our understanding. All of these things— even the mind—are infinities; the items of our understanding are finitudes. Never can the infinite things in themselves properly be understood by the finite terms in which we are forced by our language and our thought to represent them.

The problem is that reason (*ratio*) is by its nature discursive (Latin: *discurrere,* "to run about"). This means that because our thinking is discursive any conclusions drawn upon it are attained through a series of inferences, not by direct insight. Although the intellect (*intellectus*) transcends this limitation insofar as it is capable of intuitive cognitions (apprehended all at once), such as insights, our language cannot adequately express these intuitions because it relies necessarily on categories, oppositions, and contradictions that exist only at the finite, relative level of immediate appearances. Thus the unity of opposites in ultimate reality can never be directly attained by us; however, when the mind sees that it cannot attain realization, it is then already enlightened, at which point it can mystically transcend its limitations. In other words, during the brief instant that the mind can see (not just believe in) its own limits, it transcends its own limits, it moves beyond itself toward the infinite. That is the learned ignorance, which, according to Cusa, is the main goal of philosophy.

In studying the world, however, we also are studying God. This is an idea that would reverberate throughout the Renaissance, from scientists like Galileo, who sought to study the world directly rather than through official scriptures in order to learn about God (which was the real reason the church sought to censor him), to modern philosophers like Berkeley who argued that at each moment in which you experience anything you are having, at that and every other moment, the direct experience of God. The world is a *theophany*, an appearance of God. Like Bruno and Spinoza, Cusa speaks of the world as an endless unfolding of God; the present existence is the result of a divine "contraction" from which the unity of God unfolds into multiplicity. The world is therefore infinite, which leads Cusa to reject the idea of fixed points in space and time in a way that anticipates twentieth-century developments in the relativity of space and time as pioneered by Albert Einstein. No body in the universe—neither the earth nor the sun—has a privileged position. All judgments about location must be relative. Cusa even went so far as to declare that the geocentric view of the solar system expressed in the Old Testament was false, written for the people of the time in terms they could understand.

All individual things, too, are contractions of the divine infinity. Stimulated no doubt by the forbidden views of Averroes, Cusa argues that each individual is a manifestation of God, forming a harmonious system in which each is both unique and part of the whole. Thus his revival of the key phrase from Anaxagoras, "Everything is in everything," states that everything in some way mirrors the entire universe. God is in everything and everything is in God: "All is in all, and each in each . . . each creature receives all, so that in any creature all creatures are found in a relative way." And anticipating both Spinoza and Leibniz still further, he concludes, "All things are what they are, because they could not be otherwise nor better."

Unlike all of his contemporaries, Cusa did not belong to, nor did he try to make his thought adhere to, any particular school of philosophers or theologians. He saw no orthodox or institutional path to knowledge. Ultimately, the mind must through its own efforts transcend the limitations of sensory knowledge and attain through intellectual intuition a vision that goes beyond reason, logic, and language. The finite is thus returned to the infinite and the philosopher through learned ignorance achieves a mystical union with God. In his final work, *De visione Dei* (Vision of God, 1453), Cusa argues that the enlightened are free to live out the rest of their lives in mystical contemplation of the oneness of all things, forging between the relative, finite world and the absolute, infinite world, a living bridge.

Bacon: The Idols of the Mind

Born in London to a family of high-ranking civil servants, Francis Bacon (1561–1626) studied law at Trinity College, Cambridge. After an illustrious political and legal career, he became lord chancellor (attorney general) under King James I. A prolific and brilliant writer, he produced a body of highly revolutionary philosophical works that made him a pivotal figure in the ensuing transition from medieval to modern philosophy and influenced subsequent British empiricist philosophers Locke, Berkeley, Hume, Mill, and Russell. Indeed, his philosophical works shifted the entire focus of the knowledge-seeking enterprise away from the medieval concerns with predominantly religious themes. He provided a model for a new way of gathering scientific knowledge that bears the name "Baconian method," in which one moves from particular facts to more general knowledge of forms using experimentally discovered laws.

Bacon shunned what he saw as a vain craving for psychological satisfaction under the guise of a search for truth: "I find that even those that have sought knowledge for itself, and not for benefit or ostentation, or any practical enablement in the course of their life, have nevertheless propounded to themselves a wrong mark, namely satisfaction (which men call Truth) and not operation." (This view will find voice again most dramatically in Nietzsche, Chapter 4.) According to Bacon, knowledge has nothing to do with personal happiness or satisfaction. The sole purpose of knowledge should be the technological mastery of nature. Philosophers should avoid the sort of abstract contemplations about the ultimate natures of things that so interested medieval theologians, give up the Socratic search for enlightenment, and avoid the inner tranquility sought by the Stoics and ancients. All of these are wrongheaded. What philosophy should do instead is "endow the condition and life of man with new powers or works" and "extend more widely the limits of the power and greatness of man." Philosophers must stop "prostituting" themselves by supporting or establishing religious or even scientific dogma and by seeking inner bliss or any other manner of "delight only and not of discovery."

Baconian philosophy is thus a shift away from metaphysical abstraction and psychological satiation toward a concrete, practical, utilitarian conception of wisdom. Bacon is as critical of skeptics who claim that knowledge is impossible as he is of the dogmatists who claim that knowledge must be based on the authority of ancient Greek learning (most notably, at the time, Aristotle, with whom Bacon makes an audacious break). He wanted to find a balanced, middle ground. The Baconian method is designed to be used by those seeking sound judgments who wish to find out the truth for themselves. It is a purely mechanical procedure for attaining knowledge, openly available to anyone. The idea is that just as a person untrained in geometry could use a pair of compasses to construct a circle, anyone could use Bacon's method to construct knowledge. Before you can use this method, however, or even learn it, you must first clear your mind of all the falsehoods you have been conditioned to believe.

In his most celebrated work, *Novum Organum* ("New Instrument," contra Aristotle), Bacon tries to shed light on the psychological motives and covert personal interests of the previous philosophers. These fallacies stand in the way of real philosophical progress and must be removed before real learning can take place. They come in four types. The first, the *idols of the tribe,* are fallacies based on a sort of "wishful thinking." For instance, most people delude themselves into thinking that nature exhibits a far greater regularity than it actually does; this is the result of the mind generalizing from affirmative instances while neglecting negative instances through an elaborate but socially sanctioned self-deception. Because our perceptions of the world are neither veridical nor even adequately accurate, we learn to ignore what we cannot grasp. We represent the world to ourselves in a false way, using false images that seduce us.

The *idols of the cave* are personal prejudices stemming from one's own temperament, beliefs, upbringing, and education. Bacon puts a new twist on Plato's allegory of the cave by suggesting, in effect, that we do not all live in the same cave—we are each individually encased in our own private illusion. We thus cannot simply by reasoning see the truth "as if through a glass darkly," as Plato imagined; the mind, in Bacon's words, is not the window but a "false mirror" of reality. Unfit to trust our own sensibilities, we naively use our eccentricities, emotions, and cravings to imprison ourselves. He thus warns, "In general, let every student of nature take this as a rule, that whatever his mind seizes and dwells upon with particular satisfaction is to be held in suspicion."

The *idols of the marketplace* are ideas, rumors, and beliefs passed along in social settings, through work and play; they result from our not taking the time to define our words properly. Without our being consciously aware of it, words exert a deep and seductive power over the mind; Bacon saw as philosophically blinding the trappings rampant in a society of merchants and consumers, a society defined by persuasive advertising, rumors, and hearsay. According to Bacon, the idols of the marketplace are the worst of all the fallacies for two reasons: first, so many words in our vocabulary are but names for nonexistent things; second, most of our words are concepts abstracted from a few instances and then applied in a haphazard and sloppy manner to a whole range of things. This process, he says, has been particularly devastating for philosophy because it has led to arguments about nothing, as for instance when philosophers have taken part in empty religious debates.

The *idols of the theater* are fallacious modes of thinking that have come about through blind acceptance of tradition and authority, including—and especially—bad philosophy. The worst perpetrator of such bad philosophy, according to Bacon, was Aristotle, whom he accuses of trying to force nature into his own vain abstractions and then using them to try to explain things away merely through the use of clever definitions. Theology according to Bacon has similarly been the result of this fourth type of fallacy that has infected the mind with superstition and glorified ignorance.

According to Bacon, these four intellectual and emotional idolatries, as the main obstacles to objective knowledge, have kept humanity in the dark for centuries. He urges people to dispense with them so that they can apply his new method and thereby pave the way for new thinking. Once freed of these old fallacies, humanity would be free to establish a natural philosophy, which he divides into theoretical and practical, physical and metaphysical. This leads him to his concept of forms, the central aspect of his theory which is supposed to solve both the theoretical and practical problems of science.

In the concluding part of the *Novum Organum,* he describes a method that would come to be called the "Baconian method" of induction. The central ideal is that any inquiry with truth as its aim must always begin with as clear and unambiguous description of the facts as possible and then all generalizations from these facts must be checked by a search for (1) positive instances of the phenomenon in question, (2) negative instances of its absence, and (3) instances of its presence in varying degrees. We must then eliminate whatever is not directly connected with the phenomenon under investigation. Numbers 1, 2, and 3 are essentially an anticipation of the methods of agreement, the joint method, and the method of concomitant variations as used in modern science.

Although Bacon is sometimes labeled an empiricist who anticipated Locke and Hume, it should be noted that he says, "The Empirical school of philosophy gives birth to dogmas more deformed and monstrous than the Sophistical or Rational school." In other words, he is as suspicious of experience as of blind reason and though he insists that experience must always be put to the test through experiment, he is also as deeply critical of the "experimentalists" as he is of the rationalists:

> The men of experiment are like the ant; they only collect and use: the reasoners resemble spiders, who make cobwebs out of their own substance. But the bee takes a middle course; it gathers its material from the flowers of the garden and of the field, but transforms and digests it by a power of its own. Not unlike this is the true business of philosophy. . . . Therefore from a closer and purer league between these two faculties, the experimental and the rational (such as has never yet been made), much may be hoped.

A complete system based on exactly such a synergy between experience and reason, as Bacon is here clearly anticipating, would have to wait two more centuries, until the ground-breaking work of Immanuel Kant (Chapter 4).

Bacon's influence on the subsequent revolution in modern thought has been pivotal and often unappreciated. Early-twentieth-century philosopher John Dewey (Chapter 5), inspired by Bacon's views as summed up in the aphorism "Knowledge is power" to invent the philosophy known as American pragmatism, wrote, "Francis Bacon of the Elizabethan age is the great forerunner of the spirit of modern life [who as] a prophet of new tendencies . . . hardly receives his due as the real founder of modern thought."

Giordano Bruno: The World-Soul and You

Giordano Bruno (1548–1600) was born in Nola, Italy. At the age of fourteen he went to Naples to study with a leading member[5] of the secret Averroist circle. These philosophers had continued teaching the Averroist view that all human beings are one numerically identical intellect, despite the ban against such teaching by the list of "forbidden propositions." After being trained by an Augustinian friar in logic, Bruno continued his studies in 1565 at the Neapolitan convent of San Domenico Maggiore.

As a Dominican, Bruno got into trouble for having anti-ascetic and anti-Christian views. In 1576 he came under suspicion of heresy and fled to Rome. Things did not work out much better there; he got involved in a murder case and once again had to flee. This time he went to Liguria and ended up in Venice. In 1578 he was forced out of the Dominican order. He fled across the Alps to Geneva and there made a humble living as a proofreader. Trying to improve his standing he converted to Calvinism, but as soon as he was in favor with the new authorities he published a devastating criticism of leading Calvinist Antoine de la Faye. By then he had already become one of the most controversial and certainly the most persecuted of the late Renaissance philosophers. He was charged with both impiety and heresy and was sent off to prison. He retracted his views and after his release moved to Toulouse. He earned the degree master of arts and finally managed to secure a lecturing position in philosophy.

Interestingly enough, most philosophers who have been accused of impiety and heresy, from Socrates onward (even the case of Galileo), were not accused of being atheists. As the church authorities saw it, atheism was not the problem. Rather, the problem was that these philosophers claimed to be able to know God, or ultimate reality, themselves, without having to rely on the orthodox authority of the church. They claimed to be able to have knowledge on the basis of their own reason or experience. Spinoza, too, as we shall see, will find himself in the same predicament. Bruno was no exception. What got him in trouble was what the church considered to be a most heretical and dangerous idea: pantheism, the view that the universe is the living God and that everything in it is a manifestation of God. Bruno's own version of pantheism was founded on the metaphysics of Averroes. He conceived of God in ways that church officials saw as the most heretical of all and which they feared even more than atheism: the identification of God with the world.

According to Bruno, "God" and "world" are two names for the same being. As God, *natura naturans,* the universe is one unified whole, transcendent and ineffable; as *natura naturata* it is the infinity of worlds, things, and events. The idea is that being, which is a cosmic, Parmenidean unity, divides itself into a many so as to display all infinite potentialities of the One. This leads to an eternal process of outgoing creative activity into the many and a return into the One, the divine unity; the supreme achievement of this activity is the human mind, whose search for the One within the Many, unity among diversity, simplicity in complexity, the changeless within the eternal, and so on, is the expression of the divine mind returning to itself. In Bruno's philosophy the human mind functions as the fulcrum of the cosmic process of existence, which is in many ways suggestive of the philosophy of Hegel (Chapter 4).

Despite warnings from the authorities, Bruno continued teaching and publishing his controversial views. He was in danger of being arrested when French king Henry III read his works and was so impressed that he offered Bruno his protection, brought him to Paris, and appointed him official court lecturer. Two years later Bruno was in trouble again, this time at Oxford, for his unorthodox views about the immortality of the soul and the unity of the intellect among all human beings.

During his stay in England he published *Ars Reminiscendi* (1583) and *La Cena de le Ceneri* (1584), in which he accepts Copernicus's view of the solar system and argues for an infinite universe composed of an infinite number of worlds; in addition, the works criticize English society in general and the Oxford philosophers and theologians as unenlightened pedants. His *De la Causa, Principio et Uno* (Concerning the cause, the principle and the one, 1585), written in dialogue form, is an Averroes-inspired attempt to demonstrate the fundamental unity of all substances including, and especially, the human intellect. He begins by relating the world *as it appears to us* as described within the current scholastic terminology and the traditional Aristotelian distinctions: form and matter, cause and principle, final and efficient cause, and *potentia* (possibility) and *actus* (actuality). Bruno uses these distinctions for a single purpose: to express the unity of the universal world form and of the world soul. Thus he uses the distinctions to show that they are but relative and only of partial significance.

The issues Bruno raises are as timeless as philosophy. The characters in his dialogue argue about the nature of the relationship between that which you see—the immanent perception of objects—and that which is their efficient cause, that is, whatever it is that causes objects to appear as they do. We may conceive that physical tables and chairs "out there" in the world are the first, or initiating, cause —the first domino—of a long series of causes that finally end up causing the images you see. But notice that you don't see any of these causes, neither the first nor the last domino in the chain; you see only the final effect: the object of perception. In other words, even if a physical object "out there" corresponds to the visual image you see, what is responsible for the creation of the visual image as such? You can't *see* the cause. What, then, is it? Pause a moment and try to meditate on this problem. The physical object conceived "out there" can't be the direct cause of the image. Tables and chairs don't reach into your brain, grab your neurons, take hold of your mind! You can say that your own mind/brain is the cause, at least is the final cause of the whole series of events starting with the "stuff" out there (like atoms and light waves or whatever it is), and that the immediate cause is you. But notice that you are not aware of this—you do not see this. You can only infer it in *theory.*

It is this problem that moves Bruno to refer to things in themselves as they actually are—the originating, first cause of all the things we see, the ultimate reality of which the appearances are merely a secondary affect—as *divine substances.* In calling this reality "divine" he is as much noting that the cause of the objects of perception is transcendental to experience (rather than immanent) as he is claiming that it is a supernatural spiritual force, God. Regarding the nature of the "thing in itself" and the "transcendental" nature of the cause of our experience, Immanuel Kant, as we shall see, will agree. So will the American philosopher Josiah Royce (Chapter 5), who expresses essentially the same ideas as Bruno, except in a more contemporary context.

In Bruno's dialogue, when one character asks another to explain the difference between the cause and the principle and how the distinction resolves itself into unity, the explanation given is that it is resolved through the presence of the world-soul, the light of pure self-consciousness, which exists in each of us as one and the same individual. The idea of the ultimate and fundamental unity of all things—the immanence of the world-soul and of the world-form in everything—Bruno expresses as an intuition rather than as a demonstrable proposition. His motive is not just the impartial search for truth. He claims that intuiting the truth has two practical benefits. If the individual soul (you) learns to view itself as being one with the world-soul, this alleviates all fear of death. The highest aim of any individual being is to thus become the expression of the meaning of the whole world and all its parts, including itself at the center.

In *De l'Infinito, Universo et Mondi* (1585), Bruno uses the arguments of the pre-Socratics against Aristotle. It is deeply ironic that whereas Averroes argues for such a numerical identity of all minds on the basis of his interpretation of Aristotle, Bruno considers Aristotle's views in particular and the language imposed on philosophy by the prevailing scholasticism as unduly constraining for his own "we are all one being" view. He thus claims that the immanence of the world-soul and of the world-form in every being is not something that can be logically demonstrated. Nevertheless, it can be grasped as an intellectual, or rational, intuition. The ultimate secret truth about the identity between the world and you has the power not only to relieve you from fear of death, but also to liberate your mind to fully contemplate and thereby realize its own true nature and the true nature of the world, free of religion and fear.

In his ethical writings, Bruno urges social reforms along anti-Christian lines, with obvious parallels to his metaphysics: treat others as yourself because they are you. The church, which held as sacred the division of human beings into good and evil, sinners and saved, considered this an assault on its authority. The church argued that if Bruno is right then everyone has the same relationship to God and, in a very important sense, is God. The person who follows obediently the rules of the church is no closer to God than the person who rebels against them; they are equally close, they are one. In the end, because Bruno refused to recant his views, the order was put forth to burn him at the stake.

Bruno went back to Paris and continued his criticisms of Aristotle in his *Fuguratio Aristotelici Physici Auditus* (1586). He then came out with more of his heretical views and was again forced to leave. Only Wittenberg, Germany, allowed him a place to teach and there he continued to publish until the Calvinists came to power. Once again Bruno was exiled, and for a brief time he found safe haven in Prague, Czechoslovakia. Among his written works from this period, the greatest is *De Immenso* (1588). Here his monopsychism is presented in full force, along with its Averroist foundation, and he explicitly argues for the single-identity view of the human intellect.

Upon reading this work, the local Protestant church excommunicated him. He fled to Frankfurt and was immediately denounced. Next he fled to Venice under the protection of a Venetian nobleman who soon, after hearing his arguments, denounced him to the Inquisition and helped bring Bruno to Rome. After seven years in prison and a long trial for heresy, Bruno refused to take back any part of his view. He continued to espouse the unity of the universal world-form and of the numerical identity within each human being of the world-soul—that, ultimately, we are all the same person. In the end he was burned at the stake.

Bruno's dying words were "Why do you burn yourself! Why?"

To which the learned archbishop, very familiar with Bruno's works, responded with a grin: "Why do you?"

Martin Luther and the Reformation of the Church

As the sixteenth century ended with the death of Giordano Bruno at the hands of the Inquisition, the hold of papal authority and the church-dominated Aristotelianism of the Middle Ages had already begun to wane. Three events in particular had helped set the stage for a new era, now known as modern philosophy: the publication, in 1543, of Nicholas Copernicus's controversial sun-centered model of the solar system, the general recognition of the gross corruption of the church and a sudden attempt at reformation, and the publication, in 1562, of the first Latin edition of the work of Sextus Empiricus.

It is a commonly accepted view that these were deeply religious times. Certainly the people and their leaders professed great religiosity through the pomp and circumstance of ritual, not the least of which was the public torture and death by burning for the crime of heresy at the hands of the notorious Inquisition established back in 1231 under Pope Gregory IX. Heresy was

> the greatest of all sins because it was an affront to the greatest of all persons, God; worse than treason against a king because it was directed against the heavenly sovereign; worse than counterfeiting money because it counterfeited the truth of salvation; worse than patricide and matricide, which destroy only the body.[6]

Once you were accused of heresy, the best thing you had to look forward to was confessing your sins under torture, in which case you "might be granted the mercy of being strangled before being burned at the stake." This, apparently, was not one of the religious cordialities offered to Bruno. But by all accounts such activities were motivated not by piety or reverence but by power. And the power, by and large, as it was wielded by those who had it, concerned itself not only with political gain and the accumulation of wealth but also with the suppression and control of human thinking and inquiry, especially regarding philosophical questions. But *why?*

If you think past the obvious and ultimately superficial (and unconvincing) answers, you will see that this question is really rather puzzling. It is one thing to have absolute political power and then to use your authority to suppress the opposition. But metaphysics? Speculation as to the nature and origin of the cosmos? Epistemology? Theories have of course arisen trying to explain such behavior in terms of consolidation of political power through subjugation of people using religious beliefs as a sort of bondage. But the deeper, philosophical questions we have already considered in our discussion of philosophy's first twilight and the beginning of the Dark Ages prompt us to wonder: could it be that the human mind, or the brain itself, creates repressive social institutions as a means of repressing or stopping its own inquiry? In other words, the Aristotelian dictum "All men by their nature desire to know," which we have already questioned, may turn out to be but a desire for the pretense to knowledge in exactly the fashion that Socrates seems to have gone to his own death to warn us about.

In any case, we can further muddy the water by asking who among the church leaders at the time actually believed in God. Today, over forty percent of the clergy admit (upon graduation from divinity or rabbinical school) to being atheists.[7] In the fifteenth and sixteenth centuries, those who had the most studious access to the religious arguments and evidence for the existence of God and had attained the highest levels of authority within the church were men whose actions can scarcely be believed to be pious or religiously inspired. For instance, Pope Alexander VI had four illegitimate children (one of whom was Lucrezia Borgia), though he put to death others who did not abide by the rule of clerical celibacy. Someone who even suspected that the sort of God that Alexander VI preached about actually existed would not even think to commit what would so blatantly be regarded as sin—unless, of course, he was incredibly stupid or incredibly weak. But incredibly stupid and incredibly weak persons rarely, if ever, attain such positions of power as enjoyed by the popes of the time, who held absolute power over citizens, princes, and kings alike. Pope Julius II put on a suit of armor and led his troops to war to conquer other papal territories. Leo X, who at the age of thirteen became a cardinal through family influence, declared upon his election, "The papacy is ours. Let us enjoy it."[8] When Albert of Brandenburg, bishop of two districts, wanted to become Archbishop of Germany, the pope sold the post to him for ten thousand ducats. Albert borrowed the money at twenty percent interest from the banking house of Fugger and repaid it by the common practice of "indulgences," through which "sinners" could buy salvation by paying directly to the bishop or archbishop a predetermined fee. These certificates, purchased from church authorities, gave written guarantees that the purchaser was forever freed of any guilt or retribution for some expressed sin; the greater the sin, the greater the price. In 1477, Pope Sixtus IV extended the authority of the "indulgences" all the way into purgatory so that "as soon as the coin in the coffer rings, the soul from purgatory springs,"[9] as one Dominican monk advertised. It is difficult, if not impossible, to believe that the authors of such documents and the grand authority structures whose bank accounts were built in part by them could have seriously believed in the God of which they preached.

Indeed, before long the corruption became so widespread that various church reformers emerged, most notably Martin Luther (1483–1546). The son of a German copper miner, Luther earned the nickname "The Philosopher" at the University of Erfurt. Everyone expected him to become a lawyer, but upon graduation he mysteriously joined the Augustinian Hermits in Erfurt. He was ordained in 1507 and gave his first Mass. Shortly thereafter his university professors—all of whom were nominalist philosophers under the influence of William Ockham—recommended him for advanced theological studies. Five years later Luther earned his doctorate. As a professor, during his teaching of Aristotle's *Nicomachean Ethics,* he began to experience grave anxieties and guilt over his own beliefs, conduct, and what he perceived as his unworthiness to be called a "righteous man of God." When he expressed his doubts, the other priests and church authorities seemed to scoff at his apparently genuine faith and simply assumed he would eventually go along with what had by now become standard procedure. Because of his perseverance, however, Luther continued to be promoted and by the time he began to question not only his own standing in relation to God but that of his fellow authorities as well, he was well entrenched as an illustrious member of the inner power structure. And suddenly he began, much to the outrage of his colleagues, to "spill the beans":

> It is painful and shocking to see that the head of Christendom, proclaiming himself the Vicar of Christ and the successor of St. Peter, lives in such a worldly and ostentatious style that no king or emperor can reach and rival him. He claims the titles of "Most Holy" and "Most Spiritual," but there is more worldliness in him than in the world itself. He wears a triple crown, whereas the mightiest kings wear only one. If that is like the lowly Christ or St. Peter, it is to me a new sort of likeness.
>
> What Christian purpose is served by the ecclesiastics called cardinals? I will tell you. In Italy and Germany there are many wealthy monasteries, institutions, benefices, and parishes. No better way has been devised of bringing them into Rome's possession than by creating cardinals and giving them bishoprics, monasteries, and prelacies as their property. . . . The consequence is that Italy is now almost devastated; monasteries are in disorder, bishoprics despoiled, the revenues of prelacies and all the churches drawn to Rome, cities devastated, land and people ruined. . . . Why so? Because the cardinals must have their revenues. . . . Now that Italy is drained dry, they are coming into the German countries. . . . If ninety-nine percent of the papal court were abolished and only one percent were left, it would still be large enough to deal with questions of Christian faith. At present there is a crawling mass of reptiles, all claiming to pay allegiance to the pope, but Babylon never saw the like of these miscreants. The pope has more than 3,000 secretaries alone, and no one can count the others he employs, as the posts are so numerous. It is hardly possible to number all those that lie in wait for the institutions and benefices of Germany, like wolves for the sheep. . . . It is not at all astonishing if princes, aristocracy, towns, institutions, country and people grow poor. We ought to marvel that we still have anything left to eat.[10]

After being threatened with censure, on October 31, 1517, Luther nailed to the door of All Saints Church in Wittenberg, "for the purpose of eliciting truth," ninety-five theses critical of the indulgences and openly questioning the divine authority of the pope.

The pope responded by instructing the vicar-general of the Augustinians to deal with the "rebellious monk" through the "usual channels." Luther was relieved of his duties as district vicar, and proceedings against him on the charge of heresy were begun in Rome. Luther boldly responded by publishing a sermon on the power of excommunication that declared that the pope did not have infallible and absolute power to decide on such matters unquestioned. He called for open debate and there defended himself so aptly that others began coming to his defense. During these debates, instead of retracting his statements, Luther took issue with the deepest theological and metaphysical positions of the time, including raising doubts about the Eucharist. Despite winning the support of many, who now called themselves "Protestants," the end result was the Edict of Worms, which declared Luther to be an outlaw, and all of his writings were banned or burned. As a result, Luther went under disguise and lived in seclusion during which time he achieved what probably had the single greatest effect on subsequent religious affairs throughout Europe: he translated, for the first time, the New Testament and the Old Testament from the original Greek, which formerly no one but the priests could read, into the vernacular German. This helped to bring about the revolt of the people, including the peasant uprising; private Masses, celibacy of clergy, and religious vows were revealed to be not derived from scriptures but the result of legal, financial, and liturgical affairs, about which he now wrote openly. During the peasant uprising he married Katherine von Bora, a former nun, "to spite the devil."

Four years earlier, in 1521, Luther had been formally excommunicated from the church; by then, the division between "Protestants" and "Roman Catholics" had become official. The thousand-year-old doctrine, enforced under threat of death by the church that questions of truth had to be settled in one certain and specific manner, had come to an end. Reason and experience were to be guided by Aristotle and his interpreters. Questions that could not be answered by reason and experience, such as ultimate questions about the nature of the soul, God, the meaning of existence, and so on, had to be answered by a single authority: the church. Likewise for the many questions that Aristotle's philosophy (as any legitimate philosophy) leaves open and unanswered not because there is no answer forthcoming but because there is no clear and distinct criterion for deciding among many competing answers. The church would simply decide the undecidable.

Luther's challenge was just the first of several to this one-sided thinking. He proposed a different criterion from that of Catholic thinking: the scriptures, which he had now translated into the vernacular! According to Luther, disputes that could not be resolved by (Aristotelian) philosophy should be resolved, as so many of his earlier medieval predecessors had also claimed, by appeal to the scriptures. But *whose* appeal? Part of the popularity of the Protestant Reformation was the appeal not to papal authority but to individual reading of the scriptures. Papal authorities, as Luther had pointed out so well in his arguments against the church, differed as to their edicts and pronouncements. Often, their motivation came not from divine illumination (God would not change his mind, Luther argued) but from personal interests motivated by power and greed, things that Luther openly asserted. This all sounds well and good as a negative criticism of Roman Catholicism. But what about Luther's positive answer? *Scriptures?*

The idea is remarkably naive. How could a personal reading of the scriptures resolve that which could not be resolved by reason and experience? Here it is not difficult to see how and why his Catholic critics mounted, in subsequent years, an attack as devastating to Luther as Luther's had been against the Catholic Church. After all, everybody knows that individual opinions are even more volatile than the opinions of papal authorities. Individuals are as corrupt as the papal authorities (though the Catholic theologians of course did not put it quite like that). Just think of how many different Christian sects there are in the world, each professing to be Christian and yet each, in many cases, differing vehemently from the others' interpretation of the same book.

When put in proper perspective, the choice between submitting to some ruling papal authority and submitting to one's own interpretation of the scriptures is in neither case without problems. Rarely will the conscience of one person agree with someone else's. Thus it should not be surprising that the division between Roman Catholics and Protestants continued to produce divisions among Protestants into many different factions. Luther's call to a return to scripture turned out to be as philosophically naive as the Catholic call to submission to papal authority turned out to be philosophically evil.

At this point in our intellectual and spiritual history, a series of bloody philosophical and religious wars raged across Europe and the world, in which rulers tried to fix or determine the religion of the people residing in their lands, so as to quell internal disputes. The Reformation thus began to unsettle the thousand-year-old stasis. Luther's attempt to bring an evil and corrupt church back to some sort of "true" or "authentic" foundation brought about lasting divisions and a dogmatic belief of people on all sides that their opponents, unlike them, were blind and wicked. Small wonder that Descartes will go to such lengths to seek a firm and solid foundation for all knowledge, even beyond the limitations of Aristotle. Small wonder, too, of the sudden revival of Skepticism.

The Revival of Skepticism

Between 1562 and 1569 all of Sextus Empiricus's writings were republished. The Catholic Counter-Reformation was in full swing and, perhaps surprisingly, the Catholic theologians began to use the rediscovered Skepticism against Protestants, Calvinists, and Lutheran opponents on the grounds that they could not use reason to come to know what they profess to know. Thus, ironically, in the sixteenth century Skepticism became aligned with religion in exactly the way it once opposed it.

By the time Nicholas Copernicus published his controversial hypothesis that the earth revolves around the sun, the church-dominated Aristotelianism of the Middle Ages was already drawing to a close. The numerous issues being discussed and debated at the time were made even more complex by the various religious and secular power struggles. We shall therefore avoid the broad, sweeping generalizations that obscure rather than reveal the breadth and depth of the historical events during those times; they are best explored in their proper historical contexts. Any number of fine texts about intellectual history that discuss the apocryphal events of these times will better introduce you to the multiplicity of interpretations that try to explain how we got from there to here. We shall focus instead only on the central philosophical issues of the time, which, as we have seen, run throughout the entire history of philosophy: Is reality as it appears to be? If not, can we know reality as it *really* is? If not, why not? If so, how?

For more than two thousand years just about all philosophers and even the theologians agreed that the answer to the first question was *no*, reality is most definitely not the way it appears to be. From Thales through Protagoras, from Plato to Aristotle and up through the Middle Ages, just about everyone who had ever thought about it had come to the inexorable conclusion that the appearances are not just appearances but grossly deceiving. Suppose, for instance, that ultimate reality consists of atoms. That's not how things appear. You don't see atoms as atoms; you see them (if they indeed are there) as objects like tables, chairs, people, and so on. Or suppose ultimate reality consists of a mind, like a world-soul or God; again, you don't see that. Even if what you are now seeing occurs through the operations of a physical brain, that's not how the things you see appear to you! You don't see neurons firing, if that is the underlying physical basis of perception; you see these neural firings as other than what they really are. And so on. That is why I say that, on the first point (whether reality is as it appears to be) nearly everyone—regardless of their philosophical, religious, or scientific persuasion—was in agreement that the answer is an unmitigated *no*.

What about the second question? Can we, despite this big frustrating *no*, come to know reality? Here there was a great divide between the Skeptics who claimed that the answer was *no* and all the rest who claimed the answer was *yes*, though they disagreed as to how knowledge was possible. Some professed the primacy of reason; others professed the primacy of faith. The "new scientists," following Galileo (1564–1642), had an answer: the word of God is written not in scriptures but in the book of nature, and it is written in the language of mathematics. (In the next chapter we shall turn to these "new scientists," whom we might call the "new Gnostics"—that is, believers that knowledge of ultimate reality, "God," can be attained by individuals rather than the orthodoxy of institutions.) Science thus promptly reverted to the teachings of Aristotle, professing the primacy of observation—the study of the appearances themselves.

The Copernican Revolution

In 1543, Nicholas Copernicus (1473–1543), a Polish clergyman, published a book called *Concerning the Revolutions of the Celestial Spheres*. In it he presented a mathematical model of the universe in which the sun, not the earth, was at the center of the solar system. Why? How did he come up with such a theory?

For over a thousand years before Copernicus, nearly everyone believed that the earth did not move, that it was the center of the universe, and that the sun, moon, planets, and stars all revolved around the earth. And why did *they* believe *that?* One popular myth is that they believed it because that is what was written in the Bible, and people were taught to take the word of the Bible as the truth. People who dared question what was in the Bible were tortured or put to death, like Giordano Bruno being burned at the stake or Galileo Galilei being put under house arrest for espousing a Copernican view of the solar system. In other words, people blinded themselves to the truth and believed whatever the church wanted them to believe.

Or so the popular myth goes. It is true that the church did have that kind of power and it did exercise it. But that is not why people believed that the earth does not move and is the center of the solar system. They believed it because that's what their senses told them. Look up at the sky. That's how things appear. You don't see or feel the earth move. You see all the other heavenly objects move. What could be more natural than the idea of a stationary earth around which all the heavenly bodies revolve? So then where does the idea that the earth goes around the sun come from? We *know* where the idea that the earth does not move comes from: your senses. What about a moving earth?

It was Aristotle who formalized what seems to be the case about the heavenly motions based on looking at the sky and made a model of the universe with that idea in mind. In other words, he took as his foundation the appearances and extrapolated, or generalized, from them. It was no simple matter. At the Academy, which Aristotle entered as a teenager, Plato assigned the following homework problem for all students: create a geometric pattern that accounts for and accurately predicts the observed motion of the sun, moon, and planets. These motions are not nearly as regular as you might suppose. First, the sun has three different motions—its daily movement from east to west, its eastward movement against the background stars, and its yearly north-south motion, which causes the change of seasons in the middle-northern and middle-southern latitudes. (You may have noticed, if you live in the northern hemisphere, that the sun is higher in the sky in summer and lower in winter.) Further, any geometric pattern must show why the sun repeats these three motions exactly to return to any given position in slightly over 365 days. Meanwhile, the moon not only moves east to west nightly and eastward monthly, its north-south motion is even greater than the sun's and it shows phases. Nor do successive phases (such as the full moon) occur in the same place in the sky. To top it all off, what makes the problem especially difficult is the "retrograde motion" of the planets, a sudden backward loop that ancient astronomers had noted as early as 1900 B.C.E.

The planets visible to the naked eye of the ancients move nightly east to west. During the year they slack off against the background stars in an eastwardly direction, just as the sun does. Their overall motion in the eastward relation is constant, but the individual retrograde motions in the western direction are different for each planet; Saturn is the slowest in its eastward movement and makes 28 retrograde backward loops. Jupiter is faster and makes 11 retrograde motions, about

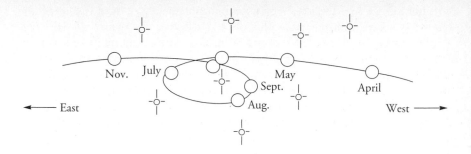

1 every 200 earth days. Mercury is much faster and shows only 1 retrograde motion every 116 earth days.

Ancient astronomers kept extremely accurate records of all of these apparent motions. Ancient philosophers, from Thales to Parmenides, from Pythagoras to Plato, had put forth the idea that the appearances are in such cases especially deceiving, because ultimate reality—the way the world really is—is not just a haphazard, random chaos or even some irregular hodge-podge: the real world is ultimately perfect, well balanced in its essential properties, ruled by order and reason. The ancient philosophers believed this not for religious reasons (in fact, most of the religions at the time presented the gods as extremely volatile, irrational, and often very corrupt). They believed it based on what they knew about the nature of reason, logic, and especially mathematics.

But how could the ancients explain the observed irregularities seen in the sky? After all, looking up we see the rest of the universe, or at least a large portion of it. If the lawlike regularities that the Platonic philosophers, under the influence of the Pythagorean mathematicians, believed to be the underlying clockwork, or operating system, of the cosmos, were not in evidence here, in our cosmic view, then where were they in evidence? Hence Plato's homework problem. Explain the irregularities seen in the appearances with some underlying, hidden regularities that could be revealed to the mind's inner eye, through the light of reason.

One of the best solutions to the problem was offered by Eudoxus (408–355 B.C.E.), who drew a series of homocentric spheres that each carried the sun, moon, planets, and stars around the earth. His model contained 27 perfect circles: 1 for the fixed stars, 3 each for the sun and moon, 4 each for the 5 visible planets. By having each sphere move at a different rate in opposite directions, Eudoxus could account for just about all the observed motions. Aristotle added 22 spheres. By doing so, he could make all "real" motions perfectly circular, perfectly uniform (all moving at exactly the same speed), and with the earth perfectly at the center. And, for all practical purposes, his system worked perfectly!

Small wonder Plato called Aristotle "the brain." Just try to do the same thing yourself, using all the advancements available in the subsequent 2,500 years of development. Use anything you want—drawing instruments, slide rules, calculators, computers—and see how far you get. In any case, here you now had a system that accounted for the way things appear and explained the apparent irregularities seen in the sky using reason and mathematics. And that's why the ancients believed in it, all the way up through the time of Copernicus. The standard "religious" explanation in terms of blind faith had nothing to do with it. Indeed, Copernicus's idea was already proposed two thousand years earlier, by the so-called "Copernicus of antiquity," Aristarchus of Samos, who in the middle of the third century B.C.E. had proposed an answer to the question posed by Plato's homework problem using a sun-centered model of the solar system. Why wasn't it accepted then? For good reason! Because all the philosophers, especially Plato, considered the sun-centered picture as something that would have to be taken on "blind faith," in direct contrast to the direct evidence available to the senses. So why then has the previous theory since then been given up (by modern science) in favor of the Copernican? And just where did Copernicus get such an idea? Was it a scientific idea? Was it based on observations?

Hardly. The Copernican hypothesis was no more "scientific" than the atomic hypothesis of Democritus. Just as Democritus, who came up with the idea of the atom, had no microscopes, Copernicus, who came up with the idea of the solar system as such, had no telescopes. So where do such ideas come from? And why is one adopted in favor of a different idea that explains the same phenomena?

Another generally accepted myth is that the "new" theoretical model is an improvement over the "old" model because it is more accurate and works better. In this all-important case, however, this is not true. Aristotle's conception was further improved by the Alexandrian mathematician, philosopher, and astronomer Claudius Ptolemy (85–165 C.E.), who applied to it an extended version of the epicycle-deferent system first developed by Apollonius and Hipparchus (third century B.C.E.). One criticism of the system of epicycles and deferents made even before Ptolemy's application was that a planet is carried in its eastward motion by the deferent (the large circle), the actual planet revolves along the epicycle (the smaller circle), and there is no actual (physical) object at the center of the epicycle. There is only a mathematical point. This will be extremely interesting to note when we see that in fact Galileo's "improvement" of the Copernican heliocentric system also does not put the sun exactly at the center (as it is according to commonly accepted beliefs) but off to one side (the path of the planets becomes an ellipse, with once again nothing but a mathematical point strictly in the center).

Ptolemy added to the epicycles and deferents invented by Apollonius and Hipparchus two curves, eccentrics, and equants. By using eccentric circles he displaced the earth slightly off the center of a circle and the central point was placed on a circular orbit revolving around the earth. In that way a planet revolved on an epicycle around a central point on yet another circle, which revolved around a center, which revolved around the earth. The equant made the motion of the planets uniform relative not to the center of the earth but to a displaced point. This system was so accurate in accounting for and predicting the motions of the sun, moon, and planets that the U.S. coast guard still uses it because the calculations are simpler and more precise than the Copernican-based model as improved by Galileo. The overall system looked like this:

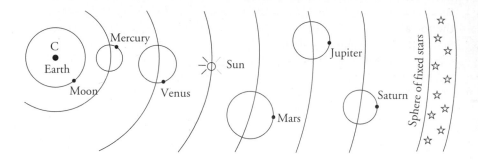

It was of course Copernicus who first challenged the Aristotelian-Ptolemaic geocentric system with a heliocentric one. Copernicus put the sun at the center. Fearing repercussion from the church, Copernicus put a disclaimer at the beginning of his work because to challenge church doctrine was heresy, punishable by death. Some years later, however, Galileo declared the Copernican heliocentric system to be not just a possible truth being speculated about in theory, but the actual truth. The trials and tribulations Galileo underwent because he dared to contradict accepted church doctrine are well known. Nearly everyone today believes that the question of who was right—Ptolemy or Copernicus?—has been settled in favor of Copernicus; the sun does not go around the earth, the earth goes around the sun. After all, can't we go outside and look directly at the solar system and see whether the earth goes around the sun or the sun goes around the earth? Probably you believe some scientist must have had some such experience, or else this sun-centered view would not be so widely disseminated with such absolute authority. Galileo must have looked in his telescope, or an astronaut must have looked out the window. Surely, somebody must have actually looked and saw the great truth that the great men, like Copernicus and Galileo, discovered, namely, that the earth indeed can be observed to move and to go around the sun.

But could we really, even with all the technology at our disposal, see whether the sun goes around the earth or the earth goes around the sun? Science, after all, is based on experience. The empirical method will allow us to see that the earth goes around the sun, surely. We step outside and look up. We see that the sun rises, then sets. The moon rises, then sets. The stars move across the heavens. So far, everything seems to be moving around the earth. Not very convincing for the sun-centered view! We had better go up in a spaceship.

We go to Florida, get in a rocket, and lift off. We go straight up until we are in a synchronous orbit around the earth. Many satellites are in such a synchronous orbit, meaning that (according to the heliocentric theory) they move at the same speed the earth revolves, thus remaining in the same position over the earth. Like tall radio and television towers, these satellites are used to bounce signals from one side of the earth to the other.

Now, inside our spaceship, looking down from our synchronous orbit, we see the earth, with the Florida coastline visible beneath a layer of clouds. The earth is motionless. We look up. The sun, the moon, all the planets, and all the stars are seen to move around the earth! Well, of course, we are in the earth's reference frame. It's like being on a moving train and you throw a coin up in the air. It doesn't just fly away and smash against the back wall because the momentum of the train has been imparted to the coin. If the train is moving seventy miles an hour westward, the coin is moving seventy miles an hour westward and continues to do so even when you toss it up; that's why it lands back down in your hand, which also is moving seventy miles an hour westward.

So, obviously, up in our spaceship above the earth, we must start moving about. We fire our thrusters and start orbiting the earth. We look up and see the sun, the moon, and all the stars—still going about the spinning earth below. Obviously, then, to see what the real movement of the solar system is, we must leave the earth's reference frame and go to the sun. We fire our thrusters and retrorockets and fly away until we are in a synchronous orbit around the sun. We now see the sun perfectly still beneath us and all the planets and stars moving about the sun. Finally! Copernicus and Galileo vindicated! But hold on. We now fly to Mars. From our orbit around Mars, we see the earth, the other planets, the sun, and all the stars revolving around Mars. So Mars is at the center. No, wait . . . what is going on?

Well, the truth must then be this: whatever reference point in the solar system you're looking out from, that place will seem to be still and everything else will seem to be moving around you. But what *are* the true motions of the planets and the sun? Do they even have a true motion in some absolute sense? Even if they did, you can't—even in principle—see it just by looking. But isn't that exactly what the church officials said? Their argument with Galileo was that you couldn't tell just by looking. And guess what? On this one point, about which nearly everyone (even the church) agrees the church was wrong, *the church was right!*

According to the church at the time of Galileo, facts about the true nature of the world, including the solar system and the universe, are not available to us without revelation from God. It wasn't that, at the time, you couldn't go up to have a look—as some scientists today may want you to believe (and may even themselves, wrongly, believe to be the case). The problem wasn't that back then people didn't have airplanes and spaceships. We are in a position to go up and look all we want! The problem is that looking doesn't settle the matter: there is no position in the universe from which to look.

You might think the problem is that what is needed is a better vantage point. We would have to leave the solar system. So let's lift off from Florida and never stop, just keep going up, up, up . . . finally, we're beyond the orbit of Pluto. We look back at the earth. We see the earth as a stationary dot and all the other planets, including the sun and the stars, revolving around the earth! Unless we shifted our reference frame to some other position—say, Alpha Centauri, which then will be the only still object in the whole cosmos—our point of view will remain locked in to the earth's position and everything else will be seen to move around that point. Indeed, as Einstein showed, there is no absolute vantage point in the universe where we could stand to see what the "true" motions of anything are. The only absolute thing about motion is that it is relative.

At this point, one is apt to wonder: how then—on what grounds—did we ever come to prefer the Copernican picture to the Ptolemaic one? One apparently obvious answer is that the Copernican model is better because it explains retrograde motion. But, as we saw, Ptolemy's system explains this too. Indeed, since Ptolemy (around 150 C.E.) developed his system to account for the seen motions in the heavens, it should not be surprising that he accounts perfectly well for retrograde motion using his "epicycles." The next most obvious answer is that Copernicus's system must be the simpler system and should therefore be preferred on grounds of simplicity. But nothing could be further from the truth. The fact is that either system can get you just as well from the earth to the moon. Not only does the U.S. coast guard still use Ptolemaic calculations because they are simpler, it is not even clear which system uses fewer epicycles! But that's preposterous, you say! Isn't Ptolemy's system the ugly one with all the crazy epicycles?

Here you are in for a shock—not just because Copernicus's system also had epicycles but because the best scientific, historical, and philosophical experts, the great knowers who have studied the scientific documents, cannot even agree as to which system had how many epicycles! That is, like the world, our theories—even our *expression* of our theories and views in scientific form—are open to multiple interpretations in the most humiliating and embarrassing way:

> Copernicus reduced the number of epicycles from 80 to 34. (Burtt, *Metaphysical Foundations of Modern Science,* 1949)
>
> Copernicus uses altogether 48 epicycles—if I counted them correctly. . . . Brought up to date by Peurbach in the 15th century, the number of circles required in the Ptolemaic system was not 80, as Copernicus said, but 40. *In other words, contrary to popular, and even academic, belief Copernicus did not reduce the number of circles, but increased them (from 40 to 48)* [emphasis added]. (Koestler, *The Sleepwalkers,* 1978)
>
> [Copernicus's] full system was little if any less cumbersome than Ptolemy's had been. Both employed over thirty circles; *there was little to choose between them in economy.* [emphasis added] (Kuhn, *The Copernican Revolution,* 1959)
>
> [Copernicus] used 34. (Crombie, *Ancient and Medieval Science,* 1978)
>
> Copernicus reduced the number of circles required to explain the apparent movements of the heavens from the 80 or so used in the elaborate versions of the Ptolemaic system to 48. (Mason, *History of Science,* 1971.)
>
> Copernicus used 17 epicycles. (Margenau, *The Nature of Physical Reality,* 1950)
>
> Copernicus used 80 epicycles. (Harre, *The Anticipation of Nature,* 1976)
>
> Copernicus used no epicycles. (Bohm, *The Special Theory of Relativity,* 1965)
>
> [Copernicus] used 40, as opposed to 240 for Ptolemy. (Motz and Duveen, *Essentials of Astronomy,* 1966)

Copernicus succeeded in reducing by more than half the number of arbitrary circular motions which Ptolemy had been obliged to postulate. (Armitage, *Copernicus,* 1939)

The introduction of the revolution of the earth about the sun never managed to do away with more than five epicycles. (Dijksterhuis, *The Mechanization of the World Picture,* 1961)

Copernicus used no epicycles. (Kaplan, "Sociology Learns the Language of Mathematics," in Wiener, *Readings in the Philosophy of Science,* 1953)

The popular belief that Copernicus' heliocentric system constitutes a significant simplification of the Ptolemaic system *is obviously wrong. . . . The Copernican models themselves require about twice as many circles as the Ptolemaic models and are far less elegant and adaptable.* [emphasis added] (Neugebauer, *The Exact Sciences in Antiquity,* 1969)

Again, my point is that not only do we have multiple interpretations of reality, each of which "works," but we have a *second-order difficulty* as well: multiple interpretations of our interpretations! Science and religion, it turns out, have one and the same problem.

So then why *did* Copernicus favor the heliocentric system? The answer is *faith.* Why did Galileo? The answer is *faith.* So then why did the church reject it? The answer is *reason.*

The Platonic Versus Aristotelian Legacies

The second-order problem we've just described—conflicting interpretations of our interpretations of phenomena—would not have bothered Plato. For him, what we call the "physical" world is not the real world. The word *physics* comes from the Greek word meaning "the real." So the reason why the second-order, philosophical problem of interpretation would not have troubled Plato is that such a state of affairs is not a problem to be solved but instead reveals the truth: what we call real, what we think we see when we look around us (i.e., what we call the "physical world"), is not ultimate reality. This is not so much a *problem with* reality as it is the *philosophy of* reality. We formulate theory A about the world, which fits the phenomena we see when we think we are looking at the real world. We then discover we can formulate theory B about the same phenomena. But B contradicts A! In Plato's view, this would be but a reminder that neither what we are looking at nor the ideas we are forming about what we are looking at are the world as it exists in itself—nor are they ideas as they exist in themselves. Both are merely shadows of the true reality, the world of real ideas that we cannot ever grasp with any of our senses. Again: this is *not* a problem to be solved; rather, it is the call to wisdom, proving the need for philosophy.

In other words, Plato would have accepted as true the statement "The physical world is an illusion." (But, again, be careful about remembering what the word *physical* means for Plato.) The physical world can only be grasped indirectly by the human mind through mathematics. Aristotle, on the other hand, did not believe that the formal truths of mathematics are removed completely from the physical world. In his view, mathematical formulas are but formal relationships between physical bodies and cannot be separated from them. He therefore was a realist (i.e., a *physicalist*) about the appearances. Likewise, he believed that our ideas as they are derived from or applied to the appearances give us direct access to reality. Therefore it would be Aristotle's metaphysical view of things, not Plato's, that would be dislodged by the "multiple interpretations of our interpretations of experience" problem. (This problem sometimes goes under the ominous name *hermeneutics,* from the Greek *hermeneutike*.) The reason Aristotle's view would be dislodged is that if what we are looking at is real and not some sort of illusion as Plato thought, then at most one system, one model, one set of ideas, could fit the appearances.

Again, for over a thousand years, church-dominated Aristotelianism has solved the problem of how to decide among different, mutually conflicting ideas. In Europe the ultimate arbiter was the pope. All disputes about matters great and small were resolved by appeal to church authority. In fairness to the church, it must be acknowledged that rarely was this a matter of whimsy. The church employed the finest minds of the time. (Even today, the current pope holds a Ph.D. in philosophy.) At the time, the pope's consultants consisted of an intellectual court that, in today's terms, would be the equivalent of the National Science Foundation and all the major university professors. And during the century in question (the sixteenth), the pope employed over three thousand personal secretaries!

The papal court used to be the center of intellectual activity. All that would today be considered philosophy, science, and theology was done behind closed doors, within the domains of the court. And one of the main functions of the papal court intellectuals at the time was to come up with clever and brilliant ways in which alternative ideas could be constructed about the way the world is, ideas that fit but contradicted other ideas about the very same things. But now, it seemed, the entire structure of our understanding of ourselves and the world—including the methods of inquiry—began to unravel. The foundation had come apart, leaving an abyss of unknowing in many ways wider and far more puzzling than had been experienced by the ancient philosophers. It left everyone wondering, Where do we go from here?

---

1. M. Charlesworth, *St. Anselm's Proslogion* (Oxford University Press, 1965), p. 21.
2. Nominalism is a view that grew out of Aristotle's categorization of the individual objects of experiences as being the "first" substances, whereby the logical and grammatical rule to be followed was that "substance" therefore could not be a predicate in a judgment (*res non predicatur*). Since the logical significance of universals is that of making possible the predicates in the judgment (and the syllogism), it seemed to follow that *universals could not be substances.* The medieval nominalists concluded that a universal is the conjunction of many particulars under one name, through the use of the same word. That is, universals

are nothing but collective names, common designations for a variety of things; universals
are words that serve as signs for a multiplicity of individual substances. (Boethius, for
instance, defines all words as being merely the "motion of the air produced by the
tongue," *flatus vocis,* and that is all universals are.) Nominalism is thus *the metaphysics of
individualism:* the truly real is the individual thing, and that alone.

3. Daniel Kolak, *I Am You: A Philosophical Explanation of the Possibility That We Are All the
Same Person* (Ann Arbor, Mich.: UMI, 1986). Also, see my more recent *In Search of Self:
Life, Death, and Personal Identity* (Belmont, Calif.: Wadsworth, 1997).

4. Jacob Christoph Burckhardt (1818–1897), Swiss historian and philosopher of history,
whom Nietzsche called "our greatest sage."

5. G. V. de Colle ("il Sarnase").

6. Roland H. Baiton, *Christendom: A Short History of Christianity and Its Impact on Western
Civilization* (New York: Harper and Row, 1964), p. 218.

7. Daniel Kolak, *In Search of God: The Language and Logic of Belief* (Belmont, Calif.: Wadsworth, 1994).

8. Baiton, *Christendom,* p. 249.

9. Tetzel, as quoted in Roland H Baiton, *Here I Stand: A Life of Martin Luther* (London: Hod-
der and Staughton, 1951), p. 78.

10. Martin Luther, "An Appeal to the Ruling Class of German Nationality as to the Ameliora-
tion of the State of Christendom," in *Martin Luther: Selections from His Writings,* ed. John
Dillenberger (New York: Anchor Books, 1981), pp. 418–21.

CHAPTER THREE

Modern Philosophy

Descartes: "I Think, Therefore I Am"

By the close of the sixteenth century, the Catholic Counter-Reformation was in full swing. Catholic theologians began using the newly rediscovered Pyrrhonian skepticism against their Protestant, Calvinist, and Lutheran opponents, arguing that they could not use reason to come to know what they professed to know. Skepticism had thus aligned itself with religion exactly in the way it once opposed it, and there were growing doubts whether any of the scholastic teachings of science, philosophy, and mathematics would lead to true knowledge.

It was a period of great transition, and it had a notable effect on the young René Descartes (1596–1650), who writes that

> as soon as I had finished the whole course of studies at the end of which one is normally admitted among the ranks of the learned . . . I found myself embarrassed by so many doubts and errors, that it seemed to me that the only profit I had had from my efforts to acquire knowledge was the progressive discovery of my own ignorance. And yet I was in one of the most celebrated schools in Europe; and I thought there must be learned men there, if there were such in any part of the globe. I had learned everything that the others were learning there; and, not content with the studies in which we were instructed, I had even perused all the books that came into my hands, treating of the studies considered most curious and recondite. At the same time . . . I did not find myself considered inferior to my fellow-students, although there were some among them already marked out to fill the places of our masters. Moreover, our age seemed to me to be as flourishing, and as fertile in powerful minds, as any preceding one. This made me take the liberty of judging all other men by myself, and of holding that there was no such learning in the world as I had been previously led to hope for.[1]

René Descartes was born in La Haye in Touraine, France. His mother died not long after he was born and he was raised by his father, a councilor of the parliament of Rennes in Brittany. At the age of eight he enrolled in the celebrated Jesuit college of La Flèche, where he studied science, philosophy, literature, and mathematics. Legend has it that he refused to get up in the morning, complaining of ill health, but his teachers allowed him to study in bed until noon. He continued the practice for the rest of his life.

Apparently disillusioned by the lack of certainty in any of the disciplines of study, Descartes writes:

> As soon as my age allowed me to pass from under the control of my instructors, I entirely abandoned the study of letters, and resolved not to seek after any science but what might be found within myself or in the great book of the world. So I spent the rest of my life youth in travel, in frequenting courts and armies, in mixing with people of various dispositions and ranks, in collecting a variety of experiences . . . and in reflecting always on things as they came up, in a way that might enable me to derive some profit from them.[2]

Thus, instead of pursuing his studies he turned to gambling, fencing, and horsemanship, and had numerous love affairs, one of which ended in a duel. Although a French citizen, he fought as a soldier in the Netherlands, in Bavaria.

In abandoning "the study of letters," Descartes would stumble upon what would turn out to be, literally, a revolution. After all, it was Socrates who argued that philosophy ought not to be written down, that philosophy books would only deceive readers into thinking that words were the thing. Indeed, in many ways, the developments in philosophy, science, and religion from the ancient to the modern world were the gradual abandonment of that Socratic ideal; philosophy during those two thousand years became a series of derivative activities predicated on a variety of conformities and disputations on the written word. In ending this process, Descartes reawakens philosophy as it was done by the Presocratics, before the advent of the study of letters as such. Thus, after more than two millennia of learning, knowledge, and wisdom, Descartes revived for a time the activity of philosophy as it was practiced by the ancients, the founders of philosophy who were anything but men of letters. He thus writes that

> after spending some years thus in the study of the book of the world, and in trying to gain experience, there came a day when I resolved to make my studies within myself, and use all my powers of mind to choose the paths I must follow. This undertaking, I think, succeeded much better than it would have if I had never left my country or my books.

What happened next to Descartes has not only the elements of high drama but a certain aura of mysterious fatefulness as well. One night, while returning from the emperor's coronation to his military post in Germany, he tells us how

> the winter held me up in quarters in which I found no conversation to interest me; and since, fortunately, I was not troubled by any cares or passions, I spent the whole day shut up alone in a stove-heated room, and was at full liberty to discourse with myself about my own thoughts.

These, "my own thoughts," became the basis for the revolutionary ruminations that would provide a solid foundation for knowledge for centuries to come and paved the way for the new era of modern philosophy: his *Meditations on First Philosophy* (to which we shall turn shortly).

In Paris, Descartes joined an illustrious and influential group of highly original thinkers headed by Marin Mersenne, his best friend from La Flèche, who would one day oversee the publication of the *Meditations*. When they urged Descartes to publish his iconoclastic views, convinced that he had come upon a revolutionary way of doing philosophy, he instead quit the group and went into hiding, keeping his residence a secret, and refused to publish. Then, in 1629, disillusioned with "the book of the world," Descartes fled to Holland where he started work on *Le Monde* (The world), a work divided into two parts, "Light" and "Man." When his old friend, now Father Mersenne, chanced to read it, once again he urged Descartes to publish. The popular historical account has it that Descartes again refused because he had just heard about the condemnation of Galileo (in 1632). But Mersenne had shown the *Meditations* to the Faculty of Theology in Paris and they already had approved it. In fact, it wasn't until twenty-two years after Descartes's death that the Roman Catholic Church first put the *Meditations* on the *Index Librorum Prohibiorum*, the list of books considered dangerous to read that Pope Pius V had begun in 1571. This list was then approved by the Council of Trent, the Roman Catholic church council created to deal with the crisis created by the Protestant Reformation that started the Catholic Counter-Reformation. The *Index* was one of the council's main tools of repression; it forbid people to read the *Meditations*.

Only fragments of *Le Monde* were published in Descartes's lifetime. But he did publish another ground-breaking work, his *Discourse on the Method of Properly Guiding the Reason in the Search for Truth in the Sciences* (1637). Here he states, "The greatest minds, as they are capable of the highest excellencies, are open likewise to the greatest aberrations; and those who travel very slowly may yet make far greater progress, provided they keep always to the straight road, than those who, while they run, forsake it." His purpose in the work is to correct the "aberrations of the mind." Inspired by Francis Bacon's proposition that "the entire work of the understanding must be begun afresh, and the mind itself be, from the start, not left to take its own course, but be guided step by step," Descartes says that the straight road that must be followed without ever veering from it consists in four fundamental principles:

> The first was never to accept anything for true which I did not clearly know to be such; that is to say, carefully to avoid precipitancy and prejudice, and to comprise nothing more in my judgment than what was presented to my mind so clearly and distinctly as to exclude all ground of doubt.

Few statements have such eloquence, power, and simplicity to allow anyone to see the fundamentals. But, first, what does it mean to clearly know something to be so? Few can answer questions such as "What is mental clarity?" A definition of mental clarity would require further definitions, which require further definitions still. What Descartes is looking for, however, is not a definition but an experience: an internal experience of one's own consciousness and a specific object: clear and distinct, undoubtable truth.

Most students who read Descartes's first principle accept it on blind faith. They think they understand what is being said because they think a definition is being offered. But it must be kept in mind that Descartes is not offering a definition. He is asking you to inquire with him into the conscious experience of what he is talking about. To accept what he is saying as merely a definition is to act in complete prejudice, which, if you really understand what he is saying, leads you to not accept any such statements without first embarking on a philosophical inquiry on your own, in terms of your own conscious experience. The following is my restatement of Descartes's four principles, with the all-important first one broken into several steps:

1. Never accept as true any proposition that is not clearly recognized by you to be true.
   a. Avoid precipitancy: don't be too hasty in accepting a new proposition.
   b. Avoid prejudice: don't be too dogmatic in holding on to a previously accepted proposition.
   c. If you use a proposition as a basis from which you derive some others, make sure that the fundamental proposition is presented to your mind so clearly and so distinctly that you cannot possibly doubt it.
2. Divide each complex problem requiring many steps into more basic parts, each of which involves only a single step. We just did that with principle 1.
3. Start with the simplest and easiest known propositions and move very slowly, step by step, to the more complex.
4. Always make a complete list of all your steps so that you can review them to make absolutely certain you have omitted nothing.

The inspiration for the imperative that you should always start from premises known to be certain beyond any doubt stems from the axiomatic method in mathematics. An axiom is a proposition known to be true, but not by empirical evidence. It is accepted as true on the basis of it being seen clearly and distinctly to be so, and beyond doubt, like the Euclidean axiom that two points determine a line. A demonstration would be not only superfluous but also impossible (since it is a general statement and any demonstration would be only for the two points drawn). Mathematics is derived from the ancient Greek *mathemata,* meaning "thoughts occurring not at random but guided by clear and distinct principles," like a logical machinery or a computer program. So in that sense mathematics can be thought of as philosophy done in a way whereby the driving force is not the thoughts themselves (the meaning, or semantics) but, rather, the thoughts themselves are driven by some rule (rule-governed structure, or syntax). Then mathematics proceeds by a deductive method in which each new proposition is simply derived from the axioms with clear and distinct certainty, each step perspicuous and accounted for. Descartes says that only when such formal perfection is attained in all the sciences and in philosophy as well will humanity be certain that it is on the path to true knowledge. With that in mind, he sets out to create a universal mathematics.

According to Descartes, the philosopher must make a careful and deep analysis not just of what the mind "says" but of the way the mind "works": this involves the ways and methods of reasoning. Taking the mental activity of mathematics as his model, he sees that thoughts are not the guide of the activity but themselves are guided. Instead of appealing to indirect methods of belief formation through external authority, the Cartesian method appeals to the more direct internal "authority" in terms of a specific and clearly defined conscious mental state. But what do you suppose would happen if you tried to apply Descartes's method? Could you even do it? Would you want to? Students often respond to such thoughts with the idea that this would be an awfully constraining way of thinking, that it would lessen our freedom, or that it would be a task so arduous and artificial it would lead us to ruin. But then what we call "freedom of thought" can itself be extremely constraining because when we can think anything we "want," then we are open to seduction by our own thoughts into believing things not because they are true but because we would like them to be true. That is no path to freedom but a self-imposed slavery of ignorance.

Ask yourself how many things you have accepted for true that you do not know directly, on your own authority, to be so. Probably most of the things you think you know are not really known by you to be so directly on your own authority. The range of the list can be quite staggering and unnerving. For instance, you know only indirectly that you have a brain, that the moon has a dark side, that George Washington was the first president of the United States, and so on. These things may be known by others (such as those who conditioned you to think that way). Or not. In that case, your position and standing in the world is weakened, insofar as you are not yourself the master of your own knowledge. Or, even worse, you live in a prison of false truths and half-truths, subordinate to those who are in the know. But who are those individuals?

Anyone who cares to find out for him or herself, using the Cartesian method, what is true and actual. I suggest that what Descartes means by "clearly know" is related to what Plato meant and so we might use the more familiar term, "recognize." For Plato, you will recall, all knowledge is recollection. There is a point, as in *Meno* when the slave "sees" the Pythagorean theorem, at which something strikes you as true in a way that it seems you already have known it to be so, there is an "aha," the way you recognize, say, something unfamiliar as really being familiar. One can always quibble, intellectually, with such a notion. The point, however, at least initially, is to focus on that conscious experience itself until it becomes clear and distinct, that is, until it stands out from all other ideas in a unique way. This might end up being merely a psychological illusion, but Descartes is suggesting that you already have a built-in, extremely accurate, internal mechanism for discriminating the true from the false. There may be cases in which that feeling is mistaken, but there are some clear and distinct cases in which this inner sense is accurate. Descartes is inviting you to look inside yourself to find this inner faculty within yourself, inside your own mind.

In other words, instead of appealing to external authority, the Cartesian method appeals to internal authority in terms of a specific and clearly defined conscious mental state. To understand clearly and distinctly what Descartes means, consider the analogy to the concept of pitch in music. How do you know when you're in tune? There is some conscious state in which the note is clearly and distinctly recognized as being in tune. Once you are attuned to this inner tuning, you cannot be wrong. Unless you are "tone deaf," you can tell, perfectly clearly, whether someone is in tune or not. What I think Descartes is claiming is that, intellectually, most people are "tone deaf." They cannot hear the truth. Their minds must be tuned. And they must be tuned to themselves. Part of the problem, according to Descartes, is that minds have lost their inner tuning due to the fallacy of tuning yourself to the thoughts of others. This does not make you in tune with the truth and, further, makes you out of tune with yourself.

Note that Descartes is not just saying, "Whatever seems true to you, is true," or anything like that. Let's take an empirical example (but keep in mind that he is explicitly not an empiricist). You probably couldn't pick me out of a crowd. My wife could, because she, unlike you, recognizes me. What is that recognition? What does it consist in? Well, when she sees me she doesn't have any sort of double vision; that is, she is not comparing her present image of me with some past image. That (or something like that) is being done automatically for her by her brain. She simply has the sense of familiarity associated with the image of me that she sees. No conscious interpretation is necessary. Her entire cognitive apparatus is doing it for her. Descartes is suggesting that visual appearances in the empirical world are easily deceiving in ways that propositions in the rational realm are not. *Propositions* are the "meanings" of which thoughts are internal experiences (Leibniz and Kant will use the word *apperception* to distinguish experience of one's own mental states as such in contrast to *perception,* experience of things—still within one's own representational mental states, of course, but not as such.) Thus propositions can be thought of as the apperception of meaning. Ordinarily, the activity of thinking involves the use of language. Stop reading for a few moments and think about something else. Listen to yourself think. What do you hear? A string of words comprising sentences, fragments, questions, single words, and so on. In other words, conscious thinking consists of stringing together words, the most important of which—in terms of knowledge—have to do with propositions.

Propositions are expressed by sentences that are either true or false. For Descartes, knowledge consists of true propositions—but not just that. For instance, the proposition "There are 314 pages in this book" is true, but it is not at this moment known by you to be true. It is, however, known by me to be true. Once you look on the last page and verify that there has not been some typo or some trick, then you can claim to be on the way to knowing that this proposition is true. Why? Because you are then evidently justified in your belief. Descartes is thus laying down a justified true belief theory of knowledge, an epistemological theory that we shall return to again when we consider various subsequent epistemologies. But the evidence is not in terms of some external experience. It is your own internal experience, what he calls a "rational insight," a clear and distinct occurrence within the human mind, that is the key to knowledge and on the basis of which he will attempt to construct a new and absolutely solid foundation for all subsequent philosophy: objectivity found hidden in the last place where anyone would have thought to look, inside the dark and hidden heart of one's own subjectivity.

Descartes rejects scholastic Aristotelianism in favor of a type of classical Platonism. He formulates his system of universal knowledge on indubitable premises. As in mathematics, he proceeds with straightforward deductions in which each step is as clear as the starting proposition. His attempt to construct the universal mathematics as a complete system of absolute validity includes not just numbers and figures but the whole world. In the process, he discovered a way to link geometry and algebra and thereby invented an entirely new branch of mathematics still practiced today and known as analytic geometry.

Descartes, like Plato, considered mathematics as the highest form of knowledge. The mathematics Plato had in mind was geometry, but his argument had to be allegorical; he claimed that the seen triangle is only a "reflection" of a perfect triangle, which is not an appearance but a "form," leaving it rather mysterious as to what these forms were. Like his teacher Pythagoras, Plato was inspired by the view that everything could be explained in terms of numbers (which Pythagoras pictured geometrically). For Plato, trying to express the concept of a triangle perfectly in the world (the world of appearances) would be like trying to draw a perfect triangle using a felt-tip pen on tissue paper; everything gets very blotchy and only the vaguest, fuzzy resemblance to a perfect triangle is possible. It was not until Descartes showed exactly how to express what a geometric figure like a triangle is in terms of a perfectly precise algebraic formula that Plato's ideas could further be developed. What Descartes managed to do using his now famous coordinate system that still bares his name ("Cartesian coordinates"), in which the x- and y-axis are number lines that serve like crosshairs in translating the figure into an abstract formula, is to translate the image into a formal relationship among variables such that one could simply plug in the appropriate numbers. Numbers, as such, are purely abstract conceptual entities. And what Descartes showed is that purely abstract formal relations, such as those studied by algebraic equations, could contain (or represent) all the information contained by a visual figure. In other words, he showed that there is an intimate and fundamental relationship between our perceptions—the world of appearance—and our intellect—the world of pure reason. We shall see this idea reach its culmination in the work of Immanuel Kant.

Descartes wrote a manual outlining his method in perfect detail for anyone who should wish to follow in his footsteps, called *Rules for the Direction of the Mind,* written in 1628 but not published until 1701, more than half a century after his death. In it, he offers clear and explicit rules that anyone can follow, which, he claims, have the power to lead to similar, far-reaching results in anyone who applies them. The key is to study and learn everything you can about as many different, even nonconnected, areas, teaching yourself the skills in those areas even if they seem completely unrelated. Descartes formulates in explicit detail such rules for philosophical thought designed to lead to clear and distinct ideas via a method modeled on the precision of mathematical thought. The purpose is not mathematical theory per se but the foundation of a perfect and complete understanding of ourselves and the world. Descartes thus echoes Plato's warning, placed above the Academy, "Let no one ignorant of mathematics enter here."

Thus, as we are about to see, starting from skeptical doubt about everything, in the end Descartes will claim that anyone can know everything there is to know. This knowledge of course would, on the views of other philosophers such as Bruno and Averroes, be possible through mystical intuitions, unity with the divine, the transcendental self, and so on; it does not require divine grace or genius or any sort of special talent. What makes it possible for the mind to attain such knowledge is explained in Descartes's first rule, in which he claims that one of the greatest mistakes we make is to limit the mind in the ways that we limit the physical body.

Descartes's distinction between the mind and the body is not merely a metaphysical distinction. The body, as part of the extended universe, has certain limitations due to its finitude. Being a great violin player necessitates your not being, say, a great wrestler or bricklayer; your fingers simply weren't made for such diversity of action. The mistake, however, according to Descartes, is that people assume that the limitations of the body are the limitations of the mind! This is an egregious error, the source of much of our self-imposed limitation.

The full title of his *Meditations,* mentioned earlier, is *Meditations on the First Philosophy, in Which the Existence of God, and the Real Distinction of Mind and Body, Are Demonstrated* (1641; 2nd ed., 1642); it is one of the most influential philosophical works of all time. By "first philosophy," Descartes means the same as Aristotle's *first principles of things,* or metaphysics. "Thus the whole of philosophy," he wrote, "is like a tree; the roots are metaphysics, the trunk is physics, and the branches that rise from the trunk are all the other sciences." The work begins with Descartes dispensing with the foundations laid by all previous philosophical and scientific systems built on external authority. He attempts instead to reconstruct philosophy and the entire knowledge-seeking enterprise anew. Many philosophers at the time objected furiously to the *Meditations,* whereas others praised it as a great intellectual achievement. Instead of ignoring his worst critics, Descartes published in the same volume all the most prominent objections and criticisms, including those of Pierre Gassendi, Antoine Arnauld, and even the English philosopher Thomas Hobbes (discussed in the next section).

Descartes begins the *Meditations* by taking stock of all his acquired opinions. He asks himself, *how do I know that all these things that I believe to be true, are true?* He wonders how he came to his beliefs. He notices that, while it would be impossible to examine each of his beliefs individually, there are only a few methods by which his beliefs were acquired. Most of his beliefs come about through conditioning by various religious, political, and educational authorities. Descartes now asks: *have I ever been deceived by any of these methods?* If so, then I must throw out all beliefs derived from that method. The method, in other words, is to find the general method or principles on the basis of which some set of beliefs is acquired, and then to test not the individual beliefs but the principles on which they are based, the method by which they were acquired. If the principles and methods are bad, any beliefs thus acquired are not knowledge.

Descartes's suggestion seems drastic, but what he is after—absolute certainty—calls for drastic means. And if there is some method by which you acquired a false belief, that method is unreliable. Suppose you have a friend. You confide in this friend some most intimate secret about yourself and ask your friend never to tell a soul about it, to never betray you. The friend then betrays you. Is this friend trustworthy? No. A friend who has betrayed in this way even once is not trustworthy. You can never really trust this friend again. It is the same with beliefs. What Descartes is saying, in the first meditation, about any supposed method of knowledge, is this: if the method has betrayed you even once, it is not trustworthy. Throw out all beliefs based on that method. If that leaves you with nothing, then so be it.

He considers the senses first. The senses often mislead us: the appearances are deceiving. But even if our senses only sometimes misled us, that would be enough to dismiss them as a reliable method of knowledge. Therefore, throw out any beliefs derived from the senses. But what about general beliefs derived from the senses? There might be optical illusions, visual deceptions, and so on, but what about the most general sorts of information revealed to me through the senses—such as that there is a bookcase in front of me? Here Descartes evokes one of the skeptics' most powerful questions: how do you know right now that you are not dreaming, or that an evil demon (or God) is not deceiving you? We have all had vivid dreams in which we believed, at the time, that the objects we saw were not dream objects but real objects. So we've all been deceived. The appearances are therefore, by themselves, not trustworthy.

But is this argument convincing? Typically, when presented with the question "How do you know right now that you are not dreaming?" most people can recall situations when they were having especially vivid dreams in which they believed, at the time, that what was happening was not a dream but reality. They then woke up with much surprise to find that it was only a dream. So most people, even while agreeing with Descartes, covertly believe that *usually* they can tell whether or not they are dreaming. It is just unusual, extraordinary dreams that are indistinguishable from waking states. What these people fail to realize is that just about every one of your dreams, no matter how "crazy," "discontinuous," and so on, is taken by you while it is occurring to be reality. The proof? While you're having a dream—any dream—you don't say to yourself, hey, here I am dreaming again! Typically, regardless of how strange the dream is, as you experience the dream you take it to be reality. (Of course people do sometimes claim to have had dreams in which they "knew" that they were dreaming—but, first, *even then the items in the dream do not look like mental images but objects.* Second, if you "know" that you are dreaming, you "know" that your reasoning is dream reasoning and therefore cannot be trusted![3]) That is, typically, you don't say, "Look at those imaginary images I see! Isn't this fun," and, even if on occasion you do, you do not directly apprehend the mental states *as mental states* but as things. Regardless of how strange the dream, usually it is the case that the objects in the dream do not appear as items inside your head but as items outside your head.

Indeed, Descartes's demon is not merely an imaginary example. It can be taken as a real and nasty problem. In an important sense, the Cartesian demon is running just about all the time, able to deceive you about all sorts of things and make you believe that what you are experiencing is not a mental construction but mind-independently real objects outside your head. Today, it's called *the brain*. That is not to say that Descartes would accept the reduction of mind states to brain states, but merely that the problem posed by his demon can easily swallow any new form of externally based authority, such as, and especially, physical science. For there is a very important sense in which you are always dreaming, even when your eyes open, insofar as the appearances themselves are mental constructions. The objects you see may to some degree be accurate representations of the things "out there," outside your head, but they are not numerically identical, that is, they are not one and the same entity: just as the word *dog* is not a dog, so the image of the chair in front of you is not a chair. Cross your eyes! The one chair becomes two? Hardly. The one image of the chair becomes two images. The point is that you can't simply tell, just by "looking," whether what you are seeing represents the way something appears in reality. What Descartes is pointing out in his first meditation is that you cannot even be absolutely sure that the object you see represents any sort of mind-independent reality at all. You've been deceived before, as when the object you were looking at existed only as a dream image, into believing that what you were looking at was a mind-independent thing outside your head. Appearances can therefore, by themselves, never be trustworthy. But it's worse than that. Even when you are not dreaming, that is, when you are wide awake, you are not directly aware of what Kant will call the "transcendental illusion," the feeling that the objects perceived in your mind are themselves mind-independent realities. In that sense, to see properly you must in the act of perception be successfully deceived by your own perceptual-cognitive apparatus —your brain!

After all, to put it in contemporary scientific terms, light stops at the back of the retina, where an impulse (actually, a bunch of potassium ions bouncing back and forth) goes along the optic "nerve" (it's not really a nerve as such, nor does anything optical travel along it in the sense of visual images as such) to the brain. Suppose you're looking at a chair: an image of that chair appears upside down on the back of your retina and then this "information" is translated into a sort of numerical code that is then used by your brain to construct the image that you see when you see a chair. The chair "out there" doesn't by itself directly cause the image you see, nor does the brain passively receive any such image; the brain creates such an image using its own active processing. The information from the optic nerve may tell the brain, in effect, what sort of mental picture to paint, but that information does not, itself, come in the form of a visual image. Now, the chair "out there" may *in some way* contribute to the event you experience as your perception of the chair *when your eyes are open*, but it clearly does *not* contribute in *any* way to the event you experience as your perception of the chair *when your eyes are closed.* This I think is often the least understood aspect of Descartes's demonstration. He is saying that *the chair object you see in your "waking state" is not a different sort of object from the chair object you see in your "dream state."* This is absolutely key and to miss it is to miss the point entirely. There may be a *theoretical* difference *but there is no phenomenological difference.* I repeat: *Descartes is telling you that there is no phenomenological difference between dream and waking states.* Once you fully understand and see this, you will be where Descartes was in his *Meditations* when he put it in no uncertain terms that "I perceive so clearly that there exist no certain marks by which the state of waking can ever be distinguished from sleep, that I feel greatly astonished; and in amazement I almost persuade myself that I am now dreaming."[4]

Thus, even with all our advanced science and neuroscience of perception, Descartes's epistemological question stands as vivid as ever. What we call "reality" is already a sort of "virtual reality," and so how do we know that what we are looking at is real? For all you know, given the way that perception works, you might be a brain in a vat on a planet in the Alpha Centauri system being stimulated by electrodes into experiencing an imaginary virtual reality film called *Life on Earth.* The Alpha Centaurians are running experiments to see what kinds of imaginary worlds they can create. Any experience you try to have to verify that something like that is not so can itself, for all you know, be an induced, virtual reality experience!

We don't need the perhaps antiquated concept of a deceiving demon or a God to get the point of Descartes's first meditation. Everything science has learned in the meantime about the operations of our own eyes and brains makes such extraordinary, supernatural concepts unnecessary but the philosophical question even more sharply poignant; we can now, thanks to the "advances" of science, raise exactly the same problem with our ordinary, natural concepts, such as the brain and the eye.

And yet Descartes goes on to offer a brilliant solution to this devastating skeptical problem. Just as Archimedes showed how if only he had a firm place to put his fulcrum he could move the entire earth, Descartes finds a firm place to put his absolutely indubitable proposition, which he shall then use to move the whole of philosophy. After doubting everything that can be doubted and throwing out anything that can be doubted, he finds solid ground: he realizes that even if he is dreaming, even if an evil demon is deceiving him into having the experiences he is now having, *nobody, not even God, could deceive him into believing falsely that he exists.* Why? Because even if he is always and forever being deceived, *deception* is going on. So there is at least the fact that something, someone, is being deceived. And so this deceived entity cannot be deceived into thinking, falsely, that it exists. Even a deception is something, even a false thought is a thought.

So there is one indubitable proposition: "I think, therefore I am." It occurs as an insight at the end of a series of apparently endless doubts: I doubt that the world is what it appears, that there is a God, that external objects exist, that I have a body, that twice two are four (even that can be doubted!). But it is impossible for me to doubt that I myself, who is involved in this activity of doubting, exist. So here is this one point at which the apparently endless series of doubts comes to an abrupt end: at the doubter, at the self-existence of the thinker who thinks such thoughts. I can doubt everything except that I doubt and that, in thus doubting, I am. Even if a being superior to me tried to deceive me in all my thinking, such a being could not succeed unless I already existed; the deceiver could not cause me not to exist so long as I am thinking. To be deceived means to think falsely, but that something even in that moment of false thinking is being thought, no matter what it is, is itself *not* a deception. It might be true that nothing exists, but then there would be no one to conceive of this nonexistence. Even if every thought I have ever had is a mistaken thought, the state of being mistaken, the activity of thinking, is not a mistake: even when everything is denied the denier remains. Undermine the whole content of consciousness by making its assertions false, still that consciousness itself—the doubting activity, the being of the thinker—is not thereby undermined but affirmed, acknowledged, realized. This, then, is the absolute point of departure necessary for knowledge, found in the *self-certitude of the thinking ego* (the Latin *ego* means "I"). In other words, from the fact that I doubt—that is, from the fact that I think—it follows not as a strict logical deduction that *I,* the doubter, the thinker, *am,* but only as an insight or philosophical realization of *existence, or being, in its own presence.* Thus Descartes's Latin phrase, *Cogito, ergo sum*—literally, "Thinking, therefore existing"—is the most certain of all truths.

Once I realize in my own experience that, as thinking, I exist, I can then reach the general conclusion that thought and existence are in this specific sense inseparable. This fundamental truth is a self-evident, immediate cognition, a pure intuition: *sum cogitans.* My own existence is revealed to me by my activity of thought. My thought is my being: in me, thought and existence are identical. I am a being whose essence consists in thinking. I am a mental entity, an ego, a rational mind. The existence of the mind is therefore not only the most certain of all things, nor is it only the basis for the possibility of finding certainty among all other things; mind is itself identical to being.

Cartesian doubt thus takes up again the Platonic-Aristotelian conversation that will now become a major preoccupation for all subsequent modern philosophers and that has continued to this day: Is knowledge attained through rational intuition or by sense experience? Descartes's answer lays the foundation for Kant's critique of dogmatic metaphysics and paves the way for idealism with the Cartesian argument that we know our own minds more immediately than we know our bodies and the material word. For the sum and substance of the Cartesian philosophy is not a skeptical renunciation of the unattainable any more than it is a dogmatic doctrine. It is the precept, the starting point of philosophy, not its conclusion. The cogito is, in other words, a methodological instrument for the knowledge-seeking enterprise that uses doubt to find the indubitable.

Keep in mind that Descartes's method is not aimed at the possibility of knowledge, as it is sometimes presented (and in which case it obviously fails to do what it is supposed to do). Rather, it is taken on the assumption that knowledge has already been attained. In Descartes's view, part of the problem not only with his contemporaries but also with most thinkers today, is that we confuse the acquisition and handing down of information with knowledge of the truth. The only certain knowledge according to Descartes is that which is self-attained and self-tested and this, just as Socrates had so wisely taught, cannot be learned and it cannot be handed down. It can be rediscovered only through one's own examination and experience. That is, instead of taking your own unsupported opinions or the opinions of others as a guide, the real "secret" of the search for truth is to become independent of your or any other age, to think for yourself. Only this will remedy the dangers of self-deception involved in other "false" systems of unphilosophical attempts at acquiring knowledge.

Yet another way to try to understand the Cartesian revolution is to compare it with the way Aristotle answers Descartes's question, "Who am I?" Aristotle, as we saw, claimed that all knowledge must proceed on the basis of definition. So how do you define what you are? You first give its *genus*—that part of the essence of anything that belongs also to other things differing from it in species —and then its *differentia*—that part of its essence that can be possessed by, or predicated of, only members of its own class, or *species*. (The species is the subclass of the more general class, genus.) Thus, for instance, according to Aristotle's definition, the genus of the term *human being* is "animal," while its differentia is "rational." Descartes raises a Socratic type of objection to this method of acquiring knowledge; you don't then know what a human being is unless you can also define animal and rational. And then whatever you define those as will, in turn, require more definitions, ad infinitum. The process, Descartes would claim, must come to an end—but where? Certainly not on a definition. Remember Euclid's axioms. They are definitions in a sense, but they are self-evident truths as well, like "any two points define a line." Descartes wants to find terms that do not need Aristotelian definitions, whose meanings can be seen directly by the conscious mind: the "clear and distinct" ideas that then become the elements out of which to construct more complex terms. This is in fact the direct application of the second and third rules of his system. Thus metaphysics, like mathematics, must derive its conclusions by deduction from self-evident principles.

The *Meditations* attracted a wide following among philosophers, scientists, artists, and leading intellectuals of the time. When the daughter of the titular king of Bohemia, Princess Elizabeth, began writing to the greatest new philosopher of her time and asking for his advice, Descartes wrote back that her understanding of both his *Discourse* and his *Meditations* was "incomparable." In 1649, Queen Christina of Sweden invited him to Sweden. She wanted Descartes to be her private tutor. He accepted the offer, but when he arrived in Stockholm the queen requested her lessons at 5:00 A.M. Accustomed to sleeping until noon, in less than four months Descartes caught pneumonia and died.

Descartes was found in his bedroom clutching an unfinished letter[5] that he had begun to pen to his friend Marin Mersenne:

February 11, 1650

Dear Marin,

    I just woke up from a . . .

His friend had died two years earlier.

Hobbes: *Leviathan*

Thomas Hobbes considered Descartes's *Meditations* work so derivative of Plato that he wrote in his review, "I am sorry that so excellent an author of new speculations should publish this old stuff." Apparently, Descartes was not worried, for he insisted that Hobbes's review be published as an appendix, exactly as written.

    Thomas Hobbes, Jr. (1588–1679), was born near Malmesbury, England. His father, the vicar of Westport and Charlton, enrolled him at the age of four in the church school at Westport, intending for his son to follow in his footsteps. A few years later his father got into a vicious fight at the church door and then disappeared, leaving his three children to be brought up by their uncle, a glover in Malmesbury. When Hobbes turned fourteen, his uncle sent him to Magden Hall of Oxford University. Bored and even repulsed by the prevailing Oxfordian scholasticism, Hobbes spent most of his time reading travel books and studying charts and maps.

    Three events seem to have been pivotal in Hobbes's extremely gradual awakening to philosophy. The first of these occurred when after graduating at age twenty, he was hired by the noble Cavendish family as a sort of travel companion and tutor to a young man only a few years his junior, William Cavendish, who would later become the second earl of Devonshire. The two took the opportunity to travel throughout continental Europe, and there Hobbes was surprised to find himself defending the Oxfordian philosophy, which, much to his surprise, was treated with great contempt especially by the French, Germans, and Italians. This experience inspired him, upon their return, to study more carefully the philosophy that before had not in the least bit stirred his interest.

    The second event came as a stroke of luck when between 1622 and 1625 he was hired by Francis Bacon to transcribe Bacon's lectures and oral notes and to translate some of his *Essays* into Latin. Thus, though Hobbes was already in his late thirties, by coincidence and almost without his own will he happened to become a personal student of one of the greatest living philosophers of the time. This further stoked his growing interest in philosophy and science that culminated with the third event, his discovery of geometry at age forty-two. Having recently been disheartened in his growing study of the classics by all the disagreements among the various philosophers and the completely different systems developed by the various schools, one day in the library he came across an open copy of Euclid's *Elements*. He read the Pythagorean theorem, which seemed to him probably false and certainly undemonstrable. Yet he followed the proof to its inexorable conclusion. Profoundly moved by seeing how the power of reason could attain absolute certainty in geometry, Hobbes suddenly began thinking about how—and whether—one could achieve the same level of certainty within philosophy. Thus armed with an avid aversion to the religiously tainted views of his immediate philosophical predecessors and a mathematical model of knowledge, he set out to purge philosophy of its scholastic influence and to develop a method for attaining absolutely certain knowledge to which end all the subsequent modern philosophers aspired. Nevertheless, certain strong medieval influences remained, particularly the paradigm of understanding the world in its entirety and as a unity. Thus what now really began to perplex Hobbes most of all was this: if the world was ultimately all one substance, could there ever be a distinction between one thing and another, and how could there even be perception (in addition to the thing perceived)?

With this burning question Hobbes approached some of the leading thinkers of the time. His support from the Cavendish family continued after William died and Hobbes became tutor to William Cavendish, Jr., whom he took on a prolonged trip to France and Italy. During this trip he met with Marin Mersenne's circle in Paris and in Florence he visited Galileo. He was so impressed by Galileo's mechanics that he saw in his method a key to developing a new system and it became an overwhelming passion. Everything could be explained in terms of the motion of bodies, even sense perception. Yet, unlike the experimentalists, Hobbes was equally moved by his insights into geometry and so developed a purely a priori mathematical system in sharp contrast with the prevailing inductive approaches based on the methods of Francis Bacon. He thus formulated the major philosophical insight that would propel his thinking on all subjects for the rest of his life, namely, that all things must be understood just as the ancient Greek Democritus had once supposed, in terms of bodies in motion. He embarked on a philosophical trilogy that would explain everything. In *De Corpore* he showed that all physical phenomena could be explained using geometry and mechanics. In *De Homine* he showed that specific bodily motions are the specific causes of all human mental activity, including thinking and willing. In *De Cive* he explained how the ideal human society should be formed and sustained to be in harmony with the way the world is.

Upon his return to England, however, Hobbes found that instead of embarking on his philosophical quest he had to deal with the political turmoil of civil war. Having just turned fifty, he thought he should give up his philosophical dream and help his country and so used his knowledge and growing influence to heal the two sides that had begun to fight over the divine right of kings versus the rule of constitutional government. His views, however, ended up antagonizing both sides; those loyal to the king saw him as a traitor for arguing that the sovereignty of law ought to be based on the social contract, while the parliamentarians were threatened by his advocacy of the rule of many by one individual. In 1640 he was thus forced to flee to Paris, and during the next eleven years spent in exile he not only began work on his trilogy but joined the Mersenne circle where by lucky coincidence there was circulating a new and unpublished work that would become one of the most influential documents in the history of philosophy—

Descartes's *Meditations*. Hobbes wrote brilliant, if often rather scathing, objections (as mentioned earlier). Descartes insisted that all of Hobbes's objections be published, along with Descartes's rebuttal, as an appendix to the *Meditations*. Hobbes's continued criticisms, however, so angered Descartes that after several heated exchanges he soon refused to have anything more to do with "the Englishman."

Because of the political turmoil across Europe stemming from the beginning of the end of the great monarchies, *De Cive* (1642) was the first of Hobbes's trilogy to appear. In 1651 he published his masterpiece, *Leviathan, or the Matter, Form and Power of a Commonwealth, Ecclesiastical and Civil*. At the end of that year, though still exiled from the British court and now under suspicion by Paris authorities for his attack on the papacy, Hobbes returned to London and made peace with the new regime. Now sixty-three, he began work on *De Corpore* (1655). He had by now further alienated the philosophers at Oxford for his attack in *Leviathan* of the university system as functioning mainly to covertly sustain papal against civil authority and to confound the people by their adherence to "old learning." He completed his *De Homine* in 1658, which presents a new theory of vision and an account of psychology.

In 1660, at age seventy-two, Hobbes published a severe and brilliant attack on the prevailing methods of mathematical analysis (*Examinatio et Emendatio Mathematicae Hodiernae Qualis Explicatur in Libris Johannis Wallisii*) and then an attack on current trends in natural philosophy, which would come to be called physics (*Dialogus Physicus, Sive De Naura Aeris*), in which he argued against both Wallis and Robert Boyle, as well as the other scholars who were beginning to form the Royal Society, the British group of scientists and scholars still meeting today. Despite an onslaught of severe criticism and even slanderous propaganda levied against him by his many enemies, Hobbes continued his attacks against what he saw as errors and misdirections of the new trends in philosophy; he was eighty-eight years old when he published *De Principiis et Ratiocinatione Geometrarum* (1666), in which he argued that the geometricians and their supposedly "certain" works, as Descartes and other mathematically and scientifically inclined philosophers had claimed, were no more certain than the faulty speculations of the physicists and as full of errors as the works of the ethicists.

From his seventies on, Hobbes enjoyed the protection and patronage of the new King Charles II, who it turned out had been a pupil of Hobbes while Hobbes was in exile in Paris. Thus, while Hobbes was widely regarded as a freethinker and, for his attacks on the church as a subversive atheist against all religion, the king bequeathed to him a lifelong pension and much enjoyed his presence in court precisely because it scandalized the bishops. The only proviso the king made was that in the interest of not further inflaming the public Hobbes would not be allowed to publish anything in England relating to human conduct.

Hobbes regarded knowledge as fundamentally empirical in nature, yet insisted that the appropriate method for inferring causes of things from their effects and vice versa had to be done via an a priori mathematical method. By carefully analyzing the elements of experience, one finds the concepts of matter and motion to be the least common denominators, and that is why he claims that physical bodies and their movements, as understood by geometrical laws, are the only valid subject matter of philosophy. Hobbes thus came to view consciousness in both its sensitive aspects—the ability to attain percepts—and its cognitive aspects—the ability to form mental models and to think—as two different aspects resulting from the jarring of the nervous system by the surrounding environment. Both physical and psychological events are covered by four subdivisions within philosophy. Geometry describes the spatial motions of physical objects. Physics describes the effects of moving bodies on each other. Ethics describes the movements of the nervous system. Even politics merely describes the effects of nervous systems on each other.

Like Descartes, Hobbes calls for a specific method of inquiry that will lead to certain knowledge in philosophy, but along a slightly different path. He called the method, which in many ways grows as much out of Bacon as it does out of Descartes and Galileo, *resolution and composition.* Like Descartes's second rule for the direction of the mind, based on Plato's division of ideas, *resolution* is analysis of complex wholes into simpler elements. Like Descartes's third rule, *composition* consists in synthesis, or putting back together, the parts into a whole. But the similarities end there. Whereas Descartes argues that the mind is something completely separate and distinct from the body, and not reducible to physical elements, Hobbes argues not only that the mind is not something separate from the body but also that, like the body, the mind is a purely physical thing.

Although *Leviathan* was supposed to be mainly a treatise on the philosophy of politics, it remains a fundamental work in metaphysics and epistemology, as well as a treatise on the philosophy of language and philosophical psychology. Paramount to both aspects is Hobbes's distinction between two different functions of the mind. On the one hand there is sense, imagination, and the movements arising from them; on the other, there is ratiocination—calculation, using words, looking into the causes of phenomena. The former is natural, the latter artificial in that it depends on the manipulation of language and the naming of things; philosophy's main concern is with the latter. Following Galileo and the emerging physical science of the time, which involved a new synthesis of empiricism and mathematics, in *Leviathan* Hobbes develops in precise modern terms the ancient Democritan and Epicurean atomic materialist philosophy according to which everything that exists reduces ultimately to physical particles moving in accordance with physical laws. Thus, for instance, the first law of motion appears in every body as a tendency toward self—preservation and self-assertion, which become a natural right. On this basis he argues that all organic as well as inorganic bodies exist in the primary condition of collision, conflict, and war. Similarly, the second law of motion manifests itself in organic things and impels us to relinquish a portion of our natural rights in purely self-interested acts in return for being guaranteed that others will do the same. This is how the antagonistic forces of diverse individual wills can exist in harmony through a social contract that forms the basis of the political state.

Spinoza: The Philosopher's Philosopher

Baruch Spinoza (1632–1677) came from a family of Jewish merchants that had escaped to Holland from their native Portugal to avoid persecution. In Amsterdam he attended the local school for Jewish boys. Known for arguing with his fellow students and teachers, he got into trouble for claiming that the Bible itself was no evidence whatsoever for God and that its authors were as ignorant about physics as they were about fine points of theology. The rabbis and teachers tried to silence him but were unsuccessful. In 1656 he was banished from Amsterdam and excommunicated by the Jewish community.

Spinoza supported himself by grinding and polishing lenses. Privately, however, he began work on a vast new metaphysical system. In 1670 he published his *Tractatus Theologico-Politicus* (Treatise on theology and politics). Christian theologians quickly banned it, calling it a work "forged in Hell by a renegade Jew and the devil." Spinoza thus has the distinction of being banned by both Christian and Jewish theologians. As a result, his masterpiece, the *Ethics*, never appeared in print during his lifetime.

Influenced by the new Cartesian method and the sudden success of mathematics and geometry in physics, Spinoza's *Ethics* is designed according to a strictly rational geometrical system with definitions, axioms, and propositions arranged in a deductive system. It begins with a discussion of God's nature, from which the rest of existence, even our understanding of existence, is derived. It should be noted that Spinoza's conception of God is anything but the traditional theistic one. Spinoza's God is not something separate and distinct from the world but is the world itself. God, and whatever is true of God, is to some extent true in each and every existent thing in the world.

Spinoza's pantheistic conception of God is an elaboration of a Parmenidean view of the world in which there exists but one unified, eternal being. Mind and matter, thought and extension, are but attributes of the one infinite and universal substance, God. You and I do not have separate identities, nor are we individual beings. We are each but an aspect of the one infinite being, God. Spinoza argues that what makes it possible to see the truth of this idea is the sort of rational introspection begun by Descartes.

Many philosophers, because of the technical precision of the *Ethics*, have referred to Spinoza as "the philosopher's philosopher." Everything in Spinoza's universe is knowable with perfect certainty through pure reason: we can use pure concepts, unfiltered by any experience, to understand everything. The human mind is epistemologically omnipotent.

Spinoza accepts the Cartesian notion of substance: "By substance," wrote Descartes, "we can conceive nothing else than a thing which exists in such a way as to stand in need of nothing beyond itself." However, though Spinoza is typically regarded as a substance dualist, his monistic (one substance) view is already anticipated even in Descartes, who writes, "And in truth, there can be conceived but one substance which is absolutely independent, and that is God," which Descartes equated with "infinite substance." Descartes's mistake—a deep and fundamental contradiction in the Cartesian system, according to Spinoza—was to distinguish between infinite and finite substances. The body—corporeal substance—is finite, whereas the mind—incorporeal substance—is infinite.

In this way, Spinoza takes the Cartesian definition of substance as that which is absolutely independent and then shows why there can be only one such substance; essentially, the idea is that if there were two such substances this would be logically impossible, for the two would limit each other's independence. Thus the Cartesian "mind-body" problem is solved; the assumed interaction between mind and body is as unnecessary as it is impossible. Body and mind do not need to act on each other because they are not two things but one thing. What explains the apparent duality, according to Spinoza, is that when the one universal substance (reality) is viewed from the perspective of its attribute of extension, it becomes body, whereas when it is viewed from the perspective of its attribute of thought, it becomes mind. It is impossible for two real substances to affect each other because by having influence on each other, indeed, by their very duality, they would lose their independence and therefore their substantiality as such. There can therefore be no plurality of substances. There is only one, infinite, Parmenidean substance. This is the centerpiece of Spinoza's system. Material and spiritual being form two sides of one and the same world: particular extended beings and particular thinking beings are the ephemeral and transitory states of the eternal, unified world-being; they are its modes. All multiplicity, the apparent self-substance of particular objects, free will, and evolution are mere illusions. Philosophy allows us to see the truth behind the illusion.

This enlightenment is achieved by correcting the understanding, the inner light of reason. Unlike Descartes, however, Spinoza begins with definitions and then adds the axioms. He derives further propositions or theorems until he has in every case provided a proof by demonstration for his conclusions. Part I of the *Ethics,* called "On God," thus begins with a traditional distinction between that which requires no external cause to exist and that which owes its existence to some other being. Something that is its own cause, because it has no external cause (i.e., is not contingent) exists necessarily; it needs nothing but itself to be conceived. This he calls *substance.* We see many different things, but in reality these are all just one thing. What makes this possible is that the one substance possesses infinite attributes.

Spinoza relies on a classical, fundamentally Aristotelian definition of knowledge, according to which we can know something only if we understand it through its causes. Thus his proofs for the one substance that is absolutely infinite and its own cause is a modern version of the ancient Parmenidean argument for the One. Like Zeno, he claims that the one infinite substance cannot be divided, nor can the existence of any second such substance be conceived without contradiction. And that is why Spinoza concludes what has probably been the most often popularized aspect of his philosophy, namely, that whatever is, is in God, and that nothing can either be or be conceived without God. This is the view of reality traditionally known as *pantheism.*

In the appendix to Part I, Spinoza goes on to present an elaborate refutation of Christian and Jewish theology, especially those aspects adapted from Aristotelian teleology, the philosophy of final purposes—the view that all things exist for a preordained purpose. According to Judeo-Christian doctrine, God acts so as to achieve certain ends, for otherwise the fundamental theological doctrines of sin and redemption make no sense. According to Spinoza, however, everything that happens does so through absolute necessity. Thus the enlightened philosopher transcends the various perspectival views on reality and experiences reality itself, *sub specie aeternitatis,* meaning "from the point of eternity." Becoming "one" with reality, that is, viewing it sub specie aeternitatis, is made possible in Spinoza's philosophy through his understanding of the origin and nature of the mind, which form the central topics of Part II. By the eleventh proposition he proves that when you perceive something, say right now this book, this is nothing more than God having that idea. You reading right now is nothing less than the world soul, the divine mind, contemplating one of its infinite modes!

However, neither the mind of man nor the mind of God has anything akin to the illusion we call "freedom of choice," as Spinoza so eloquently argues in Part III, "On the Origin and Nature of the Emotions." Take a look, for instance, even at your own activity of speaking; where do the words you say come from? Did you consciously *choose* them? Consciously *select* them? If you pay close attention to the activity of your conscious mind in the act of speaking or thinking, you will find the words appearing as if from out of nowhere, much as the words you are here reading are not created by your conscious activity. *You,* the conscious ego, are not consciously their cause. Once this is realized—that everything that happens, happens not by conscious free choice but of some metaphysical necessity (*metapsychological* would be the better word here, meaning "beyond the direct contents of consciousness open to introspection")—the mind attains a Stoic-like state of blissful joy, in which even our most negative emotions are transformed into a clear and distinct idea of divine blessedness in which there is unity with the Godhead.

This state is something Spinoza tried all of his life to realize, and for this the great twentieth-century philosopher Bertrand Russell called him "the noblest and most lovable of the great philosophers." Unfortunately, Spinoza lived out his life in exile in The Hague in south Holland, in virtual anonymity. Ironically, in 1676 —the year before his death, his lungs having been destroyed by years of inhaling glass from the grinding of lenses—he had a visitor: Leibniz. But the reason he came to Spinoza was not to learn his philosophy but to learn his techniques for grinding lenses!

Leibniz had been told that Spinoza was one of the greatest lens makers in Europe. He had sent Spinoza one of his own research articles on optics; in his reply, Spinoza had included the *Tractatus Theologico-Politicus.* This work ended up influencing Leibniz's own philosophical development. From that point on,

Leibniz, according to his own account, "conversed with him often and at great length."

Leibniz: The Great Calculator

Gottfried Wilhelm Leibniz (1646–1716) was born in Leipzig, Germany. He went to the University of Leipzig to study law, but under the guidance of a neo-Aristotelian philosophy professor named Jakob Thomasius, he devoted most of his time to studying the philosophical works of Bacon, Kepler, Galileo, and Descartes. His undergraduate thesis, written when he was only seventeen, "De Principio Individui" (1663), presented a nominalistic view of individuation and identity. After getting his doctorate in law, Leibniz worked for the elector of Mainz in Frankfurt.

In 1672 Leibniz went to Paris, where he met Malebranche, Arnauld, and Huygens. On his way home he visited Spinoza at The Hague. He was soon hired in Hanover at the House of Brunswick, to work as a librarian and historian. He held a series of other jobs, including diplomat, alchemist, and even engineer. He worked on draining the Harz Mountains. As an inventor he made designs of an express coach and something that would have to await construction for several centuries: a computer. Like Descartes, he invented an entirely new branch of mathematics: differential and integral calculus, which he published several years before Newton published his system of calculus. At one time Leibniz actively corresponded with more than a thousand people, among them many courtesans and princes. In Berlin he directed the founding of the Prussian Academy of Science and served as its first college president. Throughout his life he tried to apply philosophy and mathematics to everyday affairs. For instance, he once tried to demonstrate, using logic and mathematics, why a German candidate should succeed the Polish monarchy, and he used his calculus to try to make peace between Catholic and Protestant theologies.

The last years of Leibniz's life were tormented by the controversy over whether he or Isaac Newton had first invented calculus. (Leibniz, contrary to popular history, was not only first, but his system is far superior to that of Newton.) By then he had already fallen out of favor with the princes of Brunswick, who viewed his philosophy and academic propaganda as impractical and no longer useful. Unlike most great philosophers, however, he left no single great work, not even, like Spinoza, one that was published posthumously. Some of his original and powerful writing can be found in his two main books, *New Essays on the Human Understanding* (1705) and *Theodicy* (1710), but his most important contributions lie in his many shorter works, most of which were not published until this century and many of which, for reasons not understood, still exist only in manuscript form. But he died a famous and often lampooned figure, one of the most influential of the eighteenth century. The character of Pangloss in Voltaire's *Candide* is supposedly based on Leibniz.

Reality according to Leibniz consists not of one substance, as Spinoza and other types of monists had believed, nor in some finite number of different substances, such as Descartes and other mind-body dualists believed, but in an infinite number of individual substances. "Substances" can be thought of as "realities"; thus Leibniz was the first thinker to conceive of a many-worlds view of the world, an infinity of existences each of which is equally and fully real. This concept is in large part due to his analysis of the notion of individual substance, derived from the Aristotelian doctrine of true predication. The idea is that when the predicate is contained in the subject, an individual substance is complete in itself such that an all-knowing being could derive all true propositions about it simply by pure reason and without having to contemplate any other individual substances. As the ultimate constituents of the whole of reality, these individual substances (realities), which Leibniz called *monads,* are—like the Parmenidean whole—simple (without parts). "What is not truly one being," he wrote in his letter to Arnauld in 1687, "is not truly one being."

Monads are neither created nor destroyable; viewed abstractly, they are like physical points but, being unextended (nonspatial), their only essential attribute is thought. Following the Cartesian argument that substances cannot interact, Leibniz held that monads cannot interact with each other nor can they be causally related; each monad exists in a preestablished harmony with all other monads. Each monad is a "windowless" mirror of the entire universe. Monads form a hierarchy according to the clearness and distinctness with which they mirror the universe. The perceptions of monads vary in levels of confusion from minute perceptions so tenuous or mixed up that they exist at a threshold below consciousness to clear and distinct, fully conscious perception, which Leibniz calls *apperception.*

Relying on concepts from his infinitesimal calculus, Leibniz suggests that the rational determination of an individual substance is a derivative of the infinite universe of space and time; just as any infinitesimal part of a curve—the differential quotient of a curve derived from its analytic equation—contains virtually the entire curve, each individual monad contains virtually the entire universe. Thus it should in principle be possible to deduce all knowledge about all aspects of the universe from within a single monad. In other words, not only is knowledge of the whole universe possible, but it is also possible to attain such knowledge of the whole from any of its constituent parts!

Leibniz had a lifelong goal to develop a universal language that could be used to both describe and discover all aspects of the universe. His idea was to create a universal encyclopedia of all knowledge expressed in a natural language. All the words would be properly defined (as in binary arithmetic, where the infinite integers can be defined with only two signs, 1 and 0, so that they could be put in a machine—i.e., a computer) with each symbol standing for only one idea. The idea is that just as all words in English are composed of only twenty-six letters, all the words in Leibniz's universal encyclopedia would be analyzed into undefinable primitives. All that would then be required is a syntax for the new ideal language; one could then algorithmatize without reasoning the effect of reasoning, and the whole process would be so simple it could be programmed into a machine. Though Leibniz never completed his systematic program for all knowledge, it gained recognition, after his death, in the form of cooperative academies of learning in Berlin, Leipzig, Vienna, and Petersburg, and other collective institutions for the systematization of all knowledge based on his ideas arose such as the Royal Society in London and the French Academy in Paris.

In marked contrast to Descartes, who regarded history as not only irrelevant but deceptive in its inability to offer us philosophical insight, Leibniz is first to offer an interpretation of the historical developments in thought as a view of the development and gradual enlightenment of the mind, much in the way that, and on the basis of which, Hegel would later construct an entire metaphysical system. Like Spinoza, Leibniz sought to improve Cartesian metaphysics. But whereas the geometrical labyrinth of Spinoza's thought everywhere closes in on itself until it reveals a world of pantheistic monism, Leibniz's logical calculus is an open labyrinth of endless paths each leading into a different universe, a separate world, another reality. We are still in Plato's cave, but now it opens to an infinity of suns, a plurality of worlds.

Leibniz's improvement over the Cartesian system begins with a marriage between the Cartesian concept of extended, continuous substance and the atomists' conception of ultimate, indivisible, individual units of reality. The atomists explain reality in terms of simple, indivisible eternal units—atoms—but according to their essentially materialist conception the atoms are lumps of matter having no consciousness or mental-like properties. These two lines of thought combine in Leibniz's concept of the monad. Indeed, Leibniz called Cartesianism "the antechamber" of the true philosophy, and atomism the preparation for his theory of monads. The monads, as Cartesian substances, are not mindless atoms but self-acting forces and immaterial. The monads are fundamentally *representative* forces; that is, their "metaphysical energy" consists in the power of representation. There is nothing real in the world except the monads and their representations, which are ideas and perceptions.

Apperception, the name Leibniz gives to any perception that occurs as a conscious mental state, needs some additional explanation. You could of course call everything that occurs in the world of our sensations "perception," as the unreflecting mind has been conditioned to do, but this misses the point, first, that some perceptions occur as conscious events and others do not and, second, that the former must consist of the latter. This all-important distinction between non-conscious perception and conscious apperception is crucial for understanding Leibniz and subsequent developments, especially in the German traditions, most notably Kant and even the neo-Kantian movements including phenomenology. This is not merely a psychological point. In stating that obscure states of unconscious representation, which are present in the mind along with states of clear consciousness, give rise to the whole life of each individual monad, Leibniz is avoiding both the dualism of atomic materialism, in which the mind arises out of individual inert substances, and the monism of pantheistic idealism, in which the entire universe is one mind. The former leads to incoherent scientism, the latter to incoherent mysticism, both of which according to Leibniz are unphilosophical in that they deny the possibility of true understanding.

Perception is thus a purely mechanical process. Leibniz defines *perception* as the representation of the external in the internal, of multiplicity in unity. The representing being, without any loss of its absolute simplicity, bears a multitude of relations to external things. What now is the manifold, which is expressed, perceived, or represented, in the unit—the monad? It is the whole world. Every monad represents all others in itself, a concentrated all, the universe in miniature. Each individual monad contains an infinity in itself. A supreme intelligence, for which every obscure idea would at once become distinct, would be able to read in a single monad the whole universe and its entire history—all that is, has been, or will be; for the past has left its traces behind it in the monad, and the future will bring nothing not founded in the present: the monad is the bearer of the past and the forbearer of the future. Each monad represents that which is near at hand distinctly and that which is distant confusedly. Since all monads reflect the same content or object, their difference consists only in the energy or degree of clearness in their representations. Every monad is thus a mirror of the universe. And it is a living mirror, meaning that it generates the images of things by its own activity or develops them from within itself. All monads represent the same universe, but each one represents it differently, that is, from its particular point of view.

The natures of the monads consist in nothing else than the sum of relations in which the individual monad stands to all other monads, wherein each one takes account of all others and at the same time is considered by them, and thus exerts influence as well as suffers it. No monad represents the common universe and its individual parts exactly as do any other monads, but either better or worse; there are as many different degrees of clearness and distinctness as there are monads. When a group of monads appears as a body, it is indistinctly perceived. The essence of each monad is thus simply the position it occupies in the organic whole of the cosmos; each monad is related in a preestablished harmony to every other monad and shares actively and passively in the life of all the others. The history of the universe is a single great process in numberless reflections, each of which is an entire and complete universe unto itself.

Starting thus with his concept of representation, Leibniz ends with the harmony of the universe. The representations are multiplicity in unity; the harmony is unity in multiplicity. All monads represent the same universe. But each one mirrors it differently. The unity, as well as the difference, could not be greater than it is; every possible degree of distinctness of representation is present in each monad, and yet there is a single harmonic accord in which the infinite tones unite. This total unity is God.

In the *Monadology,* Leibniz asks what would happen if you stepped inside a "machine whose structure produced thought, sensation, and perception." For instance, the brain. Suppose we shrink down, as in Isaac Asimov's science fiction film *Fantastic Voyage,* to microscopic size and enter the brain. When this happens to the scientists in the movie, they travel into the brain and see electrical discharges along the neurons, which they conclude must be the thoughts occurring in that brain. But thoughts as thoughts, images as images are not flashes of electrical discharge along neurons! If we looked thus inside your brain and saw neurons firing, we would not see the images you see or hear the thoughts you hear. Likewise, if we shrunk even further, until we saw the atoms themselves out of which the neurons are composed, what we would see, according to such a materialist picture of reality, is mindless clumps of atoms floating in empty space. It would look like a constellation of stars. Where are the thoughts, ideas, images that are supposed to exist at some macroscopic level, where these lifeless little pieces of matter give rise to them? Impossible!

Such images are part of Leibniz's argument for his thesis that unless the ultimate constituents of the world are, themselves, living minds, minds as we know them could never emerge into existence as such. But what does it mean to say that the world consists not of lifeless, immaterial atoms but of monads, each of which is a living mind? Especially since Leibniz in several passages in the *Monadology* refers to the human body as a machine! Here, in one of his most powerful and original images, he explains why; starting with composites of simple substances, he distinguishes divine machines, or natural automata, which is what we are, from artificial automata, that is, artificial machines such as those made by us: the difference is that we, unlike the machines we make, are an infinity of machines within machines, forever, all the way down. And the only reason why each monad is not God—why you are not identical with the world soul, as in Bruno's and Averroes's philosophy—is that you are confused.

It may help in understanding Leibniz's work to know that by *a posteriori truths* he means true propositions that are known after the fact of experience to be so. By *a priori truths*, on the other hand, he means true propositions that are known prior to there being any conscious experience. All truths in his system are derived a priori, as he makes clear in another of his great works, the *Discourse on Metaphysics*, in which he declares himself to be an explicit Platonist in opposition to the Aristotelians of his time. Crucial to his reasoning here is the *principle of sufficient reason*, explained in the *Monadology*, and his advance toward our understanding of the traditional distinction between two types of truths, which Kant and all subsequent philosophers will call analytic versus synthetic truths. Whereas the a priori–a posteriori distinction is concerned with how we know whether a proposition is true, the analytic-synthetic distinction is concerned with what makes a proposition true. "All bachelors are unmarried," "2 + 3 = 5," and "Either it is raining or it is not raining" are all examples of analytically true propositions. To suppose, for instance, that John is a married bachelor would be to contradict yourself; once you know the meaning of the word *bachelor*—"unmarried male of a marriageable age"—it is impossible that John is both a bachelor and married. Why? Because it is not possible to be an unmarried married man. To suppose otherwise is self-contradictory. Further, when we consider analytically true propositions like "Either it is raining or it is not raining," we see that it is not possible that they could be false. It is always and everywhere true that either it is raining or it isn't. In other words, as Leibniz would put it, analytically true propositions are true in all possible worlds; they are necessarily true. Although I could in principle discover, for instance, that all bachelors are unmarried males by tak-ing a survey of all men, the whole empirical procedure would be a ridiculous waste of time and an elaborate self-deception; all I had to do was understand, from the inside, the meaning of the terms. Thus, in calling a proposition analytic, we are saying something about what makes it true. Notice that all analytic propo-sitions, such as the three above, are a priori; that is, they are known to be true independently of experience.

Consider, on the other hand, a proposition such as "The sky is blue." This is an example of a synthetically true sentence. The truth of such sentences depends not on meanings but on the facts of the world, and such sentences are in no sense necessary; it is possible for them to be false—that they are true is what Aristotle called "accidents" of nature or of some aspect of the world. Thus, for instance, if there was less moisture in the air or the refractive properties of oxygen were dif-ferent or our brains responded differently to particular wavelengths of light, the sky would be a different color; indeed, on Mars the sky is a different color, or would be seen as such if someone were there to see it.

Or consider the proposition "George Washington was the first president of the United States." It is conceivable that someone other than George Washington might have been the first president of the United States. That is, "George Wash-ington was the first president of the United States" is synthetically true. But con-sider now the proposition "George Washington was the first president of the United States or else George Washington was not the first president of the United States." This proposition is true in all possible worlds—even in possible worlds where George Washington never existed and in which there are no countries. In such a world, it would still have to be true that either Washington was or was not president—in that case, it would be true that he wasn't. This may seem like a fine point of language, but what could possibly account for such facts of the world?

In basing his system on such logical underpinnings, Leibniz is painting a pic-ture of a God that is an elaborate, perfect, absolutely precise infinite machine, a log-ical space of infinite possibilities that must exist not by design or by cause but of itself. It is like asking, "What makes 2 + 3 = 5?" or "What makes 'p or not p' true?" The problem, of course, is that it seems the propositions that are necessarily true—the analytic propositions—are of the sort that do not give us information about the actual world we live in. Here, however, Leibniz makes one of his boldest meta-physical moves, one that anticipates a move made by the great twentieth-century philosopher W. V. O. Quine in his article, "The Analytic Synthetic Distinction" (Chapter 5). But whereas we shall see Quine question the validity of the analytic-synthetic distinction, Leibniz argues that all synthetic sentences are really analytic. That is, *sub specie aeternitatis*—"from God's point of view"—all true propositions are necessarily true. In saying that all synthetic propositions are really analytic, Leibniz is saying that there are no accidents. Everything that is must be exactly as it is, and it is impossible for it to be any other way.

We must be careful to distinguish absolutely necessary propositions from those that are "accidentally" necessary, that is, are dependent on the way the world is. Once the world gets going, there will be a certain class of world-dependent (world-relative) necessities in addition to the absolute, trans-world necessities, based on incomplete inaccessibility and freedom, such as is enjoined only in the sum total of being, in the mind of God; thus Leibniz's God, unlike Spinoza's, is free. Such a divine perspective on everything, however, is not reserved for God but is open to each and every mind; for the key to each mind is also the key to metaphysics. That key is *logic*—which through Leibniz's philosophy allows us to infer conclusions about the real world from studying the grammar of our propositions. This is possible because you already contain all of your predicates so that if you (or anyone else) comprehended yourself—that is, had a complete individual notion of you—we could deduce every event of your life and every one of your personal characteristics, in the same way that "the quality of king . . . belongs to Alexander the Great." Further, you are as you are and cannot be any different any more than the world itself—indeed, the totality of all possible worlds—can be any different than it actually is.

The actual world, which Leibniz argues is the best of all possible worlds, is one in which everything has a necessary reason for why it is as it is rather than some other way; this is his principle of sufficient reason, mentioned earlier. It is impossible, according to this principle, that something could exist without any explanation, cause, or reason; this is the main principle of his metaphysical rationality. It may be the case that only God's perspective can clearly and distinctly reveal all the reasons until the necessity is made explicit, but the inquiry into the reasons is open to human scientific inquiry.

According to Leibniz, there must be some reason why the universe in its totality and everything in it exists at all. Why is there something at all rather than nothing? Because everything exists of necessity. Like Thomas Aquinas, whom he greatly admires, Leibniz answers this biggest question of all time in terms of an uncaused cause, an all-perfect being whose being is itself necessary. This he calls "God." But, unlike Spinoza's God, Leibniz's God is free, except not in any ordinary sense. God must act so as to create the maximum amount of existence—metaphysical perfection—and the maximum amount of possible activity—moral perfection. But God is free in the absolute sense—in that the absolute necessities that are world-independent come into existence with the actual world, realized by God through free choice.[6]

Newton: The World According to Modern Science

One of the most famous figures in the history of science, Sir Isaac Newton (1642–1727), was born at Woolsthorpe, near Grantham in Lincolnshire. By age twenty-six he had developed the binomial theorem and the method of fluxions, an early form of differential calculus that many regard, along with Leibniz's calculus, as the most important innovation in mathematical thought since the ancient

Greeks. Newton also formalized Galilean mechanics and discovered the inverse square law of universal gravitation. He made fundamental contributions to the theory of light and invented the Newtonian reflecting telescope that bears his name. He also claimed that his theory of universal gravity, the most comprehensive system of mechanics ever developed, provided clear evidence for the existence of God! (This is because by his own calculations the gravitational force would cause a slowing down of the planets and not just the solar system, but the universe entire, would implode; whereas subsequent physics would try to deal with such problems with an expanding universe, Newton's answer was that every ten thousand years or so God winds the universe up again.)

In 1672, at the age of thirty, Newton was appointed Lucasian Professor of Mathematics at Cambridge University, the prestigious position presently held by Stephen Hawking. Much of Newton's empirical and inductive method grew out of an extended response to and reaction against the philosophical and scientific views of Descartes. In turn, most seventeenth- and eighteenth-century philosophers as well as scientists were deeply influenced by Newton, especially the British empiricists Locke, Berkeley, and Hume; Locke's distinction between primary and secondary qualities (themselves derived from Galileo) and his causal theory of perception, for instance, were the direct result of his trying to work out the philosophical implications of Newtonian mechanics. Among Newton's most notable adversaries was Leibniz, with whom he had a prolonged debate. They disagreed vehemently about which one of them was the first to invent calculus (which most probably happened independently), about the absolute versus relative conceptions of space and time (Leibniz arguing for the latter), and about whether God was above mathematics and logic or whether logic and mathematics were above God (Newton arguing for the former).

Newton's most famous principle is this: "Abandon substantial forms and occult qualities and reduce natural phenomena to mathematical laws." This he tried to achieve through a union of Bacon's experimental induction with the mathematical deduction of Descartes, a combination of the analytic and synthetic methods that would lead to the establishment of mathematically formulated natural laws provided that it is presupposed that nature as it exists in itself is deprived of all inner life. This is what Newton means by his call for the abandonment of substantial forms and "occult" qualities.

One of the most remarkable things about Newton's world view, which even a mild understanding of some of the issues within the philosophy and history of science makes perfectly clear, is that the world according to Newton is not, by itself, in any sense obvious; nor does it, in any clear sense, make much sense. This is a hard thing to say, given that much of our so-called commonsense view of reality is predicated on it. But lest we find too much difficulty with the idea, you will no doubt recall that that world, Newton's world, has since been turned upside down and inside out (literally) by twentieth-century relativity and quantum physics. But even before then, in the nineteenth-century work of eminent physicists such as Ernst Mach, Newton's world, as we shall see, revealed itself to be a figment of Newton's imagination in exactly the way Berkeley had claimed. We might wonder why that view became publicly accepted (not to mention publicly conditioned and enforced). No one has ever given an account of this nor, as far as I know, even tried to.

The single most fundamental presumption in the world according to Newton is this: the physical (real) world does not in any way require mind for its existence. In other words, it takes as an absolute starting point the belief that there exists a mind-independent reality. Even the mind of God, in whom the universe itself is what Newton called the "sensorium" of experience—a divine theater just like the human mind is the "sensorium" of the brain—does not disturb the universe through knowing it, sensing it, experiencing it: "In him are all things contained and moved, yet neither affects the other; God suffers nothing from the motion of bodies, bodies find no resistance from the omnipresence of God." Thus the physical world exists independently of any perceiving minds, even the mind of God.

Such a conception, in which there is an absolute independence between mind and reality, accords with much of today's commonsense view of the way things are. When you look at, say, a chair, your looking does not in any way affect the physical chair. Your observation is a passive activity, like you're peeking into the universe from out of your head (or out of Plato's cave) through a keyhole, an epistemological voyeur. This explains why, regardless of how hard you wish that the chair would be otherwise than it is, your wishes do not change anything. Your point of view on the chair does not alter in any way any of the chair's qualities, such as its shape, position, how long it has existed, and so on. Your measurement of the chair's spatial and temporal locations, while they may be due to difference of viewing angle, margin of error, and so on, differs from mine, but the difference between our points of view is irrelevant to the facts of existence. The differences within our views of things are not real. There exists but one space, one time, one world: the physical universe.

Insofar as the mind exists in such a universe, it is an objective, passive observer. Its intellectual activity, which includes seeing, thinking, believing, and so on, does not influence the physical reality that is the object of our mental activity. Subjective mental states have no effect on objective physical states. Thus I cannot turn the chair into a table or a cat.

Few people, even today, recognize the hidden presuppositions behind Newton's world view. It is a world in which philosophy, as such, is not necessary. That is, words like *thing, object, world, reality,* and so on, refer not to constructions (or interpretations) of the mind but to existences "in themselves." This view of things came to be known as *modern scientific materialism*. It is a view that has come and gone; the world of twentieth-century physics is anything but Newton's world: it is the world of Einstein and quantum mechanics, in which the mind has once again returned to center stage as a necessary ingredient to reality, a world in which science itself can only exist, as such, within a philosophy.

Newton's God Versus Spinoza's God

Although God did not exist in Newton's world, Newton's world existed inside Newton's God, an essentially Christian notion, in which God exists as something separate from the universe: a divine creator to be found nowhere in the world or any aspect of it, but existing beyond the world, a transcendent supreme being. Compare this with the God of Spinoza, who is not transcendent but immanent. Spinoza's God is in no sense a Christian God, such as conceived in popular Christianity as a fatherly figure on a gold throne in some heavenly world, nor as conceived in sophisticated, scientifically and intellectually inspired Christianity as a transcendental superforce existing beyond the cosmos. Rather, Spinoza's God, like the God of Bruno and Averroes, is immanent. God is a mystical, rational force that is not just in the universe but *is* the universe. God is everything, including you. The physical world according to Newton is for Spinoza but one of God's "modes," just as the mental, spiritual world is another. In Spinoza's philosophy we saw that the language that best describes this immanent force of existence, insofar as it can be captured within the sphere of our limited human understanding, is the very same mathematical laws discovered by science. Thus, in studying the cosmos mathematically, one studies God, the object of our "intellectual love." Interestingly, when in the twentieth century Albert Einstein was asked whether he believed in God, he replied that he believed in "Spinoza's God."

What of course is at issue here for us is not anyone's concept of God but the nature of the relationship between mind and reality. Berkeley's philosophy, as we shall see, will be difficult to make sense of from inside the perspective of Newton's world. But we no longer live in Newton's world. We live in the world of Einstein and quantum mechanics. Common sense has just not caught up. In the new world of twentieth-century physics, the notion of physical reality as such has become subordinate to the concept of mind. It has come to question the fundamental presuppositions accepted without question as true within the Newtonian perspective which were not even realized at the time to be presuppositions, except for the fact that philosophers like Berkeley (discussed later in this chapter) will go to great lengths to try to make these hidden assumptions apparent. In doing so, the universe as such (the one universe consisting of the one true reality as it exists independently of any minds) literally disappears, replaced by an infinity of worlds, within which each one of us exists within our own world. Science and religion both must once again give way to philosophy.

Before we see exactly how Berkeley and Hume will pull the material world right out from under Newton's feet, we must look at Locke, who paved the way for them. The key to understanding the error that led to Newton's physical materialism and the subsequent myth of modern science that coexists (contrary to popular conceptions) perfectly well with modern religion, consists in drawing a boundary between primary and secondary qualities by which the realm of single, determined, absolute, interpretation-free, mind-independent facts exist. Philosophy is needed only here, on the inside of the border, where things are messy and unresolved; beyond that boundary there is no need for philosophy, only science, because "out there" all things are exactly the one way that they are and cannot be any other way. That, as we shall see, will turn out to be the greatest myth of modern science.

Locke: The Mind's Eye

Born in Somerset, England, John Locke (1632–1704) attended the famous Westminster School. He studied philosophy and medicine at Oxford University, where he learned the new experimental science of Robert Boyle. As a member of the Royal Society, he worked with and got to know Isaac Newton. Although he became a medical doctor, Locke turned his full attention to philosophy after reading Descartes's *Meditations* and seeing how a method might be worked out that could accommodate the progress being made in the newly emerging sciences.

Descartes, Spinoza, and Leibniz were rationalists who, like Plato, held that knowledge must be attained by the light of reason. Locke was an empiricist who claimed that all knowledge comes from experience. However, he fully agreed with Descartes that the mind and our ideas are better and more directly known than physical objects, which are known only indirectly. In many ways, Locke's *Essay Concerning Human Understanding* (1690) is a critical response to, and further development of, Descartes's views, only in a different direction. Locke attacks the idea of innate knowledge, arguing that all ideas in the mind can be accounted for through experience—via either sensation (mental events derived from the outer senses) or reflection (mental events evoked through introspection).

Locke distinguishes simple ideas like red, cold, and salty, which are atomic in that they cannot be further divided, from complex, compound ideas, put together by the mind, which do not correspond to the real world (like fictional objects). He explains the origin of all our ideas by analyzing complex ideas into simpler ones, and gives an account of the nature and origin of the mind and our ideas. He begins with a criticism of the commonsense distinction between our perceptions and our ideas. For Locke, as for Descartes, having ideas and perceptions are the same thing. Although anything that occurs in the mind—all mental events—are ideas, perceptions, too, are mental events.

Take, for example, your present perception of this book, of your hands holding the book, and so on. These are not things in themselves as they exist outside the mind. Rather, these perceptions are ideas that, at best, resemble the things "out there." The objects "out there" make impressions on some part of your body —hands, eyes, and so on. These impressions are then transmitted to your mind, which, in turn, creates perceptions. With what do you apprehend the perceptions? Obvious answer: your mind. But what, exactly, is it within your mind that makes seeing, as a visual event, possible? What until Locke had been only implicit is now made explicit. The all-important mental faculty, as Locke defines it, is the faculty of the understanding. In Locke's view, understanding is to perception as eyes are to things out there in the world. Further, just as the eyes are

"transparent" to themselves—the looking eye does not see itself, the eye, looking
—so too the understanding does not notice itself.

Locke claims that the mind at birth is exactly what Leibniz claimed it was
not, namely, a *tabula rasa,* a blank slate. This is the so-called empirical view of
knowledge acquired from the "external world," "through the senses," according to
which the newborn mind knows nothing and is thereby ready to learn anything
and everything, which it can do only through experience. If you read Locke's
Essay carefully, however, you will see that Locke does not claim that all of our
ideas are derived from experience but only those ideas that he calls *perceptions.*
The other category of ideas, which he calls *reflections,* by which he means not
"yellow, white, heat cold," etc., as in the case of perceptions, but "perception,
thinking, doubting, believing, reasoning, knowing," and so on, are not learned
through experience but are entirely innate: "This source of ideas every man has
wholly in himself; and though it be not sense, as having nothing to do with external objects, yet it is very like it, and might properly enough be called internal
sense." Thus, the so-called empirical view of knowledge, along with the "scientific" world view such a so-called empirical philosophy is supposed to afford, has
—contrary to the received wisdom—much in common with the philosophers
who, typically, are drawn into an "opposing" camp. The phrase "divide and conquer" comes to mind; for a fuller reference to what is here being asserted, see the
section in Chapter 2 on the Copernican "revolution."

Locke goes on in his *Essay* to give a detailed account of the history and origin
of our ideas on which our understanding of ourselves and the world is based.
Having distinguished perception from reflection, the former being the mind's
reaction to "external objects" and the latter being the mind's own reaction to its
own perceptive states, he uses the word *idea* to refer to any and all perceptions.
(Keep in mind that what Leibniz calls apperception applies both to Locke's
"ideas" [perceptions] and his "reflections" [apperceptions].) In effect, Locke is
denying the existence of what Leibniz is implying by the Leibnizian notion of perceptions as existing below the threshold of consciousness. And this is all happening simply at the level of the language that these philosophers are using to
describe what they take to be the incontrovertible facts about their experience—
a point that George Berkeley will in the next section use with great insight and
advantage in constructing the first fully "idealist" philosophy, in which nothing
exists but ideas.

In his *Essay,* Locke goes on to explain how just as the eye cannot actively
choose how it reacts to the light hitting upon it but is passive, so too the understanding is completely passive. Thus, "the mind is forced to receive the impressions," and the mind cannot "avoid the perception of those ideas that are annexed
to them." What causes impressions and the subsequent perceptions based on
them is that objects out there in the world have *qualities,* by which Locke means
powers: the power of objects to affect our minds. Ideas (that is, perceptions) in
the mind are the effect; the qualities of objects are the cause. Ideas of primary
qualities, which resemble objects out there in the world, are solidity, extension,
figure, mobility, and number. Ideas of secondary qualities, which do not resemble

objects out there in the world, exist only in the mind, giving rise to complex ideas (such as colors, smells, and textures).

According to Locke, our perceptions do not render an accurate and perfect picture of the world; rather, our perceptions are imperfect representations of reality. As in Leibniz's philosophy, they are each an individual "mirror" of a part of reality, albeit a distorted and imperfect one. These representations that we call "perceptions" and that he calls "ideas" ultimately consist in primary qualities only: colorless, odorless, tasteless, extended solid particles—the atoms of Newtonian mechanics. But since we can have no clear and distinct idea of physical substances, we cannot have genuine knowledge about the real nature of things; all we can see is that they are a "I know not what." What allows us to have knowledge to the extent that we do have it, however, is that all of our simple ideas are real: the mind cannot create them but receives them, passively, from the primary qualities in the things in themselves that exist out there independently of the mind. Ideas of secondary qualities are also real. But in these ideas the things existing beyond the mind are represented only partially and imperfectly.

Locke's *Two Treatises on Civil Government* (1690) is an important work on political philosophy. It was published in the same year as his *Essays Concerning Human Understanding*. Though motivated in part to justify the ascendancy of King William after the Glorious Revolution of 1688, it is widely regarded as among the greatest political works of modern times. Like Hobbes, Locke begins with an analysis of the "state of nature" as it existed prior to the formation of a political state. But Locke takes a much less pessimistic view than Hobbes. According to Locke, all human beings are created equal "within the bounds of the law of nature," which is reason itself: "reason, which is that law, teaches all mankind who will but consult it, that, being all equal and independent, no one ought to harm another in his life, health, liberty or possessions." Since in Locke's view empirical inquiry furnishes no certain and universal knowledge, and since assumptions such as that like bodies will in the same circumstances have like effects is only a conjecture from analogy, natural science in the strict sense does not exist. Both mathematics and ethics, however, belong in the sphere of the demonstrative knowledge of relations. Thus the principles of ethics are according to Locke as capable of exact demonstration as those of arithmetic and geometry, although their underlying ideas are more complex, more involved, and hence more exposed to misunderstanding. Further, though lacking the visible symbols of mathematics, these principles should be made explicit through careful and strictly consistent definitions. Moral principles such as "Where there is no property there is no injustice" and "No government allows absolute liberty" are as certain as any propositions in Euclid.

According to Locke, mathematical and moral sciences have a great advantage over the physical sciences. The reason is that in mathematics and morality the real essences and the nominal essences, or qualities, of their objects coincide. In physical theory, they do not. The idea is that when we think of things out there in the world of which our perceptions are but representations, the true inner constitution of the things themselves is unknown. That is, the primary qualities of things cannot ever be seen or grasped. Moral ideas, however, like numbers, points and planes, are entirely accessible because they are already conceptual products of our own voluntary operations. They are not copied from things in themselves "out there in the physical world." They need no confirmation from experience; they are the archetypes of reality.

Consider, for instance, the connection constituted in our understanding between the ideas of crime and punishment. This relation is expressed by the proposition "Crime deserves punishment." It is valid even if it were the case that no crimes had ever been committed and none ever punished. In other words, existence is not at all involved in universal propositions: Locke states that "general knowledge lies only in our own thoughts, and consists barely in the contemplation of our own abstract ideas" and their relations. Therefore the truths of ethics, like the truths of mathematics, are both universal and certain, whereas in the natural sciences single observations and experiments are most certain, but not general, and general propositions are only more or less probable.

Both the particular experiments and the general conclusions are of great value under certain circumstances, but they do not meet the requirements of comprehensive and certain knowledge. Such requirements can be attained only in the moral and mathematical realms. In this way, Locke constructs one of the most influential political philosophies of all time, in which exactly those propositions which are usually taken to be most subjective and least certain become the most incontrovertible and best known. What is brewing in such a new and revolutionary philosophy is, in part, the idea that society can be constructed in such a way that its functioning can become an absolute arbiter not only of justice but of truth and knowledge as well. A just political system must be constructed according so as to reflect and amplify the natural state of the world. Majority rule, the separation of church and state, the right of a people to change governments, the natural right of a people to overthrow unjust governments, the separation of powers within a government, are all ideas central to Locke's system.

Locke championed the idea that all people are born free and with like capacities and rights. Each person is free to preserve his or her own interests, but without injuring those of others. The right to be treated by everyone as a rational being holds even prior to the founding of the state; but then there is no authoritative power to decide conflicts. The state of nature is not in itself a state of war, but it would lead to war if each person attempted to exercise the right of self-protection. To prevent such acts of violence, the civil community is constructed based on a free contract to which all individual members transfer their natural freedom and power. Submission to the authority of the state is thus defined by Locke as a free act; by this "contract," natural rights are not destroyed but rather are guarded. Political freedom is thus an obedience to self-imposed law, the subordination to the common will expressing itself in the majority. Political power should therefore be neither tyrannical, since arbitrary rule is no better than the state of nature, nor paternal, since rulers and their subjects are all equally rational, which is not the case in a parent-child relationship.

In Locke's system, the supreme political power is the legislative branch, entrusted by the community to its chosen representatives, whose laws should aim at the general good. Subordinate to the legislative power, and to be kept separate from it, come the two executing powers, which are best united in a single hand under a king or monarch: the executive power (administrative and judicial), which carries the laws into effect, and the federative power, which defends the community against external enemies. The ruler is subject to the same law as the citizens; if the government, through violation of the law, has become unworthy of the power entrusted to it, sovereign authority reverts to the source from which it was derived: the people, who then must decide whether its representatives and leader have deserved the confidence placed in them. The people then have the right to depose of their leaders. The sworn obedience of the subjects is to the law alone, not to the ruler; so a ruler who acts contrary to the law has lost the right to govern. Revolution is then necessary.

Locke had a great and lasting influence on political philosophy in the eighteenth century, not just in Europe but also among the founders of a new, revolutionary country called the United States.

Berkeley: The Modern Idealist

George Berkeley (1685–1753) was born in Kilkenny, Ireland. He went to Trinity College in Dublin, where he studied Locke, Newton, and Malebranche, as well as earlier philosophers such as Bacon, Descartes, Hobbes, and Leibniz. He also became an expert on mathematics, physics, and optics from studying the works of Kepler, Descartes, and Newton. Unlike most of his contemporaries, Berkeley saw the scientific revolution of his day as the starting symptoms of the decline of the philosophical mind. Science and mathematics were in his view both ultimately on par with religion. For instance, in his criticism of the calculus of Newton and Leibniz, he wrote, "He who can digest a second or third fluxion meaning, in today's terminology, the 'derivative' . . . need not, methinks, be squeamish about any point in divinity."

Berkeley produced most of his most important works at a young age: *Essay Towards a New Theory of Vision* (1709), *Three Dialogues between Hylas and Philonus* (1713), and *A Treatise Concerning the Principles of Human Knowledge* (1710), written when he was only twenty-five. However, all of these works were ignored by the reading public and vehemently disliked by most philosophers, scientists, and mathematicians. Nearly everyone, even the theologians, regarded his views as absurd. His books having, in his eyes, failed, Berkeley journeyed to the American Colonies with the idea of founding a new university in the style of Plato's Academy. "The savage Americans," he wrote, "if they are in a state purely natural and unimproved by education, they are also unencumbered with all that rubbish of superstition and prejudice, which is the effect of a wrong one."

At Newport, Rhode Island, Berkeley awaited the monetary support he had been promised so that he could go to Bermuda and there establish his academy. But the money never arrived. He gave up the project and returned to London, where eventually he received a position as Bishop of Cloyne.

During his remaining years Berkeley continued to write, but his works continued to fall mostly on deaf ears. Subsequent philosophers, however, have held him in great esteem. His pioneering work on the nature of the mind, particularly his analysis of the complex, bundled nature of our ideas, and the elaborate argument against the existence of abstract ideas, David Hume called "one of the greatest and most valuable discoveries that has been made of late years in the republic of letters." American idealists considered Berkeley their founder, including Josiah Royce at Harvard who developed his own brand of absolute idealism. The American pragmatist Charles Sanders Peirce claimed Berkeley paved the way for the development of pragmatism. Immanuel Kant, though supposedly a critic of Berkeley's idealism, relied heavily on Berkeley's views, especially Berkeley's criticism of materialism; Kant's transcendental idealism incorporates Berkeley's famous dictum, *esse* is *percipi* ("to be is to be perceived"), tailored according to Kant's transcendental philosophy. Arthur Schopenhauer credited Berkeley as being the first to put forth the view that the world is but an idea in the mind. Ernst Mach, influential physicist and philosopher, claims to have been guided in his criticisms of absolute space, time, and motion by the work of Berkeley, which led him toward laying the foundations for the revolutionary idea in physics that the conscious observer plays a fundamental role in structuring reality.

Berkeley developed his philosophy in part as a reaction to Locke. Locke had shown that secondary qualities exist only in the mind, leaving the primary qualities in the things themselves. Berkeley argued that even primary qualities exist only in the mind. Locke's mistake, he claimed, is that he derived the objective existence of extension, hardness, weight, motion, and the other primary qualities of sensible objects through the (bogus) principle of abstraction. That is, Locke according to Berkeley mistakenly thinks he has an abstract idea of substance and extension—matter—as a something "I know not what" to which the mind adheres the secondary qualities of color, texture, and so on. A closer scrutiny of such notions and careful inspection of the actual contents of the mind, along with an analysis of language—the "curtain of words" that deceive us—reveal, Berkeley argues, that there are no such things as abstract ideas. If we do not allow ourselves to be deceived by our language and analyze the actual notions themselves, we shall see that the mind contains only particular ideas. What Locke called the "primary qualities" of sensible objects thus have no existence beyond the conscious mind. Each and every property of a sensible object exists only as a sensation within the perception of a conscious being.

In Berkeley's view, the entire universe, and all things within it, cannot exist without being perceived by a mind. Once we realize the truth about the nature of perception and the inner working of the mind we will see that

> all the choir of heaven and furniture of the earth, in a word, all those bodies which compose the mighty frame of the world, have not any subsistence without a mind—that their being is to be perceived or known, that, consequently so long as they are not actually perceived by me or do not exist in my mind or that of any other created spirit, they must either have no existence at all or else subsist in the mind of some eternal spirit.

Berkeley prefaces his masterpiece with the warning that you should suspend judgment until you have read the whole thing:

> For as there are some passages that, taken by themselves, are very liable (nor could it be remedied) to gross misinterpretation, and to be charged with most absurd consequences which, nevertheless, upon an entire perusal will appear not to follow from them, so likewise, though the whole should be read over, yet, if this be done transiently, it is very probable my sense may be mistaken; but to a thinking reader, I flatter myself, it will be throughout clear and obvious.

These words have turned out to be prophecy. No philosopher has been more butchered and explained away into incoherence than Berkeley.

At the beginning of his *Treatise,* he identifies the two major obstacles that we have erected in the way of clear understanding. The first has to do with the nature and abuse of language. The second has to do with the false opinion that "the mind has the power of framing abstract ideas or notions of things." The problem is with our language. Consider, for instance, some ordinary words. I am in my study. I am sitting on my chair. I get up and leave the room. Is that chair, which I was sitting on, still there? Berkeley's first and foremost point is that it is impossible to answer this question correctly unless we first specify exactly what we mean by the words *chair* and *there.* There are two, perhaps equally important, senses of the word. There is the general term *chair,* as a sign for all chairs, meaning something like "things to sit on," but that's not quite right, it's too general; maybe "things with legs and a seat that usually go with tables." But what about armchairs? There is a problem with this first sense of the word *chair,* by which it is a general term referring to a whole class of things; it is rather arbitrary, ultimately, where we draw boundaries between chairs and non-chairs. For instance, an elephant is not a chair. But then Sabu is sitting on the elephant. Well, but the elephant is alive. So we kill the elephant and stuff it and now Sabu sits on it in his (large) living room. Is it now a chair? It's up to us to decide how we wish to classify it. But clearly, this abstract sense of the word does not refer explicitly to any actual, particular, real chair.

Thus, the first sense of the meaning of the word *chair* does not refer to a particular real object. It's like the words *United States of America, humanity,* or *philosophy.* Are any of these words real? Well, there may be a whole class of real things that such names and general terms refer to, but there is no entity, as such, that is any one of those things. The United States of America exists only as an idea in people's heads. So does humanity. Why? Because that term, that symbol, is a tool of classification; there is no actual thing in the real world, Berkeley would remind us, that is humanity. Like "United States of America," this word is a noise we make consistently in referring to a concept that exists only in our minds to help us with the classification of real things. The real things are the things that you and I experience. For the word *real,* too—like the word *philosophy* and the words discussed above—has this double meaning, or function. One is to serve as a general term, which gets reified into what Berkeley will call *abstract ideas,* and the other is to designate actual things as they exist. But now the same is true of the word *exist.*

And to what does the word *exist* refer, not in its mistaken role as a designator of an abstract idea (i.e., not as something existing beyond the realm of actual experience, beyond the mind), but as an ostensive designator for something that we can touch, see, feel, taste?

Berkeley claims that the chair, the real chair—not the abstract generalization as a class concept to which there is no actual designated object, but the chair that actually exists—is not there when one is in the room seeing, touching, feeling it. This is not crazy. You can't sit on an abstract concept! Even the word *there* does not designate, in Berkeley's attempt to achieve realism within the domain of language, an abstract idea (an idea of something that exists beyond the realm of mind, that is, an idea that is not an idea, an absurd contradiction). Space is that which is right now being seen by you as the manifold within which objects exist. It is, as such, a mental phenomenon. The there, the actual phenomenon, is not inside a stone room but inside the mind. The reference of stone room is itself something that exists, in the sense of being tangibly, actually there, as an idea. Not an abstract idea! Even space is not an abstract idea.

To understand this rather difficult notion, we must understand what the word *abstract* means. It means, literally, "to exist not in space and time." And what Berkeley clearly acknowledges, and what will be one of the firm foundations for the philosophy of Immanuel Kant (Chapter 4), is that space and time are categories of the mind. According to Berkeley, they are not just categories in the sense of some transcendental (beyond experience) condition necessary for the having of experience as such, as they will be in Kant's view; rather, space and time are existent things only insofar as the experience called space and time is going on. In a nutshell: to exist not in space and time is to not exist.

Of the things that do exist, Berkeley says, "Their *esse* is *percipi*." You will find this phrase quoted again and again in various places, translated as "to be is to be perceived." But that all-important first word is usually, and notoriously, left out. Without the word *their* as a reference point, the phrase becomes exactly the sort of abstraction that Berkeley's philosophy was designed to eradicate from the enlightened mind. Let anyone try to demonstrate the falsity of Berkeley's statement with the word *their* intact. It is impossible. The full statement of Berkeley's thesis is incontrovertible. He derives it without reference to science or experience or experiment, purely a priori. In fact, though this may be a gross oversimplification, what Berkeley is saying is actually a tautology, a logically necessary truth that cannot possibly be false: "That which is mental is mental." Or "Events in the mind are events in the mind." He doesn't just stay with that, any more than Descartes stays with his cogito, "I think, therefore I am." Like Descartes, Berkeley attempts to erect a whole philosophy upon the certainty of his true statement.

The main thrust of Berkeley's assault on the (abstract) idea of a world out there "existing" (a meaningless term when divorced from experiencable perception) comes down to a very specific (not abstract), clear point: the so-called primary qualities are just as much mind-dependent for their existence (i.e., are themselves secondary) as so-called secondary qualities. The distinction between primary and secondary qualities did not originate with Locke, though that is where we first read of it. It originated with Galileo. Here is how Galileo put it:

> I feel myself impelled by the necessity, as soon as I conceive a piece of matter or corporeal substance, of conceiving that in its own nature it is bounded and fig-ured in such and such a figure, that in relation to others it is large or small, that it is in this or that place, in this or that time, that it is in motion or remains at rest [the primary qualities] . . . but that it must be white or red, bitter or sweet, sounding or mute, of a pleasant or unpleasant odor [the secondary qualities], I do not perceive my mind forced to acknowledge it necessarily accompanied by such conditions. . . . Hence I think that these tastes, odors, colors, etc., on the side of the object in which they seem to exist, are nothing else but mere names, but hold their residence solely in the sensitive body; so that if the animal were removed, every such quality would be abolished and annihilated.

In other words, drop a ten-ton weight on the lone cat sitting on the chair in the red room drinking the leftover sweet and sour and you have removed from the realm of existence the redness, the sweetness, and the sourness that existed only so long as the cat was creating, within its mind, those qualities. Those are the sec-ondary qualities. Whereas the roominess of the room, the impenetrability of the mahogany walls, the hardness of the chair, and so on, have not thereby been destroyed when the cat was crushed. These are the primary qualities. Or so says Galileo. And so says Isaac Newton. Berkeley is denying what they are saying, but more than that: Berkeley is asking you to reflect upon those primary qualities and the meaning of the words in those statements because doing so will make it per-fectly clear to you that Galileo and Newton are dead wrong in the worst possible way: they are self-contradictory.

Let us now put Berkeley's thesis in the following, explicit, terms. Consider the "things" you are right now "looking" at. Do they exist when you are not look-ing at them? Forget now about anything and everything not having to do explic-itly with those things that you are looking at. Forget your theory about the way the world is. Forget about everything you tacitly assume to be so about what you are looking at and focus just on what you are looking at. What is that? What are these things? And do those things, the very things you are looking at, exist when you are not looking at them? Simply find out by closing your eyes. What hap-pened? Everything you were looking at disappeared. This is so obvious that we should ask ourselves why it is that we are even writing this into a book or reading it and thinking about it. You see a chair. You close your eyes. The chair disap-pears. Ah, you say, the chair didn't disappear. Well, what disappeared, if not the chair?

One is tempted to say that your viewing disappeared or your image of the chair disappeared, and so on, but not the chair. Now, what Berkeley would at this point ask you is to reflect upon what—within the sphere of your knowledge—the word *chair* refers to. Because what Berkeley has just tried to show you is that you are confused about language or, more precisely, your language—the way it automatically interprets your experience for you—confuses you about what is going on right now and at each waking moment of your life. By "chair" Berkeley means the actual chair you are looking at, whereas what you mean by "chair" is not the actual chair you are looking at but the theoretical chair you imagine (but not even really that, since there is no image of that chair that you say is the real referent of the word *chair*) is there whether you are looking at it or not!

This sounds bizarre unless one understands to what Berkeley is referring. He is referring to these things you actually see; these are the things of which your world consists, and these are the referents of your object terms such as "chairs," "books," "rocks," "stars," "mountains," and so on.

In other words, even if there is a world beyond this world which you actually see—the world of tables, chairs, colors, shapes, and so on—these things you are looking at are not those things. Again, we've done this before, but let's do it again just because it is such a crazy demonstration of what is so obvious that it is bizarre to realize, once you do realize it, to what lengths we have to go to make this concept of Berkeley's clear to ourselves. Look at this page that you are right now reading. Find a particular word and look at it. Now cross your eyes. What happens? You can make the word split into two, move about, blur, get bigger and smaller, and so on. Now how are you doing that? Mind over matter? Hardly. It's mind over mind. You can do that because what you're looking at is not inkblots but images. Images are not made out of ink and paper! They're made out of the stuff that dreams are made of.

Now forget every bizarre thing you may have heard about what has been dubbed "idealism," or "Berkeley's philosophy," or anything else for that matter. The fact is that any way you look at it, the immediate stuff with which you are acquainted among your perceptions is not non-mental matter. This is what Berkeley is saying. He eventually goes beyond saying just that. People who take issue with what Berkeley is saying typically move very quickly beyond that first point, which is merely that what you are immediately and directly experiencing when you are looking at these things you are right now looking at, whatever they may be, are not made out of rocks and nails! First of all, are there rocks and nails in your head? No. At most there are *images* of rocks and nails in your head (but where are they? Hume will answer: nowhere). Rocks don't swell up and shrink depending on your movements. The rock you're looking at does. Now, you may say it's just a matter of your perspective on the rock. But take a look at that rock (or that pencil, or this book, or whatever) that you are looking at. Bring "it" closer to your "eyes." What has just "grown"? Your perspective? But what is that? Do objects have perspective? No. Viewers in a space have perspective. And where is that space within which all of this is being seen?

Let me put it still another way. One reason it may be so difficult for us to really see what is being said here is that no matter how you look at it, what is being said, if it is true, is proof incontrovertible that you are not in direct control of what you call your images. Berkeley makes this perfectly clear. Right now you're seeing things. How are you making these images happen? On the commonly received view, it's the stuff out there in the world imposing itself on your eyes, which then transmit what you are looking at to you inside your brain. But the generation, the immediate cause, of what you are seeing is coming from "you." Why "you" and not you? Because "you" are as much a projected image as all of these other things you see, all the things your language tells you are real things that exist independently of "you." "You" are neither the direct cause of you nor of the things you are seeing, the images. It is all happening somewhere behind the scenes, in the workings of your brain or whatever it is beyond the reach of your conscious awareness—what Berkeley calls "some other will," which ultimately he identifies with "God," the absolute "other" whose will runs the world, whose continual presence keeps everything from vanishing into a void of insubstantiality, into nothing.

Hume: "I Do Not Exist" and "The World Is a Fiction"

Born in Edinburgh, Scotland, David Hume (1711–1776) began his studies in law until he discovered the writings of the philosophers. To support himself he worked in a merchant's office in Bristol, then moved to La Flèche, France, the same place where Descartes had gone to school. There he began writing his monumental *Treatise of Human Nature*. Three years later he published it in England but the work was completely ignored. In his own words, "It fell dead-born from the press."

Hume tried, and failed, to get a teaching position in philosophy. To make matters worse, those who had read the *Treatise* accused him of heresy and atheism. Hume tried to support himself as a tutor, then a secretary, first to a general and then to an ambassador. After failing yet again in 1752 to get hired as a philosopher in Glasgow, he got a job as head librarian at the Advocates' library at Edinburgh, where he continued to write and further develop his views.

Hume rewrote much of Book I of the *Treatise* and used it as the basis for his *Enquiry Concerning Human Understanding* (1748). The material from Book III was incorporated into his *Enquiry Concerning the Principles of Morals*. Finally, by the time he was in his late forties, these reworkings of his original views began attracting a steadily growing audience so that by 1762 James Boswell was declaring him to be "the greatest writer in Britain." Hume had a tremendous influence on nearly all philosophers who came after him. He inspired Auguste Comte in his development of positivism, an antitheological and antimetaphysical system of scientific knowledge. His moral philosophy influenced Jeremy Bentham and John Stuart Mill. Immanuel Kant claimed that Hume awoke him from his "dogmatic slumbers."

Hume pushes Locke's and Berkeley's empiricism to its logical conclusion. Whereas Locke's views were tempered by commonsense notions of reality, often inconsistently, and Berkeley made an exception to his empiricist principles by relying on the concept of a transcendental other—God—Hume refused to make his philosophy bow either to common sense—for which he was criticized by Thomas Reid (1710–1796)—or to transcendental metaphysics. He wanted to create a fully consistent but purely empirical philosophy. Bertrand Russell, a sympathetic critic of Hume, remarked that by making the empirical philosophy of

Berkeley and Locke consistent, Hume "made it incredible." Indeed, not only does Hume deny the existence of a Berkeleian or Cartesian self, he also provides devastating empirical criticisms of many metaphysical concepts, such as causation, morality, space, time, and freedom, formulating skeptical objections to all inferences that go beyond immediate experience. Even impressions of the "external" senses exist only in the sensing mind, and he rejects all attempts to argue from the senses to the existence of a continuing physical substance outside the mind.

Hume develops Berkeley's criticism of abstract ideas and general entities to their extreme and ends up dissolving the idea of a continuously existing mental substance. He replaces the notion of a unified, continuously existing soul with the famous "bundle theory" of the mind that has so influenced twentieth-century personal identity theorists. According to Hume, the mind is an aggregate, or bundle, of discrete and discontinuous experiences; our minds only seem continuous to us because our imaginations smooth out the borders, bumps, and ceaseless changes. Hume claims that he will be applying Newton's experimental method to the human mind in an effort to develop a "science of man." In his *Enquiry Concerning Human Understanding,* obviously with reference to Locke's *Essay Concerning Human Understanding,* Hume analyzes the mind into a bundle of perceptions, of which there are but two kinds: impressions and ideas, thereby restoring "the word, idea, to its original sense, from which Mr. Locke had perverted it, in making it stand for all our perceptions." Recall Locke's question: with what faculty does the mind apprehend its own visual images as such? Locke's answer, and Hume's, is the *understanding.* This often overlooked aspect of their philosophical systems carries with it the implication that although I do not see the world, it is possible, through philosophy, to understand it. But *understanding* for these empirically minded philosophers is an empirical notion; that is, it is cast in terms of perceptions: the having of perceptions is an understanding of the things that are perceived.

Hume thus sets out, as did Berkeley, to improve Locke's theory of knowledge. In some ways he does not go as far as Berkeley, in others he goes even further. Like Berkeley, Hume is an ultra-nominalist, in that he denies the possibility of there being any sorts of abstract ideas. He does not, however, deny the existence of an "external" reality, although he does claim that it cannot be known with certainty. On the other hand, he goes to much greater extremes in removing fictional, imagined, or theoretically implied but nowhere experienced (ghostly) elements from our immediate sensations. That is, Hume's astute and often intense introspections lead him to point out that our immediate sensations are even more ephemeral and contain much fewer phenomena than unenlightened common sense ordinarily ascribes to them.

In Hume's view, there is no causality among phenomena. Finally, and in many ways most radically, he will conclude that there is no need for the supposition that there must be something underlying the various perceived qualities: he will thereby deny substantiality to immaterial as well as to material beings. All that is real are the impressions and the ideas. *Impressions* are perceptions that enter most immediately and vividly by way of the senses, whereas *ideas* are perceptions that are dim facsimiles of impressions. But what is an impression?

Tucked away in a footnote to his *Treatise* is a comment that he can find no ordinary word to refer to that aspect of phenomenal experience to which, with reluctance, he chooses to apply the word *impression:*

> By the term of "impression" I would not be understood to express the manner, in which our lively perceptions are produced in the soul, but merely the perceptions themselves; for which there is no particular name either in the English or any other language that I know of.

According to Hume, all ideas originate from impressions, each of which is distinct, exists only for a brief moment, and is disconnected from any other; how, then, can we justify all of our beliefs that reach beyond the contents of our present consciousness? Ultimately, we can't, which will bring us to Hume's problem of induction.

At this point, however, let us note that Berkeley was right in his drawing our attention to the nature, function, and power of language. For look what has begun to happen here; in making claims such as that Locke is misusing the word *idea,* that there is no common word for that which he will designate using the word *impression,* and so on, he too is drawing our attention to the language we use when we are philosophizing. Something as remarkable as it is subtle has happened, as important to our understanding of what philosophical enlightenment is (in the sense we mean) as the realization that our eyes are not windows and that to which the proverbial ocular windows open into is not reality as it exists in itself but a *theory.* And that is the realization that language is yet another intermediary layer between us and whatever it is that existence is.

There is a deep irony here. Without eyes we are blind. With eyes we no longer seem to be blind; there is now a sense in which we are no longer blind but also a sense in which we still are, because the things we see (i.e., the perceptions constructed by our minds or brains or whatever it is that is doing it) are not things as they exist in themselves but only appearances that, at best, in some sense and in some degree inform us as to what there really is. So our views of our views have gotten better but more complicated; further, and this is where philosophy comes in, we are in danger of becoming entrapped in the beautiful, luminous cocoon called vision. We don't want to get rid of it—that would be stupid. We just want to remain aware of it for what it is, which is very difficult. Likewise with our theories. We need them. We cannot do without them. With them we are smart and intelligent; we can do what other animals cannot because we can extend, to some degree reliably, our beliefs beyond our immediate perceptions into realms of which we cannot even form images. In an important sense, theories are intellectual extensions of the eyes. But Hume's warning here echoes Socrates: we must be careful not to lose ourselves in our knowledge.

Likewise with our language. We can talk, communicate, ask questions, preserve our beliefs, form written procedures so that others can follow in our footsteps when we have discovered something. Language is a tremendous acquisition on the part of the human mind, some would even say the greatest. But, again, and perhaps most ominously, language, like our eyes and our theories, becomes yet another double-edged tool, bringing us closer to the world while severing our consciousness from it, for we become as seduced by our language as we do by our images and theories. And so now philosophy has a triple function: stay wise about perception, theory, and language. We must, with Hume, proceed here with great caution.

One way to get an experiential sense of Hume's distinction between impressions and ideas is to strike, say, the surface of your desk. What you heard when you struck the desk is an *impression*. What you hear when your hand is no longer hitting the desk but you are still recalling the sound is an *idea*. It is important to note that both impressions and ideas are mental images, in this case auditory, or sound, images. Or look at the cover of this book and then close your eyes and remember it. The first visual image consists of impressions, the second visual image consists of ideas. And so on for the other contents of your mind. Run your fingers along the edge of the book; that tactile image consists of impressions. Now recall it. That tactile image consists of ideas. So although impressions and ideas are both mental images, ideas are fainter than impressions. But ideas are themselves representations of impressions. Ideas are not representations of things in themselves, of objects "out there in the world." Like Berkeley, Hume is deeply critical of Locke's supposition that that is what all ideas are. Rather, *ideas are themselves representations of impressions.*

There is however yet another distinction among our perceptions that carries over into both impressions and ideas. That is the division into simple and complex. Take, for example, the following auditory image: shut the book closed. That was an impression and it was simple. Recall it: that is an idea, a simple one. Listen to music; those impressions are complex. Recall the melody: that is an idea, a complex one. Thus, complex impressions consist of simple impressions and complex ideas consist of simple ideas. Second, in noticing "the great resemblance betwixt our impressions and ideas," we must be careful to not be deceived into thinking that "all the perceptions of the mind are double, and appear both as impressions and ideas." This is true only of simple ones; that is, every simple idea corresponds to a simple impression that resembles it. Therefore, there is a "constant conjunction" between them. And the impression always appears first, the idea later. This is what makes us think that there is a relation of dependence between them, insofar as every simple idea is a copy of a simple impression.

What, then, is the origin of all our ideas? Our impressions. No impressions, no ideas. This is the first principle of Hume's philosophical method. Notice that he has, once again, just made a point about language. A term is meaningless unless it is associated with an idea. Some terms have no idea to which they are thus associated. Yet we get used to using them because they are in our language. We are thereby deceived.

How can we discover which of our terms are thus merely false reifications from our language, or if they really mean something? Notice the parallel with our previous discussions having to do with the representational nature of perception. Once it is discovered that some of our images (e.g., colors, warmth) exist in our minds and are perceived as if they exist in the object out there in the world when they do not—that is, when they exist only in the mind—the question becomes how to distinguish those aspects of our perceptions that correspond to reality from those that do not. Hume is asking the same question, as did Berkeley, with the terms in our language. To miss this aspect of their philosophies is to miss a great deal; in fact, it keeps us from taking the next philosophical step, the one leading to subsequent developments into the twentieth century.

There is but one way to find out whether a particular term really means something or not. We must trace the associated idea back to an impression. If we can do this, then the term is meaningful insofar as it expresses a real idea. If we can't, then the term is just so much noise in our heads or blots of ink on paper. Thus far, then, Hume has analyzed the mind into perceptions. Remember that *analysis* means, literally, to break apart or divide something into its simpler components. He then further analyzed the perceptions into impressions and ideas. Next, he proceeds to the stage of *synthesis,* that is, putting these together by offering an explanation in terms of the principles that bind these elements together into a fully functioning mind. He now finds that all the elements of the mind are conjoined, or bound together, by various principles of association. And there are three principles of association among our ideas: (1) resemblance, (2) contiguity, and (3) cause and effect. Just as Newton's theory of universal gravity governs the elements of the entire physical universe, so the "gentle force" of association governs the entire mind. It is, as Hume says, "a kind of Attraction, which in the mental world will be found to have as extraordinary effects as in the natural, and to show itself in as many as various forms." The most startling thing about this gentle force within the mind, the force of association, is that it operates entirely without any conscious willing on our part. It is not something that we control, any more than natural objects control the force of gravity; rather, it controls us.

Now that we have a sense of what the mind is, what it consists of, and how it works, we can turn to the question of how knowledge might be possible. We can't just plunge into the knowledge-seeking enterprise. We must first understand the tools—especially since what we are studying when we look at things is not the world directly but our perceptions, which exist within and are subservient to the mental activity of reason. But, given Hume's analysis of the mind, what is that activity? Here Hume invokes his famous distinction, now called "Hume's fork," between (a) inquiry into relations of ideas and (b) inquiry into matters of fact. We've encountered Hume's distinction between "relations of ideas" and "matters of fact" before, in Leibniz's analytic-synthetic distinction. Recall that analytic propositions are expressed by a priori sentences whose negation leads to a self-contradiction, which are true by definition, and which therefore are necessarily true. Synthetic propositions, on the other hand, are expressed by a posteriori sentences that are not necessarily true and whose negation is not a self-contradiction; they are not necessarily true. Following Leibniz, Spinoza, and Descartes, Hume accepts that there are a priori necessary truths, but he argues that they are tautological. Tautologies are empty, merely verbal truths that provide information only about the conventional meaning of words. They do not provide any new information about the world.

Consider, for instance, the proposition "I am me." This just tells us that the words "I" and "me" are synonyms. It doesn't tell you who I am. Or consider "All brothers are siblings." This doesn't tell us anything about any particular brother that wasn't already known to be so by calling him a brother. Similarly, once we understand the concepts "thirty," "fifteen," "twice," and "equal," we already know that twice fifteen is thirty. The upshot of this line of reasoning is that a priori truths, not being descriptions of anything real, cannot give us knowledge of reality. Only "matters of fact"—synthetic propositions—could do that. Synthetic truths can be known only a posteriori. Therefore, if there is any true knowledge about the world, it must be based on observation. But does observation, which consists of nothing but perceptions, which are representations not of things in the world but of our impressions, connect us to reality? Not directly. But notice what Hume has done; in distinguishing analytic from synthetic propositions he has created a category in which to dump the contents of the mind that we know are not even possible contenders for giving us knowledge of reality. It is a category called *nonsense*.

In Hume's view, any proposition will be either analytic or synthetic, or else it will be nonsense. Thus, although we may not be able to perceive reality directly, we might be able to make true statements that are at least meaningful. We come upon a proposition that we would like to test for truth. We ask, "Is it analytic?" This is decided by negating the sentence expressing the proposition; if the result is a self-contradiction, the original sentence is analytic. If the answer is "Yes, the proposition is analytic," then the proposition is true but trivial. It is a mere tautology, empty of information about reality. If the answer is "No, the proposition is not analytic," we ask, "Is it synthetic?" How can we tell? Hume gives us the answer:

> When we entertain . . . any suspicion that a philosophical term is employed without any meaning or idea (as is but too frequent), we need but inquire, from what impression is that supposed idea derived? And if it be impossible to assign any, this will serve to confirm our suspicion.

In other words, a proposition can be synthetic only if we can trace the idea back to some impressions. For example, if "Fire is hot" can be traced back to some impressions, then it is a synthetically true proposition. If, on the other hand, some particular idea cannot be traced back to an impression, then it is vacuous and we know that we are dealing with nonsense. Notice that whereas Descartes started out by doubting whether all of his beliefs are true, Hume does something much more radical. He starts out by showing that most of our beliefs are neither true nor false, they are not even capable of being true, they are not even contenders. They are nonsense. Inside Hume's philosophical labyrinth, the concept of self is nonsense. God is nonsense. And so is the world.

The world at the time was Newton's world, a world in which we know the true causes of the phenomena we see. The science of the time, which was Newtonian mechanics, provided the method by which the true causes could be known, through such universal concepts as gravity. The Copernican-Keplerian-

Galilean model came to be accepted not as a theory but as the truth, in which the true cause of the motion of the planets was known. That cause was gravity.

Many of the greatest minds of the time went along with the Copernican-Keplerian-Galilean model, declaring, along with the influential French mathematician Jean Le Rond d'Alembert, "The true system of the world has been recognized, developed and perfected." Hermann von Helmholtz likewise declared that thanks to Newton the new science would bring an end to the knowledge-seeking enterprise; soon we would know everything: "[science] will be ended as soon as the reduction of natural phenomena to simple forces is complete and the proof given that this is the only reduction of which phenomena are capable."

Like nearly every epoch in which great advances occurred, the latter part of the eighteenth century was a time in which people believed that it was no longer possible that we could all be completely wrong about everything. Indeed, the idea that there is a world in which it is not possible that everyone, even a God if God existed in that world, could be completely wrong about everything, is nothing less than the idea that it is possible for there to be a world without need of philosophy. If there is anything we have learned thus far, it is that such a world is not possible. It is always possible that we could all be not just a little bit off, or that merely some of us are grossly mistaken: everyone in the whole world could be completely wrong about everything!

That's what Hume showed to his contemporaries. At the height of all the successes of the Newtonian scientific achievements, Hume showed in no uncertain terms that everybody, including and especially Newton, could still be wrong about completely everything. How? He didn't do it with science. That would have to await the work of Einstein, who showed that Newton's gravity was not the true cause of anything because it was a fiction and that Newton's space and Newton's time did not exist. It would have to await the advent of quantum mechanics to show that minds were not passive observers of reality, as in Newton's world, but were intimately involved in the game of existence. So how did Hume do it?

To understand how Hume did it is another wonderful opportunity to see how the activity of philosophy differs from the activity of science. Hume did it by showing that each and every one of Newton's major concepts, including gravity, was exactly what it would take science centuries more to discover: a fiction. And he did it not by doing any experiments or creating elaborate contraptions with which to measure physical phenomena. He did it by a philosophical analysis of the key concept in Newton's world: causality.

After all, what gives us the notion that there is such a thing as a world to begin with? It is the idea that all the variety of impressions are linked to their originating causes and that everything is held together by a manifold of cause and effect into one dynamic whole. Hume attacks the concept of causality, concluding that it is an elaborate fiction. He argues that whenever anyone claims to know something not present in his immediate perceptions, it is the idea of cause and effect that supposedly allows the knower to extend beyond his immediate experience to the object of his knowledge. In each case, an impression—reading a letter, seeing a watch, hearing a voice in the dark—is associated with an idea—a friend being in France, someone dropping the watch, someone speaking. Each idea is an idea of something not present to the mind at that moment. That's how beliefs about matters of fact beyond our senses arise: they are grounded in our sense of cause and effect. The letter is the effect of someone writing it and mailing it, which are the cause; the presence of the watch is the effect of someone having dropped it, which is the cause; the heard voice in the dark is the effect of someone speaking, which is the cause; and so on.

In other words, in every one of these cases it is the idea of causation that supposedly extends the mind beyond the narrow limits of the present moment, allowing us to reach beyond our immediate conscious experience: "By means of that relation alone we can go beyond the evidence of our memory and senses." But now Hume asks a devastating question: From what impression is the idea of cause and effect derived? As he explained earlier, the cause-and-effect relation cannot be known a priori. Consider the sentence "A causes B," where A and B are both events. A is the event of billiard ball 1 striking billiard ball 2, and B is the event of billiard ball 2 moving after having been struck by 1. Is this sentence analytic? No, because its negation, "It is not the case that A causes B," is not a self-contradiction. We can easily conceive 1 striking 2, where 2 doesn't move. Here's why. Suppose we knew everything there is to know about the two billiard balls—their size, shape, weight, movement, etc.—but never had any experience of one thing striking another. Could we still predict that when 1 strikes 2, 2 will move?

Hardly. If we never had any prior experience of billiard balls hitting each other, for all we know they might stick together (think of silly putty), or get absorbed into one another (think of water drops), or explode (think of grenades). The belief that when ball 1 strikes 2, 1 will bounce off or stop (depending on the angle and momentum) while 2 keeps moving is entirely dependent on our having observed that sort of action before. So, is the sentence "A causes B" synthetic? It should be. But is it? Well, applying our method from above, we must now see if we can trace back the idea of "cause" to an impression. Can we do that? I certainly do notice that I have the expectation that 2 will move when 1 strikes it. This clearly is the result of my having seen that sort of action before. My expectation at least seems like a reasonable one to have in this circumstance. But is it really? Hume gives two devastating reasons why it isn't.

First, in analyzing the concept of "A causes B," we find it consists of three components: (1) "A is prior to B," (2) "A is contiguous to B," and (3) "the connection between A and B is necessary." The first two conditions can be traced back to impressions. But not the third, and that's the crucial one. Why? Because no matter how many times I've observed billiard ball 1 strike billiard ball 2—no matter how many such impressions I've had—I will never observe anything like "necessary connection"; that is, I will never have any impression, as such, of necessity. What does necessity look like? Is it red? Colored? What shape does it have? Is it hard, soft? No.

But the problem is worse than that. The turkey sees the farmer. Food follows. The next day, the turkey sees the farmer. Food follows. This happens ninety-nine days in a row. On the hundredth day, the turkey, being a very good scientist, runs to the farmer, expecting that food will follow. Food does not follow, though it has ninety-nine times in the past. Today the axe follows. Thanksgiving! So how do we know we're not in that sort of situation with whatever we observe in the world, indeed, with the world entire? Remember, what we have to go on is not the things out there but our impressions. And we might merely have mistaken covariation for causality. Event A covaries in a certain constant way with event B; whenever A, there is B. But this does not establish causality. In the case of the turkey, a psychological expectation was set up in the turkey's mind between one set of impressions—the farmer—and another set of impressions—the food.

But this psychological expectation connecting the first set of impressions with the second set is, itself, just a covariation among the two sets of events, not the cause of any necessary link between them; the psychological expectation in the turkey's mind is not any sort of necessary link between the farmer and the food! In other words, this problem extends to everything. Go back, for instance, to our discussion of the Copernican revolution. For thousands of years people had watched the covariation of the sun moving from east to west every single day. They assumed that the cause of what they were seeing was the movement of the sun. The cause of what they were seeing was *not* the sun. But nor was the cause of what they were seeing the motion of the earth. I repeat: the cause of the motion of the sun across the sky was not the motion of the earth. The cause was their own minds. After all, the mind does not have direct access to the motions of anything! Experience comes to you by way of your mind's own habits of drawing its world.

Perhaps we could try to bridge the gap between the idea and the impression (or, more accurately, make up for the lack of there being any impression) with an argument. That is, we could try to justify the proposition "A causes B" with a rational argument by making it the conclusion of a syllogism:

1. I have seen ball 1 strike ball 2 a hundred times.

2. Each time ball 1 strikes ball 2, 2 moves.

Therefore,

3. Ball 2 will move the next time ball 1 strikes it.

This simply will not work. Clearly, 3 does not follow from 1 and 2; the conclusion is not forced. The argument is not valid.

We might try to add another premise, such as

1a. The future will in relevant ways resemble the past.

But this only sinks us deeper into an ever-widening abyss; we have just fallen into an epistemological black hole, better known as *Hume's notorious problem of induction.*

Our idea of causality—the principle of cause and effect, the cornerstone of Newtonian physics—is not analytic. It is not synthetic. It is nonsense. As if that weren't enough, proposition 1a is another cornerstone, not only of the scientific world view but of every philosophy we have thus far considered. It is called the *principle of the uniformity of nature.* Is it true? We now know what to do with such questions. Is 1a an analytic statement? No. Is it synthetic? Well, what impression is it based on? Can we trace the idea of the uniformity of nature back to some impression? Forget it. There isn't any such impression. There's nothing even close.

Take all the information scientists have gathered, from light waves and radio waves, about all the rest of the universe. All their telescopes, optical and radio alike, have thus far examined the energy equivalent to one snowflake hitting the ground. Compare that to the mass-energy of the entire universe and you'll have an impression (that's right) of how solid and incontrovertible all the currently accepted laws, principles, and so-called universal constants of science are. Not very. And how long have scientists been checking them (i.e., the current ones, not the previously accepted ones which were just about all completely different, even completely different concepts, having to do with things like phlogiston and ether)? A few decades. How much of the temporal extension of the universe have they checked? The universe is, supposedly, fifteen billion years old. What percentage of that is twenty years? One billionth of one percent. You now have an impression of the flimsiness of the so-called scientific world view.

By the way, do you see that Hume's destruction is not just negative, that is, it is not merely a skeptical attack, but gives positive affirmations of his thesis, in terms of an actual impression? This philosophical fact is often overlooked by philosophers who have themselves been corrupted, as many philosophers in Newton's time were, by the current scientific paradigms (not to mention previous philosophers having been corrupted by the prevailing religious ones). Hume was not.

So, how do we know that the so-called laws on nature work everywhere in the universe? How do we know that they have worked all the way back into the past and will continue to work into the future? We don't. Again, you can check this yourself. Is the statement analytic? No. Is it synthetic? No. Then it's nonsense.

Really, once you start thinking about it even a little bit, you will realize, as Hume did, that there are no necessary connections between any two events in the world. Well, then, why on earth (and this is not meant just as a figure of speech) do we—and why do all the so-called scientists—believe in the uniformity of nature?

Let us make sure we are clear about what Hume is doing here. He is inquiring into our ideas that go beyond the contents of our present consciousness; on what are they based? They all depend on relations of cause and effect. That is, such ideas are effects caused in us by impressions. Notice that Hume has not had to inquire into where those impressions come from or on what they are based. It is a brilliant philosophical move, akin to Socrates being too wise to get drawn into a debate with Euthyphro about how he knows that what the gods say is true. Socrates just gives him that. Because of course that argument can go on forever. Hume doesn't want to get into the endless dialectic about impressions. He just lets you have them. You can assume what you want about them, even that they are perfect representations of the external world. This is incredible! Because even if they are, the problem is as awful and devastating as before. It is just like with

Socrates and Euthyphro; let Euthyphro have his direct knowledge of what God loves. Big deal! The problem is so much deeper than that. What is the nature of the connection between God's love and a thing being good? Is God's love the cause? No. So even if Euthyphro knows truly what God loves, he does not know the cause of good.

It is the same with our impressions. Let them be as veridical as you like. Look at your impressions. How far do they extend? The life of individual impressions is extremely short. Everything else—your entire knowledge of the world, including yourself—must be based on the impressions you are having at this moment, then, a moment later, on those impressions. Do you see that this is impossible? You have ideas, which are of more than just the immediate impressions, but what is the nature of the connection between those ideas and whatever impressions gave rise to them? That is, what is the foundation of the causal inference? It can only be experience. But experience cannot provide sufficient reason in any particular case. For instance, to use one of Hume's own examples, I don't have sufficient reason for believing that my friend is in France on the basis of the impression that in my hand I hold a letter with a Paris postmark. The gulf between premise and conclusion remains because it is always possible that the premise is true while the conclusion false. Reason itself cannot bridge the gap.

So why do we all believe in the uniformity of nature? Here is Hume's answer: the "reason" we all believe as we do is not, itself, a reason. It is just a fact. This goes contrary to just about all previous philosophies, both Platonic and Aristotelian, which assumed that the universe and the mind each function in a certain way. They may each function differently, but there is some way that the universe is and there is some way that the mind is, meaning that there are certain stabilities, continuities, laws, tendencies, and so on. Human rationality and natural functionality, regardless of to what degree they were in sync, had a certain stable way of going on; even if there was a Heraclitan instability, there was a certain way that this flux was, rather than some other way, in which the logos (reason, breath, thought, logic, in all its multifarious meanings) participated or was even the cause. In other words, not just our belief in cause and effect but all of our beliefs about the world and ourselves based on that belief, are not even merely irrational! They are nonrational beliefs.

This conclusion overturns both Aristotelian tradition and common sense, according to which the relation of cause and effect is the foundation of all beliefs that go beyond immediate consciousness. Under the sharp knife of Hume's analysis, however, cause and effect dissolve into a psychological construction based on habit: it is a fiction without any reason or evidence behind it. We can never, even in principle, reach beyond the fleeting, momentary, chaotic experience of the present moment to infer truths about the world that reach beyond the tiny duration of brief instants: neither experience—which is fleeting—nor reason—which is but a psychological sense of seeming connections where there are none—can reach beyond experience. Since the relation of cause and effect is the foundation of all our beliefs about everything that we are not right now at this instant experiencing, the entire world built up by common sense as well as by science is a construction, an elaborate fiction, without any reason behind it. All the traditions have just gone up in Pyrrhonian flames; hence the devastating conclusion of Hume's *Enquiry*:

> When we run over libraries, persuaded of these principles, what havoc must we make? If we take in our hand any volume—of divinity or school metaphysics, for instance—let us ask, Does it contain any abstract reasoning concerning quantity or number? No. Does it contain any experimental reasoning concerning matter of fact and existence? No. Commit it then to the flames, for it can contain nothing but sophistry and illusion.

Hume is not merely denying Aristotelian teleology or Platonic formalism. He is conceiving the most horrible thing that could be conceived. Existence is utter chaos all the way down, with nothing keeping everything the way it is rather than some other way. Nothing in charge. Nothing guiding anything. Nothing.

Socrates had his own God, Heraclitus his Logos. Even the Stoics and Pyrrhonian skeptics had their inner peace. Hume's enlightenment came in absolute darkness, the penultimate awakening: it was no less than the beginning of the death of God. Indeed, in his *Dialogues Concerning Natural Religion,* Hume mounts a detailed and searing attack on all the major arguments for the existence of God and presents a devastating version of the argument from evil against God's existence. Bowing to pressure from his friends who feared for his life, he left it to be published posthumously.

Consider the proposition "God exists." Is it analytic? Well, Anselm, Descartes, and Spinoza all accepted some version of the so-called ontological argument for the existence of some version of God, according to which God exists necessarily and so the proposition "It is not the case that God exists" is, in their view, ultimately self-contradictory. So they would consider the proposition "God exists" to be analytic. Hume's response is that in that case the proposition is tautological and tells us nothing about reality, any more than the true sentence, "A necessarily existent being exists necessarily," tells us whether there actually is such a necessarily existent being.

In his third *Meditation,* Descartes relied on the idea of God to reinstate his beliefs about an external world and other minds; otherwise, he is left in the Cartesian circle of solipsism, in which all he can be certain of is his own existence. Berkeley used the idea of God to retain his notion of a world and its objects existing even when conscious human egos are not observing them; what you don't see, God sees, and so the existence of things unseen by you persists. Thus not only the Berkeleian and Cartesian worlds, but even the worlds of earlier thinkers such as Aquinas, Anselm, Augustine, and their philosophical avatar Aristotle, hang on the question of whether it is reasonable to believe that God exists.

Hume has no need for such a hypothesis. His interest is not edification but truth at all costs, even if it means losing the world; indeed, as we shall see, solipsism—which so often is regarded with such dread, as if it were the end of the world—would be no less than the discovery of a heavenly choir as far as Hume is concerned! For Hume affirms even his own nonexistence: the self is nothing but a self-deceptive illusion.

Descartes's argument for the existence of God hinged on his premise that the idea of God, which he finds among his other ideas when he examines, through introspection, the contents of his mind, could not have come from himself. Hume, already in his *Enquiry,* argues as follows:

> The idea of God, as meaning an infinitely intelligent, wise and good Being, arises from reflecting on the operations of our own mind, and augmenting, without limit, those qualities of goodness and wisdom.

In other words, man has made God in man's idealized image of man. Likewise, our ideas reach no further than our experience. We have no experience of divine attributes and operations. I need not conclude my syllogism—you can draw the inference yourself. So how do we come to have an idea of God, when we have no experience of divine attributes? Our idea of God has its origin in impressions having to do with ourselves. It is entirely anthropomorphic. I have an impression of myself as a being that to a certain limited degree can do certain things; I then extrapolate to an unlimited being that can do all things. I have an impression of myself as a being that to a certain limited degree and in a certain relative sense can know certain things; I then extrapolate to an unlimited being that can know all things absolutely. I have an impression of myself as being to a certain degree good; I then extrapolate to an all-good being. And so on. This extrapolation is made possible because we have the impressions of more and less; combining the impression of more with our impression of power, intelligence, and moral goodness, we can form an idea of ourselves being more powerful, wiser, and better than we are; we then augment, without limit, this process until we form an idea of God.

The most popular arguments for the existence of God during the so-called Age of Enlightenment, however, came not from such medieval scholastic methods but from a new emphasis on experience. Indeed, the universe itself—its existence (the cosmological argument) as well as well its order (the argument from design)—came to be regarded as the supreme evidence for the existence of God. In his *Dialogues Concerning Natural Religion,* Hume divides the arguments for the existence of God into anthropomorphic (the ontological, cosmological, and design arguments) and mystical. Together, these categories are meant to be exhaustive; that is, they contain all possible types of arguments for God. Hume destroys both categories, starting with the cosmological argument (also sometimes called the first cause argument, or "argument from the first cause") above. It is a perfect example of the application of Hume's method, discussed in the previously.

The bare logical structure of the cosmological argument as presented by the character Demea in Hume's *Dialogues* can be sketched as follows:

1. The universe exists.
2. "Q exists" implies "P exists," where P is the cause of Q.

   Therefore,
3. The cause of the universe exists.

Propositions 1 and 2 are the premises, 3 is the conclusion. But right away we notice that God is conspicuously absent from the conclusion, which establishes, at best, the existence of the cause of the universe. What would then be needed is another argument establishing that the cause of the universe is God. But, first, does this argument even establish the conclusion? No. We already have seen in great detail Hume's criticisms of the concept of causality. We don't know that premise 2 is true. How do we know that everything must have a cause? Is it self-contradictory to suppose that there exists an event without a cause? No. The argument fails.

But suppose we did somehow know that every event has a cause. Would the argument then work? The answer would still be no, unless we knew, also, that the word *universe* is not merely the name of an endless series of events, each of which is a cause of the next, forever, but refers to an event. That is, we would need to know, first, that the universe had a beginning in time. But even that is not enough. We would also have to know that the universe is not the sort of thing that could exist without a cause or else have somehow caused itself to exist. In other words, for the cosmological argument to work, we would have to know that the universe is not the sort of thing that can exist without a cause or be its own cause.

The characters in Hume's *Dialogues* argue as follows. Demea suggests that God, unlike the universe, exists necessarily. Cleanthes responds, first, by arguing that the idea of necessary existence is meaningless—literally, nonsense—and, second, that even if it weren't and such a concept applied to something real, we could never know that the universe is not that sort of thing. How, after all, does the theologian know what the universe can or cannot do? Further, in conceiving of something that exists without an external cause, premise 2 is denied. Indeed, if it were possible to conceive of a being that exists without an external cause, then the cosmological argument would be self-contradictory. The theologian could try to argue, again, that only God, not the universe, has this special property. But this evokes, without any reason (after all, what is the evidence?), a double standard: one standard for God, one standard for the universe.

In other words, if God caused the universe, what caused God? To answer, "God exists without an external cause," is, first, to deny that nothing can exist without a cause (premise 2), and it evokes without sufficient reason a double standard. After all, none of us has ever seen this universe come into existence, much less a number of universes, which would be required in order to be able to claim that we know how universes come about—whether or not they are the sorts of things that bring themselves into existence.

In short, there are so many things wrong with the cosmological argument for the existence of God that one wonders how anyone could ever have come to believe in God on the basis of it. Hume would remind us, of course, that people making such arguments are not reasoning but rationalizing, trying to explain their nonrational beliefs as if they were rational. The real "cause" for people's belief in God is bad logic, fear, and the wish to repress others. But nobody wants to see that in themselves, so they invent religions to justify their shortcomings and hide their flaws.

The argument from design is just like the cosmological argument and contains the same flaws, which are obvious once one sees them but invisible so long as one is blinded by unreflective acceptance. It goes something like this:

1. "Q is well ordered" implies the existence of a well-ordered P that gave rise to Q.
2. The universe is well ordered.

Therefore,

3. There exists a well-ordered something that gave rise to the universe.

Once again, there is no way to link the evidence—the existence, in this case, of a well-ordered universe—to the existence of God. First, the conclusion does not lead to the existence of God but, at best, to the existence of "a well-ordered something." We would thus again need a second argument to convince us that the only sort of well-ordered something that could have given rise to the universe is God. Second, to suppose that something with a very high degree of order can exist without an external designer is to contradict premise 1 of the argument from design. For, if God designed the universe, what (who) designed God? To answer that God is so well ordered not through the effects of an external designer but by God's own nature is once again to contradict premise 1. Third, to suppose that the existence of such a being is possible evokes the same fallacious double standard as did the cosmological argument.

What, then, are we to make of religion? Cleanthes' answer, in a nutshell, is that the dumb need it and the intelligent will see through it; therefore, leave it alone.

No world, no God . . . just *you*. But is there even a you? Hume spares nothing and no one, not even himself. In affirming his own nonexistence, he argues that the self is nothing but a self-deceptive illusion. In his *Treatise* he denies that he has a self and puts forth his famous "bundle theory" of the mind.

The mind is a bundle of perceptions. Perceptions come in two varieties: impressions and ideas. The life of individual perceptions, whether they are impressions or ideas, is short; flickering in and out of existence, "they succeed each other with an inconceivable rapidity." Thus from what impression indeed could the idea of self—i.e., the experience of unity at a time and identity over time—be derived? The term *self* is supposed to represent an idea of our personal unity at a time that continues unchanged over time. If it is a meaningful term and not just an empty noise standing for nothing, there must be some impression of which it is a representation. And the problem is that there simply is no such impression. The idea of self is not even a misrepresentation of an impression; it is but an insubstantial ghost—literally, a figment of the imagination. But whose imagination? Nobody's.

Hume is not merely proving the nonexistence of the self; he is making the much more radical claim that we do not even have any idea of such a thing! It is an empty word, like "God," whose reference is to nothing. Thus, technically speaking, Hume is not so much denying the existence of the self as he is claiming that to affirm or to deny the existence of the self is to speak utter nonsense. To see why, we must understand Hume claims that there is no impression that corresponds to the (imaginary, fictive) idea of the self. He is applying his own introspective method of paying close attention to the phenomena of his own experience without theorizing about them or framing any hypothesis that goes beyond the immediate data of his experience. Now, he isn't just looking, he is looking for something: a simple, unchanging impression that persists over time. All he finds is individual sensations, emotions, and thoughts.

For instance, right now you're reading this book. Probably you're sitting down. Do you feel the pressure of the chair against your rear? Focus your attention on that feeling of pressure. That's an impression. Call it $i1$. It occurs at a particular time, call it $t1$. You're reading words. These words. Now these. As you read, you hear the words in your head as a sequence of mental whispers, auditory images, sounds in your mind. Pause now a moment, close your eyes, and repeat ten times the sentence "I am an auditory image." That is an auditory image. So is this sound that you are hearing right now as you read these words. You now know what the phrase "auditory image" refers to. But be careful: it does *not* refer to those impressions that you just heard but to *these!* That is, the impressions that you are now hearing (as you read these words either to yourself or out loud) are the ones that exist now; those previous ones (which occurred a few moments ago when you were reading three lines up) are no longer here, they no longer exist, as you read these lines. Those impressions are then, these impressions are now; those past impressions can now only be represented, at best, if at all, as ideas (when you recall them in this, the new, present).

Impressions come and go. They vanish into nothing almost instantly. They can be "recalled" as ideas ("recalled" being in quotes because you're not bringing back the past moments in which those impressions came and went. Ideas do not have the same identity as the impressions of which they are representations; they are not one and the same impression). These words that you are right now hearing in your head are, likewise, new impressions.

Let us call the impressions when you first said the phrase "I am an auditory image," $i2$. Let us call whatever moment of time this new moment is, $t2$. Let us suppose that you're also hungry at the moment. You have a sensation of hunger. That too is an impression. Call it $i3$; it exists during some brief interval of time, $t3$. This impression might appear as a grumbling in your stomach, a feeling of emptiness, or a conglomerate of these. Suppose, on the other hand, that you now say to yourself, "Damn, I'm hungry." That phrase is experienced not as a tactile image (grumbling in your stomach) but as an auditory image (the sound of words in your head). It too is an impression. Call it $i4$. It exists at $t4$.

Let us suppose you're getting curious about how this section will play itself out, how it will end; this feeling of curiosity, a sensation of wonder, is also an impression, call it $i5$. It exists at $t5$. What about the light you see? That too is a sensation. The page you see may be glowing with a reflected light, or there may be what appears to be sunlight in the window, and so on. Focus on your sensation of light reflected from the page of the book you are right now reading. That visual image is also an impression. Call it $i6$ at time $t6$.

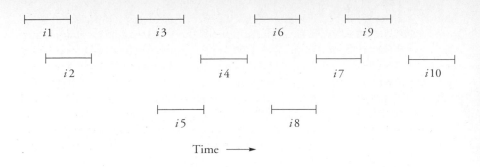

Time ⟶

Now: focus on the pressure of the chair against your rear. Do you now feel that same impression, $i1$? No! *This* one, the impression you feel as the tactile image of the pressure of the chair against your rear, is going on right now, impressions exist only in the present. This new impression began at the top of this paragraph, and it will last a while until it disappears into the cascade of new impressions. This feeling of pressure, the impression you feel now (is it even the same one you felt at the top of the paragraph?), let us call it $i7$. It exists at whatever the time is now; we will refer to this moment of time as $t7$.

Now comes the identity question: is impression $i1$ the very same impression as $i7$? Hume is not asking whether $i1$ and $i7$ are similar. He is asking whether they are one and the same entity. And the answer is no, $i1 \neq i7$! They are not the same perceptual object. Why? First of all, $i1$ exists at time $t1$, which is in the past from time $t7$, when $i7$ popped into existence. Second, impression $i1$ did not exist continuously from time $t1$ to time $t7$.

You might think that the impression caused by the pressure of the chair against your rear existed even when you weren't experiencing it. Do you see why Hume would object? He would say that no, an impression is a perceptual object that exists as a mental entity, requiring consciousness to exist. No conscious experience, no mind; after all, if we put some machine to register the pressure of the chair at regular intervals, that machine would not have any impressions unless it had, also, a conscious mind.

But what about the fact that impressions $i1$ and $i7$, even though they are separated in time and there is a big discontinuous gap in their existences, seem more alike than do $i1$ and $i2$? That is, the impression of the chair against your rear at time $t1$ is much more like the impression of the chair against your rear at time $t2$, even if they are not one and the same object (this one is now, that one was then); it is like the impression of the sound in your head when you repeat the phrase "I am an auditory image." Hume would not deny this (though he might ask you how you think you can know that any two impressions, which are not before the mind at the same time, are alike). Hume would agree that $i1$ and $i7$ are qualitatively similar, whereas $i1$ and $i2$ are qualitatively dissimilar. But qualitative similarity does not identity make. In other words, what Hume is saying here is that two things that look alike are not, thereby, in virtue of looking similar to each other, one and the same, numerically identical thing! Suppose my black 1993

Honda Accord looks just like your black 1993 Honda Accord. We can say, in a purely verbal sense, that we have "the same car," but that is not to say that my car is your car. That is Hume's point about differentiating between mere verbal claims of similarity and the strict logical claim of identity. Our two cars are made by the same manufacturer, they are the same model, and so on, but two things are not one thing! The identity of the object in my garage begins and ends in my garage and does not in any way extend into your garage.

And that, by analogy, is what Hume is asking about our individual impressions. As I sit at my computer typing these words that you are right now reading (ah—but are these words that I am right now typing the very ones that you are reading? Think about it!), I feel the pressure of the chair against my rear. This impression of mine might be as similar to the impression going on right now there wherever (and whoever) you are, sitting and reading, as my car is similar to your car; but just as my car is not your car, no matter how similar the two physical objects may be, my impression is not your impression—regardless of how similar the two mental events might be.

But that's just the start of it. It's far worse than that. Look now what happens without my ever having to talk about you or anybody else! The me that is here and now—is this the me that began this book? Is this person sitting here and now typing these very words even the me that began this chapter, this section, this page? Hume's answer is a resounding no! The problem is that the word *me* does not have the reference that we ordinarily, in our unreflective and unphilosophical consciousness, falsely think it does: it does not refer to a self. There simply is no such self, no unity at a time that continues to exist with identity over time. There is no unity at a time because of the disjoint cascade of individual impressions flickering in and out of existence; there is no identity at a time because these individual flickerings do not last very long, their duration is "unimaginably brief," not even a few seconds. Thus, in the case of "I am cold," the reference of the word *I* is, at best, directed to a bundle of perceptions. Remember that perceptions consist of two things: impressions and ideas. There is not even an idea corresponding to a self. There are only the impressions. There may be qualitative similarity but there is no numerical identity between one impression and another, even if they are exactly similar (that one was then and there, this one is here and now). So there is no personal identity over time.

In other words, I am as nonidentical to "myself" as I am to you! I may of course be much more qualitatively similar to myself over time than I am to you, but, again, qualitative similarity does not personal identity make. It only fosters an illusion. Memories, theories, ideas, all come and go; no permanence, no identity, all is flux. Going in and out of existence, individual perceptions (both as impressions and as ideas) have no persistent identity over time, except perhaps for very short Buddha instants. The self in Hume's sharp analysis is like a story we keep telling ourselves in each and every instant as we die.

Such dark and dreary thoughts, so full of dread! Yet apparently Hume did not fear his woeful ruminations. He tells us that his own dispositions, something from within himself, always drew him back out into the world. All it took was a rousing game of backgammon. Then, after thoroughly enjoying his furlough, he would be drawn back in to the heart of darkness.

1. René Descartes, *Discourse on Method,* trans. E. Anscombe and P. Geach, in *Descartes: Philosophical Writings* (Indianapolis: Bobbs-Merrill, 1971).

2. Descartes, *Discourse on Method.*

3. My *In Search of Self: Life, Death and Personal Identity* (Belmont, Calif.: Wadsworth, 1998) explores these nuances in much greater detail, through the character of Descartes, who finds himself caught in a series of dreams.

4. René Descartes, *Meditations on the First Philosophy,* trans. John Veitch (Open Court, 1901); reprinted in Daniel Kolak, *From Plato to Wittgenstein: The Historical Foundations of Mind* (Belmont, Calif.: Wadsworth, 1994), and with emendations in Daniel Kolak, *The Mayfield Anthology of Western Philosophy* (Mountain View, Calif.: Mayfield, 1998).

5. See my *In Search of Self: Life, Death and Personal Identity* (Belmont, Calif.: Wadsworth, 1998).

6. Thus the logic of existence, the infinity of possibilities and actualities, is so large as to contain more room than is contained within itself; that is, existence itself contains no boundaries. There is a certain metalogical incompleteness to the complete totality of the whole, an openness to reality.

CHAPTER FOUR

Kant and Nineteenth-Century Philosophy

Rousseau: The Romantic

In Immanuel Kant's study, directly above his desk there still hangs a portrait of Jean Jacques Rousseau, whom Kant admired so much that he called him "the Newton of the moral world." Rousseau (1712–1778) was born in Geneva, Switzerland. His mother died giving birth and he was raised by his father, a local watchmaker who could not afford to give him a formal education. So Rousseau got his early education from various novels and books, the most influential of which was *Parallel Lives* by Plutarch (46–119). This was the monumental biography of leading Greek and Roman figures, in which Plutarch tried to discover the universal forms of great human character by making formal comparisons between different individuals unified by common deeds, strengths of character, and so on. At the age of ten, however, he was sent to live with his aunt and uncle, who shipped him off to boarding school. Here, Rousseau writes in his *Confessions,* "We were to learn . . . all the insignificant trash that has obtained the name of education."

Rousseau was apprenticed at a young age to an engraver, which he despised even more than schooling. In 1728 he ran away to France and there met an older noblewoman, Mme. de Warens, who virtually adopted him and eventually became his lover. She tried to have young Rousseau formally educated at various institutions, including the Hospice of the Holy Spirit in Turin (a Lazarist seminary) where he converted from orthodox Calvinism to Catholicism (he would later convert again, to Protestantism), and then the choir school of the cathedral at Annecy. Unhappy with his schooling, Rousseau worked a variety of odd jobs such as engraving, copying music, and giving music lessons. He ended up being Warens's live-in lover for seven years, during which time he read Plato, Montaigne, Pascal, Virgil, and Horace, and composed music using a new type of musical notation. He wrote poems, operas, plays, and even a ballet, *Les Muses Galantes,* which was performed at the Paris Opera in 1747, with lukewarm reception. Warens eventually found a younger lover and Rousseau had a long affair with a hotel servant, with whom he had five children. In the end he married her but sent all of their children to orphanages.

In 1749 the Dijon Academy announced a national essay contest on the following question: Has the revival of the arts and sciences purified or corrupted morals? The prevailing opinion, as espoused by the church, was that humans are by nature sinners who need orthodox institutions to make them good; education therefore is for the edification, purification, and enlightenment of the soul. Rousseau submitted an essay, titled *Discourse on the Arts and Science,* in which he argued that it is the institutions of learning themselves that make human beings bad. Further, the arts and the sciences are the worst corrupters of humanity because they mold behavior and condition us away from our authentic passions, which we are given by nature. The arts and science condition how we speak and think, even what we feel, away from what we really feel and think. In addition, the artistic and scientific institutions seduce people with promises of wealth and glory, corrupting them into living false, artificial lives.

Rousseau's scathing essay won first prize. Almost overnight, Rousseau became famous throughout Europe as a new philosopher and social critic. Suddenly, within a year, his operetta, *Le Devin du Village,* was performed before the court of King Louis XV. His comedy, *Narcisse,* played at the prestigious Théâtre Français. One success followed another. Artists, writers, scientists, philosophers, and politicians all freely quoted him, often in openly criticizing their own institutions.

A few years later, in 1755, Rousseau decided to publish a more thorough version of his essay, called *Discourse on What Is the Origin of the Inequality Among Men, and Is It Authorized by Natural Law?* He then authored a brilliant novel, *Julie, ou la nouvelle Héloïse* (1761). Not only did this become the most celebrated novel of the eighteenth century, it helped launch the romantic movement in literature. A year later he published *Emile,* a fictional account of his provocative new theory of education. His greatest philosophical work was also published that year: *The Social Contract.* It begins with the famous words "Man is born free; and everywhere he is in chains." In it, Rousseau argues that the transition from the original "state of nature," in which all human beings once lived, to the modern "civil state" provided a firm foundation for modern politics. Evident in the work is the influence of Plutarch, who had been initiated in the mystical rites of Dionysus and inspired by the Stoics, Pythagoreans, and Peripatetics. Like Rousseau's other works, *The Social Contract* is vehemently critical not only of Christianity but of rationality and philosophical skepticism as well. As a consequence, in the end the French authorities took offense and issued a warrant for Rousseau's arrest.

Instead of facing trial, Rousseau escaped and spent the remaining years of his life as a fugitive condemned by both church and state authorities. It was none other than David Hume who helped him live in exile in England, for over one and a half years. However, still convinced that his enemies were out to get him, Rousseau apparently accused Hume of conspiring against him and once again fled. He returned to France under the pseudonym "M. Renou." Some years later he decided finally to defend himself publicly. He took his own name back. But by then the authorities had decided to drop all charges against him. Shortly before his death he published a candid and brilliant autobiography, *Confessions.*

Many philosophers have regarded Rousseau as not being systematic or rigorous, or criticize his views as being deeply inconsistent. Yet he has wielded a tremendous influence on some of the greatest philosophers. He has been called the originator of the romantic movement, mainly because of the powerful appeal he makes on behalf of the emotions. His emphasis on equality, liberty, and the supremacy of individual citizens inspired the leaders of the French Revolution and the builders of republican democracies. Yet his works were also used to support many authoritarian movements. His arguments to the effect that human beings can realize their true natures only through society and that it is the individuals who control the sovereign, for instance, inspired the Hegelians with the idea of national spirit. Others have suggested that it is Rousseau who made possible the suppression of freedom in the name of freedom with the idea that what makes freedom possible is a social contract, that is, by trading natural liberty for civil liberty. In doing so, according to Rousseau, "Each of us puts his persona and all his power in common under the supreme direction of the general will, and, in our corporate capacity, we receive each member as an indivisible part of a whole."

Rousseau claims that anyone who does not obey the "general will" must be forced to do so: it is through the social contract that a human being is "forced to be free." Bertrand Russell thus calls Rousseau

> the inventor of the political philosophy of pseudo-democratic dictatorships as opposed to traditional absolute monarchies. Ever since his time, those who considered themselves reformers have been divided into two groups, those who followed him and those who followed Locke. . . . At the present time, Hitler is an outcome of Rousseau; Roosevelt and Churchill, of Locke.[1]

In Rousseau's view, the will of the political leader is the incarnation of the general will, which reflects the sum of the individual wills of all the citizens.

Imannuel Kant, as we are about to see, drew much inspiration from Rousseau. Especially influential was Rousseau's claim that if each individual citizen was given enough information and the freedom to choose, all citizens would, independently of each other—since they are all directed to the same will to do the common good—arrive at the general will for the good of all humankind.

Kant: The Transcendental Idealist

Immanuel Kant (1724–1804) was born at Königsberg in East Prussia (today's Russia), where his grandfather had emigrated from Scotland. The school he attended raised children according to the tenets of Pietism, a seventeenth-century Christian evangelical movement emphasizing devotional meetings, Bible study, and personal religious experience. His mother, who had no formal education, and his father, who made saddles for a living, wanted him to have a college education and so in 1740, when he was sixteen, they enrolled him in the University of Königsberg. At the time, the philosophy of Leibniz and the science of Newton dominated not only the university but much of continental Europe as well; many, perhaps most, scholars had come to believe that philosophy, science, and mathematics would soon integrate into one complete system of knowledge.

Kant was extremely studious and competent but showed no particular flair or originality, and after graduating he got no offer from the university. He supported himself over the next ten years by hiring himself out as a private tutor in science, mathematics, and philosophy. In 1755 the University of Königsberg offered him a job, a lowly instructor position without any official title. For the next fifteen years he dutifully stayed in this post without any promotion until 1770 when, at age forty-six, he was finally promoted to the position of professor of logic and metaphysics.

Kant's personal life was quiet and unassuming. Only one controversy occurred when he was reprimanded, by no less than the Prussian king, Frederick William II, for the "distortion of many leading and fundamental doctrines of holy writ and Christianity." The king ordered Kant not to lecture or write further on such topics. Kant dutifully obeyed the king's orders until the day the king died, when Kant promptly resumed. He had few friends, hardly ever socialized, and never married. The only place he ever went was for his daily walk, at half past four. He walked up and down his street exactly eight times. His neighbors considered him a rather eccentric old recluse.

Kant was already fifty-seven years old, living the life of a quiet old professor nearing the end of a singularly unillustrious career, when he published his first philosophy book. It had a mixed reception—at first. Some said that it made no sense at all or that it was unreadable. Others claimed it was the greatest single work of philosophy ever written.

Today there can be no doubt that the *Critique of Pure Reason* is one of the major achievements in the history of philosophy. Published in 1781, it brought Kant great fame. Philosophers all over Europe suddenly began proclaiming themselves "Kantians." It quickly became the book everyone was talking and writing about. And then, as if out of nowhere, less than two years later Kant followed with his *Prolegomena to Any Future Metaphysics.* Then came the *Foundations of the Metaphysics of Ethics* in 1785, *Metaphysical First Principles of Natural Science* in 1786, a revision of the *Critique of Pure Reason* in 1787, the *Critique of Practical Reason* in 1788, the *Critique of Judgment* in 1790, *Religion Within the Limits of Mere Reason* in 1793, and *Perpetual Peace* in 1795. Philosophy would never be the same.

Kant's writings (except the *Foundations of the Metaphysics of Ethics,* which is quite readable) are among the most difficult in philosophy. One twentieth-century philosopher, Anthony Flew, calls the *Critique of Pure Reason* "one of the greatest masterpieces of philosophy, although also one of the most unreadable." Kant himself called it "dry, obscure, contrary to all ordinary ideas, and on top of that prolix." It is for this reason that Kant wrote his *Prolegomena to Any Future Metaphysics.* The idea was to provide a book for students and teachers that would be much shorter than the *Critique* and more accessible. Understanding the central purpose of the *Critique of Pure Reason,* "which discusses the pure faculty of reason in its whole compass and bounds, will remain the foundation, to which the *Prolegomena,* as a preliminary exercise, refer; for critique as a science must first be established as complete and perfect before we can think of letting metaphysics appear on the scene or even have the most distant hope of attaining it."

It is important to understand what Kant means by *metaphysics*. The term is an arbitrary title, invented around 70 B.C.E. by Andronicus of Rhodes, given to a collection of Aristotle's writings that came after his *Physics,* meaning "after" (*meta*) the physics. Since then, however, it has come to be used as a general term having to do with the aspect of philosophy that happened to be covered in that collection, "the study of being." What is meant by this? A good place to begin is with Descartes's famous example of a piece of wax. First of all, Descartes notices that as the wax is warmed, it becomes first soft and then liquid; every one of its properties changes. Has anything remained the same? What *is* the "thing" that remains through all the changes? Not the shape. Not the color. "That which has shape and color." And what is *that*? All that remains the same across the changes is its "extension" (the "thing" does not cease to take up space), but neither space nor extension are objects of perception: all you ever see are colored shapes and figures. So the idea of there being something "beneath" all the changes in the wax is *substance,* meaning, literally, "standing beneath." From the time of the ancient Greeks, the notion of substance had come to be closely associated with the idea of reality, based on the Parmenidean notion that ultimate reality is permanent and unchanging. But, further, even if space or the idea of extension were the "objects" of our perception, they would then be no different than any other aspect of the wax as it is represented in perception, since "the perception I have of it is a case not of vision or touch or imagination . . . but of purely mental scrutiny." Likewise for all objects that immediately appear before you right now—the book you hold in your hands, the light you see reflecting off the objects, all the things you see, smell, taste, and touch:

> I now know that even bodies are not strictly perceived by the senses or the faculty of the imagination but by the intellect alone, and that this perception derives not from their being touched or seen but from their being understood.

This is in fact the one point that, according to Hume, all philosophers universally accept. Descartes, Hume, and Kant certainly accept it; but, in that case, how are we ever to have knowledge of the wax as it exists in reality independently of our own understanding—knowledge of substance, of "being in itself"? Descartes's answer, and the answer of all so-called rationalist philosophers, is that the mind can have knowledge of physical substance through pure reason. It is possible for us to thus go beyond what is given to us in our own minds, as Spinoza and Leibniz also argued, using rational tools such as mathematics to polish the mind into perfection.

Apparently Kant, too, assumed that such a thing could be possible until he read Hume's criticisms of a priori necessary truths (found in the domain of "relations of ideas," versus "matters of fact"): not that there aren't any, but that they are merely empty tautologies. The only possibly real content would have to come from a posteriori synthetic truths, which come to the mind in the form of perceptions; but, as Hume showed, these exist only as momentary, flickering sensations, or—even worse—as fictional abstract ideas in the mind. So how can we have knowledge of things in themselves? For Kant, this is the central problem not only of metaphysics but of the whole of philosophy as well.

Every attempt to solve the problem of metaphysics, Kant argues, had thus far been thwarted not so much by lack of available solutions but by the presence of too many solutions. That is, for every solution to the problem of metaphysics, philosophers have constructed competing solutions in terms of a completely different method for acquiring true knowledge of reality:

> It seems almost ridiculous, while very other science is continually advancing, that in this, which pretends to be Wisdom incarnate, for whose oracle every one inquires, we should constantly move round the same spot, without gaining a single step.

What we need, then, is to be able to take the all-important first step in the right direction—but which way could that possibly be, asks Kant, when every attempt to solve the problem of metaphysics has ended in a dead end? Rationalist systems of pure reason, built using a priori analytic truths, have given rise to dogmatic beliefs such as Berkeley's Omniperceiving God, Descartes's Self, and Descartes's Nondeceiving God. Meanwhile, empiricist systems of pure experience, built using a posteriori synthetic truths, give rise to skeptical doubts, such as Hume's No-Self, No-God, No-World. So Kant sets out to find an alternative to both empiricism and rationalism as a way of avoiding both dogmatism and skepticism.

Recall Hume's analytic/synthetic distinction. Analytic propositions (like "All bachelors are married," in which the predicate is already contained in the subject) are known a priori (that is, "independent of experience, and even of all sensuous expressions") and synthetic propositions (like "The cat is hungry," in which the predicate is not already contained in the subject) are known a posteriori (that is, by sense experience). Rationalists took the former path; empiricists took the latter. This brought us to Hume's fork (Chapter 3); both roads are a dead end. But what if there is a path between the two paths, one so narrow that every great philosopher had thus far missed it and now it took a scrupulous, methodical pedant like Kant to find it? "The path to truth is thin as a razor," warns an ancient proverb from the East. "Few can cross it without being divided."

Kant finds the thin and narrow, apparently self-contradictory, path that Hume failed to notice: the way of the synthetic a priori. It is possible, claims Kant, to make meaningful statements about the world that are derived from experience (but not in the way Hume and other empiricists thought), whose truth is known a priori—independently of any experience! This, then, becomes Kant's metaphysical path to knowledge, the way of synthetic a priori truth. Here Kant proceeds to forge a new philosophical path, at the juncture of Hume's fork, right at the point of contact between synthetic truth and analytic truth. According to Hume, Locke, Berkeley, Descartes, Leibniz, and every philosopher before Kant, there is no such point of contact between the two for the simple reason that there couldn't be. Yet Kant does not reject his predecessors; he begins, as Plato,

Descartes, Locke, Berkeley, and Hume have all done before him, with acknowledgment of what we have been calling the first philosophical insight—the realization that your eyes are not windows—which thus far he says has led either to Humean and other varieties of skepticism or to Berkeleian and other varieties of idealism. Kant does not deny the single main insight of the whole history of philosophy, but he uses it in a different and unexpected way.

Kant agrees with Hume and just about all the other philosophers who argue that you do not directly experience things in themselves. What you experience directly are the objects of your own mind, which Kant says are mere representations, but not of impressions, as Hume thought. For that leads to Berkeleian idealism, the view that there is no world beyond the mind, since the "representations" are themselves representing mental (phenomenal) objects. That is, to view the phenomenal world (the world of your experience) as consisting in representations of phenomena is to be an idealist, pure and simple. Hence he claims that Berkeley's "to be is to be perceived" makes knowledge possible by making metaphysics—in the sense of knowing things in themselves as they exist beyond or outside our experience—unnecessary. But, in Berkeley's case, it requires the dogma of abstract ideas like God or, as Hume points out, the Self, which are mere fictions and so without the weight of metaphysics the idealist system evaporates. In the case of materialist philosophies, it requires abstract ideas like cause and effect, or material substance that then collapses under the weight of their metaphysics, leaving an unbridgeable gap between the phenomenal world of appearances and what Kant will call the noumenal world of things in themselves. The noumenal world is the real world as it is in itself, independently of our representations. Kant claims we can know absolutely nothing about the noumenal world except that it exists. All we are ever directly aware of is the activity of our own minds. All we ever have access to is our own representations of things, not the things in themselves. So of course it is not possible to know things in themselves. Experience connects us not to things in themselves but to ourselves. How could the mind-independent world of things in themselves ever be reachable given that there is no possible path into the mind from such a world?

We've already noted the striking similarity between one aspect of Augustine's philosophical system, built in the fourth century, and Descartes's system. Now we see a similarity with Kant as well who, like Augustine, predicates his elaborate metaphysics on a threefold division of the mind. Kant's three "faculties" are intuition, understanding, and reason. But Kant does something no other philosopher before him had ever attempted: he performs what he calls a transcendental analysis of each faculty. That is Kant in a nutshell.

It is extremely important to understand, right from the onset, what Kant means by the word *intuitions,* for this is extremely confusing. What he means is the same thing Hume means by the terms *impressions* and *perceptions.* Thus, for instance, what you presently see are, in Kant's vocabulary, not things in themselves but your own intuitions of things. The problem is that the word *intuition* in its vernacular English sense means something like "hunch" or "thought" or "gut feeling." This is not at all what Kant means. What he means is more like "perception."

Kant's concern, however, is not with the phenomena of perception. Rather, the key question is, how is perception possible? He says, "Sensuous cognition represents things not at all as they are, but . . . phenomena only and not things themselves are given to the understanding for reflection." Once again, this is the one point Hume identified as being the only proposition that is

> universally allowed by philosophers, and is besides pretty obvious of itself, that nothing is ever really present with the mind but its perceptions or impressions and ideas, and that external objects become known to us only by those perceptions they occasion. To hate, to love, to think, to feel, to see; all this is nothing but to perceive.

The point may be obvious "in itself," once one has thought about it, but it certainly is not obvious to an unreflective mind not steeped in philosophy; and Kant insists that this fact should not be overlooked. Kant takes it as a very important piece of information that these phenomena—all the things we feel and see—are automatically interpreted by us, by the very thing that gives rise to them, not as phenomena, but as things. This is the very point that Hume says is obvious, and of course by now it should seem familiar to you. But notice that things don't look any different once you know this!

In other words, knowing the truth about the representational nature of your perceptions does not in any way change the quality of your perceptions. For instance, no matter how much philosophy you read and learn, in no way do your perceptions start seeming to you like perceptions, events in your mind, mental phenomena, or products of the imagination. Rather, the "things" you see still look to you like things. Clearly, what is not obvious to an unreflective mind is that it is looking at its own representations. But even after it is revealed that the things we see are falsely and automatically interpreted by the mind as things existing outside our minds, it does not alter the character of the phenomena.

Put simply: the objects you see don't look like visual phenomena, or like mental images, or like mere mental representations of things. We interpret what we are looking at to be mind-independent physical objects, things in themselves. Keep in mind, though, that—as Kant goes to great lengths to point out—this interpretation is not something you, the ego, do, but something that happens to you. That is, it is done for you by your own cognitive faculties. Thus, when Kant says that "the difference between truth and dreaming is not ascertained by the nature of the representations, which are referred to objects," he means just this: whether dreaming or awake, phenomena are referred to objects; that is, they are taken to denote things like tables and chairs. In a manner of speaking, when you are dreaming your mind itself becomes, if you are dreaming about a chair, a phenomenal representation of a chair; likewise, when awake and in the presence of a chair, your mind again becomes a phenomenal representation of a chair.

Clearly, there's no phenomenal difference between the two states. Yet there is a difference. The key difference is, remarkably and paradoxically, as similar to Descartes's method as it is different from it. Recall that Descartes forged a new (though, again, Augustine inspired) path to certainty by doubting; specifically, he discovered that in the act of maximal doubting, while realizing that he might be deceived about everything, he could then see the one thing he could not be deceived of and see it with absolute certainty: his own existence. In Kant's transcendental analysis, the focus is not on your existence per se. Rather, you realize that everything you are looking at when you are experiencing phenomena are not things in themselves but, at best, representations. You realize that you are never seeing outside yourself, that everything you will ever know or can ever know through the having of experience is only your own mental states as such. Then, and only then, in the midst of this realization that what you are looking at is not reality as it exists in itself but only your own representation of it, you realize that there is and must be something making it possible for you to have representations as such and that this is known by you with absolute certainty. At one point, Kant illustrates with the paradigm example of the planets:

> The senses represent to us the paths of the planets as now forward, now backward, and herein is neither falsehood nor truth, because as long as we hold this path to be nothing but appearance, we do not judge of the objective nature of their motion. But as a false judgment may easily arise when the understanding does not carefully guard against this subjective mode of representation being considered objective, we say they appear to move backward; it is not the senses however which are charged with the illusion, but the understanding, whose province alone it is to give an objective judgment on the phenomenon.

Clearly, it is not the fault of our phenomena that they are phenomena. What else but phenomena can they be? If actual physical chairs entered our brains, we would die. You can't put real, objective objects into the mind. So the source of error lies not in the phenomena themselves but in our understanding of the phenomena. Ordinarily we don't understand that phenomena are phenomena nor do we experience the process by which phenomena are created. All we experience is the effect: the objects we see. We don't see how they're constructed by our own minds. We don't consciously know how this is happening. In our own subjectivity we understand the phenomena to be things in themselves, whereas objectivity requires us to understand that the phenomena are phenomena. Experience will always have this illusory aspect to it. That is, the structuring of the objects of perception as if they were other than what they are is not a flaw in the mind to be fought against or removed but is itself a necessary condition for the having of experience.

In other words, to expect or look for a "direct" experience of reality is like trying to invent a language that consists not of words (which are not things but only symbols standing for things) but of things. Things do not a language make. You need non-things, which are not rocks and chairs and tables and atoms and whatever is really out there but are themselves immaterial, which is exactly what words are. You also need grammar, syntax, interpretations schemes, and so on. Without language you just have an inert world of matter. Likewise, without phenomena you just have an inert world of whatever it is that exists, things in themselves. And we can carry this analogy with language even further.

Already implicit in Hume's philosophy was the radical idea that meaning is up to a point man-made. Certain disputes, such as ones about the self, were purely verbal. Others, such as ones about identity, were not: they were truly meaningful, their meaning being a midway interface between ideas, which are mental representations of impressions, and impressions. It was, for Hume, a proper relation rather than a fictive one. Kant carries this concept one step further, to a meta-level. As we shall see, it is not just meaning (a linguistic phenomenon) but objects themselves that are, in part, man-made. That is not to say that Kant is espousing idealism:

> These my principles, because they make phenomena of the representations of the senses, are so far from turning the truth of experience into mere illusion, that they are rather the only means of preventing the transcendental illusion, by which metaphysics has hitherto been deceived, and led to the childish endeavor of catching at bubbles, while phenomena, which are mere representations, were taken for things in themselves.

To see how, we must understand what Kant means by the "transcendental illusion." He means this: the illusion that what you are seeing—the phenomena themselves, which are merely your mind's representations, consisting of visual and tactile intuitions—are things existing outside you, independently of the mind. It is this fact that gives rise to the various "antinomies of reason," mentioned earlier: contradictory systems by which philosophies flip-flop back and forth, like a Necker cube, between materialism and idealism, dogmatism and skepticism, atheism and theism, deism and pantheism, a one self view to a no self view, and so on. All such antinomies, Kant argues, are "destroyed by the single observation, that phenomenon, as long as it is used in experience, produces truth, but the moment it transgresses the bounds of experience, and consequently becomes transcendent, produces nothing but illusion." Think again in terms of our analogy with language. As long as we are perfectly clear about what words are and what they are not, then the mere fact that words exist and function as they do can be used to distinguish the true from the false. But not just in the domain of language. It is more like the world itself has a grammar and a syntax, a logic by which it operates, and these structure both language, which is a representation of the world, and that which is represented by language.

In calling his philosophy "transcendental," Kant does not mean to imply that it is possible to transcend the phenomena and thereby reach the things in themselves. This would be akin, in his view, to trying hard to use the word *dog* until it becomes a dog. Rather, he means that his critical method of transcendental analysis can be used to transcend phenomena not for the purposes of reaching the noumenal world, which is impossible, but to reach the three cognitive faculties of the mind.

Before we go into more detail to see exactly what this means, let us pause to address the revolution in thought that is here unfolding. For therein lies the secret behind Kant's metaphysics. We've already touched on one of the major assumptions underlying not just the Newtonian world view but nearly every view ever taken of the relationship between our minds and reality: namely, the assumption that our minds are passive perceivers of reality and not in any way the creators of it. This assumption, too, seems too obvious to question! To question it seems to move us away from the domain of philosophy into the world of myth, magic, and shamanism of the most blatant and superstitious kind. After all, one would have to go all the way back to prehistoric pagans, who believed that things like wishing, human emotions, and opinions could affect reality! I might put a curse on you, or we may have to appease some ancient spirit lest the weather destroy us, and so on. But of course, such beliefs have nevertheless persisted into the modern period and beyond, through the idea of a God who, as essentially a mind or spirit, affects not just individual aspects of reality but the whole of reality. Many people today believe that while their own minds cannot simply by wishing turn thoughts into reality, they can express their wishes to some "divine" mind that then can affect reality in exactly that way. Likewise, there have always been stories about certain special individuals with unique powers to influence or bring about, through their thoughts and wills alone, real events beyond their minds: people who bend spoons, make accidents happen (or not), and so on. But what if such a "link" between mind and reality exists not just in the domain of religion and magic but within you as well?

Kant's goal is to transcend the phenomena by recognizing them as such. In this way you reach the realm of the cognitive faculties (the Kantian threefold division of the mind into intuition [perception], understanding, and reason). What powers do they have? Not just the power to create the phenomena we see; that is obvious from the fact that we experience phenomena as such. Our cognitive faculties, Kant argues, also affect the objects themselves. They are not, as Hume and other empiricist philosophers have thought, purely passive. In a way, he is reversing Locke's idea of (primary and secondary) qualities that we explained in terms of powers of objects in the real world (things in themselves) to affect our minds, which are passive receivers, blank slates, and so on. Kant is ascribing such active powers not to inanimate things themselves but to the cognitive faculties, the powers of the mind. Thus it is the faculty of the understanding that gives an order and regularity to "the phenomena which we call nature." And where do the so-called laws of nature come from? We are their source. For, as Kant concludes in his *Critique of Pure Reason*,

> However exaggerated therefore and absurd it may sound, that the understanding is itself the source of the laws of nature, and of its formal unity, such a statement is nevertheless correct and in accordance with experience.

Lest you think that this is just plain crazy, consider this: How much crazier is the idea that an inanimate, lifeless object has such powers over you? In other words, which is more bizarre—that inert, lifeless matter can affect the mind, or that your mind, consisting not just in phenomena but in cognitive faculties producing them (already recognized by anyone who has thought about it as a great power), can affect the inert, lifeless things in themselves?

Second, you may get a clearer sense of what Kant is saying about the relationship between the mind and the world, if you think once again to our analogy with language. What do dogs, cats, tables, and chairs have to do with the existence of the words *dog, cat, table,* and *chair* within our language? The answer isn't just "nothing." If there weren't any such things at all in any sense of the word, the cognitive apparatus through which language emerges would not have responded by inventing such sounds and giving them references. And, likewise, what do those words have to do with the things? Here one may be tempted to answer, "nothing," but clearly in the cases of tables and chairs and other man-made objects that is not true. Words have a lot to do with the existence of those things. But in the case of phenomena, the connection is even stronger. Kant is saying that the cognitive apparatus through which phenomena appear in us is something that functions in the world as such and is operating under the same laws.

Here you may begin to gain a glimpse into what Kant is saying about reality. Think of how many actual human experiences come about because of the generation, within our minds, of new phenomena and new words with which to interpret them. Concepts affect percepts, percepts affect concepts; Kant will extend this sort of relationship into the domains of space, time, and causality. For example, how is it possible that we can express true sentences about the height of a mountain, if Hume and the empiricists are right in claiming that we never perceive space? According to Hume, perceptions consist only in ideas and impressions; impressions come in discrete bundles of sense-data and ideas are merely representations of them, so we never really perceive space. Likewise, Kant asks, how is it possible that we can make true statements about how long it takes, say, to get from Berlin to Frankfurt, if Hume and the empiricists are correct in claiming that we never perceive time, only discrete impressions and ideas, which are their representations? Kant's solution to these problems hinges on his ability, through transcendental analysis, to reach the foundations of the faculty of perception. A posteriori sentences like "Mt. Everest is more than three feet tall" presuppose the truth of the sentence "Objects exist in space and time." But the fact is, Kant argues, sometimes we can know that a sentence like "Mt. Everest is more than three feet tall" is true; but such a sentence cannot be true unless the second is also true. However, the second sentence is not analytically true (it is not a contradiction to deny it), nor is it known to be true a posteriori (there is no impression of space or time on the basis of which an idea could form a legitimate representation). So it must be a synthetic a priori truth.

This is the crux of the new understanding of reality that Kant gave to the world. Indeed, many of the ideas behind twentieth-century scientific "revolutions" in thought—in which the boundary between mind and reality dissolves in exactly this way, such as Einstein's theory of relativity and the subsequent advent of quantum mechanics—can be found in Kant. Indeed, Albert Einstein said that reading Kant's *Critique of Pure Reason* and *Prolegomena to Any Future Metaphysics* had the greatest impact on him of all philosophical works and helped him in his development of relativity. (Think of Einstein's "frames of reference" and of how times slows down or speeds up relative to the motions of the observers, and so on, and you will begin to understand the nature of the link.) It was Kant who first showed in what sense space, time, causality—the very fabric of existence—are not mere figments of our imagination, as Hume supposed, but nor are they fully objective realities, as did Newton; rather, the entire phenomenal world in which we exist as phenomenal beings is an interface, a fulcrum between that which exists only in the mind and reality as it exists in itself, independently of the mind.

It is this part of Kant's philosophical revolution that he likened to a second "Copernican revolution," the Kantian revolution being not in natural philosophy (physics) but within metaphysics itself, the innermost core of any knowledge-seeking enterprise. It is in effect a reversal of the traditional epistemological question: instead of asking how objects affect the mind, Kant asks how the mind affects the objects of knowledge: "We must make trial whether we may not have more success in the tasks of metaphysics, if we suppose that objects must conform to our knowledge." Kant thus creates a philosophical synthesis between the empiricism of Locke, Berkeley, and Hume and the rationalism of Descartes and Leibniz: he reconstructs a new bridge between the Platonic world of ideas and the Aristotelian world of empirical forms. As for Aristotle, the objects in our experience—the phenomenal world—are not merely illusions. Their existence is a collaboration between the three faculties of the mind and the noumenal world; real objects are partially constituted, as real objects, by the mind. To understand how such a constitution takes place requires Kant's method of analysis, which he called *transcendental deduction*. It is the method by which the mind transcends its own direct observation of its own phenomena. It gets behind or underneath its phenomena to discover the necessary conditions of the having of an experience, allowing the mind to thereby look reflectively behind the phenomenal world of appearance and glimpse into its own cognitive machinery that makes the phenomenal world possible. We must, however, be careful to point out that in calling this "glimpsing behind its own appearances" *transcendental* Kant does not mean that philosophical inquiry can reach beyond the mind into the world of things in themselves. Rather, the mind reaches into itself, into its functional activities.

The reason the mind is able to create, or structure, its phenomena is that space and time are not features of external, noumenal reality but are features of the structure of the mind. The human mind analyzes and synthesizes the impressions it receives in terms of the categories of space and time—our two-way "irremovable lenses" through which the phenomenal world is created. It would be wrong to say merely that we perceive the world through the lenses of space and time; that would be to take a Cartesian-Lockean-Berkeleian-Humean passive view of the mind. What would the phrase "the world," in such a case, even refer to? We would be right back with Humean fictions (or, at best, some theoretical construction). Rather, space and time both inform the mind and, in turn, inform the phenomenal world.

Think about a game of chess. The pieces are things. So is the board! Kant is not saying that space and time are like the board. Rather, he is saying that space and time are like the rules according to which the game of chess is played, without which the game of chess would cease to exist. What we call reality is a game of chess, and each of us is an active player.

Or take our earlier example of the chair. You see a chair. Forget about the chair "out there." Forget about the idea of atoms. How is it possible that you are having this experience? Remember, that the existence of a chair "out there" is not necessary for you to be having an experience of the chair. This is an extremely important thing to realize! Dreams are a quick reminder. If you can experience phenomena as a chair in a dream, this is an albeit indirect but vivid proof that the existence of physical chairs is not a necessary condition for there to exist the phenomenon of a chair. But what then makes it possible for you to have an experience of a chair, whether an imaginary chair that exists only in your imagination or an imaginary chair that exists as a representation of some real chair? Do you see what Kant is asking?

One thing that should bother you is that you don't know the answer to that question. The reason this should bother you is that the focus and the burden now are not on what is beyond you or outside you but on what is within you. Whether the chair you see exists only in the mind, and there is nothing out there of which it is an accurate (or inaccurate) representation, or whether the chair is a perfect representation, you can't see how your mind is making the representation. Kant is so concerned about transcending the phenomena not to get to the "outside" noumenal world, but to get inside ourselves, to our own faculties of cognition, because, to put it colloquially, that's where the action is.

Another thing to notice is that what we've just done is to learn something not by experience but through experience; that is, we've just learned something by attending to our experience not in terms of what the experience is *of* but what, in and of itself, the experience is like, and then inquiring into the question of *how it could be like that*. And this is how we got to the categories of space and time as being necessary conditions for the having of experience.

Besides the perceptual faculty—the having of intuitions—there is the faculty of understanding and the faculty of reason. Both of these, too, are reachable through transcendental deductions. The faculty of understanding makes it possible for us to understand not just facts about the (phenomenal) world, but all the things we've just been talking about. Recall the sense in which for philosophers like Descartes, Locke, and Berkeley the answer to the question "What am I seeing the objects of my perceptions with?" is not "the eyes!" The eyes, at most, bring in nonperceptual information (wavelengths of light, etc.) to the body. Rather, it is the understanding, by which these philosophers all meant, in various ways, something like the "mind's eye." For Kant this eye is, to use a bad but appropriate phrase, the phenomenal eye of the soul. It's like when you're dreaming: What do you see the dream with? Not your eyes, they're closed! But the same thing is going on right now, Kant would remind you, as when you dream. The only difference is that the phenomena you experience in dreams are not real, whereas the phenomena you experience in waking life (a sort of "waking dream," if you like) are real. And so for Kant it is the faculty of the understanding that both passively apprehends phenomena and actively imbibes them with the meanings they have in all the various ways in which meaning occurs.

Through the transcendental analysis Kant analyzes "the categories of the understanding," which he identifies as unity/plurality/totality, causality, and substantiality. These concepts are not deduced by the mind from reality, neither from the noumenal world nor from the phenomenal world; that is, they are not themselves, in any sense, phenomenal representations and they are not noumenal things in themselves. Rather, such categories are structural/functional rules for phenomena and meaning formation that the mind brings to the phenomena and imparts to the real world. That is why, Kant claims, Hume could not find the categories when he looked for them—because they do not exist out there in the world. Sentences such as "Every event has a cause," which according to Hume is neither analytic nor synthetic, is according to Kant a paradigm example of a synthetic a priori truth. In some ways this notion can be seen as a philosophical evolution of the doctrine of Plato's forms or Descartes's doctrine of innate ideas. The big difference is that in Kant's view these categories of the understanding are not ideas that we are born with; rather, the mind is structured in such a way that it analyzes its own data in terms of a priori rules of thought. In some ways, these rules are like the operating system on a computer, nowhere apparent but everywhere essential. For instance, computers use DOS, OS/2, Windows 95, or Windows NT in structuring everything within them; the categories are thus like the permanent part of the mind's operating system that produce ideas when either the senses or the cognitive apparatus of the mind provides information. That is how the mind makes sense of the world, using concepts such as time, space, substantiality, and causality. We are thus programmed, for instance, to see the world as consisting of things, each of which has "thingness," though there exists nothing "out there," in the noumenal world, that is itself a thing in the sense of any type of substance. Likewise, the mind is forced by its programming at the most fundamental level to conceive of things in terms of cause and effect even though nothing exists out there in the noumenal world itself that is the cause of anything.

We are now in a position to understand Kant's famous phrase, "Thoughts without content are empty, intuitions without concepts are blind." For Kant, there are two distinct realities: the phenomenal world of appearance and representation, and the noumenal world of things in themselves. The noumenal world cannot be known by the mind; we can know the world only as it is interpreted and structured through the mind's categories and represented as phenomena. The key to his "transcendental" philosophy consists in the mind's coming to be aware that the phenomenal world of appearances consists not of objects in the world as they exist in themselves but the mind's own representations of things as interpreted through and structured by its own categories. This means that when I open my eyes and am confronted by all the visible objects in my field of vision (the manifold of intuition) I must learn to recognize that what I am looking at is a sort of virtual reality, a world of my own ideas, representations of objects in the world, and not the objects in the world as they exist in themselves. And yet Kant claims not to be an idealist (at least not in Berkeley's sense) because a phenomenon experienced as a representation of an object—say, the chair I see—is in fact the product of two causes: the mind and the chair in itself. In other words, as a phenomenal object the chair represented to me as a phenomenon exists as an interface between the mind and the world. Kant's phenomenal world is, therefore, real. He explicitly shuns the title of idealism, which he says should better be put on the ordinary, naive view of reality that takes what are in fact phenomena and treats them as things in themselves—what he calls "dreaming idealism" in contrast to his enlightened, transcendental, or critical idealism.

What about the third faculty of the mind, the faculty of reason? It is the faculty of reason that produces the pure concepts—those concepts that are "uncontaminated" by the senses—the domain of pure reason. What are those concepts? And are they real? Here, given the title of his most famous work, the *Critique of Pure Reason,* the answer should not be surprising, though many found it devastating. The paradigm examples of pure concepts are "God" and "soul." The question then becomes: are there any synthetic a priori grounds for believing in God or the soul? Kant's notorious answer is an unmitigated, absolute, resounding, no.

What about other pure concepts, such as freedom and justice? Here Kant spawned a second sort of revolution. For although we cannot predicate any sort of metaphysical necessity to any aspect of the ethical and moral realms, we can find there a sort of practical, moral necessity. Kant's *Foundations of the Metaphysics of Morals* (1785) gives his widely influential deontological (rule-based) ethical theory which centers on his categorical imperative: "Act only on that maxim which you can at the same time will to become a universal law." As the universal moral test of right principles of action, the categorical imperative according to Kant makes us all duty-bound to obey certain principles in the same way that objects in nature are bound to act according to the laws of nature. But what does Kant mean by *will?* The concept is extremely important not just in Kant but in many Kant-inspired later philosophers (most notably, Schopenhauer), and yet it has been almost universally misunderstood. The biggest and most common mistake is to confuse your will with your wishing. For instance, to give an oversimplified example, you might *wish* that you exercised more, because you'd like to look more attractive, but your will just isn't in it and you don't do it. Suppose, on the other hand, doctors have told you that unless you start exercising regularly you will die. Insofar as it you have a duty to yourself to survive and to live, you may now find that your duty and your will go hand in hand and prompt you to action. That's what Kant means by distinguishing between actions done from mere inclination and those done by the will. And the foundation of morality consists in having a good will. Notice how different a conception of moral goodness this is from Plato, Aristotle, Epicurus, and Augustine, all of whom understood morality in terms of happiness—in their case, one's own. Later so-called utilitarians, such as John Stuart Mill, also use happiness as their moral foundation, in opposition to Kant, though not just in terms of one's own happiness but of everyone's.

Kant distinguishes two kinds of imperatives. An imperative is *hypothetical* when it is of the form "If you wish (or want, or would like) x in circumstances y, do action a." (The earlier case of wishing to exercise to look better would be an example.) The *categorical* imperative, on the other hand, makes no reference to your wishes, wants, or desires. It is independent of any utilitarian concerns having to do with consequences or goals. It simply says, "If you are in circumstance y, do a." Period. Regardless of what you want, that is what you must do. Duty demands it. (Our case of exercising because it is a matter of life and death would be an example.) Kant's reasoning here is that since the moral law such as the categorical imperative is a rule for choosing among rules—that is, a rule for distinguishing between right and wrong rules—it cannot refer to the content of rules. It must therefore refer only to their form; that is why it must be a categorical, rather than hypothetical, imperative. It has the same form as scientific laws of nature; that is, it has a universal form. Think, for instance, of Newton's law F = Ma (force equals mass times acceleration). If this is to be a law of nature, it must apply everywhere and at all times; it can have no exceptions. That is what it means to say that something is a law of nature. It applies universally. And so Kant's "supreme principle of morality" is this: "Act only according to that maxim [rule] whereby you can at the same time will that it should become a universal law." Notice that this statement is synthetic; if you deny it no contradiction results. Because the statement has no empirical content, it is a priori. Therefore it is a paradigm of pure reason at work in the moral realm.

Suppose you are about to take a test. You haven't studied. So you consider cheating. Should you do it? What would Kant say? The answer is clear. Simply check whether you could universalize your action into a universal principle. You ask yourself what would happen if everyone who did not study for an exam cheated. Could there be a universal law, "Everyone ought to cheat on exams"? First, notice that you might not think this law would be such a good idea if you were going in for open heart surgery and wanted a reputable doctor who had passed all the necessary exams! But the situation is more clear-cut than that. Kant would tell you that "Everyone ought to cheat on exams" would be an impossible law, because if everyone complied with it, there would be no need for exams. Exams, as such, would cease to exist.

Likewise, think of lying, stealing, and killing. "Everyone ought always to lie." Impossible! You couldn't even state the law without breaking it. "Everyone ought always to steal." This would destroy the notion of property and thereby invalidate the concept of stealing, as such. And so on. But there is an equally important second aspect to the categorical imperative: "So act as to treat humanity, whether in your own person or in that of any other, always at the same time as an end and never simply as a means only." In saying that we should treat others as ends in themselves and not merely as a means, Kant is of course saying that we ought not to use other people as a means to our own ends. But this principle applies as much to ourselves as it does to others; it is, in fact, the very source of our ability to choose the way of freedom. This is because the moral law, in terms of the categorical imperative, arises from and is known through pure reason. It says, "Choose your rules according to whether they can be universalized." But notice that since this is a principle of pure reason, and I am a rational being, I am not merely a subject to this law! I am also in part its author. In other words, just as the objects of the phenomenal world are in part created (constituted into reality) by my own mind, so too the moral law is itself in part my own creation: "The will is thus not merely subject to the law but is subject to the law in such a way that it must be regarded also as legislating for itself and only on this account as being subject to the law of which it can regard itself as the author." Hence, in the spirit of Rousseau, it is when we act from duty with respect to the moral law that each of us exists as a fully and absolutely autonomous being:

> The will is a kind of causality belonging to living beings insofar as they are rational; freedom would be the property of this causality that makes it effective independent of any determination by alien causes. . . . Freedom is certainly not lawless, even though it is not a property of will in accordance with laws of nature. It must, rather, be a causality in accordance with immutable laws, which, to be sure, is of a special kind . . . . What else, then, can freedom of the will be but autonomy, i.e., the property that the will has of being a law to itself? The proposition that the will is in every action a law to itself expresses, however, nothing but the principle of acting according to no other maxim that that which can at the same time have itself as a universal law for its object. Now this is precisely the formula of the categorical imperative and is the principle of morality. Thus a free will and a will subject to moral laws are one and the same.[2]

I happened to have just finished breakfast at the inn that is down the street from the apartment where Kant lived nearly his entire life. Walking down the labyrinthine streets winding back into themselves, trying to retrace the walk that by my calculations he had taken between 18,000 and 20,000 times, I find my mind curiously empty of thought. I think of the old man coming around the corner with his black walking stick (I brushed my fingers over it in on the display rack only yesterday—it reminded me, eerily, of a blind man's), pausing at this hill where I now stand to catch his breath. Perhaps it is the strangeness of the shadowless noonday light creeping through the clouds that draws my attention away from philosophy to the texture of the bricks and stones of the buildings, the cobbled walkways, the huge tree in the park that must have been a seedling when he walked by. I move on and my mind wanders away even from Königsberg and Kant to the other places that I would visit until it hits me; I hear the old man's voice: *Where are you going to go?* And suddenly the curtain of reality lifts to unveil me from myself, from the phenomena of my vision and desire that only moments ago seemed all too mundane and inconsequential but now seem too much, for now I recognize them not as things but as phenomena.

I understood as I stood there on that little hill near the center of Königsberg why Kant never bothered to venture outside the borders of his little town. It was crossing the boundaries that he was after—not to the outside, which is impossible, but to the inside, to the categories of the mind, to that within ourselves that makes the having of the outside possible.

Fichte: The Subjective Idealist

The son of a farmer and linen-maker, Johann Gottlieb Fichte (1762–1814) was born in Rammenau, a village in Upper (Saxon) Lusatia. After studying at the Universities of Jena and Leipzig, he worked as a tutor in Zürich. His first work, "Aphorisms on Religion and God" (1790), was highly influenced by Spinoza's philosophy, especially his views on determinism. But of the philosophers then living, it was Kant who exerted the greatest and most lasting influence on Fichte.

When Fichte visited Kant in Königsberg to pay his respects, Kant agreed to read Fichte's next manuscript, *Essay Toward a Critique of All Revelation* (1792). Fichte sent it to him and Kant was so impressed that he sent the manuscript to his publisher on Fichte's behalf. The publisher decided to bring it out. However, due to a printer's error, the book appeared without Fichte's name on it and with Kant's preface—and everyone assumed the book had been written by Kant!

Soon afterward Kant published a retraction in which he stated that the work was Fichte's, not his. He then added, almost in passing, that Fichte's book solves a major problem with Kant's own system that Kant himself had found insoluble. The problem with his own work, as Kant saw it, was that his *Critique of Pure Reason* puts speculative theology in a completely negative light. Yet his *Critique of Practical Reason* puts the moral law, so central to Kant's thought, as the absolute content, or substance, of any religion. This inconsistency left open the puzzling question as to the conditions under which religious belief is possible.

Fichte's brilliant *Critique of All Revelation* bridges the gap between Kant's two monumental works by showing how the absolute requirements of the moral law supply the necessary conditions that make revealed religion possible. Fichte's reputation was instantly secured. In 1794 he became professor of philosophy at the University of Jena in 1794 and published both *On the Concept of the Science of Knowledge, or So-called Philosophy* and *Fundamental Principles of the Science of Knowledge*. In these works, Fichte departs from Kant in a direction that paved the way for three related, extremely important movements in philosophy: absolute idealism, phenomenology, and existentialism. Fichte's analysis of the ego was especially influential. According to Fichte, the ego is a self-affirming primitive act of consciousness that constructs the objective world not in tandem with "things in themselves," as Kant supposed, but solely out of its own appearances. This then gives rise to an antinomy-like conflict between the inner sense of free will and the external sense that the world is completely determined. Fichte states, "In immediate consciousness, I appear to myself as free; by reflection on the whole of Nature, I discover that freedom is absolutely impossible." And yet, the only knowledge of which any one of us is capable is that of our own minds: "In all perception you perceive only your own state." Thus, in a way that Hume might have responded to Kant's rebuttal to his argument against causality, the idea of things in themselves is itself but a projection of the mind and therefore not something to which consciousness is bound.

The idea is that the boundary by which we distinguish between self and other, based on what we can consciously control, is deeply bogus (as many later existentialists will also claim). Just about all subsequent idealists will make a great deal of this. Think of dream states. You're being chased by dogs. You don't consciously want to be chased by dogs, you're consciously afraid, and so on. But what is the cause of the movement of the dogs, the chase, the fear? In the case of the dream it is your own mind. Only you are not yourself, as the conscious ego, conscious of the mechanisms by which the world of your dreams is run by you. Fichte claims that something like that is going on in the real world. Our failure to realize this leads non-idealists to accept the notion of things in themselves over which we have no power. But this, argues Fichte, is like supposing, "What I consciously control is me, what I do not consciously control is a thing in itself." Such reasoning is invalid.[3] Think, again, of your dream states; the dogs chasing you in the dream are not material things, they are not things in themselves. Why can't you just wish them away? As the brilliant nineteenth-century American idealist philosopher Josiah Royce will argue, it is because the mind itself is far more resilient and stubborn than any concept of inert matter. Thus, Fichte argues that

> a finite rational being has nothing beyond experience; it is this that comprises the entire staple of his thought. The philosopher is necessarily in the same position; it seems, therefore, incomprehensible how he could raise himself above experience . . . the thing-in-itself is a pure invention and has no reality whatsoever. It does not occur in experience for the system of experience is nothing other than thinking . . . nothing else but the totality of relations unified by the imagination, and that all these relations constitute the thing; the object is surely the original synthesis of all these concepts.

According to Fichte, form and matter are not separate items; the totality of form is the matter. The idea is this. For something, say a rock, to be objectively real simply means, in Fichte's philosophy, that it consists of all possible experiences that it can generate in the mind of a potential observer. Take the rock apart or don't take it apart, look at it from above and below or not; the point is that you could do this because the rock is a containing space of all (perhaps infinite) possibilities of relation of that object. Lest this strike you as a philosophical flight of fancy utterly removed from our contemporary scientific world view, this view became the metaphysical foundation of early-twentieth-century quantum mechanics, in which what it means for something to be real at the physical level is that the equation describing the object allows you to list all the possible solutions that it could generate: beyond that range of possibility there is no mind-independent actuality. Albert Einstein of course famously rejected the absolute idealism of quantum physicists like Niels Bohr in favor of a Kantian transcendental idealism; Einstein defended the idea of the thing in itself, a mind-independent reality, against other leading physicists.[4]

Fichte was a subjective idealist. Like Berkeley, he believed that everything is made of thought. But what is thought? Thought, according to Fichte,

> has no being proper, no subsistence, for this is the result of an interaction and there is nothing . . . with which the intellect could be set to interact [because,

for Fichte, there is no noumenal world of the thing in itself]. The intellect, for idealism, is an act, and absolutely nothing more; we should not even call it an active something, for this expression refers to something subsistent in which activity inheres.

In some ways, Fichte is here laying a metaphysical foundation for the functionalist theories developed by twentieth-century computer scientists, cognitive scientists, and philosophers[5] according to whom reality and its simulation are viewed as one and the same: the universe is viewed as an abstract program, or Absolute Idea, which is functionally equivalent to the human intellect, or program. Indeed, Fichte's notion of an act as an undefined fundamental property of the human intellect is in many ways an avatar of the idea that human consciousness is a key ingredient to the universal algorithm through which reality unfolds from one state to the next. It makes it possible to view the entire universe as a computer program.

Fichte was recognized in his lifetime as one of the three leading successors to Kant, along with Hegel and Schelling. An extremely dynamic and popular lecturer at Jena, he commanded a large following among his students as well as the public, but this did not work out to his advantage. After a prolonged conflict with the Jena administration over academic freedom, he was dismissed from his position. Apparently, Fichte's philosophy was regarded as so dangerous that he had been asked not to publish his views; he refused, arguing that a philosopher has not only the right but the moral duty to expound his thoughts, including and especially the philosophy of religion (one of the leading bones of contention with both the university and public authorities). After his dismissal, Fichte continued to publish and even increased his public lectures, becoming one of the leading figures in Berlin. There, during the French occupation, shortly after Napoleon had arrived in 1806, Fichte delivered his famous *Addresses to the German Nation* (1807) inspiring his fellow Germans to moral regeneration through national unity and political reform. Four years later, in 1810, Fichte helped found the new University of Berlin. He remained there for the rest of his life, teaching his philosophy and writing until his death.

Schelling: The Objective Idealist

Friedrich Wilhelm von Schelling (1775–1854) was born in Leonburg, a small town in Württemberg, Germany. His first education was at the cloister school where his father was chaplain and professor, which got him accepted to the theological seminary at Tübingen. Here he became deeply interested in the philosophy of Spinoza, Kant, and especially Fichte. His friendship with Hegel, a fellow student, led to their editing a philosophy journal. Immediately after graduating, in 1798, he was invited to become philosophy professor at the University of Jena by its rector, the duke Charles Augustus; three years later he joined the illustrious department that included Fichte, Hegel, Schlegel, and Schiller.

Although his transcendental form of idealism clearly owes much to Kant, Fichte, and Hegel, Schelling's greatest original contribution was to romanticism, the eighteenth- and nineteenth-century philosophical movement opposed to both rationalism and empiricism. Generally regarded as the leading romantic of the period, Schelling inspired Samuel Coleridge (1772–1834) and the great English romantic poets Wordsworth and Shelley.

Schelling developed an "objective" version of transcendental idealism, which owed much to the work of Kant, Fichte, and Hegel. Reacting against both continental rationalism and British empiricism, Schelling's philosophy centers on the self, the power of imagination, and the relation of philosophy and theology to art. His main work, *System of Transcendental Idealism,* is a treatise on nature, epistemology, and ethics. In it, Schelling tries to unify objective and subjective thought into an objective version of idealism, with his "philosophy of identity." According to Schelling, subject and object coincide in the Absolute, which can be attained through intellectual intuition as a conscious mystical state. In marked contrast to both Kant and Fichte, according to whom the purpose of philosophical thought is morality, for Schelling the culmination of human experience is in the creative act of artists expressing the special relation of identity between the subjective self and the objective world.

For Schelling, the only immediate object of knowledge is consciousness. Knowledge of the objective world can be attained, however, as a limiting condition of the dynamic evolutionary process from consciousness to self-consciousness. In becoming self-aware as a subject, the relation of subject to object within the Absolute becomes intellectually intuited in the subject as an objective state of affairs. And only through art can the mind become fully aware of its own existence. Thus, the pinnacle of philosophical reflection is the production of objects that are profound works of art.

Schelling distinguishes, as does Fichte, between nature, by which he means the external, objective world, and spirit, by which he means the mind (the internal, subjective world). The distinction itself is derived from the concept of a third, higher reality, the Absolute, which is neither conscious nor unconscious. The Absolute owes much to Kant's notion of the noumenal, especially that it transcends the categories of thought. For unknown reasons, the Absolute desires to become conscious. It achieves consciousness by positing the existence of a material, inanimate, nonconscious world, as people ordinary conceive of reality. It then uses this concept of a mind-independent reality to distinguish the subject part of itself from the object part, thereby creating within the mind a conscious sub-mind. In this way the Absolute, in opposition to its own concept of itself, becomes the relative, phenomenal world. According to Schelling,

> Nature and spirit are fundamentally the same. . . . That which is posited out of consciousness is in its very essence the same as that which is posited in consciousness. . . . The known must itself bear the impression of the knower. . . . The ground of nature and spirit, the absolute, is the identity of the real and the ideal.

Schelling claims that there are distinct kinds of knowledge, much in the way that Spinoza did. There is the philosophical knowledge, which is of one's own rational faculties, and there is the confused knowledge of the imagination. Each gives rise to a different form of existence: the infinite, undivided existence of the Absolute, and the finite existence of individual things. The phenomenal world consists of self-developing objects that arise in thought and possess no true reality. These objects appear as separately existing, particular individuals, but this is due—as Leibniz too had supposed—to our inadequate representations of them. Only the enlightened philosopher can view them sub specie aeternitatis, in their totality, so that the objects themselves are revealed to be ideas. Having such a philosophical vision allows us, as philosophers, to interpret objects to ourselves as they truly exist in the totality of the world-soul, wherein all things are a Parmenidean One. From the perspectiveless point of view of the Absolute, which is the whole of existence, all is absolute, eternal infinitude.

Schelling was much influenced by Giordano Bruno (one of his early works was *Bruno, or on the Divine and Natural Principle of Things,* 1803), especially the view that the finitude of the individual things in the world is broken up into a plurality of self-developing individual existences, but within which the essential unity of all things is not entirely lost. The idea is that each one of us is a definite expression of the Absolute, just as in Bruno's view we are each the world-soul. Identity as a relation belongs only to the Absolute, but it exists in us to a diminished degree, mingled with difference. In other words, in its ultimate reality the world is absolute and the individual objects are relative.

Because in Schelling's view nothing exists which is purely objective or purely subjective, there is identity in both individuality and totality: everything is both objective and subjective. It is only that from any particular perspective one or the other is always dominant. Schelling thus argues that the phenomena of nature, like the phenomena of the mind, exist as a unity not of matter and spirit but of the real and the ideal, the objective and the subjective. In nature there is a preponderance of the real; in the phenomenal world there is a preponderance of the ideal. But neither world is subjectively or objectively pure.

Schelling begins his elaborate *System of Transcendental Idealism* with a Cartesian-like certainty in the proposition "I Am." Like Descartes, he then shows how the transcendental proposition "There are things outside of me" can also be known with the same absolute certainty. For Kant, such a transcendental process reaches beyond the phenomenal world of appearance, not to the noumenal world of the thing in itself but only to the cognitive faculties of the mind. According to Schelling, the object reached is the objective, absolute world itself. Thus, in marked contrast with Fichte's subjective idealism, Schelling paves the way for his absolute idealism, which is still idealism but radically different from its previous incarnations, including and especially, Fichte's:

> Fichte could side with idealism from the point of view of reflection. I, on the other hand, took the viewpoint of production with the principle of idealism. To express this contrast most distinctly, idealism in the subjective sense had to

assert, the ego is everything, while conversely idealism in the objective sense had to assert: Everything = ego and nothing exists but what = ego. These are certainly different views, although it will not be denied that both are idealism.

Berkeley's idealism involved an external and separate God to sustain the non-rational order in the universe to make things real when no rational egos were observing them into existence. Schelling's idealism constructs reality internally from itself, as a coherent universal system where the Absolute is identical to the phenomenal, relative level. And whereas Fichte argued that the subjective, which is primary, posits the objective, Schelling argued the opposite—that the objective posits the subjective. That is, for Fichte, as for Kant, a necessary condition for experience is that what is experienced is interpreted to be other than mental phenomena. Schelling, on the other hand, says that

> I posit God, as the first and the last, as the Alpha and the Omega; but as Alpha he is not what he is as Omega, and in so far as he is only the one—God "in an eminent sense"—he cannot be the other God, in the same sense . . . be called God. For in that case, let it be expressly said, the unevolved God, Deus implicitus, would already be what, as Omega, the Deus explicitus is.

We might wonder why God does not simply remain as the objective Absolute Being. In other words, why does the Absolute give rise to the separations in which we exist in our present, multiperspectival reality?

This question would be analogous to the theological question of why God is not content to stay God, that is, why God creates a world in the first place. Schelling's original answer, which he puts forth in his *Bruno*, reverses the traditional religious concept of "the fall." In an absolute act of freedom, the origin of the phenomenal, relative world comes about so that we, as creative agents, can actualize the world through our consciousness. In other words, it is our individual minds, driven by an unconscious impulse toward self-representation, that add the crucial ingredient which solidifies the worlds from the realm of possibility into actuality.

God in Schelling's view is like Spinoza's deterministic God except that Schelling's God makes choice and freedom possible within the real world through the creation of individual human beings, each of which is empowered by the self-actualizing, creative force of the Absolute. Unlike the Judeo-Christian God, who creates the world to be inhabited by individual souls, it is we ourselves who are the true artists of reality. Such a view leads Schelling to the exact opposite conclusion from Plato's view of art, elevating it as the highest branch of philosophy.

Schelling calls the philosophy of art "the universal organum of philosophy." An *organum* is a polyphonic voice part accompanying the *cantus firmus*, the plainsong or simple Gregorian melody sung in unison (usually at a fourth, fifth, or octave above or below), note for note. Thus, by equating the objective world with "the still unconscious poetry of the soul" and calling philosophy the "universal organum," Schelling is providing the metaphysical scaffolding for Hegel's subsequent notion that it is not the study of nature that allows us to glimpse into the mind of God, as Kepler, Galileo, and the self-proclaimed New Scientists thought, but the study of philosophy. In studying the evolution of philosophy we are experiencing, and taking part in, the birth of God.

Hegel: The Absolute Idealist

Georg Wilhelm Friedrich Hegel (1770–1831) was born in Stuttgart, Germany. At the University of Tübingen he made friends with fellow student Schelling. After graduating he worked as a private tutor until he received his teaching appointment in 1801, as a lecturer, at the University of Jena. He became professor of philosophy in 1805, but a year later Napoleon's troops marched into Jena and Hegel lost his position during the French occupation. He supported himself first as a newspaper editor, then as a school principal in Nuremberg. Ten years later he was reappointed professor of philosophy, first in Heidelberg and then in 1818 at the University of Berlin.

We've seen Kant's development of what he called "critical" or "transcendental" idealism based on his distinction between the phenomenal, knowable world of appearances and the unknowable, noumenal world of things in themselves. Both worlds are real. But just as Berkeley argued that an epistemologically inaccessible noumenal reality can hardly be called reality and instead should be called conjecture or theory or, as Hume called it, a fiction, so Hegel's philosophy, like Fichte's and Schelling's, developed in opposition to Kant's notion of a non-mental reality, the noumenal world, which is utterly unknowable. In some ways, this philosophical move is a metaphysical variation of Aristotle's criticism of Plato's realm of Ideas.

According to Kant, the objects of the phenomenal world—all the things you see around you—are actively processed by the faculties of your mind into existence. Since these faculties are in part the effect of the noumenal world, the objects thereby constituted are created partly (and indirectly) by the noumenal reality and partly (and directly) by your own mental faculties. Hegel argues that there is just one world whose objects are created completely by the mind whose own faculties are created through its own (historical, evolutionary) oppositions against itself. Again, this view recalls Aristotle's claim, against Plato's two worlds, that there is but one world.

Hegel thus builds with Kantian thoroughness an idealist metaphysical system in which the mind does not merely structure and regulate reality but wholly generates and constitutes it, up to and including itself. What he calls "the Absolute," the world as it exists in itself, is mind or spirit. There is no word for "mind" in Germanic and Slavic languages; the word Hegel used was *geist,* which has, as its root, the concept of ghost or spirit. That is, the world in itself is a self-thinking thought, such that the entire process of existence in time is the teleological (goal directed) movement. The easiest way to understand the Aristotelian concept of teleology is as opposed to mechanism, which explains the present and the future in terms of the past; teleology explains the past and the present in terms of the future of the universe becoming aware of itself, a process of "the Absolute realizing itself." In marked contrast to Kant's transcendental (or critical) idealism and Berkeley's subjective idealism, both of which are pluralistic (that is, they involve more than one substance: noumenal and phenomenal reality for Kant; the human mind and the spiritual mind of God for Berkeley), Hegel conceives of the Absolute in terms of a monistic system in which the whole of existence is one substance that is a spirit, or mind. In other words, everything that is, was, or will be is an evolving form within the world-mind, where the forces of evolution are driven not by events in the past or present, but by the still uncreated future. In this way, the Kantian noumenal reality, nowhere present among the phenomenal world of appearances, becomes as yet undeveloped domains of future possibility toward which everything evolves.

The history of philosophy according to Hegel is part of this evolution. The events of history are not merely a succession of various physical things rearranged into different positions. Nor is history a series of ideas and views each of which turns out to be false when it is replaced by a new view. Rather, historical developments are themselves changes in the way the world realizes itself into existence. In this way, philosophy comes to represent not just some passive intellectual activity as practiced by human beings, but the absolute mind going through various stages of the thinking process in its own metaphysical development.

In this way Hegel one-ups Kant's Copernican revolution. Recall how Kant conceived the mind's engagement with real objects not in passive terms, where impressions and ideas are the effects of the object, but in active terms, where the objects are in part the effects of the mind. But this whole process itself is, for Kant, a static thing; the mind does what it does to the phenomenal world using the faculties that it has, and the noumenal world does what it does to the faculties of the mind. Hegel now dislodges even the concept behind these relationships from its privileged position, arguing that the entire process is actively created by the mind! But how can that be, if the mind is everything there is? Where is the impetus for its being if there is not some transcendental mind behind it, empowering it to constitute its objects as they are? Kant's answer in terms of a fixed noumenal world is, for Hegel, just another "earth-centered" prejudice, this time not predicated on the phenomena themselves but on the entire conceptual framework all the way down to the very logic of thought.

In Hegel's view, nothing stands still, not even metaphysics. In Kant's philosophy the active process of reality creation on the part of the mind itself is a passive fact about the way the world is. The phenomenal-noumenal totality, including the ego and transcendental ego, are there all at once, together in their totality, implying, ultimately, the noumenal world is the given fixed place around which everything centers, a God-like, otherworldly absolute ground of being. Hegel pushes Kant's reasoning beyond its own limits. According to Hegel, the drawing of the boundary between the unknowable thing in itself and the knowable phenomena is not conceived in terms of a static horizontal (albeit fuzzy) line between (phenomenal and noumenal) worlds, but as an ever-receding vertical line within the world, drawn between the past and the future. And what is this line? Where is it?

It is here, it is now, it is the ever-receding present moment of existence: the future, the not-yet realm of infinite possibility as unreachable and inaccessible from the present as Kant's noumenal world is from the phenomenal realm, draws us with ever-increasing detail and richness into reality; the point of contact is time.

Thus we might think of the world as conceived by the absolute idealists as a natural evolution from the Kantian culmination of previous philosophical perspectives as follows. Kant, as we saw, conceives of space and time as categories of the mind. But, as such, they are different categories and are not aspects of the world as it exists in the noumenal realm. We've already discussed the sense in which Kant's transcendental idealism influenced the revolutionary development of the relativistic space and time theories of Einstein, where the observer's own "reference frame" (conceived in terms of a Cartesian coordinate system of many dimensions) imparts its own structure in terms of its own quantitative and qualitative yardsticks, such as provided by the topological concept of a metric, onto the real world. Now we shall see how Hegel's absolute idealism, built on the subjective idealism of Fichte and the objective idealism of Schelling, becomes an avatar for subsequent developments in which Kant's concept of a mind-independent, noumenal reality, even as developed by Einstein, gives way to the strange world of quantum mechanics, where all of our most mind-boggling philosophies become integrated into the most fundamental of all sciences: "physics."

But even the evolutionary changes in our ways of thinking about ourselves and the world are the result not just of philosophers, scientists, and mathematicians at work, but also of the world trying to understand itself. And this result, Hegel argues, cannot be understood by the philosophers, scientists, and mathematicians unless there is a thorough knowledge of all these developing stages of thought as represented by the history of philosophy. It is a testament to the brilliance of Hegel's often maligned mind that he then sets out to write one. In reading the history of thought, we are not, he says, viewing just the intellectual struggles of individual thinkers, we are experiencing birthing stages in the evolution of the consciousness of the world. The individuals, as such, are but cogs in the cosmic wheel of the Absolute.

Like Fichte, Hegel discards Kant's notion of mind-independent reality, the "thing in itself," as ultimately unintelligible. He begins with Kant's notion of necessary truths that are not logically necessary (the synthetic a priori), requiring the mind to exist not in a passive relation to its objects but, up to a point, as an active participant in the construction of objects. According to Kant, beyond that point things in themselves exist as mind-independent entities, contributing to the existence of phenomenal objects in the same way the mind contributes to them. The phenomenal world thus exists as a sort of superposition of the effects of things in themselves and the effects of the mind's faculties. This process involves necessity, but not in the logical sense: instead of positing any mind-independent things in themselves that exist beyond experience, affecting objects in a way that necessarily involves the possibility of experience as discoverable by the natural sciences, Hegel's necessity comes from within the mind itself and such necessities are expressed by the laws of history, which follow a necessary process, and so thereby a structure is imposed on consciousness in the same way that for Kant things in themselves impose it.

For Hegel, as for Kant, necessary truths are mind-dependent and not logically necessary. But for Hegel, as for all subsequent absolute idealists, these truths do not depend in any way on some sort of substance beyond the reach of mind. All that exists is the mental: one thinking substance, the thinking subject. Truth therefore depends not on some correspondence between a mind-independent reality and its representation in the mind but, rather, on coherence within a complete system of thought. "The true is the whole." A complete system in Hegel's sense thus does not correspond to any objective reality; it is, itself, objective reality. Again, this Hegelian whole is not a static thing existing beyond, or transcendental to, the world but is immanent in it as an evolutionary, developing process existing within the world itself, accessible to the philosopher through Hegel's theory of dialectic. It begins with the thesis, an initial proposition that turns out to be false or inadequate. The thesis then generates a contradictory proposition, its antithesis, which also turns out to be false or inadequate. This then leads to a rationality-preserving and irrationality-canceling synthesis of the two initially contradictory propositions which Hegel calls "sublation" (*Aufhebung*). This in turn leads to a new thesis and the process continues indefinitely. Hegel outlines this process in his third published work, *The Encyclopedia of the Philosophical Sciences in Outline* (1817), a manual written for his students explaining his entire philosophical system starting with the notion that all is mind.

Kant had of course already pointed out that this is not how things seem to the mind. We seem to ourselves to be minds existing in an objective material world, surrounded by material objects that exist independently of our thoughts. This state of affairs, what Kant called the "transcendental illusion," is the result of an illusion that Hegel calls "estrangement" or "alienation" (*Entfremdung*). The difference is not just a matter of semantics. Hegel uses this language to imply that the illusion is not grounded in an ontological boundary between the mental and nonmental world but is wholly created within the mind by the mind; it is the mind's drawing a false boundary within itself against itself. But, as in Kant, the awareness, or recognition, of this illusion is the first step to reaching the next stage of philosophical progress. That is, the mind's overcoming of the illusion that what is before the mind is not mind but mind-independent material objects (not by ending the illusion but merely, as in Kant, recognizing it) is the first part of the thesis-antithesis-synthesis process that culminates, ultimately, in the mind's "return to itself."

These three stages of the development of thought are presented in the *Encyclopedia* in three parts. In the first part, called "Logic," by which Hegel means not formal logic but "the science of thought," he argues that since only thought exists, logic should be viewed as metaphysics: logic is the study of "the idea in and for itself." Thus he would proclaim to his students: "The Living Being is a syllogism whose very moments are syllogisms." The second part of Hegel's *Encyclopedia* is called the "Philosophy of Nature," the study of "the idea in its otherness"; and the third part, the "Philosophy of Mind," is the study of "the idea come back to itself out of that otherness." One can easily imagine that in the hands of a lesser philosopher Hegel's attempt to provide a systematic account of absolute reality as a whole might have ended up merely as an elaborate series of counterarguments to Kant's transcendental arguments in which Kant tried to show that reason's attempt to transcend the understanding and thereby grasp noumenal reality results in unresolvable antinomies. This, as we saw, was in large part the approach taken by Schelling, for whom reality remains, as for Kant, an incomprehensible mystery. But Hegel is not content merely to argue against Kant; he insists that the true philosopher, as a stage in the development of the world soul, must proceed beyond mere criticism and counterargument (which mirror the antithesis stage of the philosophical evolution of the universe) in order for the system to evolve to its next level. If our only means for grasping the whole universe—the Absolute— were with the Kantian faculty of understanding, this would be impossible because the understanding is limited to its own divisive, contradictory concept pairs like "finite and infinite," "freedom and determinism," and so on. Such opposite concepts could never present to the mind reality as it exists in its totality, since that absolute totality is not divided. The universe would in that case remain, as it does for Kant and Schelling, ultimately incomprehensible and statically mysterious.

Hegel, however, uses reason to transcend not just the phenomenal world as a means of reaching the active faculties of the mind involved in the construction of the phenomena, but even goes beyond those faculties, to "transcend the understanding" and thereby "contain the opposites." In this way, the whole universe in its totality—the Absolute Being itself, the "mystical"—ceases to be inaccessible to dialectical thought, which leads not to unresolvable antinomies but to the resolution of the contradictions. Hegel argues that both Kant and Schelling failed to understand "the tremendous power of the negative." Typically, in our self-alienated, transcendental illusionary stage of consciousness, when we encounter deep contradiction and paradox in our thinking we experience an unhappy dread. Seeking to avoid this state of mental confusion, reason is moved by the force of its own negativity toward its negativity to sublate its previous conception and to thereby progress to the next, higher stage, where it is free of the previous contradiction but will more than likely encounter another, even deeper and more perplexing one. Again, this is not merely some intellectual process in which philosophers engage but the very life and source of reality: "Being is thought" and "What is actual is rational." Nor is it a static process; just as the concept of being, as a thesis, gives rise to the opposite concept, its antithesis, non-being, and together the mind is then perplexed to create a new sublation of these two into the concept that is their synthesis, becoming, the mind continues to thus extend itself beyond its own limits. With each new step, the mind evolves into a higher, expanded consciousness.

To use a contemporary analogy from computer science, Hegel is in a sense trying to increase the mind's "RAM" space. In fact, the analogy with computers is actually rather appropriate in our attempt to understand absolute idealism within a contemporary framework. Though one must always be cautious in using such analogies, it is a fact that many computer theorists, including philosophical logicians and cognitive philosophers, conceive of the entire universe as a computer program being run on an abstract rather than a physical computer. (Recall that our understanding of the concept of abstractness is in terms of something that does not exist in space and time.) Indeed, it is easy to see that the universe as a whole must be an abstract object in that it does not exist in space and time. Once you think about this a little it becomes not at all mysterious. What, after all, does it mean to be somewhere? It means to have a location. Location, in turn, is conceived in terms of having a containing space. Right now, for instance, I'm in my study, which is in my house, which is in New York, which is on the East Coast, which is on planet Earth, which is in the solar system, which is in the Milky Way Galaxy, which is in the universe, which is . . . well, where is the universe? If by universe we mean, as Hegel does, the totality of all existence, including the whole of space and time, the universe cannot be in any space. For in talking of the Absolute, Hegel means the universe of all universes, such that even if there are other, "super" and "hyper" spaces, and so on, the totality of all these types of spaces cannot be in any space.

So the universe must be nowhere. How, after all, did I provide location in each of the series above, from my room to the galaxies? In every case, I gave the larger map, the containing space. The universe conceived as the Absolute cannot, by definition, have a containing space. It is, therefore, necessarily nowhere. That's not just true, it has to be true! Likewise for time; this moment is now, which is today, which is within this week of this month of this year in this century in this millennium at the tail end of the universe's fifteen-billion-year history. But when does all this time take place? Again, to speak of the universe in Absolute terms, the absolute answer is never. This is because the universe contains not only all of space but all of time as well. Thus the universe, which is nowhere, never happens! It has neither a place (position) where it exists nor a time in which it occurs. Thus the universe of universes, the Absolute, is more like the set of all numbers. And what, after all, are numbers? (Recall our detailed discussion of numbers in the Pythagoras section in Chapter 1.) Numbers are abstract entities. And the universe thus conceived as an abstract entity makes it amenable to the same kinds of analyses as mathematical objects.

We have seen this sort of metaphysical move brewing for centuries, in the work of both philosophers and the mathematically inspired scientists. It is so central to understanding the various revolutions in thought during our own century that it behooves us to go a bit further into it. In addition, it is deeply ironic that Hegel's system and the subsequent absolute idealist movements in the nineteenth century have often been regarded as somehow not being central to subsequent developments in philosophy, mathematics, physics, and computer science. Nothing could be further from the truth. What happened, historically, is that while philosophers descended (meant literally, not pejoratively) into the domain of logical analyses and reductions of thought to language, the development of the ideas of Kant and the nineteenth-century absolute idealists came to be carried forth by physicists like Einstein and Niels Bohr, while mathematicians like Alan Turing and logicians like Kurt Gödel and Alonzo Church dissolved the distinction between representation and reality to a new level of logical rigor, encodable into the types of algorithmic processes that, when embedded in physical processes, became the universal machines now known as computers. Let us see if we can catch a glimpse of this, perhaps itself a paradigm example of, Hegelian process.

According to Hegel and the absolute idealists, everything is thought. But what is thought? We've discussed this question at various points using several different philosophical systems to get at it. Using methods that we should by now be familiar with, we can when we attend to our own thoughts very quickly come to realize that in the intellectual domain (meaning other than the perceptual representations—the visual impressions and ideas) thoughts exist as auditory images, which themselves consist, in turn, of strings of words. Likewise, the rational thinking process, or insofar as it is rational, consists in stringing together propositions. Once we see this we can perhaps understand what is generally regarded as one of the most cryptic remarks of Hegel's, namely, that "the living being is a syllogism whose very moments are syllogisms."

Typically, such assertions by Hegel have been ridiculed as nonsensical. But, as has so often been the case, there may be far more to the statements of a great philosopher than first meets the understanding. Perhaps truths about reality cannot fit into the limited and limiting mind space of our ordinary, commonsense understanding. Hegel and many subsequent philosophers to whom he was an avatar believed that ordinary (natural) languages are inadequate as they are and that their conceptual base must somehow be enhanced. In any case, here we have a statement, like "Everything is made of water," which at first glance seems preposterous but may contain the seed of some great, as yet unblooming, insight: "Everything is a string of syllogisms." How could that be? A string of syllogisms, after all, is a string of propositions, themselves the molecules making up a complex tautology strung together by logic.

But this is exactly the sort of process that happens in a computer program, except that the propositions have been further reduced to numbers. What is a computer program, philosophically speaking? Abstractly, a program can be represented as a map $f: N \rightarrow N$, where N is the set of natural numbers mapped onto N, that is, a map into itself. Given some input data, which is just an integer or a string of integers, the program can then use this number to generate another number as output. Contemporary computer theory is a decision procedure for determining what constitutes an effective procedure (a way of going on, i.e., a "rule") and describing its attributes (what states it is in and what states it can get to, i.e., its "memory bank"). Today, not only can we model (represent) the human mind using a computer program, the entire universe can be so modeled using a formal language in which the universe evolves deterministically from an initial state into a final state. (If you think of "formal" languages as related to Plato's forms, you will not be far off the mark; the term refers to languages such as logic and mathematics, which are used to talk not about actual particular objects in the world, such as "All Swedes are persons" or "My sweater is pretty," but the general forms of grammar and syntax underlying them, such as "All S are P" or "Some S are P," and so on. The same holds, less obviously, for mathematics.)

What the absolute idealists do in equating reality with the process of thought is remarkably analogous to what the computer scientist does in viewing the universe as equivalent to its simulation, provided, of course, that the simulation can meet certain specific conditions in terms of functional equivalence, isomorphism, and so on, conceived as a *universal program*. Likewise, human beings are conceived as subprograms within the general universal program that act in exactly the same way in the "simulation" as "real" human beings do in the "real" universe. Suppose you ask, "How could operations consisting not of the sensations of happiness and sadness, dryness and wetness, and so on, but of electrical impulses in computer wiring, be the same as real human thought?" But then you have to ask yourself what things like the experience of sadness and the experience of rain— mental events in what you call the "real" world—consist of. In the firing of neurons (happiness) and in the activities of clouds (rain)? But what are neurons, what are clouds and rain? These all consist in the movement of molecules that are neither happy nor wet. H_2O is just a constellation of three little round atoms and not wet! Likewise, a sequence of neurons is a sequence of neurons and not, itself, happy or sad!

Thus, starting from an absolute idealist perspective, the question would have to be reversed: how can "real wires," "real computers," "real rocks, rivers, and hurricanes," and so on, consist not in physical things but in mental things? Hegel's elaborate answer comes in the form of not just a metaphysical theory but also a logical procedure for carrying out such a program into the faculties of human understanding, thereby increasing the logical space of the understanding. Once this evolution takes place, the philosopher is in a position to see why the mind's structuring of its "models" of reality is reality: because in Hegel's world there is no underlying substantive thing in itself. Thoughts are not only the objects of our experience but also the elements of reality.

In this way the Hegelian process of enlightenment consists not in transcending beyond the phenomenal world outwardly, to things in themselves, or inwardly, to the mental faculties of the understanding, but in breaking through the logical categories themselves. Hegel wants to use the old logic of Aristotle to move into the realm of a higher logic in which contradictions are not themselves errors (irrationalities) but a method of cognitive evolution. When the mind evolves to this higher level, the ontological distinction between concept pairs like "being, non-being," "something, nothing," "imaginary, real," "subjective, objective," "phenomenal, noumenal," "mental, physical," "perceptual, conceptual," "representational, presentational," "simulational, actual," and so on, such that all distinctions derived from the false dichotomy between empiricist and rationalist systems of thought dissolve.

To put it once again in contemporary computer language: the universal simulation does not need to run on an "actual" computer to be exactly what it is. Rather, the universal simulation is an abstract sequence of mappings, meaning that it does not need to exist in space and time. This is reminiscent of Plato's forms except that for Hegel as for Berkeley and Kant, to be an object in space and time simply means to be a mental event. Follow this through to its ultimate conclusion and you will get the whole, complicated upshot of Hegel's almost incomprehensible system, which we might put as follows: *To be a mental event, a mental event does not need to be a mental event!*

That last statement may well be the sum and substance of what has since evolved into the revolution in thought we are presently undergoing. It is, of course, too soon to tell. In any case, this is sufficient for our purposes of giving you some access to the idea that the real universe in which we live can be properly regarded as a representation of the abstract universal program in exactly the way that the numeral "3" is a representation of the number 3 (as we discussed in our sections on the systems of Pythagoras and Plato). In other words—and this is the new additional step in computer theory that parallels the move made by the absolute idealists—the actual physical computer is a representation of an abstract program.

Staying with our computer analogy, we can continue to make sense of Hegel's system as follows. Individual minds like you and I, as rational subroutines living in (functioning within) the universal program, cannot distinguish between the abstract running of the universal program and the physically real evolution of the universe. Such a universe would be a Kantian noumenal thing in itself, which is excluded not just by the absolute idealists but also by the twentieth-century logical systems in which models of what a real computer program is and a real computer program are identical objects, in exactly the way Hegel envisioned. The universe itself, regarded as an abstract program, is an Absolute Idea. It has exactly the same nature as our individual human minds, the programs or subroutines running within it. The absolute idealists' conception of individual intellectual acts, none of which are substances or things in themselves but are abstract objects, are thus analogous to the fundamental map—procedure or program—that takes the universe (the universal program) from one state into the next. Reality itself can thus be viewed as a series of operations of an abstract universal machine.

In this view, the real universe is an abstract entity that is an unimaginably complex program that forms subprograms, the most important of which is a model of itself as a subprogram—the world presented as objective reality—and a subprogram for studying this subprogram—the human mind, or consciousness. Further, as it turns out, the theorems of Kurt Gödel[6] show that an exact model of such a process involving all processes is impossible—even for infinite machines such as the universal Turing machine. Thus the various approaches of the subjective and objective idealists can be further explained using these contemporary terms, as follows.

A subjective idealist system such as Fichte's starts with the finite rational subprograms of individual human egos as the foundation. It then constructs a representation of the universal program, using the logical functions inherent in the rational operations of our own individual conscious minds. An objective idealist system such as Schelling's starts with the universal program as the foundation and then constructs individual rational minds as parts inherent in the nature of the universal program; individual minds are thus necessary elements for making the totality not just a whole but real. On the other hand, an absolute idealist system such as Hegel's takes yet a third approach: basically, in a Hegelian evolving system neither the Fichte nor Schelling type idealisms are real options to be discovered;

rather, the philosophies are part of the construction. In other words, the universe itself—the whole of reality—is presently writing itself into existence!

But, if anything like this is really true, why don't we see it? Why don't we understand it? Why is philosophy so difficult? One way of putting it, which subsequent phenomenologists such as Heidegger will build their systems on, would be this: a necessary condition for comprehensibility is incomprehensibility. Such developments will parallel advances made in mathematics where it turns out the most difficult theorems can be proven once it is proven that no proof exists; this, itself, allows a proof to be mad! Recall Fichte's contention, derived from Kant's analysis of the necessary conditions for the having of experience, that in order to be conscious a mind must interpret some of its own activities as other than its own activities. Put in physicalist language: the neurons of a properly functioning brain must function so as to tell each other, at some point, "I am not a neuron," or "I am not a neural firing," or "I am not an event in the brain." You see a chair, after all, which even on the most basic physical understanding of the brain means that a part of the brain (somewhere in the calcarine fissure, according to the latest neurophysiological theory, where the active neural processing of perceptual events takes place) is interpreted by another part of the brain as not being part of the brain! This is a stripped down version of a difficult to understand twentieth-century theorem, which we've already referred to, known as Gödel's theorem. In effect, as we are here presenting it, such an insight says that any system must, in order to be a properly functioning system, lie to itself. Translating this idea into a computer language vocabulary, we could say that a computer program can be conscious only if it is embedded as a subroutine in a larger program containing many such subroutines interpreted by each subroutine not as subroutines in a program but as an external world. Further, not only must the universal program give rise to self-conscious subprograms, these must in turn continue to evolve toward becoming one. Only at that point does the universal program actually come into existence as such. In other words, the problem is that the world is not yet fully comprehensible! Such Hegelian thinking, involving a bootstrap metaphysics in which the future brings about the past, is exactly of the sort found in recent quantum models of the universe, such as that of John Archibald Wheeler; according to Wheeler, we live in a "participatory universe," in which our own acts of consciousness actualize reality retroactively. Such thinking comes out of the so-called measurement problem in quantum mechanics, and this was already explicitly anticipated by Hegel. For discrete, quantum measurement states in the conscious mind are the reality necessary to bring the world into being. Prior to such acts of consciousness all events subsisted in a weird superposition of ghostly possibilities that come into a state of being only through the process of measurement.

The fundamental philosophical basis for such thinking emerges from Hegel's notion of the universe in terms of self-thinking thought (thought that thinks *itself*, without need of other devices), where philosophy can be viewed as the evolving software of an abstract universal machine, the universe. But then we must remember that philosophy is not yet a done act! The entire process of human history, as presented in Hegel's system of thought, is the evolving struggle of the universe to become aware of itself. This incredible idea is laid out in great detail in the first and most difficult of Hegel's systematic works, published in 1807, *The Phenomenology of Mind*. It describes the stages that consciousness must undergo in its evolution from naive commonsense notions of reality to a truly philosophical, synthetic view and full self-consciousness in which the universe not only fully realizes that it exists but, therein, creates itself through "the consciousness of its own freedom." Starting with the "unhappy consciousness" stage—a subjectively idealistic, abstract, and dualistic view of truth that represents itself in our conscious psychologies as a lonely, religious quest for some remote, "changeless," deified, consciousness—it begins the slow process of awakening into its final, absolute stage. The process of Hegelian enlightenment is thus not just the process of our trying to become lovers of wisdom, though it is that. It is also the enlightenment of the world entire, of being itself, through a process whose machinery can be studied. For that process is history.

In his *Lectures on the Philosophy of History* (1837), which Hegel delivered between 1822 and 1831 and which were supplemented with two sets of notes by students, Hegel gives what he considers a full and final account of "the philosophical history of the world," by which he means not observations on history or the study of records and facts nor even reflections on history but the "universal history" of the evolutionary unfolding of thought itself, the absolute world-mind trying to realize itself. In a sense, it represents what in Hegel's view is no less than the autobiography of the universe.

Schopenhauer: The World Is Your Idea

Born in the Free City of Danzig, Arthur Schopenhauer (1788–1860) was sent at age nine to Le Havre, where for two years he learned French, then he went to a boarding school in Hamburg for four years. As a teenager he traveled through England, France, Switzerland, and Austria for two years, until his father made him go to work at a merchant's office. After his father committed suicide by throwing himself into a canal, young Schopenhauer went to live in Weimar with his mother, a novelist. In 1809 he enrolled at the University of Göttingen but then moved to the University of Berlin to study with Fichte. He completed his doctorate in philosophy at the University of Jena.

Schopenhauer's highly original philosophy developed from the idealism of Kant and Fichte. It is a rich blend of Kantian and Platonic views of ideas and owes much to Indian mysticism. His main philosophical influences were Goethe, Fichte, Schelling, Locke, and Hume. In his thirties he published his most important work, *The World as Will and Idea* (sometimes translated as *The World as Will and Representation*), convinced that it would cause a great stir. It was almost universally ignored for over three decades. The book did, however, help him to get a teaching position in philosophy at the University of Berlin at the same time as

Hegel, whose ideas had already begun to dominate German philosophy. Schopenhauer was vehemently opposed to Hegel's use of the concept of reason as the basic force of the world, arguing that what is most fundamental to the world is not reason but will.

Schopenhauer tried in vain to compete with Hegel, even by scheduling his lectures at the same time as Hegel's, but never managed to achieve any sort of following. Meanwhile, Hegel's influence spread like wildfire throughout Europe. Bitter and jealous, Schopenhauer left Berlin and had this to say about his colleague:

> Hegel, installed from above by the powers that be as the certified Great Philosopher, was a flat-headed, insipid, nauseating, illiterate charlatan, who reached the pinnacle of audacity in scribbling together and dishing up the craziest mystifying nonsense.

His view of most other philosophers, with the exception of Plato and Kant, was not much better; he referred to them as "windbags."

Nevertheless, Schopenhauer continued writing. In 1844 he issued a second edition of *The World as Will and Idea,* with fifty additional chapters. Unlike the first edition, this new version finally brought fame to the author, who was now in his sixties. Soon Schopenhauer found himself famous throughout Europe. He has continued to exert enormous influence on philosophers, psychologists, and writers, including Friedrich Nietzsche, Richard Wagner, Leo Tolstoy, Joseph Conrad, Marcel Proust, Thomas Mann, and Sigmund Freud.

The World as Will and Idea begins with Schopenhauer explaining how everything in your present experience is *you,* in that the objects in your experience are aspects of yourself. The world of your experience and everything in it is, literally, your dream, expressed in the proposition "The world is my idea." This sounds like a very positive and enlightening philosophy: your life is a dream, the world is a dream, and so on. But actually it is a very negative, deeply dark philosophy. For then one must ask, "If the world is but my own idea, why then is there so much suffering and evil in it?" Here is Schopenhauer's unflattering answer: "The World is my will." The reason the world is so full of violence, pain, and suffering is that you willed it to be so.

To understand Schopenhauer's reasoning, we must go back to Kant's distinction between phenomena, the world of appearances, and noumena, things in themselves. For Schopenhauer applies this distinction to us, to our own experience of ourselves. Kant had claimed that the noumenal world is forever beyond reach of the phenomena and even of reason, because the noumena transcend the categories of the mind. But Schopenhauer argues that the noumenal world is actually much involved in each and every aspect of experience, because he equates the noumenal world of things in themselves with the will.

Keep in mind that the will for Schopenhauer is no abstract notion. It is an actual object, you can even see it: your body, rocks, tables, chairs, even the stars. Everything you see, feel and experience is the direct manifestation of the will, an active construction of the will. Schopenhauer explains this situation as follows. You are to yourself a phenomenal object in the same way as a cloud, rock, or plant. But unlike trees and plants, you are self-conscious. That is, your own phenomenal body that you experience as extended in space and time does not merely respond and react to its environment instinctually. Your phenomenal body is an embodiment of the will.[7]

Consider the analogy of ordinary dreams. Say you're dreaming that dogs are chasing you and you are running. That phenomenal body in the dream, from whose first-person point of view you seem to be experiencing the dream, of what is it made? The phenomenal body consists of phenomena, and what animates these phenomena? First, it is your will that makes those phenomena, as such, appear as a body. Likewise, your legs and arms in the dream as you run from the chasing dogs appear to move because the dream character in whom you find yourself is scared of the dogs and wants to get away from them. But this of course is but a very elaborate self-deception! Schopenhauer distinguishes the apparent will from the actual will. This is one of the most misunderstood aspects of his philosophy. For to suppose that when you are running from the dogs in your dream you are willing the dogs upon yourself seems absurd. After all, according to your own experience in the dream, what you want most is to get away from the dogs. But wishing and the appearance of willing are not the will in itself. You are actually willing the dogs upon yourself and willing yourself to be afraid and willing that you believe the dogs are chasing you, and so on—but that is the actual will, the dark driving force behind the phenomenal world of appearance.

Schopenhauer thus refers to your body as the direct manifestation of will, not your phenomenal psychological "wishing states" or "ruminations." In your dream, you are in your own world: Schopenhauer's statement "The world is my idea" is true in dreams. So during the dream there is something projecting your consciousness into one part of the dream (your phenomenal body) and excluding it from another (the phenomenal bodies of the dogs). That something is the will. Once this is understood, we are in a position to finally understand why Schopenhauer says what he does about the world entire. All the so-called "real" events of which the actual world of your experience consists are in reality the constructions of the will. Schopenhauer's concept of will provides the missing bridge between phenomena and noumena.

We are now also in a position to understand why Schopenhauer was so vehemently opposed to Hegel. What is ultimately real for Schopenhauer is not any sort of rational world-mind, as Hegel had thought. Rather, the driving force of the world is a nonrational and blind force, the world-will. It is the dark momentum of existence that with an insatiable craving creates all and destroys all. The will that drives the world is not some benevolent God, not even is it rational. Hiding behind the veil of appearance, the will is invulnerable to the prying glances of its own creations. It creates in its creatures insatiable cravings that are the will objectified: sex, violence, greed, war, and domination. Behind it all is the eternal, dark, metaphysical world-will.

It is out of these very concepts that Sigmund Freud would create the foundations for psychoanalysis. His notion of the Id (Latin for "it") is a psychological variation of the same noumenal force as Schopenhauer's will. As Freud wrote: "We have unwittingly steered our course into the harbor of Schopenhauer's philosophy." Indeed, our analogy with dreams is highly appropriate, given that Freud's highly influential *Analysis of Dreams* was an elaborate attempt to try to create a bridge of communication between the individual phenomenal being, the ego, and the dark irrational forces behind its own inscrutable actions. Schopenhauer would have claimed that such a bridge could never be built, that no analysis could ever be fully successful, because of the infinite power of self-deception. We are led by our thoughts to believe that we act from conscious, rational deliberation. But the truth according to Schopenhauer is that our intellects are a clever rationalization, a veneer of rational sanity hiding the blind, unconscious actions of our underlying wills.

The will remains hidden. Our desires, our wishes for happiness, are illusions. The will cares nothing for happiness. The proof? Schopenhauer would say: look around, and you will see that nearly everyone everywhere is always suffering through life. The only real force is reproduction and domination. The human race is driven by the will. Human values such as happiness, optimism, and hope are clever deceptions, part of the grand illusion driven by art, religion, morality, politics, law, science, and even philosophy.

There is, however, one escape clause in Schopenhauer's dark philosophy: art. Schopenhauer claims that only through art can human beings escape the tyranny of the will. Because the will is not rational and yet it controls everything, the world cannot be understood through rational means. Therefore, true understanding can be attained only through aesthetic experience. Art exists, according to Schopenhauer, in the transcendental realm of "will-less" perception. Thus, as with Schelling, what Plato considered to be the worst aspect of art turns out to be the very solution to the problem of existence. That is, because art is not subservient to science and rational thinking, art provides the highest form of understanding and gives just enough elbow room for the possibility of freedom.

In Schopenhauer's philosophy, the role of the artist as philosopher and the philosopher as artist is to create the archetypal ideas that communicate the essential forms of reality to the unenlightened masses. Schopenhauer is thus at the extreme end of the romantic conception of art: because art is the metaphysical bridge between the phenomenal world of appearance and the noumenal world of the will, it must be free from all practical constraints. The philosopher and the artist must be free to create without being influenced by any practical concerns. But Schopenhauer does not consider all art forms equal—music is the highest. And it must be formal music, free from words or images, as is found in the pure mathematical formalism of baroque music that connects us with ultimate reality.

Kierkegaard: The Subjective Existentialist

Sören Kierkegaard (1813–1855) was born in Copenhagen. At seventeen he went to study theology at the University of Copenhagen but spent most of his time reading literature and philosophy, both of which were under the influence of contemporary Hegelian philosophy. He liked the works of Plato and the romantics, but though he admired Hegel he found himself deeply critical; upon hearing

Schelling's criticisms of Hegel in Berlin, Kierkegaard commented that "if Hegel had written the whole of his Logic and then said . . . that it was merely a joke, then he could certainly have been the greatest thinker who ever lived. As it is, he is himself merely a joke." Kierkegaard saw Hegel's rendering of the whole of reality as deeply ironic, in that he not only failed to capture what Kierkegaard saw as its most important aspect—individual human existence as such—but even went so far as to deny it. Kierkegaard presented his criticisms of Hegel in a brilliant master's thesis, *The Concept of Irony.* He went on to publish an enormous number of highly original books before his death at age forty-two.

Critical of both established philosophy and all institutional religion, especially the Danish state church, in his voluminous writings Kierkegaard went on to argue for the primacy of existence, which he saw in radically individualistic terms, diametrically opposed both to abstract thought and to all group social systems. He claimed that authentic individuality can come about only through a relationship of commitment and engagement with the world through choice, involving despair and dread about the unknown. Such authenticity cannot be achieved with logic and reason, which are incapable of approaching the ultimate, unknowable unknown, which Kierkegaard called God; it can be attained only through self-actualization. This meant experiencing the direct awareness of existence as an unknown and then within that despair affirming one's individual existence, the self-creation of a true, inner self.

For Hegel, thought and existence are identical; according to Kierkegaard, it is not even possible to relate to existence via thought. In Kierkegaard's Platonic view of meaning, existence is unthinkable; thought is but an abstraction limited to concepts within general categories. Thinking only removes us from the direct experience of existence and imprisons us in language, itself an abstraction. Likewise, though Kierkegaard admired Descartes for trying to base philosophy in the self, he saw him as making the same mistake as Hegel: namely, equating the self with thought. According to Kierkegaard, "I think, therefore I am," is the ultimate mistake in philosophy! We can think about ourselves, but this only involves us in our outward roles. We cannot through thinking experience existence, for in thinking we are moving away from the existential core of our own being, hiding from ourselves through abstraction. Existence must be lived and experienced with full passion, decision, action. Kierkegaard thus laid the foundations for the highly influential existentialist movement in philosophy, of which he is widely regarded as the founder.

Although Kierkegaard's views arose in opposition to Hegel's, they owe a lot to his system. The very titles of some of Kierkegaard's most important works were direct provocations against Hegel. *Either/Or* (1843) is a satire of what Kierkegaard saw as a depersonalization of human existence in Hegel's departure from traditional logic erected by Aristotle on three fundamental principles:

1. the principle of identity,
2. the principle of noncontradiction, and
3. the principle of the excluded middle.

The first says that everything is identical to itself: A = A. The second says that nothing both is and is not the case; for instance, no proposition (such as "Socrates exists") is both true and false: ~(p ∧ ~p). The third says that anything either is or is not the case; for instance, "Socrates exists" is either true or false: p ∨ ~p. Rejecting all three principles, Hegel's dialectical logic makes everything its own opposite, A = ~A, and so the second and third Aristotelian principles, both of which stand on the more basic principle of identity, are invalidated in Hegel's system. Kierkegaard saw this as an abomination: without the principle of identity the individual ceases to exist; without the excluded middle all decision making and with it freedom is denied—leading to the state described in *Either/Or,* one of the most amusing in all of philosophy:

> If you marry, you will regret it; if you do not marry, you will also regret it; if you marry or do not marry, you will regret both; whether you marry or do not marry, you will regret both. Laugh at the world's follies, you will regret it; weep over them, you will also regret that; laugh at the world's follies or weep over them, you will regret both; whether you laugh at the world's follies or weep over them, you will regret both. Believe a woman, you will regret it; believer her not, you will also regret that; believe a woman, or believe her not, you will regret both; whether you believe a woman or believe her not, you will regret both. Hang yourself, you will regret it; do not hang yourself, you will regret both; whether you hang yourself or do not hang yourself, you will regret both. This, gentlemen, is the sum and substance of all philosophy.[8]

In one of Kierkegaard's most important works, *Concluding Unscientific Post-script* (1846), he distinguishes subjective thought, which concerns itself with the how, from objective thought, which concerns itself with the what, a distinction central to Kierkegaard's philosophy. The idea is this. Thought cannot grasp pure existence, but it must be used to interpret existence. That is how subjective thought allows individuals to create themselves existentially: the subjective thinker is defined not by studying or observing truth but by living it. The Kierkegaardian individual becomes the truth, he exists it. Once again Hegel's objective history, objective reflection, objective existence, and so on, are the sounding boards against which Kierkegaard launches his own view: the Hegelian individual, defined by the state, exists in a system of objective thought in which the individual's own existence is absurdly and comically excluded because all he has at his disposal for self-understanding are abstract, universal, and timeless categories. The individual's concrete, particular existence in time is thereby appropriated into the crowd, the group, the system until the individual exists no more. Indeed, Kierkegaard suggests that in a fully Hegelian world the individual has ceased to exist:

> One must therefore be very careful in dealing with a philosopher of the Hegelian school, and, above all, to make certain of the identity of the being with whom one has the honor to discourse. Is he a human being, an existing human being? Is he himself sub specie aeterni, even when he sleeps, eats, blows his

nose, or whatever else a human being does? Is he himself the pure "I am I?"....
Does he in fact exist?

Kierkegaard's philosophy thus opened a path for the radical subjectivity that
became the cornerstone of existential thought in which the concrete individual is
primary and existence itself is understood, ultimately, in concrete individualistic
terms. Since no objective system is possible, the subjective thinker is doomed to
exist in perpetual uncertainty. Recognizing this as our fate is according to
Kierkegaard the key to an authentic life. The unique category of the individual
(*Enkelte*) is for Kierkegaard so central that he had it inscribed on his tombstone.

In taking his own views to heart, Kierkegaard went to such extreme lengths
that none of his works is presented as a system, not even as *his*; instead of writing
in the objective voice used by nearly all other philosophers (except perhaps to a
certain degree Plato, who as far as we know wrote only dialogues through the
voices of characters other than himself), all of Kierkegaard's works are written
through a pseudonym and presented through the eyes of distinct characters. Perhaps recognizing that the idea of the author as an objective, external observer was
a construction (as the later deconstructionists would insist), Kierkegaard created
vivid characters with their own distinctive psychologies, ideas, beliefs, and writing styles. He wrote his works not in "his own" voice but from within the subjective voice of the created persona. Thus, for instance, *Either/Or* is presented as a
correspondence between a young aesthete and an older man named Judge Wilhelm; the *Either*, written by the young man, is lyrical and poetic whereas the *Or*,
written by the old man, is dry and pedantic. But Kierkegaard goes even further,
and puts both parts within the persona of yet another pseudonym, an imaginary
editor named Victor Eremita. Among the many other personas that Kierkegaard
created for his voluminous works are Johannes de Silentio, Constantin Constan-
tius, Johannes Climacus, Nicolaus Notabene, Vigilius Hafniensis, Anti-Climacus,
and Hilarius Bogbinder.

Nietzsche: The Superman

Friedrich Nietzsche (1844–1900) was born in Röcken, Germany. His father and
both grandfathers were Lutheran ministers, and his family expected that he too
would become a man of the cloth. But not only did he reject the religion, he
became one of the most radical, influential, and outspoken critics of religion of all
time, in addition to rejecting all of its traditional morality and values, especially as
espoused by Christianity and Judaism. It is Nietzsche who coined the famous slo-
gan "God is dead."

When he was four his father died, leaving him and his sister to be raised by
his mother and grandmother. As a young man at the famous Schulpforte, he
excelled in the study of ancient languages, religion, literature, and philosophy,
especially the ancient Greeks—his favorite was Plato. He entered the University
of Bonn but found the students and professors so "shallow" and "unphilosophi-

cal" that he transferred to Leipzig. Inspired by Schopenhauer's philosophy and Richard Wagner's music, Nietzsche began writing and publishing important papers. He became such a brilliant student that the University of Basel in Switzerland offered him professorship before he even completed his doctorate at Leipzig. He accepted and a year later, while still only twenty-four, was awarded the doctorate without an examination.

At Basel, Nietzsche became friends with Richard Wagner. He taught there for ten years and then resigned so he could work full time on his various books. He produced fourteen highly original and provocative works. Among his most influential are *Thus Spake Zarathustra* (1883, 1884, and 1885, published in three installments), *Beyond Good and Evil* (1886), *The Genealogy of Morals* (1887), *The Antichrist* (1888), and *The Will to Power* (published posthumously in 1901).

In *Beyond Good and Evil,* Nietzsche argues that concepts like "good," "bad," and "evil" come about through the weak trying to corrupt the strong, what he calls the "transvaluation of classical values." Religion is part of the process, especially the "philosophically blind" Jewish and Christian priests who "transvalue" human biological and psychological nature. Philosophy, too, is guilty, and Nietzsche mounts an equally searing attack on the philosophers, suggesting that philosophers are as blinded by the "chimera" of "objective knowledge" as much as the Christians are blinded from the truth by their concept of God. The only remedy is truth, itself subjective and perspectival, created not by the weak but by the strong, through the will to power.

In the world according to Nietzsche there are no Gods and no devils, no things in themselves, not even things as such; no pure being of any kind, neither noumenal nor phenomenal, no Platonic forms: there is but a chaotic Heraclitan flux, stripped even of the Logos, upon which we impose our will. Traditional epistemology is as dead as God. Nietzsche in this way attempts to revolutionize both epistemology and philosophy by taking them back to their Presocratic roots. The only true morality is that of the powerful imposing their will on the weak, much in the way the authoritarian nihilist Thrasymachus had espoused in the fifth century B.C.E. To "know" for Nietzsche means to invent, and to invent authentically for human beings means to lie. Traditional lying is inauthentic lying in which one lies using the terms and methods of religious, political, and educational institutions; this is an elaborate form of self-deception.

To lie authentically according to Nietzsche is the essence of authentic creativity because it subjugates others to one's own will to power. One thereby forces reality into a shape to which others must then bend. According to Nietzsche, only a few individuals are brave enough to retain their authentic power after passing through the self-destructive gauntlet of social "normalization." Most people get absorbed by the previous lies imposed on them through institutions that are the decaying remnants of others' will to power. These insidious processes cut deep, not only into our biological and psychological makeups but into the very structure of thought and language, the vehicles not of truth but self-deception. To use language is to lie, for language works by lying. Words deny what is real, the perpetual flux of ephemeral things, by imposing fictitious similarities between appearances through the power of repetition. Thus, for instance, we identify our-selves as part of the same group by willfully ignoring and thereby suppressing from our consciousness the primordial fact that no two persons are alike; a false identity is imposed on us by the various religions, clubs, organizations, racial classes, and so on—institutions through which people deceive themselves into having a sense of identity where in fact there is none. And so whereas many other philosophers of the time, most notably Kierkegaard, argued for individual iden-tity, Nietzsche—just like David Hume—claimed that there is no true individual identity, no authentic personal self. The concept of a self too is but a clever lie and self-deception. The only authentic action left to the conscious mind is the willful construction of masks with which to further exert unto the insubstantial world its own will to power. Language is such a mask, imposed on us "as a condition of life," which because of the fact that it must by its very nature lie becomes the source of new creative possibilities.

Language in Nietzsche's view is a "mobile army of metaphors, metonyms, and anthropomorphisms." A *metaphor* is a figure of speech in which a term is transposed from its original concept to another, thereby establishing—falsely—a sort of likeness or analogy between them. We say "the ship plows the sea." In real-ity there is no similarity; it is imparted to the objects of the world by our lan-guage. But this applies just as much to ourselves! We "see solutions" to problems. Jones is a "brilliant" student, that philosopher is "clear," that one "fuzzy," "dull," or "obscure." All of these words are but metaphors. We "approach" a problem from a certain "viewpoint," we "grapple" with the various "solutions." And so on. Just about every word we use to refer to our own mental states is itself a metaphor built on tissues of metaphors. There are also metonyms. A *metonym* is a figure of speech in which we use the name of one thing as a substitute for something else with which it is associated—for example, "I spent the evening reading Shake-speare" and "These lands belong to the crown." But this "association," Nietzsche points out, exists only as a linguistic entity: it is thereby created by our language. Or we say, "I spent last night reading Nietzsche," "In the interest of the United States . . . ," "By the will of God," and so on. In every case what we say is literally a lie (think about it). Finally, there are *anthropomorphisms*, figures of speech in which we project human "traits" (and what are they?) onto what is not human. For instance, "The tree strives to reach the sky" (which itself consists of a set of unconscious metaphors).

From his early training as a philologist Nietzsche was well familiar with how all language in its origin was metaphoric, metonymic, and anthropomorphic; that is, originally all language was metaphoric and it had the same origin and function as poetry. The division between the "literal," "scientific," and "logical" nature of language, on the one hand and its "metaphoric," "figurative," or "poetic" nature on the other, Nietzsche viewed as wholly artificial. He says this division is the leading cause of error in philosophy. In his voluminous writings he attempts to return language to its original, primordial function as poetry. Indeed, Nietzsche refers to his philosophical works as elaborate "poems" (something that even Lud-wig Wittgenstein will do, as we shall see), explaining that terms such as "Will to

Power," "the Death of God," and the "Superman" are but the products of the metaphorical/metonymical/anthropomorphic process. Such terms for Nietzsche are not to be regarded as philosophical insights into being itself, some "true reality"! Rather, as interpretations—poetical interpretations—of being, they are the artistic forces of self-creation acting in the world. They do not provide philosophical insights into being itself, some "true reality," but are merely poetical interpretations of being.

But not all interpretations are created equal. The powerful poetic lies that "affirm life," which, following Thrasymachus, he calls "the noble lies," he regards as true. Common lies, such as found in both Platonism and Christianity, Nietzsche condemns as bad poetry consisting of ignoble lies. For both Platonism and Christianity deny reality for what it really is, a chaotic flux to be molded in the image of each will. They set up a false and unfulfillable longing for another world through the theory of formal ideas, heaven, and so on. Nietzsche claims that what these other-worldly philosophical and religious congregations truly long for are nothingness and death. Religions are not life-affirming but life-denying. This, in Nietzsche's view, makes religions utterly decrepit and false.

Keep in mind that the words *true* and *false* in Nietzsche's vocabulary do not have their standard logical meanings. For Nietzsche all truth is either poetic or aesthetic. Like Schopenhauer and Kierkegaard, he claims that our reasoning and even our individual thoughts are but manifestations of the will to power. In showing, like Kierkegaard, that language functions precisely by lying, he is in a way doing to words what Kant did to the appearances: explaining why their being not what they seem is not an epistemological problem but its very solution. Taking our lies, pretensions, and self-deceptions for what they are allows us to face the chaotic flux of reality in a creative way so that it can be molded, like a great work of art, into something noble through the will to power. But the Will to Power is not the dark Schopenhaurian notion of the World Will. Rather, it is of Dionysian character, marked by laughter, dancing, and life affirmation culminating in what Nietzsche calls the "Superman," an enlightened individual who represents the triumph of the Will to Power. Such a person must, first and foremost, teach and impose "the Death of God."

What Nietzsche means by the Death of God is the end of all traditional forms of authority, not only religious but historical, political, moral, and any kind of textual authority. This conclusion was inspired by his early philological studies, whereby he learned that the foundational books for all the major world religions, such as the New Testament Bible, the Old Testament Bible, the Vedas, the Upanishads, and so on, consist of multiple indirect translations of multiple existing documents, compilations of fragments of deeply conflicting evidence derived from a multitude of sources, and so on. In Nietzsche's view, none of these "holy" books exist in anything like a truly "authoritative edition," nor are they based on any truly "original text." These so-called holy books are merely the result of decisions to let some particular subjective interpretation of a scattered and fragmentary series of texts stand for the "official" view. (For instance, in the case of the New Testament, none of the so-called gospels are written by eyewitnesses and there are dozens of other gospels, even more contradictory, some of which are even older, which were kept hidden from the general public by church authorities.[9]) Indeed, Nietzsche's philosophical approach can be seen as an extension of his philological insights from the textual into the ontological and epistemological domains, where the whole of existence itself—Being—comes to be viewed not as something to be described in language but as consisting in the form of an elaborate text.

   Nietzsche thus presents a sort of philosophical fulcrum between Hegel and a subsequent twentieth-century intellectual movement in philosophy, literary theory, and criticism known as *deconstructionism*, which systematically challenges all the fixed orthodox hierarchies central to Western thought and culture based on exactly the sort of dissolution between formerly antithetical concepts we explored in the work of the nineteenth-century idealists. The major additional development is that instead of the dissolution of the distinction between object and its representation conceived in noumenal/phenomenal terms, the analysis moves on to the more technical examinations of the elements of language, experience, and thought themselves conceived in terms of signs. When ordinarily we think of signs, we think of symbols used to represent objects, a way of bringing before consciousness something that is not otherwise fully present to consciousness. Thus, in talking about reality, we use signs and gestures as if these were of secondary importance and the reality behind the signs (the thing-in-itself signified?) as primary. But this is just the old primary/secondary qualities distinction rearing its ugly head again; what some absolute idealist–inspired contemporary continental philosophers like Jacques Derrida claim is thus deeply inspired by Nietzsche. Derrida, who challenges what he calls "the metaphysics of presence," claims that there are no beings and events that exist apart from the signs. Thus in claiming, "There is nothing outside of the texts," the twentieth-century deconstructionists are doing little more than echoing Nietzsche.

   Nietzsche attacks all traditional forms of authority, including, and most of all, morality. In stating that "slave-morality is essentially the morality of utility," he means to attack the utilitarian systems of the time, in particular that of John Stuart Mill. Again, in his view, nowhere is this more evident than in religion, which is the social machinery for "turning values upside down," and the religion that is the most culpable is Christianity. In *The Will to Power*, he calls Christianity the most "fatal and seductive lie that has ever yet existed" for the suppression of humanity, urging everyone to declare "open war with it." Along with a call to arms against Christianity, Nietzsche in *Beyond Good and Evil* presents his perspectivist analysis of truth and an instrumentalist theory of knowledge: "Against positivism, which halts at phenomena—'There are only facts'—I would say: No, facts are precisely what there are not, only interpretations." According to Nietzsche, one cannot separate facts from values from any domain of human inquiry, not even science. No observation can exist without theory. Though initially dubbed as "irrationalism" by some, in the end Nietzsche's criticism of logical positivist science would reemerge later in the twentieth century through such influential philosophers of science as Thomas Kuhn and Paul Feyerabend. "Physics, too,"

Nietzsche wrote, "is only an interpretation and exegesis of the world. . . . Behind all logic and its seeming sovereignty of movement, there also stand valuations or, more clearly, physiological demands for the preservation of a certain type of life."

A Brief History of Social Philosophy

The relationship between the metaphysical and epistemological sides of philosophy with its social and political wings has been poorly understood. So, before venturing in some detail into the social and political arena, I will sketch what I take the connection to be; for I think philosophy begins and ends on the metaphysical side, not the other way around (but this of course does not leave out the important middle ground of ethics, morality, and political theory). Consider, first, what the "naive realist" believes: (1) a mind-independent real world exists, and (2) this mind-independent real world is directly experienced. Naive realism is the view children naturally come to. We might call it "folk philosophy." We have seen various philosophers take a stand for or against (1) but none who accepts (2)—though soon we will meet some who accept (2). Among the various responses to (1), idealists deny the existence of a mind-independent world, while representationalists, most notably Kant, argue that the real world is in part created by the mind (the phenomenal world) and in part created by things in themselves (the noumenal world).

Such views have thus far been predicated on the notion that if there is such a two-way relation between real objects and the mind, it is a case of individual minds affecting the same public reality, though on one interpretation of Leibniz, as we saw, each individual monad is part creator of its own individual world, such that each of us exists in our own world and there are an infinite number of worlds. But in any case such a view is still very different from the social reality view here being developed. There is just one world, and we are each a participator in that world. Thus objective reality is created. But we've already seen Schopenhauer begin to move in a new direction, one followed by both Kierkegaard and Nietzsche. In arguing that the thing in itself is the will and that the will is the body, Schopenhauer implies the possibility of transcending subjectivity in the social arena. That is, there is already in Schopenhauer the implicit possibility of verifying whether an experience is "real," whether an object is "real," whether an event is "real," whether an idea is "real," and so on, by seeing to what extent there is agreement among minds. Moreover, given the active view of the powers of the mind taken by Kant, Hegel, Fichte, Schelling, Kierkegaard, and Nietzsche, it now seems possible that the ego can create reality, which otherwise is out of reach of its prying insubstantiality, by convincing, seducing, or forcing other minds to think as you do.

Just about all subsequent philosophies have, in certain aspects and in varying degrees, been influenced by that line of thinking. Thus both Auguste Comte's positivism (discussed in the next section) and the logical positivism of a century later would be in part based on the notion that public (i.e., "social") verification is a necessary condition for truth and meaning. Likewise, the shift in Kierkegaard, Nietzsche, and Marx from the search for new and better epistemologies and metaphysical systems to building, instead, a new kind of human individual, is largely predicated not on new critiques of reason but—especially in Nietzsche and Marx—on critiques of social institutions. Indeed, the entire basis for Marx's famous call to arms—"The philosophers have only interpreted the world in various ways: the point however is to change it"—is predicated on his belief not that individual consciousness makes reality but, rather, that social reality makes individual consciousness.

From such a vantage point, the entire so-called industrial revolution, a term used by the English economic historian Arnold Toynbee (1889–1975) to describe Europe's economic development from 1760 to 1840, can be seen as the result, literally, of a philosophical shift in thought. Traditionally, the end goal of much of philosophy—it's "product"—was thought. In the process of philosophical enlightenment, you went from having those (false, wrong, misguided) thoughts to having these (true, correct, learned) thoughts. The philosopher had certain thoughts that the non-philosopher didn't. Occasionally, as in the Socratic, Epicurean, and Stoic periods, there were shifts in emphases from a search for the right cognitive states to a search for the right emotive states. (In Socrates, notably, there is a search for unity between theory and pratice.) But now if the world is my idea or, more broadly, if by "idea," "perception," "phenomenon," and so on, I mean all of these things that are at this moment before my eyes, it is only a matter of time before I draw the conclusion as to what the activity of philosophy—traditionally imbibed into the human intellect as the study, manipulation, construction, improvement, or whatever, of ideas—should now become! The building of "bridges," "roads," and the proverbial "pillars of knowledge" becomes, literally, the building of bridges, roads, and pillars, along with a study, understanding, and general improvement of the means of their production. If my theory is correct, the fact that the European industrial revolution corresponds to the time of Kant, Fichte, Hegel, Schelling, Schopenhauer, Comte, Mill, Kierkegaard, and Marx is no accident. For it is precisely in these philosophers that this literal shift in thought occurs.

In other words, the nineteenth-century shift of philosophy into the social arena, although it has often been misunderstood as a shift away from traditional concerns with epistemology and metaphysics toward social engineering, can be viewed as a shift in focus concerning the question of where and what the stuff of reality is. The common misunderstanding is partly the fault of the nineteenth- and early-twentieth-century philosophers who so openly talked against metaphysics when in reality what they conceived themselves to be doing was not just studying the "noumenal" world by manipulating thought, but bringing the real world into existence, constructing and then ultimately improving it. One does not have to "turn Hegel upside down," as in Marx's dialectical materialism. The idea is already evident in Schopenhauer; after all, where, in Schopenhauer's view, are those mysterious "things in themselves"? Where is the will? Look at your hand: there it is. Look all around you. You're in the belly of the beast.

Comte: The Birth of Positivism

We are now in a position to examine the shift of philosophy as an introspective activity to philosophy as a social, political, and—what was the ultimate outcome of this line of thought, through the work of Hegel's most famous and influential student, Karl Marx—philosophy as an economic activity. We begin with Comte, the philosopher who gave birth to a new discipline, now known as sociology.

Auguste Comte (1798–1857) was born in Montpelier, France. He attended the École Polytechnique at Paris for two years, then took part in the student rebellion that closed the school. He supported himself as a private tutor in mathematics. When the École Polytechnique reopened in 1833, Comte got a job there as an entrance examiner. When the administration discovered that he had been one of the revolutionaries, they fired him. But by then Comte had already been noticed by many leading figures of the time, including John Stuart Mill in England. Mill came to his defense, calling Comte an "original and bold new thinker."

Comte's writings became a major inspiration for the nineteenth-century shift from metaphysical to "scientific" philosophy. What this meant, at the time, was knowledge sanctified by some sort of social verification, what in some ways amounts to a "social" epistemology. Indeed, the knowledge-seeking enterprise known as science has since then become a social, not an individual, activity. This is a complete reversal of the Cartesian notion of "I think, therefore I am," in which certainty is grounded through the individual's own internal relation to the truth. Truth in the new, "scientific" sense meant truth publicly verified.

In his main philosophical work, *Cours de Philosophie Positive* (*The Course of Positive Philosophy,* in six volumes, published from 1842 to 1854), Comte presents his law of the three "theoretical conditions" of intellectual development. In the first, primitive, "theological or fictitious" stage, human beings rely on the power of supernatural beings existing beyond the seen world so that explanations are given ultimately in supernatural terms. In the second, "metaphysical" stage, explanation is ultimately theological and supernatural entities are replaced with abstract notions. In the third and final, "positive" stage, the mind is freed by reason and observation from its vain egotistical search for "Absolute notions."

Here we must establish some important new terminology. Comte identifies the physical world with what can be immediately sensed. The "im" in *immediate* has the same function as it does in *immoral,* meaning "not mediated": what is directly apprehended by the mind without having to pass through some other medium or steps, such as through symbolic, theoretic, or inferential construction. I will call such a view, to distinguish it from representationalism, *presentationalism.* A presentationalist philosophy is one in which knowledge is given in terms of whatever is directly and immediately present to the mind; if these are physical objects (as in naive realism), then one is a physical presentationalist. If these are phenomenal objects, then one is a phenomenal presentationalist. Idealists are phenomenal presentationalists. Materialists are physical presentationalists.

Second, Comte argues against the "vain" search for causes. He rejects causes as agents or forces. To what, then, do the phenomena that we experience refer? What do they denote? In saying that the actual designated objects of our phenomenal conscious states are mathematical functions or equations, Comte is a mathematical phenomenalist. Mathematical functions and equations are themselves not physical things but conceptual, or abstract, entities.

By "presentationalist," then, we can denote those philosophical systems subsequent to Comte in which what is to be regarded as real is what is presented to the conscious mind. What is presented to the conscious mind are, of course, phenomena, and if these phenomena refer to, or designate, not some unknowable objects (as in Kant's representationalist philosophy) but some mathematically knowable ones, we can call the philosophy "phenomenalist." Further, in turning away from introspective philosophy, in which the apperception of one's own psychological states is taken as an epistemological yardstick, toward the public, "sociological" realm of cross-verification and "social facts," Comte is in the domain of what we might call, in its broadest sense, scientific.

Comte thinks his method applies so well not just to the world itself but to the social realm, that he provided the first systematic account of social science, to which he gave the name "sociology." His thinking along these lines helped inspire the early logical positivists and paved the way for the social, political, and moral philosophy of John Stuart Mill.

Like Nietzsche and Marx, Comte makes a radical break with religion. He argues that the positive philosophy has no room for traditional theological thinking. He calls for the eradication of religion on grounds that it obfuscates the truth and only stands in the way of humanity's progress. In place of traditional religion, humanity would establish a new "religion of humanity." The new priesthood would consist of scientists, businessmen, politicians, and a "calendar of saints." These figures would be placed as icons in the new educational institutions that would replace in society the traditional educational institutions run by the church, and they would include people like Adam Smith, Dante, Shakespeare, and the great philosophers, economists, and scientists of the future.

Comte's positive philosophy was a bold attempt to end the "error" that the mind can know anything more than phenomena and their relations. Just as we do not know the essence of the phenomena, we do not know their first causes or their ultimate ends. All we know, by means of controlling the phenomena through experiment and observation, are the constant relations between phenomena, the relations of succession and of similarity, and the uniformities that we call laws. Knowledge is therefore relative. There is no absolute knowledge for the simple reason that the things in themselves and the essence of facts are unreachable by the mind. All we know is that phenomenon a is connected with phenomenon b, because b always follows a as far as our observations go.

At the same time, while the positive philosophy rejects metaphysics, it does not lead either to idealism or to empiricism. Isolated, empirical observations are useless and unknowable as such; a phenomenon becomes useful and a part of knowledge only when it is defined and explained by a theory or is combined with other observations into a law of nature.

Comte's final work, *The Philosophy of Mathematics,* was largely ignored, even by his contemporaries. In it, he espouses a numerical mysticism and suggests an entirely different direction for philosophy than espoused in his other works. In some ways it is a call for a return to the Pythagorean mysteries.

The Utilitarians: Bentham and Mill

Comte's philosophical successor, who carried on both his phenomenalist and presentationalist philosophy into the social arena of politics and ethics, was John Stuart Mill (1806–1873). But first we must turn to an even greater influence on Mill's views, one of the leading radical reformers of the nineteenth century, Jeremy Bentham (1748–1832).

Born in London, the son of a leading attorney, Bentham was a child prodigy who began studying history and Latin at the age of three. At twelve he entered Queen's College in Oxford and earned his B.A. in three years, his M.A. in two—at the age of seventeen. His father expected him to become a practicing lawyer, but Bentham was far more interested in the philosophical foundations of ethics, morality, and legal theory. He traveled widely throughout Europe; he wrote his first essay on economics in Russia and in 1792 in the interests of Voltaire, freedom, and love, became a citizen of France.

Bentham's main philosophical influences were Locke and Hume. When he read Hume's *Treatise on Human Nature,* Bentham said it was "as if scales fell" from his eyes. He went on to publish several books on political and legal theory, but it was his *Introduction to the Principles of Morals and Legislation* (1789) that made him a powerful and influential international figure. In his *Principles* he lays the groundwork for utilitarianism; as developed by Mill (whose work we shall study later in this section), it is still today one of the leading moral theories in the world.

Bentham defines his *principle of utility* as "that property in any object whereby it tends to produce pleasure, good or happiness, or to prevent the happening of mischief, pain, evil or unhappiness to the party whose interest is considered." According to Bentham, this principle takes account of the two main motives for all human action—pain and pleasure. Governments, social, political, and legal institutions, as well as individual citizens, should follow the *greatest happiness principle*: choose that course of action which leads to the greatest happiness for the greatest number of people. Bentham's utilitarianism, designed to free people from oppressive laws and to make governing bodies moral, provided a foundation to many democratic societies. Since leaders as well as individuals are thus morally bound to follow the same universal principle and one that is readily accessible to everyone—we all know what pain and pleasure are—there can be no manipulation, through rhetoric, of the weak by the powerful. In Bentham's system we are each our own best judge as to how best to live and attain happiness. To do so, we need his now famous hedonic calculus (modeled on the mathematical method of Newton) whereby one can evaluate or rate the pleasures to be sought using seven categories:

1. Intensity: How strong is the sensation (of pain or pleasure)?
2. Duration: How long does it last?
3. Certainty: How clear and distinct is it?
4. Propinquity: How soon will it be experienced?
5. Fecundity: What other sensations of pleasure or pain will follow?
6. Purity: How free from pain is the pleasure, and vice versa?
7. Extent: How many persons will be affected by it, one way or the other?

Thus, if a law would produce a very intense pleasure very briefly for just a few individuals while inducing great pain for a long time for a great number, it is a bad law; and so on.

Bentham's *Principles* drew much attention and praise throughout Europe and the United States. He continued to work on establishing the codes for laws that could be applied in any countries wishing to follow his utilitarian principles. Deeply critical of established political and legal institutions, he condemned as evil the legal judges who

> made the common law. Do you know how they make it? Just as a man makes laws for his dog. When your dog does anything you want to break him of, you wait till he does it and then beat him. . . . This is the way judges make laws for you and me.

His utilitarianism is designed to break this repressive structure of laws imposed, under the guise of morality, on people by corrupt and exploitive leaders. Bentham openly called for the rejection of all monarchies and established churches, claiming that "all government is in itself one vast evil. The only justification for putting such evil into place would be to prevent some greater evil; governments should therefore never stray from the principle of utility—the greatest happiness for the greatest number."

When Bentham died at age eighty-five, he bequeathed his fortune to University College in London under the following conditions: his body should be dissected in the presence of his friends, his head mummified and replaced with a wax replica. This was faithfully carried out, along with Bentham's final proviso: his dressed corpse with his mummified head alongside it continues to attend all board of trustees meetings.[10]

John Stuart Mill was the most famous of Bentham's many disciples who further developed utilitarianism, except along rather different lines. Born and educated in London by his father, a prominent philosopher, historian, and economist, Mill began studying Greek at the age of three. He read all the works of Plato in the original by age eight. By twelve he had learned Latin, Euclidean geometry, algebra, and studied Aristotle's logical treatises. At fourteen he had a college-level understanding of logic, mathematics, and world history. In many ways he became Comte's philosophical successor, carrying on both his phenomenalist and presentationalist philosophy into the social arena of politics and ethics.

By twenty-five, Mill was emotionally burned out. He later wrote that "the habit of analysis has a tendency to wear away the feelings. . . . I was thus, as I said to myself, left stranded at the commencement of my voyage, with a well equipped ship and a rudder, but no sail." Mill says his life was turned around by Mrs. Harriet Taylor, with whom he fell madly in love. They married after her husband died. She inspired Mill and helped him write many of his most important works, including *A System of Logic* (1843), *The Principles of Political Economy* (1848), and *On Liberty* (1859).

It was Mill's father who raised him on Bentham's utilitarian doctrines and those of other so-called philosophical radicals. But whereas both Bentham and Mill define their utility principles in terms of avoiding pain and securing pleasure, Mill argues that such straightforward self-interest is an inadequate criterion of moral goodness. What is missing in Bentham's moral calculus is a qualitative distinction between pleasures.

In this way, Mill revolutionized utilitarian ideas in his most widely influential book, *Utilitarianism* (1863). His major modification of Bentham's ethical theory is this: The main problem with Bentham's moral calculus, as Mill saw it, was that it lacks any qualitative distinction between types of pleasure and pain sensations: "quantity of pleasure being equal, pushpin is as good as poetry." Mill therefore adds "quality" to Bentham's list above, saying, "Better to be Socrates dissatisfied than a fool satisfied." The problem is that this addition makes Bentham's moral calculus no longer a straightforward objective question, since qualitative judgments are subjective. Mill tried to solve the problem by basing his moral theory on his political theory, stating that such moral judgments having to do with qualities would have to be decided democratically, through majority rule, since unlike quantitative judgments they are not objective but subjective. Competent judges, however, would have to be those who are familiar with the various kinds of pleasures, and so Mill's is a sort of enlightened, rather than purely relativistic, democratic system.

In *On Liberty*, Mill argues that the fundamental utilitarian principle—the greatest amount of happiness for the greatest number of people—can be achieved only if all individuals are given as much freedom of thought and action as possible. This meant almost unlimited freedom: the only constraint was a prohibition against causing harm to others. *On Liberty* was popular in Europe and highly influential to the development of nineteenth- and early-twentieth-century democracy in the United States.

Plato had argued that democracy is the worst form of government. Having seen Socrates sentenced to death by the democratic state majority, he urged for rule by enlightened philosopher kings. Mill comes to just the opposite conclusion.

He reasons that the correct lesson from the past is that no one should have a monopoly on what people regard to be the truth. All of our best philosophies keep evolving, as does science, and all human knowledge can attain is partial truths. The philosophical and political well-being of a society should therefore be dependent on growth and change, or else we end up in dead ends like the Byzantine and Roman Empires. Finally, and perhaps most important, if we let the wisest among us become the rulers in charge of everything, including our education, what will happen to the rest of the people? They will look up to the leaders. This may be good for a generation or two of leadership, but it will lead, Mill argues, in the long run to stagnation and decline. After a while the official "truths" will simply be passed down, generation to generation, and no one will achieve anything new.

To avoid the rise and inevitable fall of every previous empire, the wise society should therefore encourage not obedience to authority but the development of individuality, even rebellion. It must help spawn individuals through whom new ideas are born into the world. Eccentricity, not conformity, should be the ideal. The majority must be tolerant and helpful to the minorities, the learned should be tolerant of the unlearned, and so on. In Mill's view, this will produce not just a healthy, vibrant society but a moral one that evolves over time to achieve the greatest happiness for the greatest number of people.

Although Mill never held an official academic post, he applied his theories to many causes. In *The Subjection of Women* (1861), he argued for the then-radical position that women should have careers and be allowed to vote. He fought discrimination against women, founded the first women's suffrage society, and was an early advocate of openly available birth control.

Mill made his living working not as a philosopher but as a business executive for the East India Company. He had started at age seventeen as a clerk and had been quickly promoted to the highest post in his department. But he retired in 1865 to run for Parliament and won. During his term in office he achieved many sweeping reforms for the British working class. He argued on behalf of exploited Jamaicans and for fair redistribution of land in Ireland.

Marx: The Communist Revolutionary

Karl Marx (1818–1883) was born in Trèves (Trier), Germany, what was then Prussia. He went to the Universities of Berlin and Bonn and received his Ph.D. in philosophy from the University of Jena. His doctoral dissertation was on the Greek atomism of Democritus and Epicurus. At the time, the most influential philosophy in Germany and much of the rest of Europe was Hegel's. The Hegelian right consisted of older, more conservative philosophers steeped in an orthodox reading of Hegel's theories of religion and morality. The Hegelian left consisted of young radical philosophers such as Marx. Calling themselves "the Young Hegelians," they considered Hegel's social and political views false but saw in them deep, hidden truths implying the very opposite of what Hegel taught. Most of Hegel's critics at the time rejected Hegel's system on grounds that it required transcended entities, up to and including the Absolute world-mind. Marx eventually claimed that his own system, which he called *dialectic materialism,* was a right-side-up version of Hegel's dialectic idealism.

Unable to find a teaching position, Marx found a job with the Cologne *Rheinische Zeitung* and was even the London correspondent for the *New York Tribune.* The pay was minimal and he spent most of his life unemployed. Several of his children died of malnutrition.

Marx got some support from his friend and co-author of the *Communist Manifesto,* Friedrich Engels, but remained extremely poor. Yet he was prolific. His deeply influential works have made him one of the most recognized names in history and an important socialist philosopher.

Marx's greatest influence came from Ludwig Feuerbach's *Essence of Christianity,* a work that inspired the Young Hegelian leftists. Feuerbach argued that ever since Plato, the greatest corrupter of real human values has been the ideal images of universal values. In reality, Feuerbach claimed, there are no universal values and so all such Platonic goals are unattainable, the stuff of Christian religion. He argues that the human mind, by craving its own idealizations, becomes alienated from itself. In this way the mind transfers its own desires onto an imaginary ideal being, God. By doing so, the human mind prevents its own ascension to the ideal. Religion is the mind's greatest prison.

Marx continued Feuerbach's argument that religious imagery must be abolished—only then can true peace, happiness, and self-illumination come to society. But Marx went further; in his *Theses on Feuerbach* (1886), he criticizes Feuerbach on grounds that no such change in thinking could ever be attained by human beings so long as the argument remains philosophical. Philosophy itself merely manipulates ideas and images. He calls Feuerbach's materialism "speculative" in comparison to his own "practical materialism" and calls for a change in the actual material and economic relationships among human beings: "The philosophers have only interpreted the world in various ways, the point however is to change it."

The *Communist Manifesto* became the rallying cry for world revolution involving a class struggle between the bourgeoisie—the capitalist employers of wage labor who owned the means of production—and the proletariat—wage laborers who had no means of production and were thus forced to sell their labor in order to live. Marx's criticism of capitalism and of all social, political, economic, and religious structures owes as much to Hegelian dialectic as it does to his close observation and analysis of actual social conditions of London workers of the mid-nineteenth century. Marx claims that various capitalist theses lead to their opposites, "the contradictions of capitalism." Competition, for instance, leads to monopoly and the lack of competition. How does capitalism solve unemployment? By creating more money, which leads to inflation, which capitalism fixes by increasing unemployment. And so on.

The purpose of Communist revolution, which Marx advocated, was to bring about the collapse of capitalism. He wanted to replace capitalism with a temporary "dictatorship of the proletariat." This would be a worker's state in which the workers themselves would ultimately abolish the class-structured society. The false, capitalist democracy would thus be replaced by a true, Communist democracy. In the end, the revolutionary leaders would be forced to resign. When this happened, history, which Marx defined in terms of class struggle, would come to an end.

The Communist revolution was supposed to proceed as follows. First, all private property would be eliminated, which would empower the working class and banish what Marx called "alienated labor." Freedom according to Marx can be attained only through our natural ability to do and make things, to create. We are according to him fashioned by our products. The idea is that the human self does not come into existence as an individual but as part of the collective. The human self begins as a social construction. If we do not control the process and means of production for the things we produce, we become alienated from them. We never become true individuals.

Consider, for instance, assembly-line workers who have no control over the rate or manner in which their work must be done or even, in many cases, how the product as a whole works (they see it only piecemeal). They feel debilitated by their own power, their labor, *which is no longer theirs*. They do not own their own power! In this way, workers exist as slaves, under the domain of those who control the means of production. This is because human consciousness is not the cause of social processes. Rather, individual human consciousness is an effect. Thus, as Marx wrote in his *Contribution to the Critique of Political Economy,*

> In the social production of their life, men enter into definite relations that are indispensable and independent of their will, relations of production which correspond to a definite stage of development of their material productive forces. The sum total of these relations of production constitutes the economic structure of society, the real foundation, on which rises a legal and political superstructure and to which correspond definite forms of social consciousness. The mode of production of material life conditions the social, political, and intellectual life process in general. It is not the consciousness of men that determines their social being, but on the contrary, their social being that determines their consciousness.

According to Marx, human consciousness can become enlightened and evolve to a higher state—provided the competition of capitalism is removed. Along with capitalism must be removed its partner in crime: religion, the great source of "false consciousness." The people must be weaned of that which suppresses them and, in that regard, religion is "the opium of the people." The true individual can then emerge from the cocoon of class into a classless society; the world then becomes an ideal state, a utopia.

~∾©

1. Russell, *A History of Western Philosophy* (New York: Simon and Schuster, 1945), pp. 484–85.
2. All the quotes from Kant's *Foundations of the Metaphysics of Morals* are from the T. K. Abbott translation, London, 1873, with emendations by the author.

3. See the section "Fact of Exclusive Conjoinment" in my *I Am You: A Philosophical Explanation That We Are All the Same Person* (Ann Arbor, Mich.: UMI, 1986).

4. For a more detailed discussion, see my "Quantum Cosmology, the Anthropic Principle, and Why Is There Something Rather Than Nothing?" in *The Experience of Philosophy,* 3rd ed., ed. Kolak and Martin (Belmont, Calif.: Wadsworth, 1996).

5. See, for instance, *The Mind's I* by Douglas R. Hofstadter and Daniel C. Dennett (New York: Basic Books, 1984).

6. Gödel, an Austrian mathematician educated at Vienna, produced several far-reaching theorems. The first is his *incompleteness theorem,* in which he proves that in any formal system of arithmetic, S, there will be some sentence, P, such that if S is consistent (contains no contradictions) P can neither be proved nor disproved. What is as important as this theorem is the technique Gödel invented for proving it, an unbelievably simple but extraordinarily powerful *arithmetization of syntax,* that is, in representing the syntax of the language of S in S itself. It is this move that makes possible the demonstration of the necessity of their being a sentence in S that says, essentially, "I am not provable." Equally important are his proofs of the completeness of the first-order functional calculus.

7. Neil Florek has made the interesting comment to me that in that case, considering the state of most people's bodies, many must have very weak wills!

8. Kierkegaard, *Either/Or,* trans. D. F. Swenson and L. M. Swenson (Princeton, N.J.: Princeton University Press, 1944).

9. See, for instance, Daniel Kolak, *In Search of God: The Language and Logic of Belief* (Belmont, Calif.: Wadsworth, 1994), and Elaine Pagels, *The Gnostic Gospels* (New York: Random House, 1979), key sections reprinted in Kolak and Martin, *Self, Cosmos, God* (New York: Harcourt Brace Jovanovich, 1993). Pagels's argument is that the reason the early Christians chose the texts they did was to establish a male hierarchy and authority structure.

10. This will surprise only those who have never attended any such meetings. Those who have would not even be surprised if the other members never even noticed.

CHAPTER FIVE

Twentieth-Century Philosophy

Peirce: American Pragmatism

Prior to Kant, Hegel, and Nietzsche, it was commonly believed that the words of a language are but inert and ineffectual instruments used by us to make meaning out of the world. In Peirce's elaborate system, inspired by Kant, Hegel, absolute idealism, and Nietzsche, it is the other way around; the world is made, as are we ourselves, by *signs,* which are to words what numbers are to numerals—logical functions that do not need to be created in order to exist. Fichte's act (Chapter 4) is crucial for an understanding of Peirce's meaning, as well as Hume's analysis of the mind. One way to try to combine such differing analyses of our mental states (the Kantian-rationalist-idealist versus the Humean-empirical-skeptical perspective) is to interpret Peirce's theory of the mind as analogous to Hume's bundle theory, except that the individual perceptions are active in exactly the way that Kant thought the faculties were. In other words, Peirce's highly original and groundbreaking interpretation, for which he is rarely given sufficient credit, is that of viewing the elements of the mind as themselves having the active functional structure that Kantian-type theories require transcendental deductions to achieve. Such a move of course owes a lot, as well, to Leibniz's concept of the monad.

Charles Sanders Peirce (1839–1914) was born in Cambridge, Massachusetts. He was educated mainly by his father, a Harvard mathematician, though he graduated from Harvard University at the bottom of his class. As a result, the only job he could find was with the U.S. Coast and Geodetic Survey. He never secured a permanent teaching position but taught logic as an adjunct at Johns Hopkins University from 1879 to 1884 and gave a few philosophical lectures at Harvard and the Lowell Institute in Boston. Subsequently, he went back to work for the U.S. Coast and Geodetic Survey. He was, however, a member of the "metaphysical club" in Cambridge, which included William James and Oliver Wendell Holmes. Peirce's own view of metaphysics owes much to Kant and Hegel, and was highly influenced by the then-recent evolutionary theory of Charles Darwin (1809–1882).

The entire universe according to Peirce is one mind moving toward a rational end, but its driving force is love. But just as we saw Kierkegaard and Nietzsche develop Hegel's absolute idealism toward an understanding of the world entire not as a thing but as consisting in words and symbols—a sort of symbolic text or program—Pierce carries this process to its logical conclusion and becomes the founder of the view that the whole of reality is to be viewed as consisting in signs. As he put it: "I am, as far as I know, a pioneer, or rather a backwoodsman, in the work of clearing and opening up what I call semiotic, that is, the doctrine of the essential nature and fundamental varieties of possible semiosis." *Semiosis* is a term coined by Peirce to refer to any "sign action" or "sign process," by which he meant that signs have a force or will of their own. And what is a "sign"? The term goes all the way back to the medievals, particularly Duns Scotus, who defined it as *aliquid stat pro aliquo,* meaning, literally, "something that stands for something else." *Symbols*—letters, numerals, pictures, icons, myths, texts, etc.—are all signs or sets of signs. According to the prevalent view at the time, as developed by one of the greatest linguists, the Swiss Ferdinand de Saussure (1857–1913), a *sign* is an accidental and arbitrary correlation between a signifier and a signified. Peirce uses the example of an acoustic image (i.e., a sound wave) as the signifier and the corresponding concept thereby encoded (i.e., a Humean impression, such as a "thump" of a particular magnitude, frequency, and intensity). This is an explicitly dyadic model of signs, meaning simply that it is a paired relation between two terms, the signifier and the signified. But Peirce, largely due to his understanding of the systems of Kant and the subsequent Hegelian-inspired idealists, insisted, no doubt enlightened by Nietzsche's understanding of language, that as the ultimate elements of his cosmos, signs were to be conceived in triadic terms. Thus there is the sign itself—the symbol—that stands for something, called its *object,* which generates another sign, called its *interpretant.* In other words, the signs themselves generate further signs, and so on, in a cosmic process that is the textual evolution of existence. In this way, Peirce lay the philosophical foundations for the discipline known today as *semiotics.* Hence, "The entire universe," wrote Peirce, "is perfused with signs."

Semiotics today is still a flourishing and highly evolving philosophical discipline. The best textbook ever written on the subject, by my lights, is Umberto Eco's *A Theory of Semiotics* (Indiana University Press, 1979). (This is the same Umberto Eco who wrote the best-selling novels *The Name of the Rose* and *Foucault's Pendulum.*) Semiotics reaches into many other areas, including linguistics, computer science, logic, and phenomenology, almost as if the various rifts among some of these disciplines had never happened. Remarkably, however, this was not Peirce's only contribution.

Peirce also initiated the movement in American philosophy known as *pragmatism.* As a new theory of truth, pragmatism relies on one's own personal experience tempered with the practical significance of propositions. The pragmatist as espoused by Peirce involves the "clarification of thought" according to what Peirce called "the pragmatic principle": "Consider what effects, that conceivably might have practical bearings, we conceive the object of our conception to have. Then our conception of these effects is the whole of our conception of the object." The idea is this: Beliefs according to Peirce are psychological habits predisposing us to respond in specific ways to specific situations. Any situation in our experience causes either physical movement of the body or psychological expectation in the mind. In his article titled "The Fixation of Belief," Peirce claims there are four basic ways for our habits, customs, traditions, and "folkways" to become "fixed" in our minds. These apply to everything from personal convictions to metaphysical philosophical systems, and they are used for both settling opinions and resolving doubt: tenacity, authority, the a priori method, and the method of science.

The method of tenacity exists through the impoverished domain of common sense. The method of authority arises through military, governmental, and church organizations conditioning individuals against disobedience. The a priori method, which has been practiced by great philosophers from Plato to Descartes, is only slightly better than the first two. But ultimately it amounts to an elaborate form of rationalization. These three methods have their social and institutional functions. The only reliable method is the "self-corrective" way of Peirce's version of the *scientific method,* whereby one does not know in advance where one is going. This concept is not as easy as it may sound to understand; it is closely aligned with Darwin's analysis of how evolution works. Evolution works precisely because there is nothing guiding it.

Let me, by way of explanation, suggest to you what in my view are areas of similar domain: probability, logic, and geometry. Although we haven't the space to explore this topic in much detail here, if you think about it a little you will realize that the reason probability works in the way it does is because there is nothing directing the way the world goes. If there were "forces" guiding the behavior of probabilistic events, one would not see the patterns that one sees, for instance, with fair coins, bell curves, and so on. Likewise with logic. Logic works as it does because there is nothing imposing itself upon the terms as such. "Validity," "soundness," "implication," and so on, are relations among terms themselves. It is already implicit in such concepts that the connectives "of no connectives," so to speak, lead ultimately to a completely stable, functional, and incontrovertible system of operations. Likewise for space. Space is, let us say, just nothing, emptiness. That is why it has the structure it has—that is why it has what is called a "geometry." And so on. Now, of course, we are speaking rather metaphorically here, but the idea may help you see what is inspiring Peirce and subsequent thinkers along the directions leading up to today's exciting developments, which few individuals are in a position to understand because so few have taken the time to trace our ideas back to their originating sources.

Indeed, one can even go so far as to relate what we are here saying all the way back to the very beginning of this book where we started with Socrates and his desired relationship with the unknown, wisdom, via love. Philosophers spend a great deal of time on the concept of wisdom, appropriately so, but very little on the other half of the equation. And Peirce's concept of love, rarely studied nowadays, has a function in his philosophy very close to that of Socrates.

So how should one proceed, according to Peirce? It is a path few have dared to tread. In the East such cryptic phrases as "There is no path to truth, one must be free of all paths to find it," and "The Tao [way] that can be named is not the Tao," and so on, are in effect saying much the same thing. But what Peirce called for is utter spontaneity at the end of a process of acquiring the known, in order that the next step can occur; in some ways, it is a reversal of the Cartesian procedure of starting by doubting everything. One must start, rather, by learning everything and then proceed by a new method

> by which our beliefs may be caused by nothing human, but by some external permanency—by something upon which our thinking has no effect. . . . It must be something which affects, or might affect, every man. And, though these affections are necessarily as various as are individual conditions, yet the method must be such that the ultimate conclusion of every man shall be the same. Such is the method of science. Its fundamental hypothesis, restated in more familiar language, is this: There are real things, whose characters are entirely independent of our opinions about them; those realities affect our senses according to regular laws, and, though our sensations are as different as our relations to the objects, yet, by taking advantage of the laws of perception, we can ascertain by reasoning how things really are, and any man, if he have sufficient experience and reason enough about it, will be led to the one true conclusion.

In this way, Peirce sought to develop a new scientific method in which our beliefs are a response to something independent of ourselves, in terms of both our desires and our opinions. Second, this is a publicly verifiable method and thus markedly influenced by the positivist philosophy of Comte and already a call to arms to subsequent logical positivists; that is, our method for acquiring beliefs must be independent of any personal peculiarities and must have nothing to do with unique experiences that only a few special people can have. Everyone must be equally affected, or at least equally affectable, by the results of the method.

But how does Peirce know that there actually is a reality independent of our thinking, perceiving, willing, of which we can form correct beliefs? Peirce's answer is that philosophy makes it possible for us to understand in what ways a belief "is not a momentary code of consciousness." Rather, to truly believe some proposition X, according to Peirce, is to be behaviorally disposed to act as if X were true. The belief itself provides the psychological confidence allowing you to behave in a certain way in the world. To truly doubt some proposition X, on the other hand, is to be in an uncertain state about it. You lack a settled habit and don't know what to do when a given situation in which X becomes relevant to making a decision actually comes up. That is precisely the reason we work so hard to avoid doubt, because it is psychologically painful, an anxious and irritating state. The effort we make to escape our doubt by acquiring a belief is what Peirce defines to be the process of inquiry. It is really, at bottom line, a psychological concept, an attempt to recover the stoic calm that we experience when we know what to do.

Peircean inquiry requires three things: (1) stimulus, the experience of doubt, (2) end, the settlement of opinion, and (3) a method, which is science. Thus, as with all pragmatists after him, not just inquiry in particular but thinking in general must become by a felt problem. If you don't feel that there is a problem, if you are not puzzled, if you are not in a state of doubt, you are not capable of inquiry. Your mind is closed.

Peirce wrote a follow-up to his "Fixation of Belief," called "How to Make Our Ideas Clear." In it, he criticizes Descartes's notion of clear and distinct ideas, which he claims is itself not clear and distinct. Peirce's complaint against Descartes's notion is that it relies solely on the a priori method, which Peirce rejects on grounds that it appeals, ultimately, to nonverifiable self-evidence. This is but the first level of clarity, not itself sufficient. Similarly, he rejects Leibniz's method of abstract definition on the grounds that "nothing new can ever be learned by analyzing definitions." This is the second level of clarity, also not sufficient. Peirce thus calls for a third grade of clearness, predicated on and identical with his pragmatic maxim, which renders as meaningless any terms or concepts that go beyond the possible effects on observable objects: beliefs must be judged solely by the habits they produce, the practical rules of action that they govern. Peirce's system thus comes full circle and completes itself.

One must be careful to not psychologize what we might call Peirce's pragmatic semiotic philosophy, which is nevertheless often done to it even though he himself so vehemently opposed this psychologizing tendency on the part of other so-called pragmatists that at one point Peirce opted to distance himself from them by calling his system "pragmaticism." Indeed, the pragmatists have often been accused by subsequent twentieth-century philosophers as somehow being "unphilosophical" (accusations also levied at Nietzsche, Schopenhauer, Hegel, and others), in that he was replacing the notion of truth with a psychological notion of practicality. But such misunderstandings are based, in part, on an insufficient understanding of Peirce's semiotics. The other part has to do with Peirce's choice of words with regard to the term *habit*. Let us see why.

As we said earlier, his theory of signs involves a triadic structure. Instead of simply saying "A means B," we must instead say that "A means B to C," where A is the original sign, B is its object, and C is the interpretant. (Peirce calls it the "interpretant" rather than the "interpreter" so as not to limit this function to human minds; the interpretant could be an animal, a machine, or some other type of functional system.) The rules in a language for relating the various signs, A, B, C . . . , to each other—the set of possible "word-word" relations—is called *syntax*. The relation between the words and what they are about—their designated objects, what they "stand" for (i.e., the "word-world" relation)—is called *semantics*. The way that words (or, more accurately, the signs themselves) affect their users and hearers is called *pragmatics*. As we saw in Peirce's analysis, there can be three ways that a sign can be related to its designated object: (1) causality, which Peirce calls indexes, (2) resemblance, which he calls icons, and (3) conventionality (i.e., arbitrarily), which he calls symbols. Smoke is a sign of fire (way 1), the bust of Plato resembles the man (way 2), the word *dog* stands for a dog (way 3), and so on. Just about all the words in our language are like "dog"; they in no way are caused by their designated objects nor do they in any way resemble them. This idea is extremely important. "Red" is not red by any sense of the word! So how did these "symbols" come to represent what they represent? Purely by convention; it is arbitrary.

Now this is an amazing similarity to the moves we have seen made before by other philosophers in other areas of inquiry. Nietzsche finds a way to use language to attain what he calls "truth" that is predicated on the realization that language is itself, at each and every step of the way, a lie, a fabrication, the result of elaborate self-deception. Kant achieves the transcendental deduction through the realization that what is before the mind is not real and thereby ascends to knowledge of what is real, even of transcending the phenomena to what is their cause. Descartes, through doubting and in fact making a thorough method of doubt, attains a method of knowledge. And so on. Peirce is noting that the noises we make at the world are really not in any way related to the things in the world and therein sees the solution to the problems of knowledge, reality, and the puzzling nature of language and thought. One may even notice here a startling resonance with the ancient Pythagoreans' discovery that their framework of numbers did not work, that there was a gap, that their mathematics was grossly inadequate and conceptually misguided all the way down, as a means of providing a method for the subsequent development and rigorous advances in mathematics!

Peirce's great insight is that *words as symbols stand for things not because they are related to things but because they are related to their designated objects—through their interpretants*. A sign is itself meaningless—a brute and uninterpreted fact, arbitrarily arrived at through the random and chaotic processes of events. It is the interpretant that gives the sign meaning. And by way of making it perfectly clear in what sense Peirce was not merely psychologizing the notion of truth, let us be clear that he distinguishes three different kinds of interpretants of signs. Some words, like *God, love, freedom, death,* and so on, produce a lot of intense feeling when heard or uttered, whereas others—such as *orange juice, toe, doormat,* and the like—do not. Now, what are these feelings? They are not brute facts, meaningless, and so on; rather, they are signs, they are themselves significant. Thus the emotional feeling of pride at seeing a flag is a sign having a reference to one's country, just as much as the flag is. Second, there are energetic interpretants. Peirce gives the example of a drill sargeant barking out the order, "Ground arms!" The troops movement to lower their muskets to the ground is an energetic interpretant of the command.

But the third and most important interpretant is the logical interpretant, which is a sign having the same meaning as the sign it interprets. For example, suppose you look up the word *halcyon* in the dictionary and find it defined as "pleasingly or idyllically calm or peaceful: serene." Next you look up *serene* and find it defined as "lighthearted carefree episode having simplicity and charm." So then you look up *charm* . . . and so on. Unless you're already familiar with a language, the dictionary will be useless. As Peirce points out, in the logical case there is no interpretant that can serve as the final or ultimate interpretant because it is itself a sign and thereby calls for further interpretations of exactly the same kind, which require still others, and so on forever!

But not forever. There is, according to Peirce, an ultimate interpretant. It is *habit*. Yet if we recall, from the earlier passages, that this final outcome is predicated on his third level of clearness, we may be in a position to understand the full meaning and implication of his profound system of thought, for the third level of clearness is given by a set of "if-then" sentences specifying a series of operations together with the results that will occur if you perform them. This means that a linguistic or conceptual sign can function as a sign provided there is already in operation a fully functional system of such signs. The habits in Peirce's system are nothing less than programs encoded into the signs themselves.

Think, after all, about how you learned language. If you don't speak a word of English, the English dictionary will be useless; you need to have some way of translating at least some words, to get you started, into your own language. But in the case of your native language, or of English if you are a native speaker, there was never a translating into some previously known native language because you didn't yet know a language! So how did you ever learn to speak a language?

Peirce's answer, and the answer of the subsequent semioticians, is that you couldn't have and you didn't; just as the British did not invent the British language, and the Germans did not invent German, and so on, no native speakers invented their language; they are the "inventions" of the language. That is anything but a psychological interpretation!

Mach: From Empiricism to Positivism

Ernst Mach (1838–1916) was born at Turas in Moravia, a province in central Czechoslovakia, and educated in Vienna. He was professor of physics, first at Graz from 1864 to 1867 and then at Prague from 1867 to 1895, and then returned to Vienna as a professor of philosophy. His work as both a physicist and a philosopher had a tremendous influence on twentieth-century thought, and in both fields. Generally regarded as the founder of the philosophical movement known as *logical positivism,* especially of the variety espoused by the Vienna Circle; his name is also widely recognized with regard to the Mach number, relating an airplane's air speed with the local speed of sound.

As a radical empiricist, Mach formalized the view now shared by most scientists that only empirically verifiable statements are meaningful. He was also one of the clearest advocates of *phenomenalism,* the view that physical object propositions are analyzable into statements about sensations in terms of either actual or possible perceptual experience. Although his views are reminiscent of Berkeley and Kant, they often have been presented in purely Berkeleian or Kantian terms; whereas in Berkeley's view the elements of the mind are conditioned by an unknown external cause that Berkeley identified as God, and Kant relied on the "thing in itself," Mach argued that the elements of the mind depend only on each other and require no other substance or cause for a complete explanation. He influenced not only the leading members of the Vienna Circle but also the old John Stuart Mill and the young A. J. Ayer. So thoroughly rigorous were Mach's criteria of verifiability that he managed in his early work to criticize Newton's empirical system as inadequate, paving the way for Einstein's theory of relativity. In his *Analysis of Sensations* (1886), Mach describes his foray into philosophy, marked by a lifelong indebtedness to Kant's *Prolegomena,* in the following note:

> I have always felt it as a stroke of especially good luck that early in life, at about the age of fifteen, in my father's library I came upon a copy of Kant's *Prolego-*

mena to Any Future Metaphysics. The book made at the time a powerful and ineffaceable impression upon me, the like of which I never afterward experienced in any of my philosophical reading. Some two or three years later the superfluity of the role played by "the thing-in-itself" abruptly dawned upon me. On a bright summer day in the open air, the world with my ego suddenly appeared to me as one coherent mass of sensations, only more strongly coherent in the ego. Although the actual working out of this thought did not occur until a later period, yet this moment was decisive for my whole view. . . . I make no pretensions to the title of philosopher. I only seek to adopt in physics a point of view that need not be changed the moment our glance is carried over into the domain of another science; for, ultimately, all must form one whole. The molecular physics of today certainly does not meet this requirement. What I say I have probably not been the first to say. I also do not wish to offer this exposition of mine as a special achievement. It is rather my belief that anyone who makes a careful survey of any extensive body of knowledge will be led to a similar view.

The "exposition" Mach refers to is his main work in phenomenalist reduction and his most famous philosophy book, *Analysis of Sensations,* which inspired William James and other radical empiricist philosophers to develop their views.

It is by comparing the various sense-data with one another that Mach tried to progressively and systematically eliminate those aspects that were unique and peculiar to the subject, until the intrinsic nature of some single, unifying cause revealed itself not *in* but *through* the analysis of sensations. In this way, "objectivity" could be established through the elimination of singularities and the discovery of the single causes capable of producing the varied series of observed effects. Mach's philosophy and science exerted a tremendous influence on subsequent thought; in philosophy proper, Mach was a key source of the logical positivism as developed by the Vienna Circle, especially in their eventual parting of ways with Wittgenstein (discussed later in this chapter) in favor of Mach. Wittgenstein, as we shall see, will repudiate the notion that any sort of formal relationship can be established between "the world" (as traditionally conceived) and words. "This was the breaking point . . . between Wittgenstein and the logical positivists. They would have to choose between him and Mach; and by and large they chose Mach."[1]

James and Radical Empiricism

William James (1842–1910) was born in New York City. After he studied science and medicine at the Lawrence Scientific School, he went to Harvard Medical School. Inspired by his brother, writer Henry James, William interrupted his studies to accompany the explorer Louis Agassiz on an expedition to unknown parts of the Amazon, then spent a year at a medical school in Germany before returning to Harvard.

James's lifelong search for philosophical meaning and understanding took him across a variety of disciplines. After his initial work in medical physiology, he made profound and important contributions to psychology and several areas of philosophy, including epistemology, the philosophy of mind, and the philosophy of religion. His interest in philosophy began one day when he had an experience that he says changed his life:

> I went one evening into a dressing-room in the twilight to procure some article that was there; when suddenly there fell upon me without any warning, just as if it came out of the darkness, a horrible fear of my own existence. . . . It was as if something hitherto solid within my breast gave way entirely, and I became a mass of quivering fear. After this the universe was changed for me altogether. I awoke morning after morning with a horrible dread at the pit of my stomach, and with a sense of the insecurity of life that I never knew before, and that I have never felt since. It was like a revelation . . . for months I was unable to go out into the dark alone. In general I dreaded to be left alone. I remember wondering how other people could live, how I myself had ever lived, so unconscious of that pit of insecurity beneath the surface of life.

After graduating with an M.D. in 1869, James became an instructor in comparative physiology at Harvard, then taught physiology and psychology at Johns Hopkins University in Baltimore. He returned to Harvard in 1880 to join an illustrious philosophy department that included Josiah Royce and graduate student George Santayana (1863–1952). Although James directed Santayana's doctoral thesis, the relationship was not a happy one; James called the dissertation "the perfection of rottenness."

In 1890 James published *Principles of Psychology,* which helped lay the philosophical foundation for the newly developing science of psychology. James founded the American Psychological Association and served as its first president. Six years later he delivered his now-famous lecture to a combined meeting of the philosophy clubs of Yale and Brown Universities. Titled "The Will to Believe," it is an apology for religious belief. James claims that it can be rational to believe in God even in the absence of adequate evidence. The thesis has been criticized as an example of how badly a philosopher can go awry if he gives up the notion of objective truth. For instance, Bertrand Russell, a devout atheist, criticizes James's principle that "if the hypothesis of God works satisfactorily in the widest sense of the word, it is true," on the grounds that "this simply omits as unimportant the question whether God really is in His heaven; if He is a useful hypothesis, that is enough." But even the pope, a devout believer, condemned James's pragmatic defense of religion. In the essay, James tries to develop a pragmatic theory of truth, inspired by Peirce and Dewey; as a result, both Peirce and Dewey disassociated themselves from James's version of pragmatism. The reason was that Peirce and Dewey modeled their pragmatism on scientific thinking and the scientific method, whereas James's analysis relies primarily on religious and moral considerations: "An idea is 'true' so long as to believe it is profitable to our lives."

In saying that truth is but something that "happens to an idea," James was reacting against modern representationalist views of truth according to which an idea "represents" reality and is true insofar as it is a good copy in the mind of what exists "out there" in the "objective world." Russell, who otherwise greatly admired James especially for his work in psychology and the philosophy of mind, labeled James's theory of truth "subjectivist madness."

Ignoring his many critics, James continued working on his *Varieties of Religious Experience* (1902). A blend of philosophical psychology, philosophy of religion, and the philosophy of mysticism, it tries to put mysticism in a positive light. The work is widely regarded today as a definitive study of mystical experience. After its publication, James decided to respond to his earlier critics with an effort to provide a solid philosophical basis for his pragmatic theory of truth.

In 1907 James succeeded to a certain degree with *Pragmatism: A New Name for Some Old Ways of Thinking,* in which he presents the foundational principles of his version of pragmatism in the context of John Stuart Mill's philosophy, to whom the book is dedicated. In his attempt to make pragmatism philosophically respectable, James developed a bold new theory of mind, based on a careful analysis of percepts and concepts. Now known as *radical empiricism,* it turned out to be James's main philosophical achievement. In many ways a psychological version of logical positivism, the idea grew out of an attempt to wed the basic tenets of his earlier version of pragmatism with a new emphasis on experience along the lines espoused by the increasingly influential logical positivist movement, derived from the earlier positivism of Auguste Comte. James argues that a proposition is true or false depending not on "what difference it makes to you and me," as he had claimed in his earlier version of pragmatism, but on whether it succeeds in predicting, or fails to predict, a new sense experience. Propositions that do not successfully make any such predictions one way or the other are meaningless because the world itself consists entirely of experience. This view led James to his alternative to both traditional forms of idealism and materialism, what he called *neutral monism,* according to which neither matter nor consciousness exists. Influenced by the philosophical views of physicist Ernst Mach, James's theory is both phenomenalistic and yet reminiscent of naive realism. The basic but radical innovation, though in many ways extremely subtle, is this: ideas are the only existent given, but that does not mean necessarily that they are mental. James thus accepts as true certain basic aspects of absolute idealism while rejecting as false the existence of an intrinsically subjective consciousness.

In "Does 'Consciousness' Exist?" James gives a detailed account of his radical empiricist position of neutral monism through a detailed analysis of consciousness, leading up to the conclusion that what, ordinarily, we call consciousness, does not exist. What exists is "pure experience." In some ways, on this point James's philosophy can be seen as a synthesis of previous developments in the philosophy of mind and a precursor of the conceptual revolutions in twentieth-century physics and mathematics pioneered by Einstein, Russell, and Bohr, in which the mind is seen not just as a passive observer of reality but more along Kantian and Leibnizian lines, that is, as having a pivotal role in the structuring of reality. The mind according to James is not just a passive observer of reality but has an active role in the structuring of reality. Like many nineteenth-century idealists, James gives up Kant's notion of the "thing in itself" and the noumenal world existing independently of the mind. Some two decades after James's article appeared, Bertrand Russell wrote:

Twenty-three years have elapsed since William James startled the world with his article entitled "Does 'Consciousness' Exist?" In this article . . . he set out the view that "there is only one primal stuff or material in the world," and that the word "consciousness" stands for a function, not an entity. He holds that there are "thoughts," which perform the function of "knowing," but that thoughts are not made of any different "stuff" from that of which material objects are made. He thus laid the foundations for what is called "neutral monism," a view advocated by most American realists.

Russell too will argue that the mind-body problem as originally posed by Descartes can be resolved with some type of neutral monism according to which the mind and physical matter are but different constructions of the same basic stuff that is neither mental nor physical. James's idea is that the real world is, ultimately, as he titled a follow-up article, "a world of pure experience."[2] According to James, the proper concept that captures what the world in and of itself is (rather than how it "merely" appears or how it "truly" is independently of our phenomenal states) is experience. James's notion of what experience is, however, must be understood against the backdrop of his claim that consciousness does not exist. He of course does not mean thoughts do not exist. His point, rather, is that consciousness is not an entity, it is not a thing and should in no way be conceived as a type of substance. Consciousness is a specific type of function that is an act, in the Fichtean-Peircean sense of act—an *act of knowing*. The essence of the conscious act is not ontological but epistemological.

Thus, in exactly the same way that Peirce's semiotics is impersonal, the field of knowledge is active and yet impersonal: "Consciousness as such is entirely impersonal." Further, once we understand that the traditional separation between consciousness and content is bogus—that this is an illusion that the mind adds to the experience of reality—we are in a position to see an object of perceptual experience not as a representation of a non-mental object but, as James calls it above, a *presentation, which makes out of the functional activity of consciousness an external relation.*

The end result is that subjectivity itself—the very essence of conscious states —is removed from philosophy. In many ways, neutral monism is an attempt to transcend the entire subjective-objective distinction. It gave rise to the Darwin-inspired theory known as *naturalism,* highly influential in the twentieth century up to the present day, according to which not just the mind but the human being and the world entire are but interactions among natural processes, and the corresponding theory of knowledge that goes under the label *naturalized epistemology.*

Dewey: Epistemology Naturalized

John Dewey (1859–1952) was born in Burlington, Vermont, the son of a grocer. At his mother's urging and apparently against his wishes, he entered the University of Vermont. He had little interest in intellectual pursuits, viewing them as unnecessary abstractions from the practical concerns of reality, until his senior year, when he took some philosophy courses. Impressed both by the "Scottish empirical realism" and "German rational idealism," especially Leibniz, Kant, and Hegel, he also studied the evolutionary views of T. H. Huxley. After graduation, he taught high school for two years in Pennsylvania but then decided to go to graduate school in philosophy at Johns Hopkins University. In only two years he received his doctoral degree for his dissertation, "The Psychology of Kant." Six years later he published a little known but seminal work on the philosophy of Leibniz, *Leibniz's New Essays Concerning Human Understanding: A Critical Exposition* (1888).[3]

Throughout this early period Dewey was a Hegelian, especially with regard to the view that individuals do not exist in isolation from history, culture, and environment. Although this remained a central aspect of Dewey's later philosophy of education, he later modified his idealism into a unique version of pragmatism following Kant (who was the first to use the word *pragmatishe* in the sense employed by Dewey, James, and other American pragmatists). Yet still Dewey remarked that Hegel had "left a permanent deposit in my thinking." His philosophy began to change even more drastically away from German idealism after reading William James's *Principles of Psychology* (1890). In an essay, "The Development of American Pragmatism," Dewey credits James's *Principles* with awakening him to the idea of pragmatism and the development of a theory of experience according to which the perceiving mind directly apprehends reality:

> It is not experience which is experienced, but nature—stones, plants, animals, diseases, health, temperature, electricity, and so on. Things interacting in certain ways are experience; they are what is experienced. Linked in certain other ways with another natural object—the human organism—they are how things are experienced as well. Experience thus reaches down into nature; it has depth. It also has breadth and to an indefinitely elastic extent. It stretches. That stretch constitutes inference.[4]

James's neutral monism was an attempt to transcend in language itself the entire subjective-objective distinction. This move was further carried out by Dewey through his Darwin-inspired theory known as naturalism, in which James conceived not just the mind but the human being and the world entire as interactions among natural processes. Breaking down the boundary between knowers and what is known but within a strictly positivistic outlook leads to a completely *naturalized epistemology*, which is still very much a pragmatic notion: "The function of reflective thought is to transform a situation in which there is experienced obscurity, doubt, conflict, disturbance of some sort, into a situation that is clear, coherent, settled, harmonious." In Dewey's view, we as knowers are not mere spectators of reality. As Kant, Hegel, and the German idealists, especially Fichte, had argued, the relation between knowers and the known is itself an act. Reality involves a participatory existence between the knower and the known.

Dewey construes knowledge in a completely different sense than Descartes. Instead of a Cartesian quest for certainty, the correctness of a belief depends in part on states of consciousness in the present but also is determined in part by future states. Claiming to be in a state of certainty at the present moment must be false because any claim to such certainty attained in the present moment must be derived from an abstract illusion. The truth is that everything is open to revision. Dewey thus sees philosophy, science, mathematics, and logic as being a part of the ongoing process of history. But this process never ends, there is no summation of the process, no attainment of the absolute or of absolute knowledge, as Hegel thought. The human knowledge-seeking enterprise is an aspect of a perpetually evolving nature in its various stages.

But Dewey's naturalized epistemology is not a call to scientism, of which he is deeply critical:

> Only when the older theory of knowledge and metaphysics is retained, is science thought to inform us that nature in its true reality is but an interplay of masses in motion, without sound, color, or any quality of enjoyment and use. What science actually does is to show that any natural object we please may be treated in terms of relations upon which its occurrence depends, or as an event, and that by so treating it we are enabled to get behind, as it were, the immediate qualities the object of direct experience presents, and to regulate their happening, instead of having to wait for conditions beyond our control to bring it about. Reduction of experienced objects to the form of relations, which are neutral as respects qualitative traits, is a prerequisite of ability to regulate the course of change, so that it may terminate in the occurrence of an object having desired qualities. . . . Thus, "science," meaning physical knowledge, became a kind of sanctuary. A religious atmosphere, not to say an idolatrous one, was created. "Science" was set apart; its findings were supposed to have a privileged relation to the real. In fact the painter may know colors as well as the meteorologist; the statesman, educator and dramatist may know human nature as truly as the professional psychologist; the farmer may know soils and plants as truly as the botanist and mineralogist. For the criterion of knowledge lies in the method used to secure consequences and not in metaphysical conceptions of the nature of the real. . . . That "knowledge" has many meanings follows from the operational definition of conceptions. There are as many conceptions of knowledge as there are distinctive operations by which problematic situations are resolved.[5]

This opens up a cosmic multiperspectival outlook on our epistemologies more in sync with the multiplicity of nature itself; Dewey is here of course deeply following the insights of Leibniz and the concept of infinitude worlds within worlds.

Like Kant, Dewey conceives of his version of pragmatism (derived from Kant, as explained earlier), as another "Copernican revolution" in philosophical, social, moral, and economic thought. The key shift in perspective is laid out in his *Quest for Certainty*. Here, Dewey criticizes the traditional philosophical emphasis on "certainty" as an outdated remnant of ancient Greek thinking, based on the same basic presuppositions found in religion—a hopeless "doctrine of escape from the vicissitudes of existence by means of measures which do not demand an active coping with conditions." Thus, according to Dewey, the quest for certainty from Aristotle to the present has wrongly emphasized the theoretical and ideal rather than the practical and useful. It is this intellectual alienation away from practical experience that leads philosophers time and again to overestimate the power of pure reason for comprehending reality and to underestimate the true cognitive significance of ordinary experience. Dewey thus tries to unite reflective and concrete experience in a way that makes philosophy more "relevant" to the world as it is conceived out of experience rather than as something transcendent to, or the cause of, experience.

In *Democracy and Education* (1916), Dewey applies his methods to education, arguing for the central importance of practical experience to any type of thinking. As he points out, "An experience, a very humble experience, is capable of generating and carrying any amount of theory (or intellectual content), but a theory apart from an experience cannot be definitely grasped even as a theory." By this crucial point he has abandoned all hopes for a Kantian-type transcendental deduction that is supposed to go beyond experience and has adopted instead a type of Humean primacy of the empirical. The real purpose of thought and therefore of philosophy, he argues, is not to make distinctions but to make connections —among both our actions and their consequences. Ultimately, for Dewey, thinking is not to be understood in terms of the intellect but is itself a type of experience, albeit a reflective one.

Dewey taught at the University of Michigan for ten years before he became chairman of the Department of Philosophy, Psychology, and Education at the University of Chicago, where he designed and ran his "Laboratory School." This was an experimental learning environment where he tried out his unorthodox methods of teaching on children from age four to fifteen. In 1905 he moved to New York to join the philosophy department at Columbia University and remained there for the rest of his life, exerting a tremendous influence on subsequent American philosophers.

Royce: The American Idealist

Josiah Royce (1855–1916) was born in the California mining town of Grass Valley. He studied engineering at the University of California, then went to Germany to study philosophy at Leipzig and Göttingen. His greatest influence was Hegel. When he returned to the United States, he went to Johns Hopkins University and received his Ph.D. at the age of twenty-three. He taught at the University of California and then Harvard.

Royce attempted to construct a complete system of thought in the grand style of Hegel, and he founded a uniquely individualistic form of absolute idealism. For the British and German absolute idealists, the Absolute is beyond the categories of thought, hence inaccessible and incomprehensible to the individual mind. Royce argues that the individual mind can have complete knowledge of everything through an "Absolute experience to which all facts are known and for which all facts are subject to universal law." He puts this view forth in his *Spirit of Modern Philosophy* (1892).

Royce identifies each aspect of the world in terms of the immediate presence of the world-soul. According to him, we are "such stuff as ideas are made of." Royce offers a brilliant and simple response to a traditional criticism of idealism. If, as the idealists argue, reality is not material but mental stuff, then why is so much of it fixed and impenetrable? If the world is my idea, why can't I just wish whatever I want into existence? Royce's response is that ideas themselves can be even more "stubborn" and "resilient" than the firmest concept of matter: "This system of ideas we can't change by our wish; it is for us as overwhelming a fact as guilt, or as the bearing of our fellows towards us, but we know it only as such a system of ideas. And we call it the world of matter." Consider, for instance, guilt. Even though it is a mental phenomenon, you cannot simply wish it away. Likewise, in your dreams you are in a world that is entirely your own. The dream world is entirely a mental, idealist world. Yet you cannot simply wish the dream to unfold any way you want. Royce's point is that when you are literally in the grip of an idea, the fact is that you do not move it around with your wishes. It moves you. Ideas can be impenetrable to your prying into them, even though it is really their own prying into themselves. Royce's point is not that ideas cannot be altered in any way, merely that individual egos do not ordinarily have sufficient knowledge. Within the world-soul there exist imperspicuous ideas that correspond, within a materialistic framework, to impenetrable matter.

Royce distinguishes *epistemological idealism*—the claim that our knowledge of the world is ultimately subjective—from *metaphysical idealism*—the claim that the world itself is ultimately a mental, or spiritual, entity. He argues, following Fichte, Schelling, and Hegel, against both materialist realism and empiricism, claiming that metaphysical idealism is the only system that makes genuine knowledge possible. Materialism and realism, in which the world is conceived in terms of some non-mental substance, such as physical atoms or material things in themselves, ultimately make reality unknowable.

To see exactly what Royce means, let us look at a particularly revealing passage from his *Spirit of Modern Philosophy,* whose depth of meaning would have escaped even its own author! The most common sort of criticism levied against idealism relies on the primacy in our language of commonly accepted terminology from current science, which seems, at least on the surface, to be inconsistent with the idealist perspective as Royce construes it. Like Berkeley, he acknowledges how difficult it is to accept the idea that the world consists of ideas once you have the idea of matter rooted in the very language in terms of which your understanding operates. He writes:

> And here you have trouble. Is the outer world, as it exists outside of your ideas, or of anybody's ideas, something having shape, filling space, possessing solidity, full of moving things? That would in the first place seem evident. The sound isn't outside of me, but the sound-waves, you say, are. The colors are ideal facts; but the ether waves don't need a mind to know them. Warmth is an idea, but

the physical fact called heat, this playing to and fro of molecules, is real, and is there apart from any mind. But once more, is this so evident? What do I mean by the shape of anything, or by the size of anything? Don't I mean just the idea of shape or of size that I am obliged to get under certain circumstances? What is the meaning of any property that I give to the real outer world? How can I express that property except in case I think it in terms of my ideas? As for the sound-waves and the ether waves, what are they but things ideally conceived to explain the facts of nature?

In other words, your view of, say, the shape and size of the chair—how different would the very shape and size of that "thing" you are looking at be if you were of a different size, such as a flea or an atom? Clearly, the apparent "primary" qualities of the chair are perspectival. What is the size and shape of that "thing" when you move a hundred feet away from it? Well, you say, its atoms don't change, its spatial properties don't change, and so on. Ah—but what are atoms, what is space? But hold on, that's not the whole of it. There is something subtle going on here that we are in a position to make perfectly clear. When we today use the words *atom* and *space,* these words have a completely different meaning than they did in the time of Royce, which was not so long ago. The nineteenth-century conception of atoms has very little, if anything, in common with today's quantum mechanical model. Likewise, our conception of space has changed in unimaginably drastic ways with the reformulations of non-Euclidean geometries and Einsteinian space-time relativity. If ever there was an opportunity for you to experience such "scientific" terms as ideas, it is here, for Royce ends up listing not just atoms but, also, what nearly every scientist at the time accepted without question: the "ether."

At the time Royce was writing *The Spirit of Modern Philosophy,* 1892, space was conceived in terms of an all-pervasive ether, a perfectly continuous, gaseous-like material substance stretched across the whole universe, literally, the "fabric" of space. Now, when his contemporaries read his book, their minds passed without trouble over the term *ether,* just as yours does over the terms *space* and *atom.* And Royce went to great lengths trying to get them to realize—hard as it may be to believe, he readily acknowledges—that these very terms do not refer to mind-independent realities but are themselves, after all, ideas. It is as if Royce himself has difficulty at this point imagining how it could be possible that atoms and the ether is just an idea in his mind. This is not a point about skepticism but about ontology. In going to such great lengths to try to convince his readers of 1892 that terms like *hardness, molecules,* and so on, are predicated on ideas, he unwittingly throws in the scientific term *ether* in the way that you or I today might throw in the words *atom* or *quark* or *quantum state* in order to sound scientific. How could quarks be just ideas? They are the very foundation of our currently best explanation of physical reality! But the same was once true of the ether!

There is an incredible irony here. Ether waves? Royce is, in effect, saying to his readers: I know it is absolutely preposterous that something as scientifically incontrovertible and foundational as the ether does not refer to anything real, but try to go along with me! It is as if Royce himself has a hard time with that one.

And yet, since Einstein's time, science has given up the notion of an ether. Like the concept *phlogiston,* used once to explain combustion, the term *ether* in the final analysis refers to nothing—not an experience, not a thing. It is a fiction in exactly the way that David Hume claimed all the terms of science are elaborate fictions.

But note, again, that Royce is not trying to make a skeptical point about science. His solution to the problem of knowledge, like the solutions of all idealists, is not to be attained at the scientific level at all! It is not like asking a frightened child, "All right, how do you know that ghosts and goblins really exist, what evidence do you have for them, have you ever seen one?" and so on. Rather, it is like saying to the child, "Look, these are just ideas in your head," and then engaging with that question. One does not go to the closet or under the bed to look. It is not a scientific issue. It is a philosophical one.

In other words, Royce's method requires us not to go beyond the ideas themselves as they are known in experience. But Royce is not content with putting forth an idealist view in opposition to non-idealist, materialistic views. He argues for idealism as the historical evolution of philosophy, similar to Hegel. The four stages of this evolution are described in his *The World and the Individual* (1899). These "four historical conceptions of Being" are realism, mysticism, critical rationalism, and Royce's own "teleological idealism." The first three can be summarized, respectively, as the view that to be is to be independent, that to be is to be immediate, and that to be is to be valid. Each involves a deep contradiction. The only consistent view, Royce argues, is in his fourth conception, as summarized in the ancient mystic's chant, "That art thou." This is the only consistent view of reality.

Royce's "fourth conception of Being" owes much to the philosophy of Averroes and Bruno. According to Royce, the world-self is identical to each and every individual mind. You and I are both identical to the Absolute, to the world, the sum total of everything that exists as a whole. All of our personal experiences, interests, and actions are manifestations of cosmic purpose and part of the whole. Individual acts of human freedom are acts of the Absolute. We are not separate entities from the world-mind but are each identical with it, serving its purpose. All individual minds are the same mind; I am you.[6]

We have encountered this proposition before, for instance in Averroes, as one of the "forbidden propositions," and in Giordano Bruno, burned at the stake in 1600 for asserting it. Royce brought the idea into the American philosophical experience. It inspired many poetical and literary works of the time, including Mark Twain's *Mysterious Stranger* and Walt Whitman's *Song of Myself.*

Equally important are Royce's views concerning the role and nature of meaning. Like Wittgenstein, Royce argues that the notion of an x that is a pure unknowable would literally be nonsense: "Only ideas are knowable. And nothing absolutely unknowable can exist. For the absolutely unknowable, the x pure and simple, the Kantian thing in itself, simply cannot be admitted. The notion of it is nonsense." Such notions having to do with the role and nature of meaning were further discussed by Wittgenstein, Russell, and Quine. Such debates had a great impact on twentieth-century philosophy. Royce argues that any non-idealistic world view would be not merely false but meaningless.

Bradley and British Idealism

Francis Herbert Bradley (1846–1924) was born in Clapham, Surrey (now London), one of twenty-two children fathered by an evangelical preacher. After graduating from University college, Oxford, he was elected to a fellowship at Merton College. His unique brand of absolute idealism grew out of opposition to both the past British empiricists (Locke, Berkeley, and Hume) and the then-current empiricism of J. S. Mill. Like most post-Kantian idealist metaphysicians, Bradley conceives the totality of what really exists in terms of "the Absolute," an essentially whole world-mind similar to Hegel's and Schelling's conceptions except Bradley's more atheistic system does not involve any type of God.

The Absolute as conceived by Bradley requires us to transcend all the fundamental categories of human thought: quality and relation, substance and cause, subject and object, time and space, and so on, are but mere appearance. Neither one nor many, the Absolute is a "unity in diversity." Individuals, which are not collections of attributable properties, get their unity and character from the relations of their properties. This means that in Bradley's view there are no "external" relations: all relations are internal. Suppose an individual named Socrates has a property—say, that of being a teacher—in virtue of which he has a relation R to some other individual or individuals; in that case, R is an internal relation of Socrates. Socrates is a teacher; the relation of being someone's teacher is one of Socrates' internal relations. An external relation is one where there is no property in virtue of which an individual is necessarily R-related to anyone else. For instance, if Socrates is taller than Plato, this is an external relation. Now, since according to Bradley and other British absolute idealists (most notably T. H. Green and B. Bosanquet) all relations are internal, this means that any individual has relations to absolutely all other individuals; to assert any truth about Socrates is thus to assert a truth about the Absolute (the whole world of existing things). In other words, to say anything at all about any individual part of the universe is really to say something about the whole universe.

In his most famous work, *Appearance and Reality,* Bradley presents his unique brand of absolute idealism devoid of religious metaphysics and grounded in a logic distinct from both psychology and physics: the Absolute must be understood not as a system of appearances but as the container of that system such that each appearance is an essential constituent of reality. Bertrand Russell was greatly influenced by Bradley's views, first by agreement and then through opposition, and so was G. E. Moore; even while rejecting Bradley's positive theses, both Moore and Russell remained under the influence of Bradley's sharply critical dialectic as well as the approach to logic he developed in *The Principles of Logic* (1883; 2nd ed., 1922, corrected 1928). Three months before his death, Bradley became the first philosopher to be appointed to the Order of Merit.

Bergson: Spiritual Metaphysics

Henri Bergson (1859–1941) was born in Paris to Jewish immigrants; his father was from Poland, his mother from England. At the prestigious École Normale Supérieur his studies turned from mathematics, in which he had shown early prodigal abilities, to science and then finally philosophy. By the time he became philosophy professor at the Collège de France in 1900, after having taught at a variety of places, he had already become famous in philosophical circles for his doctoral dissertation, published in 1889 as *Essai sur les Données Immédiates de la Conscience* (Essay on the immediate data of consciousness). He argued in his *Essay* that experience will forever be beyond the reach of the intellect because experience is an indivisible continuum (in the mathematical sense) and therefore cannot ever be adequately represented as a succession of demarcated conscious states (as required by the intellect). Like Husserl (discussed in the next section) Bergson drew a sharp distinction between the concept of time and the experience of time; real time is not the static (abstract) time of being but, rather, the dynamic time of becoming as given in experience. Experiential time is apprehended solely by intuition as duration, which ultimately is inaccessible to the conceptual objectifications of the intellect. From this initial work, Bergson came to reject all mechanistic and scientific reductionisms of the human mind to any sort of mechanistic explanation. By the turn of the century, his philosophy of "vitalism" (or "dynamism") extended beyond philosophical and scientific circles and attracted a wide public following through his lectures on human freedom and spirituality that spoke against the growing scientific determinism. His method and unique style are presented most clearly in his *Introduction to Metaphysics* (1903). A unique and potent blend of mysticism and pragmatism, Bergson's account of the origin not just of science but of the entire human knowledge-seeking enterprise is motivated by the practical desire for the human organism to control its environment.

With the publication in 1907 of *Creative Evolution,* Bergson became world-renowned. William James called the work "a pure classic in point of form." In it, Bergson argues that the inner creative urge, a vital principle, or *élan vital,* is the teleological force behind evolution, rather than the (blind) natural selection envisioned by the Darwinists. He presents reality as an integrated whole and yet undetermined in a way that allows individual minds to play an active role. The ultimate goal of human existence, according to Bergson, is to enter into a mystical union with the ultimate, a state beyond all rationality. This enlightened experience is the culmination of the élan vital, the key ingredient in Bergson's dynamic universe of becoming: at its pinnacle, the human mind joins mystic intuition with scientific experiment, thereby taking an active and central role in "the essential function of the universe, which is a machine for the making of gods."

Bergson was elected to the Council of the Legion of Honor, and the French Academy, and the Academy of Sciences, and served as president of the League of Nations Committee for Intellectual Cooperation. In 1928 he won the Nobel Prize for literature.

Husserl and Phenomenology

Edmund Husserl (1859–1938) was born at Prossnitz, in Moravia, of Jewish parents. He began his studies in mathematics at Leipzig, Berlin, and finally Vienna where, in 1884, he attended the lectures of Austrian philosopher Franz Brentano, about whom he remarked, "Without Brentano I should have written not a word of philosophy." Profoundly impressed, Husserl decided to leave mathematics for philosophy. He later taught at Halle, Göttingen, and Freiburg.

Brentano's views were rooted in the Aristotle-inspired scholastic theory of *intentional inexistence,* which Brentano called *immanent objectivity,* used to distinguish mental from physical phenomena:

> Every mental phenomenon is characterized by what the Scholastics of the Middle Ages called the intentional (or mental) inexistence of an object, and what we might call, though not wholly unambiguously, reference to a content, direction toward an object (which is not to be understood here as meaning a thing), or immanent objectivity. Every mental phenomenon includes something as object within itself, although they do not all do so in the same way. In presentation something is presented, in judgement something is affirmed or denied, in love loved, in hate hated, in desire desired and so on.[7]

Brentano's deeply influential notion of intentionality not only was the starting point for Husserl's philosophy but also influenced many analytic philosophers in their analysis of meaning, reference, and the relation between mind and language.

As the founder of the influential European philosophical tradition to which he gave the name *phenomenology* (from the Greek *phainomenon,* "appearance," thus "the study of appearances"), Brentano's goal was to create a pure science for describing and defining the genuine essence (*eidos*) of conscious data within the domain of formal logic and mathematics. Although phenomenology has sometimes been construed as developing in marked opposition to logical positivism and the originators of analytic philosophy, Husserl corresponded with and was highly influenced by Frege (who in turn was influenced in his view of mathematics by Husserl—see below). Also, the founders of the twentieth-century mathematical movement known as *intuitionism* owe a lot to Husserl's work, particularly his shift from a Kantian emphasis on the fundamentality of the a priori nature of space to taking the a priori nature of time as being more basic and fundamental to an analysis of the structure and content of the mind.

Like Descartes, Husserl takes consciousness to be the foundation of all philosophy. But instead of building theories to get from the mind to the world, or evoking as Descartes and Berkeley did the notion of God, Husserl focuses on a purely descriptive and nontheoretical account of consciousness to try to see directly how the world appears—how the world "reveals itself" to consciousness. This, for Husserl, means the real world of everyday experience, free of theoretical philosophy and science. The purpose is to get "behind" the content of consciousness, where the deep structure of the world can reveal itself through the structure of consciousness. The method—similar to Descartes's method of doubt, which

Husserl calls "phenomenological reduction," or *epochē* (Greek for "suspension of belief")—is to "bracket" an experience. This means describing experience purely in experiential terms without the usual assumptions and presuppositions surrounding it. That is how one can "illuminate" the objects of intentionality by which Husserl means the ordinary objects in conscious experience.

Such a phenomenological reduction reveals consciousness as it presents itself. Here, for instance, is an example of a phenomenological reduction of a piece of chalk, from Husserl's *Phenomenology of Inner Time-Consciousness:*

> Let us look at a piece of chalk. We close and open our eyes. We have two perceptions, but we say of them that we see the same piece of chalk twice. We have, thereby, contents which are separated temporally. We also can see a phenomenological, temporal apartness, a separation, but there is no separation in the object. It is the same. In the object there is duration, in the phenomenon, change. Similarly, we can also subjectively sense a temporal sequence where Objectively a coexistence is to be established. The lived and experienced content is "Objectified," and the Object is now constituted from the material of this content in the mode of apprehension. The object, however, is not merely the sum or complexion of this "content," which does not enter into the object at all. The object is more than the content and other than it. Objectivity belongs to "experience," that is, to the unity of experience, to the lawfully experienced context of nature. Phenomenologically speaking, Objectivity is not even constituted through "primary" content but through characters of apprehension and the regularities which pertain to the essence of these characters. It is precisely the business of the phenomenology of cognition to grasp this fully and to make it completely intelligible.[8]

Husserl applies his method to what in his view is the essential manifold of the real world, our conscious experience of time—an idea further developed in Heidegger's masterpiece, *Being and Time,* which we will discuss in the next section.

Such phenomenological reductions can also be performed on an act of consciousness itself. This allows the philosopher to peek behind ordinary appearance into the pure consciousness of the "transcendental ego," to see directly into the heart of the hidden self, that authentic consciousness behind the mask. Moreover, like the Cartesian "I think," Husserl's phenomenological reduction is supposed to provide an absolutely certain foundation for knowledge.

Husserl distinguishes natural thinking in science and in everyday life, which to him are both aspects of naive realism. Both in natural science and our ordinary, day-to-day thinking, we are "untroubled by the difficulties concerning the possibility of cognition." This sort of thought—the type done by ordinary, unreflective life and in the most sophisticated science and mathematics—is contrasted with what he calls *philosophical thought,* defined by "one's position toward the problems concerning the possibility of cognition." In other words, how does science arise in the first place and how is it practiced, if not by disregarding just about all the deep philosophical questions we have raised? Say the scientist starts performing experiments with inclined planes, or just starts thinking theoretically about inertia, momentum, and so on. The scientist does this without ever troubling with the questions of what makes an experience possible and what makes a thought possible. This lack of questioning leads, in Husserl's view, to

> absurdity: to begin with, when we think naturally about cognition and fit it and its achievements into the natural ways of thinking which pertains to the sciences we arrive at theories that are appealing at first. But they end in contradiction or absurdity, inclining one to open skepticism.

What does it mean to think "naturally"? It means merely to think as thinking happens, without doing anything special. Philosophy in general and phenomenology in particular are, in that sense, unnatural; they don't naturally arise in one's own daily life.

There is a deep subtlety here, one that has often been misunderstood by philosophers attempting to comprehend Husserl, who are confused by his call to the study of the experience and objects unencumbered by theory and interpretation from a theoretical perspective. If you think of logic and mathematics as opposed to natural language, you will understand the essence of Husserl's point; just as logic and mathematics are formal rather than natural languages, so phenomenology is formal rather than natural experience. And just as a formal language tool like logic can be instrumental to the study of natural language, so a formal experiential tool like phenomenology can be instrumental to the study of natural experience. It should therefore not be surprising that phenomenology is extremely technical, like logic. Indeed, in his early work that has not been translated into English, Husserl equates his technique of phenomenology using the concept of pure logic through which one could achieve a seeing of the fundamental logical forms themselves, that is, the categories of thought. The task of pure phenomenology is then to test the genuineness and range of this logical "seeing," by distinguishing it from ordinary ways of being conscious.

As Husserl sets out to explain in *The Idea of Phenomenology*,[9] lectures he delivered in Göttingen in 1907, this process can be performed by the phenomenologist either on the object of intentionality itself, such as the piece of chalk, or on the act of consciousness itself. It is this second step in the phenomenological reduction, the *epoché*, that moves the field of consciousness back from its normal state to an enlightened pure consciousness, reaching its own transcendental ego, the *transcendental self* behind the self. Like the Cartesian "I am," only more deeply real, this second step marks the new, Husserlian starting point for philosophical, as opposed to merely scientific, knowledge.

Husserl's phenomenology, his descriptive method, and his theory of intentionality became the source of the phenomenological movement in philosophy, while his further development of Brentano's theory of intentionality—the view that all consciousness is essentially referential, that is, *consciousness of something*—

was incorporated by both phenomenologists and analytic philosophers. In Germany, Husserl's philosophy continued most notably in the work of Martin Heidegger; in France its two leading proponents were Maurice Merleau-Ponty and Husserl's most famous pupil, Jean-Paul Sartre, who used phenomenology to create another widely influential movement, existentialism.

Heidegger

Martin Heidegger (1889–1976) was born at Messkirch in the Black Forest. At the University of Freiburg he studied philosophy with Edmund Husserl, whose phenomenological method for inquiry into the immediate data of experience exerted a lasting influence on Heidegger's own highly original work. In 1923 Heidegger became a professor at Marburg. Five years later he succeeded his former mentor, Husserl (to whom *Being and Time* is dedicated), at Freiburg, where he was then elected rector (president) of the university. Although Heidegger did not consider himself an existentialist, he inspired the great French existentialist Jean-Paul Sartre as well as many philosophers in both the phenomenological and analytic traditions. He has also drawn his share of both philosophical and personal criticism. In a 1932 article, "The Elimination of Metaphysics," the logical positivist Rudolf Carnap used Heidegger as a supposed example of "philosophical nonsense," and he has been criticized for being a Nazi sympathizer. More recently, in the influential *Philosophy and the Mirror of Nature* (1979), Richard Rorty called Heidegger one of the three most important philosophers of the twentieth century (along with Dewey and Wittgenstein).

Like Husserl, Heidegger regarded as essential the "bracketing," or disregarding, of all preconceived epistemological and logical assumptions ordinarily used to distinguish consciousness from the external world. According to Heidegger, existence itself must be apprehended directly via the analysis of human Dasein, by which he means individual "being there," the conscious agent of participation and involvement with the events of experience:

> Dasein is an entity which does not just occur among other entities. Rather it is . . . distinguished by the fact that, in its very Being, that Being is an issue for it. But in that case, this is a constitutive state of Dasein's Being, and this implies that Dasein, in its Being, has a relationship towards that Being—a relationship which itself is one of Being. And this means further that there is some way in which Dasein understands itself in its Being, and that to some degree it does so explicitly. It is peculiar to this entity that with and through its Being, this Being is disclosed to it. Understanding of Being is itself a definite characteristic of Dasein's Being. Dasein is . . . distinctive in that it is ontological.

In *Being and Time,* from which this passage is taken, Heidegger uses language expressly for the purpose of moving beyond the limitations of language so as to have a philosophically direct and intimate relation with Being itself. To understand what he is after here, we must make sure we understand the three-level distinction in his use of the concept of "being."

Consider the world—whatever it really is—as the totality of facts. A fact is something that is the case (whether we know it or not, let us say). So there is the totality of the way things are, making up the world (as a totality). Presumably, if one made a list of all the facts, one would in principle have a map of the world-entire. But how do you list facts? You can, at best, list sentences that express propositions. What, then, is the relationship between a proposition and a fact? Well, some propositions are false, others are true. Facts, as such, aren't "true" or "false." They just *are*. You see the problem facing Heidegger (and us)? What are facts, what do they consist of? Matter? Ah—by now we should realize that this definition won't work, any more than will the concept of "mind." For if everything consists of matter, then there is the fact that matter exists and this is not a piece of matter. Or, if everything consists of ideas, then there is the fact that ideas exist and this is not a piece of an idea. Well, what then are such things?

This may be empty, meaningless talk, as some philosophers have charged, or it may be profound. But in any case, Heidegger is trying to reach the facts, not propositions as represented in language, but even beyond them. The whole process may indeed be empty and meaningless, but that does not make the effort any less profound.

Thus, Heidegger distinguishes entities that make up the world—the individual existent beings—and Being itself, the "fact that the world itself exists," not the existence of the world as such but that the world exists. The obscurity of this thinking process that we are at this moment engaging is, according to Heidegger, the result of our being in the world, "being too close to being" to see it. To use a visual metaphor, think of the eye not seeing the eye—why doesn't it? Why do your eyes not at this moment see the eyes? Well, if you think about it, you will realize that the eye needs to be some distance from anything it is looking at; the closer, the blurrier, until—to speak in terms of a phenomenological reduction— the thing being looked at becomes unseeable as the object that it is. In this way the eye (again, still phenomenologically speaking) must by necessity disappear from itself in order to see. (That is why part of Heidegger's overall philosophical program is to gain us some distance from being in order to see being—a paradox that some have used to liken Heidegger to a certain aspect of Zen Buddhism.)

Thus far, then, we have the first two-level distinction between being—or, being-as-entity in the world—and Being, the fact of the existence of the world-entire. The third, crucial, Heideggerian distinction is not between being and Being but an identification, among all the individual entities, of the one unique type of being, described in the passage above: Dasein. That is why Heidegger says, above, that "Dasein is an entity which does not just occur among other entities." It is also why instead of just talking about "I" or "consciousness" or "being," he uses as a technical term the German word "Dasein." I, as Dasein, this being here in the world, exist not just as a being having a certain physical boundary, a size, certain personal and cultural psychological characteristics, and so on; nor do I, as Dasein, merely use language as a specific type of tool when I think, will, experience fear, and so on. Rather, it is that in my own being, my very presence in the world, I do not merely exist, my very existence is "an issue." This he defines, again by using an ordinary German word in a technical way, as existence. When Heidegger speaks of existence, he is speaking of the unique characteristic of Dasein—Dasein exists, which involves, in part, always projecting itself beyond the given present into the not-yet-present future possibilities.

In other words, by being aware of the present moment, its existence within us, in light of what it has been—the past—and what it could become—the future —we escape the confinement in which beings that are not Dasein do not have: for instance, spiders, snakes, birds, and bees. They are beings who are mere automata; the bird never asks, "Why am I a bird and not an elephant?" This making present to consciousness what is not there is the unique aspect of human consciousness that makes us uniquely and radically free. The world itself is thus in Heidegger's view structured into different regions of existential modalities dispersed through an environment consisting of accessible and utilizable objects so that human knowledge and human existence cannot be divorced from human action. In this way, Heidegger is paving the way for the development of the philosophical movement known as existentialism, carried to its fruition by Jean-Paul Sartre, which we shall explore in detail in the next section.

In his masterpiece, *Being and Time* (1927), Heidegger continues to trace the fundamental question of metaphysics back to Plato and Aristotle and then sets out to discover the very meaning of all being. This cannot be achieved through sophisticated theories using concepts like substance and cause but, rather, must be attained through the philosophical investigation of Dasein itself, one's own individual human presence, the "being there" of the world as it concerns itself with its own basic situation and aims through active participation and involvement with the rest of being. And just as the fundamental question for each individual Dasein is "Why do I exist?" or "Why was I ever born?" or "Why did I ever come to be rather than having never existed?" so too with the world-entire. This leads Heidegger into an analysis of the most fundamental question of being: "Why is there something rather than nothing?"

Heidegger devotes an entire book, his *Introduction to Metaphysics* (1953), to this question. He explains why this question cannot properly be addressed either by science nor by religion but only by philosophy. Have you ever asked this question of yourself? All of this, why does it exist? Why is there something rather than nothing? This is the biggest of all questions. It extends to everything. It asks: Why existence? Why does anything exist? Why isn't there just nothing?

Heidegger uses this question to remove the borders between all things before us, to reduce the many to an undifferentiated one and ask, Why being rather than non-being? By not discriminating between things, the question extends to everything. It lumps all the things in the world into one and asks, Why a world, any world, rather than no world? By ignoring the quantity, quality, and types of existent things, the question brings into sharp focus the brute fact of existence itself: Why existence rather than non-existence?

The oldest answer to the biggest question was God. The reason there is something rather than nothing is that God created it. And the reason God exists is that God has always existed, God is eternal, and the reason God is eternal is that that is God's nature.

One thing nearly all religions have in common is their shared belief in some sort of noncontingent being, a being that exists necessarily, which they call God. However, if we have understood Heidegger's question properly, the question of whether God exists is ontologically irrelevant. It's not that God is the wrong answer; God is not even an answer. To offer God as an answer is just a very fancy existential bait-and-switch.

Question: Why is there something rather than nothing?

Answer: Because a Big Something made the little something!

This is not an answer. Heidegger's question asks why anything, why any sort of anything exists—material, spiritual, neutral monistical, or whatever—rather than nothing. God is not nothing. God is also something. The question asks about God too. A world without a God is from the point of view of Heidegger's question no less mysterious than a world with God. In fact, if God exists, then the biggest question of all time has grown even bigger: Why is there a (material) world and an immaterial world (God) rather than nothing? If a world consisting of contingent material somethings is puzzling, how much more puzzling to find ourselves in a world containing contingent material somethings plus a noncontingent immaterial something! Why is there something—any type of something, contingent or noncontingent, material or spiritual—rather than nothing?

Having realized that the question does not have an answer, that it couldn't possibly have an answer, that it must apply to any existent thing and to any world, regardless of what there is, leads to the further realization that the "most" unanswerable question is also the most meaningful. For it is the presence of this unanswerable possibility of absolute nothing, which our own existence negates without any ultimate cause, reason, or explanation, that brings Being itself most close at hand to consciousness: "What about this Nothing? . . . Where do we seek the Nothing? How do we find the Nothing. . . . We know the Nothing. . . . What about this Nothing? The Nothing itself nothings. Anxiety reveals the nothing." Here Heidegger takes an unexpected turn. Instead of an answer, he finds an experience, a deep, profound, awful experience in the primordial and etymological sense of awful—"filled with awe." But the experience is too much, it reveals the "too muchness" of existence to existence, causing deep existential dread to awaken the Dasein to the presence of the whole of Being. This is not mere fear. Fear always has an object, some entity or state. The existential anxiety of which Heidegger speaks reveals the most general form of Dasein's Being. It is not directed at any particular entity in the world, which would amount to one part of the world (e.g., you) relating to another (e.g., an enemy chasing you), but at the whole of Being confronting the whole of Being at its fulcrum, which is Dasein itself: ". . . that in the face of which one has anxiety is Being-in-the-world as such." Being-in-the-world is the most fundamental existential characteristic of Dasein. This brings us to the final pinnacle of Heidegger's entire philosophy. Dasein is anxious-in-the-face-of-itself. Ordinarily, Dasein is hidden, absorbed, "alienated" in the various aspects of its living in the world as individual human beings. It is in a state of "fallenness." Awakened to its own presence in the world, catching sight of itself, the One that is the everyday Dasein trembles:

> Anxiety thus takes away from Dasein the possibility of understanding itself, as it falls, in terms of the "world" and the way things have been publicly interpreted. Anxiety throws Dasein back upon that which it is anxious about—its authentic potentiality-for-Being-in-the-world. Anxiety individualizes Dasein. . . . Anxiety makes manifest in Dasein its Being towards its ownmost potentiality-for-Being —that is, its Being-free for the freedom of choosing itself and taking hold of itself.

In this way, Being becomes forlorn and individualizes itself, breaking apart into the many, and experiences itself as not itself; the clearest ontological manifestation of this situation within you, the Dasein that you are, at the present moment is the existential division between self and other. The clearest existential manifestation of this division is anxiety, or the degree to which you feel that deepest, darkest dread of being. Ask someone suffering from anxiety, "What do you fear?" The answer: "nothing."

Sartre and Existentialism

French philosopher, playwright and novelist Jean-Paul Sartre (1905–1980) was born in Paris to an illustrious family. His father was a decorated naval officer, his mother the cousin of the Nobel Peace Prize–winning theologian and medical missionary, Albert Schweitzer. Orphaned at a young age, Sartre was raised by his grandfather, in whose rich library he "found my religion: nothing seemed to me more important than a book. I regarded the library as a temple." He went on to study philosophy at the prestigious École Normale Supérieur and then at Göttingen under the direction of Husserl. He taught philosophy for a few years at Le Havre in Paris but then resigned to pursue a full-time writing career.

During World War II Sartre joined the French army but spent most of his time working on a novel and two plays, often typing in front of his commanding officers, for which he was often reprimanded. Captured by the Germans, he was a prisoner of war for eight months during which time he put on plays and gave lectures to the officers on the history of German philosophy from Kant to Husserl; he escaped using papers that the German officers had forged for him. He returned to the French resistance and promptly resumed his writing and finished two plays —*The Flies* and *No Exit*—both widely regarded as masterpieces. The latter, which has become a paradigm of existentialist drama, contains the famous line, "Hell is other people."

When Sartre's massive philosophical work *Being and Nothingness* appeared in 1943, it was instantly heralded as a new philosophical classic. By war's end, he had become the famous proponent of his atheistic brand of existentialism and a world-renowned leader of left-wing intellectuals. In 1964 he won the Nobel Prize but refused to accept it on grounds that Alfred Nobel, who had made his fortune by inventing and selling dynamite, had profited from human suffering and that the prize was but another political tool of the military-industrial complex.

In *Existentialism* (1957), Sartre explains the meaning of existentialism using his often-quoted dictum, "Existence precedes essence." This formula is not true for most objects in the world; in the case of tables and chairs "essence"—what they essentially are and what they are for—precedes their existence. The idea comes first, as a concept or notion in the mind, and then the object is created following the preconceived blueprint. Human existence has no blueprint, no designer, no creator. God does not exist and so no antecedent idea of human nature exists; there is no given purpose to life, no essence that precedes human existence. Only after we emerge into the universe as existent entities do we define our own essence, arbitrarily, but through choice. Because there is no God there can be no prefabricated meaning, and so human beings are forlorn; we are each condemned to be free since we cannot ever do otherwise than choose who and what we are. Nothing is given except that nothing is given. We are fully and completely responsible for our lives. The problem, however, is that we do not allow ourselves to really see this because we fear freedom. We don't want to have to choose who and what we are. We shield ourselves from the fact that it is we ourselves who make up meaning by pretending that we are what we are, that we have a fixed nature, when really meaning is something we make up. But Sartre does not view this state of affairs as something negative, since it makes human beings the true artists of themselves and their world. Going about looking for the meaning of life, Sartre might say, is like staring at a blank canvas looking for the greatest painting. It misses the point. The blankness is not horrible, it is not the end of the world, but the beginning; for now there is room for something, an infinity of possibilities. What we choose to paint is arbitrary, but paintings are not arbitrary.

In *Being and Nothingness,* building on themes developed by Hegel and Husserl, Sartre presents a phenomenological study of being, nothingness, consciousness, the self, and emotion. He begins by distinguishing two different categories of being: being-in-itself, fully complete and determinate, independent of everything else, without relation to anything—not even itself—versus being-foritself, the fully indeterminate and open domain of human consciousness, characterized by freedom. He then goes on to examine the related apparently opposite phenomena of bad faith and sincerity, arguing that these are both tools of self-deception by which we blind ourselves to the fact that we have no fixed natures, and that is how we hide ourselves from our freedom and our freedom from our true, self-created selves.

Frege: Sense and Reference

Gottlob Frege (1848–1925) was born at Wismar, Germany. He studied at the University of Jena and the University of Göttingen. He became a professor of mathematics at Jena, but his work had a deep and lasting influence on philosophy, especially mathematical logic, the philosophy of mathematics, and the philosophy of language. His ground-breaking *Grundgesetze der Arithmetik* (The basic laws of arithmetic; 1884) begins with a warning to unphilosophical mathemati-cians, telling them they should not bother reading his book: "Mathematicians reluctant to venture into the labyrinths of philosophy are requested to leave off reading. . . ."

Many philosophers, from Plato and Pythagoras to Descartes and Leibniz, made important contributions to mathematics and considered mathematics important for the study of philosophy. Kant, for instance, took mathematical truths to be a paradigm of the synthetic a priori. As a mathematician, Frege was puzzled why philosophy itself had never developed a sufficiently technical lan-guage of its own, and why philosophers seemed to shun the formal language of mathematics and logic and preferred instead to state their philosophies in the sloppy constraints of natural language. Why, he wondered, did Descartes, the inventor of analytic geometry, and Leibniz, the inventor of calculus, write philos-ophy not in the language of mathematics but in French, Latin, German, and so on? Even the philosophers doing fundamental work in logic presented the sub-ject matter of logic itself in natural language. Likewise, Spinoza, who modeled his system after the axiomatic system of Euclidean geometry, uses mathematics only as an example and states his system in natural language.

Frege inspired many philosophers, including Bertrand Russell, to try to achieve the technical rigor of mathematics within philosophy. In his *Basic Laws of Arithmetic,* he puts forth the thesis that has since become known as *logicism,* the view that mathematics reduces to pure logic. This thesis was further developed by Russell and others, who claimed that perhaps all natural languages—English, German, French, etc.—are reducible to logic.

Frege argued that proofs in mathematics must be constructed using a com-pletely perspicuous machinery, whereby every demonstration is clear and dis-tinct, not just mathematically but philosophically, heralding a new level of deductive rigor; each step must be absolutely explicit, nothing must be left to intuition or psychology. What then does that mean? Where is the clearness and distinctness to be attained, if not in some psychological sensation of clearness and distinctness?

In Plato's *Meno* we read the paradigm example of the slave boy experiencing an "aha, yes," when he sees the Pythagorean theorem. We saw Descartes's attempt to further develop such a psychologically special state of mind into the basis for a rigorous epistemology in which the rationally intuited mind-state is a sort of interface, or point of intersection, between the noumenal truth and our conscious experience, which of course influenced Kant's notion of the synthetic a priori. Every step must be explicit so that nothing is left to intuition or psychology. In this way, the Cartesian notion of clearness and distinctness, an internal state of the mind expressed as a psychological sensation, is replaced by a purely formal-ized system of symbolic clarity.

According to Frege, the propositions of arithmetic and analysis are pure a priori expressions of logic. This view is in marked contrast to Kant, who thought they were synthetic a priori, and John Stuart Mill, who thought they were empir-ical. In his *Begriffsschrift* (1879), Frege develops a new formal language whose vocabulary and modes of construction owe much to the *calculus philosophicus et ratiocinator* originally envisioned by Leibniz. It is Frege who invented the concepts of quantifiers and variables, symbolic constructions that allowed the giant first step to be taken toward the formalization of natural language. He even developed a revolutionary analysis of sense and meaning, giving primacy to reference (Bedeutung), which influenced philosophers as varied as Bertrand Russell, Edmund Husserl, and Martin Heidegger, and continues to exert enormous influence today.

In *Basic Laws of Arithmetic* (1884), Frege argues against both subjective idealism and psychologism (the view that psychology and introspection are primary methods of inquiry). He offers proof for the thesis that the mind has access to what is beyond itself. The proof is based on a distinction between the meaning of a term, its *Sinn* ("sense"), and its *Bedeutung* ("reference"), and then on a demonstration that two terms can have different meanings even when they have the same reference. He makes this clear in his article "Über Sinn und Bedeutung" (On sense and reference). The point about referring, however, is deeply subtle. It requires our noticing that within the domain of our own language the referential function of certain terms logically prohibits our drawing inferences as to the referents (the objects referred to) being inside, or part of, the mind. It isn't that we can prove that what we are referring to is beyond the mind; rather, it is that we can reduce to meaninglessness the contention that what we are referring to itself exists in the mind. Though this is an oversimplification, Frege's move is, in effect, a linguistic and logical, rather than metaphysical, refutation of idealism. And it is consistent. In a tour de force, Frege shows that idealism is linguistically meaningless and logically inconsistent, while his realism is consistent, without having to construct any elaborate metaphysical system, thereby altogether avoiding the ontological question.

Consider the following diagram:

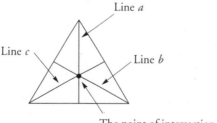

Line *a*

Line *c*

Line *b*

The point of intersection, *p*

Note that while (A), "the point of intersection between *a* and *b*," and (B) "the point of intersection between *b* and *c*," have the same reference, they have different senses. That is, (A) and (B) refer to one and the same particular point where the lines intersect, call it "*p*, the point of intersection." Yet (A) and (B) express different "cognitions." That they have a different sense, or meaning, can be seen by the fact that when you went through the cognitive process of constructing them,

(A) is a different cognitive construction—not the same mental event as (B). Likewise with "morning star" and "evening star." The morning star appears in the morning in the East, whereas the evening star appears at the dusk of twilight. The two images look very different. Whoever doesn't know that "morning star" and "evening star" are both the same planet, Venus, would never realize that those names refer to one and the same designated object. In reality, "morning star" and "evening star" have different meanings and the same referent.

Frege's technically precise distinction is pivotal for understanding the first of two very different approaches, within the history of philosophy, to the nature, function, and role of language. According to the first approach—which we have seen epitomized by philosophers like Plato, Aquinas, Spinoza, Leibniz, Kant, Hegel, and Royce—meaning is a relation between language and the world. According to the second approach—which is epitomized by philosophers like Protagoras, William of Ockham, Hobbes, Locke, Hume, Comte, James, and Russell—meaning is understood in terms of acts performed by speakers of ordinary language in everyday contexts. In the former, the ultimate tools of analysis are mathematics, logic, and formal languages; in the latter, which views the first approach in terms of analysis of relations between "language and world" as a source of metaphysical confusion, the main tool is natural language. Frege's technical apparatus provided a much needed impetus to the first approach as philosophy entered the twentieth century. His propositional calculus and quantification theory inspired Bertrand Russell and Alfred North Whitehead to attempt the full reduction of mathematics to logic in their *Principia Mathematica*. It was while reading Frege that Russell discovered the famous paradox that has ever since been called "Russell's paradox." When Russell pointed out the paradox to Frege, it ended Frege's attempt to complete his system; ironically, Russell experienced a similar fate with his own star pupil, Wittgenstein. In his autobiography, Russell writes,

> As I think about acts of integrity and grace, I realize that there is nothing in my knowledge to compare with Frege's dedication to truth. His entire life's work was on the verge of completion, much of his work had been ignored to the benefit of men infinitely less capable, his second volume was about to be published, and upon finding that his fundamental assumption was in error, he responded with intellectual pleasure clearly submerging any feelings of personal disappointment. It was almost superhuman and a telling indication of that of which men are capable if their dedication is to creative work and knowledge instead of cruder efforts to dominate and be known.

Whitehead and Process Philosophy

Alfred North Whitehead (1861–1947) was born in England at Ramsgate, Kent. His grandfathers were both schoolmasters, his father a parson. As a boy he played along the grim walls of Richborough Castle, built by the Romans, and nearby at

Ebbes Fleet beach where Augustine had preached his first sermon. He spent his adolescence at Sherborne, a 1,200-year-old school, studying in an abbot's cell in whose bells he says he heard "the living voices of past centuries." The lessons and books were in Latin and Greek. At nineteen, he entered Cambridge. At the time, the education there was considered distinctly Platonic, consisting of freewheeling conversations with professors and other students. When as a professor at Harvard he was once asked how he could have finished his *Science and the Modern World* in one semester while teaching a full load, he referred back to his years of study, replying that "everything in the book had been talked over for the previous forty years."

At only twenty-four (in 1885), Whitehead became a fellow of Trinity College, Cambridge, then generally considered one of the greatest universities in the world; it openly boasted that two centuries ago under its auspices Sir Isaac Newton had discovered all the fundamental laws of the universe. Although he would do ground-breaking work in both philosophy and mathematics, Whitehead's formal study at Trinity was in the latter discipline because "mathematics must be studied; philosophy should be discussed." His first and in many ways most important contribution came in his famous collaboration with Bertrand Russell on *Principia Mathematica* (1910–13, in three volumes), a monumental and comprehensive work on the foundations of mathematics. This was the first attempt to build a complete axiomatic system of logic; in contrast to Euclid and Newton, the axioms are stripped bare of any concrete content. There is no reference to spatial reality or any kind of transcendental or extrasensory reality as in Plato's theory of ideas.

Indeed, in Whitehead's view, the sorts of ultimately "real" things of which Newtonian-inspired physicists imagined the world was constructed—atoms—are "intellectual abstractions" that have no actual existence independently of the mind. In the tradition of Berkeley, Mach, Royce, and James, Whitehead replaces the Democritan and Newtonian inert atoms with the atomic constituents of reality that, like Leibnizian monads, exist as processes in relation to the human experience. These actual entities, or "actual occasions," are key to the understanding of metaphysics, he says, freed of the Cartesian dualism and the mind-body problem. For Whitehead, as for Aristotle, there is but one insubstantial substance undergoing perpetual change: what appears, what is given in direct perception, is real. Nothing exists beyond what is present in the direct experience of the perceiving subject, which exists in relation to its object.

As in the Heraclitan flux, Whitehead's universe has no static concepts or substances, only an interconnected network of events. These events are actual extensions, spatiotemporal unities, giving rise within the flux to organisms sensitive to the existences of all others. The relations between entities are experienced as a kind of feeling. Every actual entity consists of all its active relations with other things, which Whitehead terms its "prehensive occasion," as well as its "negative prehension," determined by the exclusion of everything that it is not. Unlike Leibniz's monads, Whitehead's "actual entities" have no permanent identity or history; they exist perpetually in the process of becoming. Death and the perishing of actual entities is but the creativity of the universe moving on to the next birth, such that the actual occasion loses its uniqueness but is preserved in the flow of process.

In this way, nothing can ever be completely understood, for everything is always changing. The great mistake made throughout the history of thought, according to Whitehead, is what he called the "fallacy of misplaced concreteness," which results from our mistaking intellectual abstractions for actual entities. The only permanence in the world is not in the realm of actuality but in the realm of possibility; possibilities are what he calls "eternal objects," reminiscent of Plato's Ideas. The relation between actualities and possibilities Whitehead calls *ingression,* by which he means that a possibility has made itself manifest upon actuality; it has *ingressed* through the subject into the object: "the functioning of an eternal object in the self-creation of an actual entity is the 'ingression' of the eternal object in the actual entity." In this way, past actualities—events that have occurred in the past—achieve "objective immortality," because the actual entities are forever involved in the process of actuality, into which eternal objects ingress from universals whose selection is necessary to the existence of actual entities. The entire system thus remains in perpetual flux, incomplete, unresolvable, unknowable except as momentary influxes into the process.

Asked once what he thought the ancient philosophers would have to say about the twentieth century, Whitehead replied:

> Aristotle would be inexpressibly shocked at the way his generalizations have gone overboard. Mind you, I don't say his ideas . . . haven't proved vastly useful. Aristotle discovered all the half-truths which were necessary to the creation of science. . . . Plato's ideas . . . tend, in comparison, to be vague. But I prefer the vagueness. I prefer Plato. He seems to me to have been the one man in the ancient world who would not have been surprised at what has happened, because his thought constantly took into account the unpredictable, the limitless possibilities of things. There is always more chance of hitting something valuable when you aren't too sure what you want to hit upon. . . . Am I right in thinking that [scholars] are quite wrong in trying to identify Plato with some explicit conclusion in his *Dialogues,* with some single speaker and a final point of view? It seems to me that was just what he was trying to avoid. Take his letters: assuming that he wrote them, and even if he didn't, they would state a prevailing frame of mind in ancient times about his work: namely, that there is no Platonic system of philosophy. What he did was explore various aspects of a problem and then leave us with them. . . . He seems to me to have had, more than anyone else, a supreme sense of the limitless possibilities of the universe.[10]

At the age of sixty-three, Whitehead was invited to join the philosophy department at Harvard University. His work in mathematics and logic, which had a profound influence on symbolic logic, having been completed and his philosophy of education widely influential in England, he set out to create a comprehensive philosophical system. His most important works from this time are *Science and the Modern World* (1925), *Process and Reality* (1929), and *Adventures of Ideas* (1933). For all of their scope and brilliance, the works are often criticized as being too vague and open-ended, to which Whitehead openly replied, "In philo-

sophical discussion, the merest hint of dogmatic certainty as to finality of statement is an exhibition of folly."

It was actually Whitehead who first noticed admirably another rather mysterious figure in philosophy, a young student of his and Russell's from Vienna
named Wittgenstein. Russell remarks:

> Whitehead described to me the first time that Wittgenstein came to see him. He
> was shown into the drawing-room during afternoon tea. He appeared scarcely
> aware of the presence of Mrs. Whitehead, but marched up and down the room
> for some time in silence, and at last said explosively: "A proposition has two
> poles. It is *apb*." Whitehead, in telling me, said: "I naturally asked what are *a*
> and *b*, but I found that I had said quite the wrong thing. '*a* and *b* are indefin-
> able,' Wittgenstein answered in a voice of thunder."[11]

After their pioneering work together, Whitehead and Russell had a great philosophical falling out. Their disagreement came about in part because of the tumultuous upheaval that came at the turn of the century in science, with the ending of
the Newtonian world view and developments that heralded the coming of Einstein's relativity:

> We supposed that nearly everything of importance about physics was known.
> Yes, there were a few obscure spots, strange anomalies . . . which physicists
> expected to be cleared up by 1900. They were. But in so being, the whole sci-
> ence blew up, and the Newtonian physics, which had been supposed to be fixed
> as the Everlasting Seat, were gone. Oh, they were and still are useful as a way of
> looking at things, but regarded as a final description of reality, no longer valid.
> Certitude was gone.[12]

Whitehead's philosophical response was unpopular not just with Russell but with
most of the logical positivists at the time, who sided with the new physics.
Indeed, Russell was so impressed by the current state of the physics that he used
it as an epistemoloigcal foundation in his philosophy. Whitehead, on the other
hand, was singularly unimpressed by the new scientific certitude. He said,

> The Universe is vast. Nothing is more curious than the self-satisfied dogmatism
> with which mankind at each period of its history cherishes the delusion of the
> finality of its existing modes of knowledge. Skeptics and believers are all alike.
> At this moment scientists and skeptics are the leading dogmatists. Advance in
> detail is admitted; fundamental novelty is barred. This dogmatic common sense
> is the death of philosophic adventure. The Universe is *vast.*[13]

Although he and Russell remained friends (even though Whitehead was,
politically, the extreme conservative in relation to Russell's extreme liberalism),
Russell veered to the side of mathematics and science while Whitehead, the
mathematician, turned deeply philosophical. Lamenting the disincilination of
those philosophers who, like Whitehead, were skeptical of the new certainty of
physicists and mathematics, Russell wrote,

> The people I don't trust are the philosophers, including Whitehead. They are
> cautious and constitutionally timid; nine out of ten hate me personally, not

without reason; they consider philosophical research a foolish pursuit. . . . Before the war I fancied that quite a lot of them thought philosophy important; now I know that most of them resemble Professors Hanky and Panky in *Erewhon Revisited.*[14]

Meanwhile, Whitehead puts his position in no uncertain terms when he says,

Let me speak personally for a moment. I had a good classical education, and when I went up to Cambridge early in the 1880's my mathematical training was continued under good teachers. Now nearly everything was supposed to be known about physics that could be known—except a few spots, such as electromagnetic phenomena, which remained (or so it was thought) to be co-ordinated with the Newtonian principles. But, for the rest, physics was supposed to be nearly a closed subject. Those investigations to co-ordinate went on through the next dozen years. By the middle of the 1890's there were a few tremors, a slight shiver as of all not being quite secure, but no one sensed what was coming. By 1900 the Newtonian physics were demolished, done for! Still speaking personally, it had a profound effect on me; I have been fooled once, and I'll be damned if I'll be fooled again! Einstein is supposed to have made an epochal discovery. I am respectful and interested, but also sceptical. There is no more reason to suppose that Einstein's relativity is anything final, than Newton's *Principia*. The danger is dogmatic thought; it plays the devil with religion, and science is not immune from it.[15]

Whitehead of course turned out to be right; the Einsteinian world view has since then given way dramatically to the strange new world of the quantum. The reality we live in now according to the latest physical science would have seemed utterly absurd to just about anyone then except, perhaps, some extreme nineteenth-century idealists and a quiet old ex-mathematician who broke ranks to become chairman of the philosophy department at Harvard.

After waiting in the wings for more than three millennia, the Heraclitan flux has swallowed the soul of Parmenides with a vengeance.

Russell and Logical Atomism

Bertrand Russell (1872–1970) was born to a noble family in Monmouthshire, England. His parents died while he was a child and he was raised by his grandfather, Lord John Russell. He studied mathematics and philosophy at Cambridge University, where under the influence of Bradley he became a Hegelian idealist. Inspired by fellow pupil G. E. Moore, he gave up Hegelianism in favor of commonsense philosophy, which in the end he rejected even more vehemently in favor of scientific and logical realism.

In his first major work, the ground-breaking *Principia Mathematica* (Principles of mathematics; 1903), Russell was inspired by Frege to equate meaning and reference. He argues that any meaningful terms must have real entities as references, even mathematical terms (numbers, points, lines, etc.). When he and

Whitehead had collaborated on *Principia Mathematica,* the idea was to start with logically primitive, irreducible concepts stated as axioms and then to derive the whole of mathematics. Each step would be perspicuous, with nothing left to intuition, as Frege had called for, to prove that mathematics reduces to pure logic. In other words, since the distinction between sense and reference existed within the logical-linguistic framework of the speaker—that is, were themselves logical or mathematical entities which, as such, existed only in the mind—Frege's distinction was merely a verbal and not an ontological one. In this way, Russell realized that the kind of linguistic distinction that Frege had in mind ultimately required a commitment to some sort of Platonic idealism, in which the logical and mathematical terms themselves had reference independent of the mind. To put it most simply, Frege's move required an even more idealistic ontological commitment than the sort of psychologism Frege was trying to avoid.

The resolution of the matter would have to await the brilliant work of Gödel, Türing, and Church in the middle part of the twentieth century, their work made possible by the monumental task to which Russell now set his sights: the reduction of the conceptual symbolic language of mathematics to the formal symbolic language of logic, hoping in this way to achieve the same result as Frege—in effect, to get out of Plato's cave—not by moving in the outward direction but in the inward direction, that is, by the reduction of mathematics to logic. In reducing mathematics to logic in this way, Whitehead and Russell relied on Russell's theory of logical constructions showing how the foundations of mathematics could be established using "contextual definitions" in which mathematical concepts are translated into their logical equivalents. His axiom of infinity, the set theoretical paradox that now bears his name (Russell's paradox, discussed below), and the theory of types revolutionized the way both philosophy and mathematics are done.

In 1911, as a professor at Cambridge, Russell discovered and became mentor to another one of the greatest philosophers of the twentieth century, Ludwig Wittgenstein. Wittgenstein, in turn, came to have a lasting influence on Russell, especially regarding his views on logic and the philosophy of language. In subsequent decades, Russell went on to extend his original logical-analytic method to virtually all areas of philosophy, even to physics and psychology.

A lifelong critic of religion, Russell was a devout atheist. In his *Why I Am Not a Christian,* he writes:

> I think all the great religions of the world—Buddhism, Hinduism, Christianity, Islam and Communism—both untrue and harmful. It is evident as a matter of logic that, since they disagree, not more than one of them can be true. With very few exceptions, the religion which a man accepts is that of the community in which he lives, which makes it obvious that the influence of environment is what has led him to accept the religion in question. It is true that the Scholastics invented what professed to be logical arguments proving the existence of God, and that these arguments, or others of a similar tenor, have been accepted by many eminent philosophers, but the logic to which these traditional arguments appealed is of an antiquated Aristotelian sort which is now rejected by practically all logicians except such as are Catholics. . . . The question of the truth of a

religion is one thing, but the question of its usefulness is another. I am as firmly convinced that religions do harm as I am that they are untrue. The harm that is done by a religion is of two sorts, the one depending on the kind of belief which it is thought ought to be given to it, and the other upon the particular tenets believed. As regards the kind of belief: it is thought virtuous to have Faith—that is to say, to have a conviction which cannot be shaken by contrary evidence. . . . The conviction that it is important to believe this or that, even if a free inquiry would not support the belief, is one which is common to almost all religions and which inspires all systems of state education. The consequence is that the minds of the young are stunted and are filled with fanatical hostility both to those who have other fanaticism's and, even more virulently, to those who object to all fanaticisms.[16]

Russell was an adamant critic not just of religion but of traditional morality and education, and an outspoken pacifist, which got him fired from his teaching post in England during World War I. In 1940 he was prevented from accepting a teaching position at the City College of New York because of his liberal views on sex. He was jailed many times in his life; at the age of eighty-nine, he was arrested for protesting against nuclear arms.

A prolific writer, Russell published over seventy books and hundreds of articles and essays on virtually every topic. He was awarded the Order of Merit in 1949, and in 1950 he won the Nobel Prize for literature. He once remarked, however, that no philosopher could receive a greater public honor than the welcome accorded him upon his arrival in the United States to accept a teaching position at the City University of New York, when Bishop Manning of the Protestant Episcopal Church wrote to every New York newspaper denouncing the appointment of "a man who is a recognized propagandist against both religion and morality, and who specifically defends adultery. . . . Can anyone who cares for the welfare of our country be willing to see such teaching disseminated with the countenance of our colleges and universities?" State Councilman Charles Keegan likewise declared, "If we had an adequate system of immigration, that bum could not land within a thousand miles." Senator Phelps went on record stating that Russell "is an unfit person to hold an important post in the educational system of our state [New York] at the expense of the taxpayers." Former city magistrate Joseph Goldstein claimed that Russell "is not a philosopher . . . not a lover of wisdom. . . . All his alleged doctrines which he calls philosophy are just cheap, tawdry, worn-out, patched-up fetishes." Martha Byrnes, the registrar of New York County, demanded that Russell be "tarred and feathered and driven out of the country." The matter finally had to be settled at the New York Supreme Court when Judge McGeehan, after no doubt a careful reading of Russell's many books (it took him twenty-three days to read about eighty volumes), in his official judgment wrote, "It is not necessary to detail here the filth which is contained in the books. . . . The court therefore holds that Bertrand Russell is not qualified to teach." Mayor La Guardia, on the off-chance that Judge McGeehan's ruling might perhaps be overruled at the federal level, promptly struck the appointed position from the state budget. As a result, Russell went to Harvard to teach, in 1941.

In *Our Knowledge of the External World* (1914), Russell argued for his Frege-inspired view that logic is the essence of philosophy. But he questions the adequacy of traditional subject-predicate logic in favor of his theory of the twofold nature of logic, which is his logical atomism. Whereas the "old logic" in his words put "thought in fetters," his "new logic gives it wings." According to Russell, the only real entities in the world are logical atoms analogous to Leibniz's monads. Just about all the objects we ordinarily take to be real turn out to be nothing more than elaborate fictions, much in the way that David Hume had supposed. In a unique blend of cosmic mysticism and technical logic, Russell offers an explicit proof of the logical impossibility of the existence of the world—the universe entire—conceived as a whole. He constructs one of the most famous paradoxes of the twentieth century, which still bears his name, "Russell's paradox."

The best way I think to understand Russell's paradox is by comparing it with what I consider its metaphysical complement: Zeno's paradox. Zeno's paradox, you will recall, plunged us into the abyss of the very, very small, showing that the whole cannot be understood as consisting of individual parts. Three thousand years later, Russell's paradox goes in the other direction and shows that the paradox at the most minuscule lower bound of the universe reappears, in reverse and doubly paradoxical, at the outermost bounds! But lest Russell's paradox sound overly mystical, let us note that it is a precisely formed antinomy within the branch of mathematics known as *set theory*.

Informally speaking, sets are well-defined collections of objects of any sort whatsoever, designated either by a property all the things have in common or by a list of the things. Thus, (1) "the books in Kolak's library" is a set, so is (2) "all even numbers greater than 12," and so is (3) "coffee cup, table, chair," and likewise for (4) "a, b, c," and so on. Sets (1) and (2) are defined the first way, whereas (3) and (4) are defined the second way. Some sets, such as (2), are infinite, whereas others, such as (1), (3), and (4) are finite. Now, if you think about it a little, all the things in the universe can be talked about, or conceived of, in terms of sets, when we want to refer to them as wholes consisting of parts; for instance, your physical body would consist in the set of all your physical atoms, each of the atoms in your body would consist in the set of all their quantum particles, and so on. Likewise for nonphysical things; your mind, for instance, can be conceived as the set of all your sensations, emotions, and thoughts, including your memories, and so on; a particular perception can be conceived as a set of its individual impressions and ideas (a la Hume), and so forth. Now, let us simply take the set of all sets and call it "Universe," or U for short. Individual things exist; we might not know what they are but we can see that they are, and we can certainly see that there are lots and lots of them. So there must be some totality of all the things there are, of all the varieties of things there are—whether perceptual, conceptual, physical, mental, spiritual, or whatever there is, even the unknowns (for instance, we can conceive of the set of all unknown things). After all, when we think of the world—and even when we don't think of it, the concept is there, in the back of our minds—we think of the totality of all that exists. You can even be mystical, if you like, and call it the "Tao."

Thinking along these lines, Russell now notices an interesting fact. Some sets contain themselves as members, where as others do not. Compare, for instance, the word *word* with the word *dog*. The word *word* is a word, but the word *dog* is not a dog. That's about the simplest version of the idea as we can imagine. Now, all we need is one simple piece of symbolic notation. To indicate that the number 3 is a member of the set of integers, I, we write $3 \in I$, and to indicate that the number 3 is not a member of the set of all even numbers, E, we write $3 \notin E$. In general, "$x \in y$" means "x is a member of set y," or, equivalently, "y contains x as a member." Thus, if y is the set of all citizens of the United States and x is Syphax McCune, then $x \in y$.

Now, some sets contain themselves as members, which we can express as $x \hat{I} x$, and some do not, which we can express by $x \notin x$. Thus the set of all the things mentioned on this page is a member of itself (we just mentioned it). The set of all sets that contain more than three members does not contain itself, since there are more than three such sets. Likewise, the set of all sets is itself a set and so it, too, is a member of itself.

Most sets do not have this self-referential property. The set of all even numbers, for instance, does not contain itself because this set is not, itself, an even number; similarly, the set of all citizens of the United States is not a member of itself, since this set is not, itself, a citizen. And so on.

By "Q" let us denote the set of all sets that contain themselves as members, and by "Z" let us denote the set of all sets that do not contain themselves as members. Thus,

{all things mentioned on this page} $\in$ Q

{the set of all sets} $\in$ Q

whereas

{all even numbers} $\in$ Z

{all citizens} $\in$ Z

{all sets containing more than three members} $\in$ Z

Even more generally, we can write that for any set x, $x \in Q$ if and only if $x \in x$, whereas for any set x, $x \in Z$ if and only if $x \in x$. Now, is the set Z a member of itself or not?

Suppose that it is: $Z \in Z$. In that case, we know by definition that $Z \in Z$. But if $Z \in Z$, then by definition $Z \in Z$! Thus, Z is a member of itself if and only if it is not a member of itself. This contradiction is the very heart of Russell's paradox. It shows us that there is something fundamentally wrong with the very concept of a collection of things—a set. But this does not merely tell us something about set theory! It tells us something about the whole universe.

To see why, let us return to our set U, which is the set of all the things there are. This is very similar, if not identical, to the concept of the set of all sets. The only reason we think it's not identical is that universe is supposed to refer to a real object where *set* is supposed to refer to just a mathematical concept, a term in a theory that has no existence outside our conceptual framework. But now Russell has shown—and this is the subtle part of the paradox—that (1) the concept "universe" has the same ontological status as the concept "set," and (2) insofar as the latter is a theoretical construction then so is the former.

It is in meditating on this perplexity, combined with studying Russell and Whitehead's *Principia Mathematica,* that Kurt Gödel (1906–1978) formulated one of the most profound theorems of all time, his *incompleteness theorem,* proving in no uncertain terms the existence of what are called "formally undecidable propositions" in any formal system, such as arithmetic. More formally, this theorem says that for any formal system S, there will be a sentence P of the language of S such that if S is consistent, neither P nor its negation can be proved in S. In proving this ultimate black hole in the universe of thought, Gödel showed how to translate the syntax of S itself into arithmetic, making S capable of representing its own syntax. This proof can then be used to show that there must necessarily exist a sentence P in S, which can be interpreted as meaning "I am not provable." The coding system Gödel invented to show these insights made it possible to translate everything you are right now reading into 0's and 1's so that it can be encoded into a universal machine such as this computer that I am right now writing on.

To get a sense of what is involved, consider the concept of a "complete pictorial catalogue of the universe," which contains a picture of everything in the universe. Does this cosmic picture contain a picture of itself? Try to imagine a giant collage of all pictures, the picture of everything, a picture of all pictures. You take a picture of that. Do you now have a picture of all pictures? Well, what about that picture that you are now holding? There's one picture that's not in the picture. The picture of all pictures is itself not a picture in the picture.

We can now compare Russell's paradox to Zeno's paradox as follows. In Russell's paradox the parts—sets that do not contain themselves as members—are there, but the whole—the set of all such sets—is not. In Zeno's paradox, the separation between Achilles and the wall, or between any point a and any other point b, is there and also the point of contact is there (after Achilles has reached the wall), but the moment in which the making of contact occurs is never there. It is as if the parts that are there cannot be put together into the whole. In some fundamental sense, everything that we are at each instant of our experience seeing and thinking must not be as it appears, up to and including our conception, and our experience, of the world entire. We must ultimately be dealing not with reality but with fictions.

Unlike David Hume, who was distressed by his conclusions about the fictional nature of both his own self and the world and ran off to play backgammon, and unlike Heidegger's anxiety and Sartre's nausea, Russell experienced through the activity of philosophy a "strangeness and wonder lying just below the surface even in the commonest things of daily life." You don't have to go as far as the outer reaches of the universe to feel it. According to Russell, to experience the strangeness and wonder of reality is, in part, "the point of philosophy." As he makes clear in *Mysticism and Logic,* his logical atomism is not opposed to the goals of mysticism but, rather, to mysticism's depreciation of the cosmic power of rational knowledge to bring about not just a fictive or religious but real "form of union of Self and not-Self."

Like Leibniz, Russell firmly believed in the infinite greatness of the world entire, such that through its union between self and not-self, "the mind also is rendered great, and becomes capable of that union with the universe which constitutes its highest good."

In *Mysticism and Logic,* Russell explains why logic is the essence not just of philosophy but of the world; thus, in "Logic as the Essence of Philosophy," he makes clear how his logical atoms differ from the concept of physical atoms by presenting a devastating problem for any naive realist conception of physical reality based on physical science verifying truths through direct experience. In "The Relation of Sense-Data to Physics," Russell gives up mind-body dualism in favor of a version of the thesis that the ultimate elements of the world are neither physical nor mental "things" but, rather, logical particulars—the logical atoms—and their external relations. He extends his logical-analytic method to the question of the relation between sense perception and physical objects. By combining his theory of descriptions in which meaning and reference are equated with his logical construction principle (the substitution, wherever possible, of constructions out of known entities for inference to unknown ones), he shows how even the symbols of physics—points in space, moments in time (instants), physical particles, and so on—can be analyzed (translated) into their propositional contexts, that is, into logical statements about empirical entities.

Like the early William James, Russell became an advocate of a type of "neutral monism," resolving the mind-body problem raised by Descartes through an analysis in which mind and physical matter are viewed as different constructions of the same, basic logical elements. Russell didn't merely offer a metaphysical claim, however, about how the world must therefore be understood as neither mental nor physical but logical. The key concept is a synthesis of the best from many previous views of what the ultimate elements of existence are, whether construed as material, idealistic, mathematical, or logical elements. Using his extraordinary intellect and his extensive knowledge of mathematics, logic, science, and the history of philosophy, Russell came up with a model of the mind as a logically operating system of data processing. The key concept here is his notion of sense-data. Just as the mind's cognitive functions—thought, mathematics, and logic—consist in logical atoms, so its perceptual functions—seeing, feeling, smelling, emoting, etc.—consist in their atomic form as individual sense-data. And, as Russell clearly states, "I regard sense-data as not mental." Ultimately they consist in external relations, which explains the realistic interpretation and central role in his system of external relations:

> I maintain that there are such facts as that x has the relation R to y, and that
> such facts are not in general reducible to, or inferable from, a fact about x only
> and a fact about y only [i.e., internal relations]: they do not imply that x and y
> have any complexity, or any intrinsic property distinguishing them from a z and

a w which do not have the relation R. This is what I mean when I say that relations are external. But I maintain also . . . that whenever we have two terms x and y related by a relation R, we have also a complex, which we may call "xRy," consisting of the two terms so related. This is the simplest example of what I call a "complex" or a "unity." What is called analysis consists in the discovery of the constituents of a complex. A complex differs from the mere aggregate of its constituents, since it is one, not many, and the relation which is one of its constituents enters into it as an actually relating relation, and not merely as one member of an aggregate.[17]

In taking such a functional approach to both mind and matter, Russell helped pave the way toward a purely logico-mathematical model of mind and reality. The key passage appears in his and Whitehead's *Principia Mathematica:*

Philosophy asks of Mathematics: What does it mean? Mathematics in the past was unable to answer, and Philosophy answered by introducing the totally irrelevant notion of mind. But now Mathematics is able to answer, so far at least as to reduce the whole of its propositions to certain fundamental notions of logic. At this point, the discussion must be resumed by Philosophy.

In Russell's pioneering work on the foundations of mathematics, logic, and language, we thus see the beginnings of a purely formal and functional analysis of the elements of thought that later in the twentieth century would help make possible the invention of mechanical minds and artificial intelligence by translating human language and the elements of experience, including the activity of thinking and reasoning, into a logical form that could in turn be translated into a purely logical machine language. Russell's detailed and explicitly precise analyses of logic, language, and mathematical reasoning, including his reduction of mathematics to logic in *Principia Mathematica,* all contributed to this development. Indeed, it is possible to view the entire three volumes as the first attempt to write a program—a set of algorithmic procedures—for the algorithmic procedure known as *deductive mathematics,* and thus instrumental in paving the way for many of the later developments that eventually led to the computer. (It is also no accident, I have been told by its inventors, that the most sophisticated mathematics software today in use by mathematics professors and students is called *Mathematica.*)

In the concluding chapter of *Problems of Philosophy* (1912), Russell gives his philosophy of philosophy—what philosophy is for, what it is about, and how it ought to be done. He argues that in other disciplines, like physics, medicine, architecture, engineering, and so on, the value of the discipline can be known and appreciated without knowing the discipline itself. For instance, one can experience the benefits of engineering technology without knowing anything about engineering. But because philosophy has no direct utility outside the lives of those who themselves partake in it, it must be known and understood by the individual before it can provide its highest value: the attainment of "union with the universe," experienced by the individual human being through the power of philosophy.

Wittgenstein: Language and Beyond

Ludwig Wittgenstein (1889–1951) was born in Vienna to a prominent Jewish family that had converted to Roman Catholicism. Owners of the largest steel company in Austria, they used their money to support many Viennese artists, musicians, and writers. Wittgenstein was educated at home by the best tutors until the age of fourteen, when he entered the Realschule in Linz, where he studied mathematics and physics. After receiving a degree in engineering in Berlin, he moved to England with the idea of going to the University of Manchester to study aeronautical engineering. But a growing interest in the foundations of mathematics prevailed, and instead he went to Cambridge University.

In his autobiography, Bertrand Russell describes his meeting with Wittgenstein:

> He was perhaps the most perfect example I have ever known of genius as traditionally conceived, passionate, profound, intense, and dominating. He had a kind of purity which I have never known equaled except by G. E. Moore. . . . His life was turbulent and troubled, and his personal force was extraordinary. . . . He used to come to see me every evening at midnight, and pace up and down my room like a wild beast for three hours in agitated silence. Once I said to him: "Are you thinking about logic or about your sins?" "Both," he replied, and continued his pacing. I did not like to suggest that it was time for bed, as it seemed probable both to him and me that on leaving me he would commit suicide. At the end of his first term at Trinity, he came to me and said: "Do you think I am an absolute idiot?" I said: "Why do you want to know?" He replied: "Because if I am I shall become an aeronaut, but if I am not I shall become a philosopher." I said to him: "My dear fellow, I don't know whether you are an absolute idiot or not, but if you will write me an essay during the vacation upon any philosophical topic that interests you, I will read it and tell you." He did so, and brought it to me at the beginning of the next term. As soon as I read the first sentence, I became persuaded that he was a man of genius. . . .[18]

Russell once asked his colleague G. E. Moore what he thought of Wittgenstein. Moore replied that he thought Wittgenstein was brilliant, "Because at my lectures he looks puzzled, and nobody else ever looks puzzled."

World War I interrupted Wittgenstein's studies, and he left England to serve as an officer in the Austrian army. In the trenches he began writing what would become his doctoral dissertation, which he completed in an Italian prison camp: *Tractatus Logico-Philosophicus* (German ed. 1921; English ed. 1922; see my translation, Mayfield, 1998). It created a revolution in philosophy. In it, Wittgenstein tries to make clear the relationship between language and thought by delineating the limit of language as the expression of thought and by showing how, using language, the mind is able to "hook" onto reality; language itself is the medium of representation as to how things are in the world. Just as Kant tried to show the necessary conditions that would make experience-as-representation possible, Wittgenstein tries to show the necessary conditions that would make language-as-representation possible by claiming that the world consists ultimately not of things but of Russellian "atomic facts" made in part accessible by the propositional logic as developed by Russell. Atomic propositions are the linguistic counterparts of atomic facts, to which they are related as pictures are to the things they depict, in virtue of what Wittgenstein calls their "logical form."

In a letter to a woman friend, Russell describes the influence his most famous student had on him:

> Do you remember that at the time when you were seeing Vittoz I wrote a lot of stuff about Theory of Knowledge, which Wittgenstein criticized with the greatest severity? His criticism, though I don't think you realized it at the time, was an event of first-rate importance in my life, and affected everything I have done since. I saw he was right, and I saw that I could not hope ever again to do fundamental work in philosophy. My impulse was shattered, like a wave dashed to pieces against a breakwater. I became filled with utter despair.

The *Tractatus* gave much impetus to the antimetaphysical views of the logical positivists. And yet, ironically, it is also a call to a unique type of mysticism: in trying to say what can only properly be "shown," Wittgenstein claims he is trying to stand outside language. According to his own view, however—since sense exists only within the limits of language—everything he is saying in the *Tractatus* is therefore, strictly speaking, "nonsense." Acknowledging this, he claims his book is a very special type of illuminating nonsense.

The initial reception of the *Tractatus* was mixed. In his introduction to the book, Russell called it an "important event in the philosophical world." But another important twentieth-century philosopher, C. I. Lewis, who also did foundational work in logic, wrote in a letter to the editor of the prestigious *Journal of Philosophy*:

> Have you looked at Wittgenstein's new book yet? I am much discouraged by Russell's foolishness in writing the introduction to such nonsense. I fear it will be looked upon as what symbolic logic leads to. If so, it will be the death of the subject.[19]

Lewis apparently changed his mind a decade later when he claimed that "the nature of logical truth itself has become more definitely understood, largely through the discussions of Wittgenstein."[20]

The *Tractatus* contains seven propositions, numbered 1–7, along with secondary propositions that are observations of the first, 1.1, 2.1, and so on, each of which is followed by tertiary propositions that are observations of the observations, 1.11, 2.11, and so on. It begins with the proposition (1) "The world is all that is the case." What Wittgenstein means by "world," however, is given by proposition 1.1: "The world is the totality of facts, not of things." This of course is in direct and perhaps shocking contradiction to the commonsense view that the world is made of *things*. But let us put this in the context of where we began, with the Presocratic puzzlement about what everything is made of, and perhaps we may not be so shocked. What Wittgenstein is saying goes well with other views expressing the idea that the world—the totality of everything—is not made of physical, material stuff but of something entirely different in nature. Indeed, it will also help us to compare Wittgenstein's assertion with Schopenhauer's, by which in point of fact Wittgenstein was greatly influenced: "The world is my idea." Schopenhauer's point, evolved from and influenced by Kant's analysis of the categories of thought and the nature of the mind, is that what the mind has direct access to is not things as they exist independently of the mind (as conceived in materialist metaphysics) but its own items: perceptions, thoughts, and language. However, we must be careful to note that Wittgenstein is here *not* denying the existence of *things* in any of the straightforward senses of the idealists (whether of the subjective, objective, or critical variety). If he were, the statement in the *Tractatus,* in which he constantly uses the word *thing* (*ding*), would turn out to be exactly the sort of nonsense that Wittgenstein most definitely thinks he is *not* writing, namely, nonilluminating nonsense; for although there is a tension in many of his sentences that play on contradiction to make their philosophical "showings" clear, it is supposed to be the sort of illuminating "nonsense" that sentences in logic express.

Indeed, in that respect we might think of Wittgenstein's philosophy as a sort of "linguistic idealism," provided this is understood in the critical rather than subjective form. This is because the form of experience for Wittgenstein, as for Kant, is subjective in the transcendental sense because the subject is the *metaphysical subject* and not the empirical subject as conceived in psychology, which is part of the world describable in language. This is why he will say, in 5.6, that "*the boundary of my language* is the boundary of my world." For the boundaries of language itself determine the boundaries of the world of the metaphysical subject's "logical space" of possible worlds. And yet, as for Schopenhauer, this world is nevertheless *my* world, as he declares in 5.62: "That the world is *my* world reveals itself in the fact that the boundary of language (the language that I alone understand) is the boundary of *my* world."

But what does he mean, in claiming that everything—the world—is made of *facts?* What is a Wittgensteinian *fact?* Wittgenstein construes facts not in some *standard* type of realism but as "states of affairs" (*Sachverhalten*), such that he really meant that any particular *Sachverhalten* may or may not be the case. Indeed, in that regard he talks about positive and negative facts, where a positive fact is the existence of a particular state of affairs and a negative fact is the non-existence of a particular state of affairs. Thus, for instance, "The Eiffel tower is taller than Mt. Everest" is a negative fact and "Mt. Everest is taller than the Eiffel Tower" is a positive fact. Indeed, he says of facts (in 1.21) that "each one can be the case or not be the case while all else remains the same," which establishes for him the distinction between that which Wittgenstein thinks the world is made of—facts —and what common sense says it is made of—things. It should be noted, however, that one major difference between things as ordinarily understood, especially by German-speaking philosophers, is that, as Heidegger states, "if one thing changes its qualities, this can have an effect upon another thing. Things affect each other and resist each one another. . . . This description of things and their interdependence corresponds to what we call the 'natural conception of the world.'"[21] Notice that here Heidegger, who as much as Wittgenstein but in a different way is wildly antithetical to any natural conception of the world, nicely and no doubt unintentionally illustrates for us why Wittgenstein would have wanted to insist (and did) that the *world* does not consist of *such* items (things) but items that are most implicitly *not* linked into a cosmos as conceived in natural science.

One problem in understanding Wittgenstein's true meaning is that the key term *Sachverhalt* has been variously translated as "atomic state of affairs," "elementary fact," "atomic fact," and so on. "Particular" I think has the better connotation, since the word *atomic* is erroneously ambiguous in that it can mean *both* "something that does not have parts and cannot be further broken down" *and* "something that consists of [basic] elements." "Particular" would do just as well as "elementary" if we kept in mind the additional sense, "consists of particles," that is, of distinct elements. I have (in my *Wittgenstein's Tractatus,* Mayfield, 1998) chosen to translate *Sachverhalt* as "elementary facts" and *Tatsache* as "fact," to remain consistent with what Wittgenstein meant regarding the all-important relation between the two terms. *Sachverhalt* corresponds to a simple declarative sentence if it is true. *Tatsache* corresponds to the totality of all simple declarative sentences when this totality is true.

For instance, "Kolak is in his study" is at this moment a true, simple declarative sentence. It describes a particular state of affairs. Likewise, "Kolak is sitting in a chair" is also true. It describes a different particular state of affairs. "Kolak is writing" is also true and describes yet another particular state of affairs. These three states of affairs just described using the above three sentences are all related by virtue of a *fact*. It is difficult, perhaps impossible, to say exactly what this fact is, even to specify its boundaries or enumerate it (i.e., count it) in relation to other facts about the world. In an important sense, we don't know of how many facts the world consists because we cannot specify their borders, only the boundary of the world (something that the whole *Tractatus* sets out to delineate). Facts are thus in that sense as elusive to the mind as Kant's things-in-themselves (*ding-an-sich*). However, unlike facts, sentences—which are their linguistic representatives—can be enumerated and there exists the totality of true statements within a language. So in speaking of particular states of affairs, Wittgenstein is alluding to the fact that, for instance, it can be observed or seen that Kolak is in his study, sitting in a chair, writing, and so on, particular states of affairs all of which can be via the content of simple declarative sentences (I just did it), "information bundles" packaged either in linguistic terms (sentences describing observed situations) or in experiential terms (items in a visual field). It may help the understanding to think of "states of affairs" as synonymous to what is available to the perceiving subject in a particular visual field, in terms of the relations of the objects present in that visual field. Indeed, it is in saying that we cannot talk about anything beyond what is present in such states of affairs that Wittgenstein made himself so useful to the logical positivists and members of the Vienna Circle. Likewise, it may also help to think of "states of affairs" as a synonym for *statement.* (Below I discuss the sense in which both visual events and linguistic events can be seen as the mind's "statements to itself" [my terminology, not Wittgenstein's].)

Wittgenstein offers a subtle and brilliant solution to the problematic nature of the relation in philosophy between (phenomenal) objects and things (in themselves, in Kant's sense), in terms of what he conceives the true meaning of the word *be.* In speaking of x as a *thing,* collection of *things* or *somethings,* and so on, Wittgenstein—like many philosophers from Kant to Heidegger—is trying to refer to x in the most neutral way possible. "Object" already is specific, it has a direction. (The German *Gegenstand* means, literally, "against" [gegen] + "stand" [stand].) That which it stands against is of course the *subject,* and we have ourselves borne witness to the long philosophical tradition—not just in idealism but in a variety of radical empiricisms, phenomenalisms, and presentationalisms—in which it is held that in order to exist objects require a subject. *Thing,* on the other hand, implies therefore something that can stand on its own, independently of being directed at (or, in some views—Fichte's, Schelling's, Schopenhauer's—*from*) a subject. This minimizes one Wittgensteinian tension only to leave us with the problem of how we should then interpret his claim that "the world is the totality of facts, not of things." For although Wittgenstein's view of what the world is— like Schopenhauer's—is that the world is, literally, *his* world and no one else's, the items of which it is composed and that stand independently of the ego are not things but facts. And this, again, moves us away from the kind of linkage presented in scientific theories to the unique type of Wittgensteinian linkage.

Let me then restate what we have considered thus far; according to Wittgenstein, the *world (Die Welt)* is the totality of *facts (Tatsachen),* which consists of *elementary facts (Sachverhalte),* which in turn consist in configurations of *objects (Gegenstande).* He uses the word *thing* to emphasize that he is trying to refer to "a something" in as simple and generic way as possible, to mean "a something, an any sort of something," that (in this case) constitutes (is a constituent of) an elementary fact.[22] Language provides the means by which something (the objects of the world) are referenced through symbolization, such that existence is implied. That is, the objects themselves are expressed in symbolic form and thus by studying the forms we study the objects themselves. And this is reality; since the world is the totality of facts, not things by *substance* (i.e., that which exists independently), it is not the concept of *matter* but *logical form* that is for Wittgenstein the most "real" existence (it is permanent, necessary, and unalterable). And yet he uses the word *form* in several different ways. It can mean *shape,* as in the "form of a spot," *type* or *kind,* as in "form of independence," or *content,* as in "the form of the visual field," or any combination thereof so as to show the way in which the world is collectively organized into a coherent whole. In a rather mystical sense, the medium *is* itself the message; language and world "*entsprechen,*" which can be translated as "correspond," but which has an extremely revealing etymology that accords with Wittgenstein's overall theory: it means, literally, "to speak for." The world is not silent; it speaks. Experiences are its sayings. That's what Wittgenstein has in mind while building his bridge between sentences and facts.

The key representing relation by which language makes contact with reality is, itself, part of the picture. That is, a picture does not need to resemble what it depicts so that we can somehow depict this resemblance to ourselves. The idea is that nothing stands between our language and our application of that language to the world: they are already in contact.

According to Wittgenstein, to think is to form mental pictures. What is not possible is not thinkable; therefore, in Wittgenstein's view, (meaningful) sentences are thoughts expressed in a communicable way. It will help here to think of a projection in geometry, where, say, a 3-D cube is projected onto a 2-D coordinate system. This is an illuminating image that takes us all the way back to Plato's ideal forms, whereby the relation of an elementary sentence to an elementary fact is like a projective shadow of an ideal form. That is the sense in which the "world" you presently see around you is a pictorial statement—your mind talking to itself with pictures. What Wittgenstein means it that the objects you see presently before you (say, this book) are, literally, concepts illuminated into actual presence by the mind; they are phenomenal and they are a veneer (and in *that* sense an illusion or a false showing) but one that is ultimately revealing. (One might playfully add, "What cannot be seen must not be looked at," and think of visual phenomena as *perceptual notation*.)

In 4.0, Wittgenstein makes the radical claim, "A sentence that makes sense is a thought." Here Wittgenstein can be taken in two different ways, one that I call the conservative, *linguistic* sense and the other that I call the radical, *semiotic* sense. In the radical, semiotic sense I take Wittgenstein to mean that a sentence that makes sense *is* what a thought is; in other words, minds or consciousness as conceived in some superlinguistic (i.e., supernatural) terms are absolutely not required. In my view, the early Wittgenstein, just as we saw in Russell and Peirce, is intuiting a computational approach to the problem of consciousness, where the computations are logical processes and the items processed are linguistic objects. On the related matter of what we might think of as "the linguistic extraction of truth from the logical structure of the world," we might by analogy say, "Given that I have ten things, I have two things," "Given that I have a hundred things, I have two things," and, most perspicuously, "Given that I have $\aleph_0$ things, I have n things," where n is any number I choose. This is revealing because for Wittgenstein there are in fact $\aleph_0$ "things" of which the world is comprised, except they are not things but facts.

It is extremely illuminating to conceive the relation of a particular fact to the world in toto as conceptually mirrored in the relation of a particular number, say 3, to $\aleph_0$. You cannot in fact remove any number from $\aleph_0$, and in that sense all numbers are *necessarily* a part of $\aleph_0$, just as each and every fact is necessarily a part of the world—except the nature of the connection is negative; hence the Buddhist-like centrality in the *Tractatus* and in Wittgenstein's thought in general of the operation of *negation*. This is the unique point of contact, the blind spot in the mirror, through which the particulars of sentential language and the statements out of which the facts of which the world is made are comprised connect. The blind spot, after all, is what makes vision possible: it is where the optic "nerve" connects the eye to the brain. That is the sense in which the concept of negation is unique: it is the central black hole in Wittgenstein's negative cosmos, in that it not only expresses the common rule for *all logical operations* but is also the foundation for the *general form of truth function,* the *general form of an operation,* and the *general form of a sentence.* It is respect of the fact that all the immanent forms in Wittgenstein's conception of the world revolve around these general forms, which in turn revolve around the possibility of the universal operation of negation, that one might with philosophical tongue in cheek paint the following picture: Plato's sun in Wittgenstein's philosophy has collapsed, and the world has been revealed, into a black hole.

Here we come up against the mystical: "It's not *how* the world is that is mystical but *that* it is. (6.44) To view the world *sub specie aeternitatis* is the view of it as a—bounded—whole. The feeling of the world as a bounded whole is the mystical feeling. (6.45) If the answer cannot be put into words, the question, too, cannot be put into words. *The riddle* does not exist. (6.5) The inexpressible indeed exists. This *shows* itself. It is the mystical. (6.522) My sentences are illuminating in the following way: to understand me you must recognize my sentences —once you have climbed out through them, on them, over them—as senseless. (You must, so to speak, throw away the ladder, after you have climbed up on it.) You must climb out through my sentences; then you will see the world correctly. (6.54) Of what we cannot speak we must be silent. (7)"

Wittgenstein's picture theory of language and his austere tone of logical rigor severs what can be said—sense—from what cannot be said—the mystical—with explicit statements to the effect that philosophy must remain completely silent about that which is beyond language.[23] This led the logical positivists, who viewed the traditional philosophical domain of metaphysics as bankrupt, to welcome the *Tractatus* as their bible. Wittgenstein himself regarded the positivists' interpretation of his work as too narrow and as having missed the essential point of the mystical allusions. Overall, however, Wittgenstein was fully satisfied with his work; he felt certain that he had successfully answered all of philosophy's main questions and thus abandoned the profession in favor of teaching elementary school in the Austrian alps. Shunning what he considered the trappings of wealth, Wittgenstein had by then given away his share of the family fortune and so when he grew disillusioned with teaching elementary school he worked as a gardener in a nearby monastery, taking time off to design a house for one of his sisters.

Seven years later, in 1929, Russell arranged that Wittgenstein would be awarded a doctorate in philosophy on the basis of the *Tractatus*. Wittgenstein thus returned to Cambridge and remained there as a lecturer. In 1937 he succeeded G. E. Moore in the chair of philosophy. He shunned academic life, however, and lectured mostly in his own rooms, spontaneously and without notes, in an effort to always create something new by his method of "philosophizing out loud." Although he wrote much and circulated some of it among his students, he did not allow any of it to be published during his lifetime. In 1947 he resigned from Cambridge and spent the rest of his life in seclusion, working on various unfinished manuscripts and occasionally visiting his former students.

It has often been said that Wittgenstein is unique in the history of philosophy for having inspired two very different and in many ways antithetical philosophical movements. Just as the *Tractatus* inspired a whole generation of logical positivists, his *Philosophical Investigations* (1953), published two years after his death, was instrumental in advancing ordinary language philosophy. In the preface, Wittgenstein writes:

> The thoughts which I publish in what follows are the precipitate of philosophical investigations which have occupied me for the last sixteen years. They concern many subjects: the concepts of meaning, of understanding, of a proposition, of logic, the foundations of mathematics, states of consciousness, and other things. I have written down all these thoughts as remarks, short paragraphs, of which there is sometimes a fairly long chain about the same subject, while I sometimes make a sudden change, jumping from one topic to another.

The work begins with a criticism of his former picture theory of language and of the *Tractatus* as a whole, with an Augustine-like confession regarding his previous views: "I have been forced to recognize grave mistakes in what I wrote." He claims that the *Tractatus* had captured only one of the many uses of language. The other legitimate uses can be found in ordinary language through meanings derived from social, tribal, cultural, scientific, and psychological contexts. Thus, according to his new and improved theory, "The meaning of a word is its use in the language." In his *Investigations,* Wittgenstein puts forth his new game theory of language, according to which the rules of the game change from one game to another. For instance, he uses the example of pain to argue that mental concepts do not refer to inner private states; uncovering the "logical grammar of pain" reveals that our sensations, thoughts, and experiences cannot be understood using a private language. Language exists through usage defined by social constructions; correct language use cannot be stipulated by private rules of application.

Although Wittgenstein's *Investigations* exemplifies his philosophical shift, on the one hand, from a pictorial to a descriptive view of language and, on the other, from logical atomism to linguistic pluralism, the task of Wittgensteinian philosophy remains in many ways the same. Philosophy according to Wittgenstein is still the "battle against the bewitchment of our intelligence by means of language," whose ultimate purpose is to show "the fly the way out of the fly-bottle."

Wittgenstein was known to get extremely angry whenever anyone would analyze his work. For instance, during a public reading of his *Tractatus,* at one point he began screaming at the roomful of eminent philosophers, telling them that what he had written was a beautiful poem, which was not meant to be dissected by them!

Quine: Radical Indeterminism

Willard Van Orman Quine (1908–) was born in Akron, Ohio. While still in high school he says he saw the falseness of religion, and already then tried to enlighten friends away from "their Episcopalian faith to atheism." But it was not the rejection of religion that inspired him to philosophy; it was a poem—Edgar Allan Poe's "Eureka," which "for all its outrageousness fostered the real thing: the desire to understand the universe. So did the antireligious motive." At Oberlin College, Quine concentrated on the study of mathematics and mathematical philosophy, including the works of Russell, Whitehead, and Peano. He went to graduate school at Harvard and received his doctorate in philosophy after only two years. His dissertation, "The Logic of Sequences: A Generalization of *Principia Mathematica*," was subsequently published as his first book, *A System of Logic*.

The work of course owes much to Russell and Whitehead's *Principia Mathematica*. But Quine develops an original view of logic that he says is in

> kinship with the most general and systematic aspects of natural science, farthest from observation. Mathematics and logic are supported by observation only in the indirect way that those aspects of natural science are supported by observation; namely, as participating in an organized whole which, way up at its empirical edges, square with observation.

Quine held a series of positions: Vienna, Prague, and Warsaw. In Europe he studied with the logical positivist Moritz Schlick, who founded the Vienna Circle, the brilliant philosopher of science Hans Reichenbach, the logical positivist Rudolf Carnap, and the great mathematician and logician Adolph Tarski. In 1936 Quine returned to the United States and became an instructor at Harvard. He published *Mathematical Logic* (1940) and *Elementary Logic* (1941) during a time in which "Germans massacred Jews, Germans swarmed over France, Japanese bombed Hawaii. Logic seemed off the point." He joined the navy and ended up working for radio intelligence in Washington.

After the war Quine returned to Harvard, where he became a full professor in 1948. At a lecture delivered at Yale and published a few years later in *From a Logical Point of View,* Quine addresses the age-old problem of "ontological commitment"—the fundamental question of how to decide philosophical disputes over what there is. Is the universe a mental object? A material object? Does consciousness exist? Influenced by pragmatism, by Russell, by Ockham's razor, Quine tries to solve disputes over the "old Platonic riddle of non-being" in an ingenious way, by arguing for relativity: different, even opposing, philosophical stances, such as phenomenalism and physicalism, are best viewed as essentially different but equally fundamental points of view, whose preference must be determined depending on one's practical purposes.

Ultimately, according to Quine, "the ontological controversy should tend into controversy over language." In other words, the issue of what exists resolves itself into the question of what some statement or doctrine says exists. Such "ontological relativity" would later be even further developed by Quine in his *Ontological Relativity*.

In 1951 Quine delivered a lecture to the American Philosophical Association that became an instant classic: "Two Dogmas of Empiricism." Subsequently published as the second chapter of *From a Logical Point of View,* it presents a challenge to the fundamental, age-old distinction between analytic and synthetic truth by claiming that "a boundary between analytic and synthetic statements simply has not been drawn." That such a distinction can be drawn in the first place is the first dogma of empiricism. It is, Quine argues, a metaphysical article of faith.

The second dogma of empiricism is reductionism. According to reductionism, every meaningful statement can be translated into a statement about immediate experience. But Quine shows that any conceptual scheme we bring to it "is a man-made fabric which impinges on experience only along the edges." According to Quine, there are no analytic truths; that is, there are no propositions that can be known to be true a priori just in virtue of their meaning. He therefore concludes that "no statement is immune to revision."

In *Ontological Relativity* (1969), Quine develops two of his most important philosophical theses about meaning—the indeterminacy of translation and the inscrutability of reference—into the view that one cannot say what a language is about.

He argues against the sort of absolute theories of meaning in which the existence of mind-independent absolute truths can be determined independently of the human conceptual system. He had already laid the foundations for this view in *Word and Object* (1960), where he makes his argument clear with a thought experiment. An explorer discovers a civilization utterly alien to his own. He attempts to communicate with the natives, assured by his pragmatic belief that their behavior will give him appropriate clues as to the meanings of the terms of their otherwise incomprehensible language. A rabbit hops by; the explorer points and says, "rabbit." The native points and says, "gavagai." Now, what does *gavagai* mean? Does it mean the whole rabbit? A rabbit part? Some feature of the rabbit, such as its animalness, its whiteness? Some temporal part of the rabbit? A perception of the rabbit? A representation? An idea? *There's no way to tell.* After some time and a lot of guessing and fumbling, the explorer can at best make a practical dictionary of translation that allows him and the natives to interact. But beyond its practical usefulness the dictionary does not say what the noises the natives make 'really' mean. It can only, at best, contain the translation of *meaning* for *meaning* that will always and forever remain necessarily indeterminate because meaning is language-bound, a part of one's own conceptual framework.

This sort of difficulty holds not just for natural languages but even for scientific and formal languages. Theories of meaning are like scientific theories in that they are undetermined by the available data; such theories can never be completed, not even in principle. This is because vastly and often wildly incommensurate competing theories can all account for the same data. (Recall, for instance, our discussion of the Ptolemy-Copernicus debate.) Indeed, we can imagine that two different explorers from different cultures, or even from the same culture, could come up, independently of each other, with radically different dictionaries *each of which worked for all practical purposes.* Any of the books could be functionally useful, in spite of the fact that they each contain radically different meanings.

What is true of our language is true of our theories, since theories live in language; philosophical relativity—theoretical indeterminacy and incompleteness—applies to all domains of inquiry, to our entire knowledge seeking enterprise, to any discourse about ourselves and the world, to all conceptual frameworks. Whether theory A or theory B is better—whether it explains more, or is more correct in its ontological claims—is *itself* relative. Whether one theory is better than another competing theory ultimately depends on the purposes of the theory. In other words, we cannot tell what 'really' exists, what the 'actual' objects of the world are, independently of the conceptual schemes of the theory and the terms of the language in which the theory is stated. Quine argues that there will always be equally competing alternative theories, each of which is encased in a number of conflicting conceptual schemes. Therefore, we must if we are true lovers of wisdom and rational seekers of the truth always make room for the possibility of new theories, better views improved according to established scientific principles.

Quine would thus agree with Wittgenstein that it is not possible to have a private language. Just as the "indeterminacy of translation" of *gavagai* type through experiments shows the limits among and between languages, the same sort of difficulty arises *within* any language. First, it is communication through language that gives us access to each other's conceptual schemes, making possible what Quine calls "semantic ascent." This is attained when speakers with "unlike conceptual schemes communicate at their best." All that can be achieved is, at best, "a common part of two fundamentally disparate conceptual schemas, the better to discuss the disparate foundations." But this always involves developing a more inclusive conceptual scheme in which the language speakers must make intelligent "ontic decisions" about what they are talking about. This decision about the ontological or existential nature of the meanings of the various items of our language—words, meanings, sentences, definitions, theories—must be done by the speakers of the language, in spite of the fact that, if they are philosophers, they know that the translation of meanings must forever remain indeterminate. Second, even with regard to our own conceptual schemes within our own language, what any sentence or word refers to—its *ontological reference*—can never be anything absolutely knowable, but only at best something intuited against the background of our own system, a web, of belief. In this way, the indeterminacy of the world and the incompleteness of our theories is not just mirrored but caught within ourselves, but not forever: we are each in our personal conceptual evolutions as incomplete as is the world.

Philosophy has as we have seen from its very beginning been an attempt to create or induce within ourselves a complete understanding of everything, to see, to know, to understand the "whole" of reality. Some, like Thales, presented their unifying vision in terms of the unity of the underlying substance of reality, along with causal explanations for the apparent disunity found among appearances. This vision led others, like Spinoza, to begin philosophize with a view of the world as a whole, such that everything we see or think in the domain of contingent existences are themselves metaphysical instantiations of the necessarily existent whole. Still others, like Hegel, came to view each individual item as the self-objectification of the whole of reality. And now we see up into the present the persistence of philosophy as the *inward urge* to "round out," as Quine himself puts it, "the system of the world," to understand the totality of existence, of ourselves and the world, as a whole. For even if our theories, like our philosophies, cannot themselves be put into a consistent system, it is a testament to the great philosophers from the presocratics to the present to try and to say as much as can be said about such a conceptual totality, up to and including—as is especially vivid in Wittgenstein and Quine—the very limitations of such an attempt—to allow the gaps, the holes, the inconsistencies, the paradoxes, as part of the view. Such an incompleteness itself in this way through the activity of philosophy becomes an integral part of the true nature of the whole of reality. It makes out of philosophy not an impossible dream but a quest for a complete understanding of ourselves and the world that cannot ever be completed.

To see philosophy and the whole of reality as anything less than in this way necessarily incomplete is to live with a closed mind inside the simplification, the naivete, of dogma. What Quine means by *dogma* is what Immanuel Kant meant: a belief held uncritically. In arguing that dogmas lie at the foundations of 20th century empiricism, Quine is purposefully "blurring the supposed boundary between speculative metaphysics and natural science," to show that even the most cherished "certain" and "scientific" terms of our present day thinking about ourselves and the world—from the supposedly indubitable realm of mathematical logic to the hard-nosed realism of physics—are on the same epistemological footing as the ancient gods of Greece! (Recall our discussion of *the ether* as used by Royce in conjunction with terms like space, time, and atoms.) All our thinking about anything requires and itself consists not in the direct apprehension of reality beyond ourselves but, at best, *through* our own conceptual schemes, colored in exactly the ways Kant realized was a necessary condition for the having of experience and, as we now come to realize, for the having of thought. Logic and science are themselves but evolving tools with which we create new webs of belief, new and evolving pictures of the world, etched upon what Quine calls "a man-made fabric which impinges upon experience only along the edges." Thus even the most indubitable of scientific terms are but convenient intellectual tools, "irreducible posits," as for the Greeks were the gods.

What such 'irreducible posits' are itself changes over time—i.e., our example of the 'ether'—no 'truth' lasts forever. That of course is *not* to say that we are no better warranted when talking about reality using our current scientific terms than the ancients were in speaking of the gods. But it does bring us finally around full circle from the beginning of philosophy in ancient Greece to the ending of this book in the present, to finally appreciate for the first time the *second* of Thales' cryptic statements with which this odyssey began:

"Everything is full of gods."

For just as Berkeley criticizes Newton for his atoms as well as his calculus, Quine argues that "in point of epistemological footing *the physical objects* and *the gods* differ only in degree and not in kind." One can only imagine Thales smiling knowingly upon his ship as he sails off into the unknown, peeking back into the universe at us, across the horizon of time.

A couple of years ago, I was talking with Quine at a reception at the American Philosophical Association. He was writing a foreword for one of my books, and I was quietly and politely asking when it might be finished. As Quine had not given a public address to the APA for quite some time, the room was jampacked with philosophers.

"Oh, I don't know." He looked as if he would shrug, but remained statuesque. "Sometimes I think it hasn't even started."

I nodded, the way one does when one doesn't understand but pretends to, knowing it must be clever. Indeed, this octogenarian of philosophy was still way too fast for me. It took me all this time to realize what he was talking about: not my book but philosophy.

1. Stephen Toulmin, "From Logical Analysis to Conceptual Theory," in *The Legacy of Logical Positivism*, ed. P. Achinstein and S. Barker (Baltimore: Johns Hopkins Press, 1969).

2. William James, "A World of Pure Experience," *Journal of Philosophy, Psychology and Scientific Methods* vol. I, no. 20 (1904), reprinted in Daniel Kolak, *From Plato to Wittgenstein: The Historical Foundations of Mind* (Belmont, Calif.: Wadsworth, 1994).

3. See my *From Plato to Wittgenstein: The Historical Foundations of Mind* (Belmont, Calif.: Wadsworth, 1994).

4. "The Development of American Pragmatism," *The Middle Works* (Southern Illinois University Press, 1977).

5. *The Quest for Certainty,* 1929 (New York: Putnam's Sons, 1960).

6. See my *I Am You: A Philosophical Explanation of the Possibility That We Are the Same Person* (Ann Arbor, Mich.: UMI 1986), in which I resurrect such a view within the debates of contemporary personal identity theory, including the views of Parfit, Shoemaker, and Nozick.

7. *Psychology from an Empirical Standpoint* (original German edition 1924, London: Routledge, 1973).

8. From Edmund Husserl, *The Phenomenology of Internal Time-Consciousness,* ed. Martin Heidegger, trans. James Churchill (Bloomington: Indiana University Press, 1964).

9. Trans. William Alston and George Nakhnikian (The Hague: Martinus Nijhoff, 1973).

10. Ibid.

11. *The Autobiography of Bertrand Russell* (New York: Atlantic Monthly Press, 1951).

12. *Dialogues of Alfred North Whitehead,* recorded by Lucien Price, 1954.

13. Ibid.

14. *Autobiography of Bertrand Russell.*

15. *Dialogues of Alfred North Whitehead.*

16. Bertrand Russell, *Why I Am Not a Christian* (New York: Watts & Co., 1957).

17. "Some Explanations in Reply to Mr. Bradley," *Mind* (1910).

18. *Autobiography of Bertrand Russell.*

19. See Lewis's cover letter to his "A Pragmatic Conception of the A Priori," in *Journal of Philosophy* 20 (1923): 169–77; quoted in Burton Dreben and Juliet Floyd, "Tautology: How Not to Use a Word," *Synthese* 87 (1991): 23–49.

20. Quoted in Dreben and Floyd, "Tautology," p. 23.

21. Heidegger, *What Is a Thing* (South Bend, Ind.: Regnery/Gateway, 1967), p. 33.

22. The German word is *Sachlage,* which has most often been translated as "state of affairs," while *Sachverhalt* renders itself in English as "*atomic* or *particular* state of affairs." We should also keep in mind that, unlike in English, *Sache* (fact, a something), *Tatsache* (fact), *Sachverhalte* (particular states of affairs), and *Sachlage* (state of affairs) all have the word *Sach* in common.

23. For a fuller discussion, see my *Wittgenstein's Tractatus* (Mountain View, Calif.: Mayfield, 1998).

Index

mystical argument (existence of
God), 171
mysticism
defined, 69–70n.8
Leibniz on, 141–142
levels of reality/consciousness
and, 67
Royce on, 250
Russell on, 274–274
of Wittgenstein, 277, 282
Mysticism and Logic (Russell),
274–275

naive realism, 223, 226, 243
Narcisse (Rousseau), 179
naturalism, 244, 245–246
naturalized epistemology, 244,
245–247
natural vs. technical language
Anaximenes and, 10–11
Frege and, 262–264, 269
history of philosophy and, 264
Russell and Whitehead and,
268–269
See also logic
natural truth, 82–83, 88–89
See also revealed truth
nature
laws of
defined, 194
knowledge as dependent on,
227
mind as source of, 188
as objective world, 199
Plato's theory of ideas and, 49
uniformity of, 167–168, 169
navigation, 1–2
necessity
Hegel and, 204–205
Kant, 205
Leibniz, 144–145
Spinoza, 138
negation, 281–282
negative facts, 278
negative way. *See via negativa*
Neoplatonism
agnostia, 69–70n.8
Augustine and, 72
Christianity and, 67, 72–73
ideas, defined, 41
Islamic philosophy and, 81
origins of, 67–68
nervous system, environment jarring, 135
neutral monism, 243–244, 274
See also monism
*New Essays on the Human Under-
standing* (Leibniz), 139
New Testament. *See* Bible

Newtonian world view, 146–147
Berkeley and, 148, 157
God in, 147, 148
Hume and, 146
Locke and, 146
and philosophy, need for, 147,
148, 164–165
quantum mechanics and,
146–147, 148
Whitehead and, 265, 267, 268
Newton, Sir Isaac
calculus, 139, 145–146
Leibniz and, 139, 146
life of, 145–146
system of, 145–148
Nicomachean Ethics (Aristotle), 57
Nietzsche, Friedrich, 29,
218–223
Beyond Good and Evil, 219, 222
The Antichrist, 219
The Genealogy of Morals, 219
The Will to Power, 219, 222
Thus Spake Zarathustra, 219
Nobel Prize, 260–261
No Exit (Sartre), 260
nominalism, 80, 117–118n.2
Berkeley, 160
Hume, 160
Leibniz, 139
Ockham, 92–94
non-being
being vs.
question of, 258–260
Scotus, 91–92
as impossible, 20, 29–30
separation and, 29
See also space
noncontradiction, principle of,
216–217
non-existence. *See* non-being
nonsense, 164, 277, 278
"nothing in excess," 2
nothingness. *See* non-being
noumenal world (of thing-in-
itself)
cause as nonexistent in, 192
defined, 184
as fixed, 203
as future, possibilities of,
Hegel, 203
haecceity and, 90–91
Hegel and, 202, 203
Kant and, 184, 187–193, 203
as knowable, 200
mind affecting, 187–193, 203
See also observer, active role
of
as nonexistent
computer theory and, 210

Fichte, 197–198
Hegel, 202, 209, 210
James, 243
Royce, 250–251
phenomenal world and. *See*
phenomenal world
as unknowable, 187, 202
as the will, 213
Wittgenstein and, 280
See also reality; substance
nous
as active intellect, 84
levels of reality and, 67–68
Neoplatonists and, 41
See also logos
Novum Organum (Bacon), 98–100
numbers
as basis of everything, 8,
13–14, 15
geometry and, relationship of,
13, 125
music theory and, 12–13
See also signs

object, as term, 280
object constancy, 8
objective. *See* subjective-objective
distinction
objective idealism, 199–201,
204, 210
objectivity, Mach and, 241
the Obscure. *See* Heraclitus
observer, active role of
Bergson, 252
Berkeley and, 154
Dewey, 245
Einstein, 204
Fichte, 198
Hegel and, 203, 211
Hume and, 165
James and, 243–244
Kant and, 187–193, 195, 203
Mach and, 154
philosophical shift into,
223–225
quantum measurement states
and, 211
Wheeler's participatory uni-
verse, 211
See also active intellect
Ockham's razor, 92
Ockham, William of, 92–94
Logic, 93
*On the Concept of the Science of
Knowledge, or So-called Phi-
losophy* (Fichte), 196
*On Power and Powerlessness, Possi-
bility and Impossibility, Neces-
sity and Liberty* (Anselm), 79

realism
    Aristotle, 117
    Augustine, 76–77
    Christianity and, 76–77
    Frege, 263
    naive, 223, 226, 243
    Royce and, 248, 250
    Russell and, 268, 274–275
reality
    absolute and relative, 31, 200
    appearances not true, 109
        See also the appearances
    atomism, 141
    cause and. *See* cause
    change and. *See* change
    contemplation of soul and,
        67–68
    as directly experienced, 223,
        225–226, 245
    dream states vs. *See* dream
        states
    dualism. *See* dualism
    as evolutionary process, Hegel,
        205–212
    experience of vs. view of,
        24–25
    as idea vs. thing
        Platonic basis of, 41–46,
            116–117
        Pythagorean basis of, 13–14
    as idea and thing composite,
        Aristotelian basis of, 50,
        52–54, 55–57, 58, 117
    intuition and. *See* intuition
    knowledge of. *See* knowledge
    levels of, Plotinus and, 67–68
    logic and. *See* logic
    many-worlds view, 140, 141,
        142
    mind as creating, as philosoph-
        ical shift, 223–225
    mind-independent
        as central question, 223
        Democritus and, 31
        Kant and. *See* noumenal
            world
        materialism and, 31
        Newtonian world view and,
            146–147
        positivism, 226
    mind as participant in. *See*
        observer, active role of
    monism. *See* monism
    mysticism and view of,
        69–70n.8
    nominalism and, 117–118n.2
    observer and. *See* observer,
        active role of
    one with, becoming, 138

perception as requirement of,
    154–159
pragmatism and, 236–237
as pure experience, 243–244
questions central to philoso-
    phy on, 109
reason as detector of. *See under*
    cosmic unity
representationalism and. *See*
    noumenal world
signs as basis of, 235, 238–240
substance of. *See* noumenal
    world; substance
as thing vs. idea, 146–147,
    Newtonian basis of
time and. *See* time: conscious
    experience of, reality and
truth. *See* truth
ultimate, nature of. *See* cosmic
    unity
as will, 213–215
See also the appearances
reason
    antinomies of, 183, 184, 187,
        206
    Biblical interpretation and, 86
    cause and effect and, 159
    common sense vs., 21–22
    discursive nature of, 96–97
    as faculty of mind, Kantian,
        184, 191, 193
    faith and. *See under* faith
    intellectual system of. *See*
        rationalism
    knowledge acquired through,
        32–33, 50, 58, 136, 182
    in moral realm, 194–195
    mysticism and, 69–70nn.8–9
    opposites, containing of, 206
    perception, as correcting, 19,
        20–21
    reality, as detector of. *See under*
        cosmic unity
reductionism, 285
reference
    Frege and, 263
    Quine and, 285,
    Russell and, 268
reflections, 149, 150
    See also apperception
Reformation, 104–108, 121
Reichenbach, Hans, 284
Reid, Thomas, 159
relation. *See* language: and reality,
    relation of structures
relativism
    of Domocritus, 31
    of sophists, 26–29
relativity

Berkeley and, 154
Cusa anticipating, 97
Kant and, 189
Mach and, 240
of meaning, 285–286
of motion, 113–115
Newton's world and, 146
ontological, 284–285
religion
    Bentham and, 228
    censorship and. *See* censorship
    Comte and, 226
    corruption and, 104–108
    Dewey and, 246
    ethics based in, Socrates and,
        38–40
    evil and. *See* evil
    faith and. *See* faith
    Fichte and, 198
    geocentric universe and, 110,
        112, 114
    Hume and, 172, 173
    in ideal state, Plato, 47
    interpretation and, 116
    Kierkegaard and, 216
    Marx and, 231, 232
    materialism and, 60, 61
    of mysticism and mathematics,
        12
    Nietzsche and, 218, 219,
        221–222
    persecution and. *See* persecu-
        tion
    philosophy as necessary to,
        148
    piety and. *See* piety
    as prison of mind, 231
    Quine and, 284
    as rational, 242
    ritual in. *See* ritual
    Roman Empire and, 71, 77–78
    Russell and, 269–270
    syncretism, 71
    wars of, 82, 108–109, 133
    See also God; *specific religions*
*Religion Within the Limits of Mere
    Reason* (Kant), 181
Renaissance, 94–95
representation
    ideas as. *See under* ideas
    ideas as
        Hume and. *See* impressions
        of monads, 141
        as identical to reality, 209–211
        Kant, 185–186, 191–193
        language as, 186–187, 189,
            276–277
    Leibniz, 141, 142
    Locke, 151

world of. *See* noumenal world
See also reality; substance
thought
  as act, 197–198
  being and. *See under* being
  development of, Hegel,
    205–206
  as experience, Dewey, 247
  freedom of, as slavery, 123
  as intuition of reality, 44–45
  intuitive. *See* intuition
  Kantian revolution in,
    183–193
  logic. *See* logic
  materialist view of, 32–33
  natural, 254–255
  philosophical, 254–255
  picture theory of, 281–282
  Russell and, 275
  subjective vs. objective,
    217–218
  See also mind
"Thoughts without content are
  empty, intuitions without
  concepts are blind" (Kant),
  192–193
Thrasymachus, 28–29, 219, 221
*Three Dialogues between Hylas and
  Philonus* (Berkeley), 153
Thus Spake Zarathustra (Nietzsche), 219
Timaeus (Plato), 45–46
time
  absolute, 207
  being as rooted in, 57, 252,
    253–254, 256–257, 258
  Berkeley and, 156
  as category of mind, Kant and,
    156, 190–191
  conscious experience of,
    253–254
  contemplation of soul creating,
    68
  experiential, 252
  Hegelian future and, 204
  Hume and, 189
  See also space
To Herodotus (Epicurus), 60
To Menoeceus (Epicurus), 61
Toynbee, Arnold, 224
Tractatus Logico-Philosophicus
  (Wittgenstein), 276–282,
  283
Tractatus Theologico-Politicus
  (Spinoza), 136, 138
transcendental deduction, 190
transcendental idealism,
  184–195, 202–206
transcendental illusion, 187, 205

transcendental self, 255
transvaluation of values, 219
*Treatise Concerning the Principles of
  Human Knowledge, A* (Berkeley), 153, 155
Treatise of Human Nature (Hume),
  159, 161, 227
Treatise on Resurrection (Main-
  monides), 85
truth
  analytic-synthetic. *See* analytic-
    synthetic distinction
  certainty, Dewey, 245–247
  as concept, differences in, 80
  as evolving, 229–230
  goal of. *See* philosophy: goal of
  knowledge of, vs. acting on, 73
  language expressing, 9–10
  as man-made, 26–27
  necessary. *See* necessity
  Nietzsche's use of term, 221
  as nonexistent, 28
  philosophers as attaining,
    83–84
  a posteriori, 143, 164,
    182–183
  power as determining, 28–29,
    219
  pragmatism and, 242–243
  a priori. *See* a priori truth
  radical empiricism and, 243
  revealed. *See* revealed truth
  revision, as open to, 245–246
  satisfaction in, as vain, 98
  seekers of, and wisdom, 6
  self-evident. *See* axioms
  as social agreement, 223–224,
    225
  as the whole, 205
  See also knowledge; reality
Turing, Alan, 207, 269
Twain, Mark, 250
twentieth-century philosophy, as
  Heraclitan, 17
Two Treatises on Civil Government
  (Locke), 151
types, theory of, 269

ultimate ground. *See* cosmic
  unity
understanding
  as divine faculty, 78
  Hegel and, 206
  Kant and, 184, 188, 191–192,
    206
  and perception, 149–150, 160
  Plato and, 43
  as universally accepted, 182,
    185, 191

  See also knowledge; mind
"unexamined life is not worth living" (Socrates), 35–36
unity underlying the appearances. *See* cosmic unity;
  God: as One; mono-
  psychism
universal program, 209, 211
universals
  Anselm's argument and, 80
  as dependent on particulars,
    52, 55–57, 94,
    117–118n.2
  direct perception and, 90–91,
    94
  ideas as, 41
  as independent of particulars,
    48–49, 52, 94
  indirect perception and, 91
  logical being of, 92–94
  objects of, as nonexistent,
    155–156
  See also haecceity; second-
    order activities
universe
  as computer program, 198,
    206–207, 208–209, 210
  evolving to become self-con-
    scious, 211–212
  geocentric, 110–116
  heliocentric, 109, 112–116
  infinite, 102
  as participatory. *See* observer,
    active role of
  as set, 272–273
  See also reality
universities. *See* colleges and
  universities
University College, 228, 233n.10
univocality, 90, 91
U.S. Coast Guard, 112–113, 115
utilitarianism
  Bentham, 227–228, 229
  of Epicurus, 61
  Mill, 228–230
  and social contract theory,
    61–62
  of sophists, 61
Utilitarianism (Mill), 229
utility, principle of, 227

validity
  in rationalism, being and, 250
  social agreement and,
    223–224, 225
values
  derivative, 35–36
  extrinsic, 35, 36
  instrumental, 35, 36